GPU Pro^5

GPU Pro^5

Advanced Rendering Techniques

Edited by Wolfgang Engel

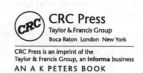

CRC Press
Taylor & Francis Group
Boca Raton London New York

CRC Press is an imprint of the
Taylor & Francis Group, an **informa** business

AN A K PETERS BOOK

Cover art: Screenshots from *Killzone: Shadow Fall* by Guerrilla Games. Courtesy of Michal Valient.

CRC Press
Taylor & Francis Group
6000 Broken Sound Parkway NW, Suite 300
Boca Raton, FL 33487-2742

© 2014 by Taylor & Francis Group, LLC
CRC Press is an imprint of Taylor & Francis Group, an Informa business

No claim to original U.S. Government works

Printed on acid-free paper
Version Date: 20140213

International Standard Book Number-13: 978-1-4822-0863-4 (Hardback)

Visit the Taylor & Francis Web site at
http://www.taylorandfrancis.com

and the CRC Press Web site at
http://www.crcpress.com

Contents

Acknowledgments   xv

Web Materials   xvii

I   Rendering   **1**
    Carsten Dachsbacher

1   Per-Pixel Lists for Single Pass A-Buffer   3
    Sylvain Lefebvre, Samuel Hornus, and Anass Lasram

    1.1   Introduction   3
    1.2   Linked Lists with Pointers (LIN-ALLOC)   6
    1.3   Lists with Open Addressing (OPEN-ALLOC)   11
    1.4   POST-SORT and PRE-SORT   14
    1.5   Memory Management   16
    1.6   Implementation   17
    1.7   Experimental Comparisons   18
    1.8   Conclusion   21
    1.9   Acknowledgments   22
    Bibliography   22

2   Reducing Texture Memory Usage by 2-Channel Color Encoding   25
    Krzysztof Kluczek

    2.1   Introduction   25
    2.2   Texture Encoding Algorithm   25
    2.3   Decoding Algorithm   31
    2.4   Encoded Image Quality   31
    2.5   Conclusion   33
    Bibliography   34

3 Particle-Based Simulation of Material Aging   35
   Tobias Günther, Kai Rohmer, and Thorsten Grosch

   3.1 Introduction   35
   3.2 Overview   36
   3.3 Simulation   37
   3.4 Preview Rendering   49
   3.5 Results   51
   3.6 Conclusions   52
   Bibliography   53

4 Simple Rasterization-Based Liquids   55
   Martin Guay

   4.1 Overview   55
   4.2 Introduction   55
   4.3 Simple Liquid Model   56
   4.4 Splatting   57
   4.5 Grid Pass   59
   4.6 Particle Update   60
   4.7 Rigid Obstacles   60
   4.8 Examples   61
   4.9 Conclusion   63
   Bibliography   63

II Lighting and Shading   65
    Michal Valient

1 Physically Based Area Lights   67
   Michal Drobot

   1.1 Overview   67
   1.2 Introduction   68
   1.3 Area Lighting Model   70
   1.4 Implementation   91
   1.5 Results Discussion   93
   1.6 Further Research   96
   1.7 Conclusion   97
   Bibliography   99

2 High Performance Outdoor Light Scattering Using Epipolar Sampling 101
   Egor Yusov

   2.1 Introduction   101
   2.2 Previous Work   102

2.3   Algorithm Overview   103

2.4   Light Transport Theory   103

2.5   Computing Scattering Integral   106

2.6   Epipolar Sampling   108

2.7   1D Min/Max Binary Tree Optimization   110

2.8   Implementation   113

2.9   Results and Discussion   119

2.10 Conclusion and Future Work   124

Bibliography   124

3   Volumetric Light Effects in *Killzone: Shadow Fall*   127
    Nathan Vos

3.1   Introduction   127

3.2   Basic Algorithm   128

3.3   Low-Resolution Rendering   132

3.4   Dithered Ray Marching   133

3.5   Controlling the Amount of Scattering   136

3.6   Transparent Objects   142

3.7   Limitations   144

3.8   Future Improvements   145

3.9   Conclusion   146

Bibliography   146

4   Hi-Z Screen-Space Cone-Traced Reflections   149
    Yasin Uludag

4.1   Overview   149

4.2   Introduction   150

4.3   Previous Work   152

4.4   Algorithm   156

4.5   Implementation   172

4.6   Extensions   179

4.7   Optimizations   186

4.8   Performance   187

4.9   Results   188

4.10 Conclusion   188

4.11 Future Work   189

4.12 Acknowledgments   190

Bibliography   190

5   TressFX: Advanced Real-Time Hair Rendering   193
    Timothy Martin, Wolfgang Engel, Nicolas Thibieroz, Jason Yang,
    and Jason Lacroix
    5.1   Introduction   193
    5.2   Geometry Expansion   194
    5.3   Lighting   196
    5.4   Shadows and Approximated Hair Self-Shadowing   198
    5.5   Antialiasing   200
    5.6   Transparency   201
    5.7   Integration Specifics   204
    5.8   Conclusion   206
    Bibliography   208

6   Wire Antialiasing   211
    Emil Persson
    6.1   Introduction   211
    6.2   Algorithm   212
    6.3   Conclusion and Future Work   217
    Bibliography   217

III   **Image Space**   **219**
    Christopher Oat

1   Screen-Space Grass   221
    David Pangerl
    1.1   Introduction   221
    1.2   Motivation   221
    1.3   Technique   222
    1.4   Performance   226
    1.5   Conclusion   227
    1.6   Limitations and Future Work   228
    1.7   Screen-Space Grass Source Code   230
    Bibliography   232

2   Screen-Space Deformable Meshes via CSG with Per-Pixel
    Linked Lists   233
    João Raza and Gustavo Nunes
    2.1   Introduction   233
    2.2   Mesh Deformation Scenario   233
    2.3   Algorithm Overview   234
    2.4   Optimizations   239

2.5   Conclusion 239
2.6   Acknowledgements 240
Bibliography 240

3   Bokeh Effects on the SPU   241
Serge Bernier

3.1   Introduction 241
3.2   Bokeh Behind the Scenes 242
3.3   The Sprite-Based Approach 244
3.4   Let's SPUify This! 246
3.5   Results 249
3.6   Future Development 250
Bibliography 250

IV   Mobile Devices   251
Marius Bjørge

1   Realistic Real-Time Skin Rendering on Mobile   253
Renaldas Zioma and Ole Ciliox

1.1   Introduction 253
1.2   Overview 253
1.3   Power of Mobile GPU 255
1.4   Implementation 256
1.5   Results 260
1.6   Summary 261
Bibliography 262

2   Deferred Rendering Techniques on Mobile Devices   263
Ashley Vaughan Smith

2.1   Introduction 263
2.2   Review 263
2.3   Overview of Techniques 264
2.4   OpenGL ES Extensions 270
2.5   Conclusion and Future Work 272
Bibliography 272

3   Bandwidth Efficient Graphics with ARM Mali GPUs   275
Marius Bjørge

3.1   Introduction 275
3.2   Shader Framebuffer Fetch Extensions 275
3.3   Shader Pixel Local Storage 279
3.4   Deferred Shading Example 283

3.5   Conclusion   287
Bibliography   288

4   Efficient Morph Target Animation Using OpenGL ES 3.0   289
James L. Jones

4.1   Introduction   289
4.2   Previous Work   289
4.3   Morph Targets   290
4.4   Implementation   291
4.5   Conclusion   295
4.6   Acknowledgements   295
Bibliography   295

5   Tiled Deferred Blending   297
Ramses Ladlani

5.1   Introduction   297
5.2   Algorithm   299
5.3   Implementation   300
5.4   Optimizations   306
5.5   Results   308
5.6   Conclusion   309
Bibliography   310

6   Adaptive Scalable Texture Compression   313
Stacy Smith

6.1   Introduction   313
6.2   Background   313
6.3   Algorithm   314
6.4   Getting Started   316
6.5   Using ASTC Textures   317
6.6   Quality Settings   318
6.7   Other color formats   323
6.8   3D Textures   325
6.9   Summary   325
Bibliography   326

7   Optimizing OpenCL Kernels for the ARM Mali-T600 GPUs   327
Johan Gronqvist and Anton Lokhmotov

7.1   Introduction   327
7.2   Overview of the OpenCL Programming Model   328
7.3   ARM Mali-T600 GPU Series   328
7.4   Optimizing the Sobel Image Filter   331
7.5   Optimizing the General Matrix Multiplication   339
Bibliography   357

V 3D Engine Design   359
Wessam Bahnassi

1 Quaternions Revisited   361
Peter Sikachev, Vladimir Egorov, and Sergey Makeev

1.1	Introduction	361
1.2	Quaternion Properties Overview	361
1.3	Quaternion Use Cases	362
1.4	Normal Mapping	362
1.5	Generic Transforms and Instancing	366
1.6	Skinning	368
1.7	Morph Targets	371
1.8	Quaternion Format	371
1.9	Comparison	373
1.10	Conclusion	374
1.11	Acknowledgements	374
	Bibliography	374

2 glTF: Designing an Open-Standard Runtime Asset Format   375
Fabrice Robinet, Rémi Arnaud, Tony Parisi, and Patrick Cozzi

2.1	Introduction	375
2.2	Motivation	375
2.3	Goals	376
2.4	Birds-Eye View	379
2.5	Integration of Buffer and Buffer View	380
2.6	Code Flow for Rendering Meshes	382
2.7	From Materials to Shaders	382
2.8	Animation	384
2.9	Content Pipeline	385
2.10	Future Work	390
2.11	Acknowledgements	391
	Bibliography	391

3 Managing Transformations in Hierarchy   393
Bartosz Chodorowski and Wojciech Sterna

3.1	Introduction	393
3.2	Theory	394
3.3	Implementation	399
3.4	Conclusions	402
	Bibliography	403

VI Compute   405
Wolfgang Engel

1 Hair Simulation in TressFX   407
Dongsoo Han

   1.1 Introduction   407
   1.2 Simulation Overview   408
   1.3 Definitions   409
   1.4 Integration   410
   1.5 Constraints   410
   1.6 Wind and Collision   412
   1.7 Authoring Hair Asset   413
   1.8 GPU Implementation   414
   1.9 Conclusion   416
   Bibliography   417

2 Object-Order Ray Tracing for Fully Dynamic Scenes   419
Tobias Zirr, Hauke Rehfeld, and Carsten Dachsbacher

   2.1 Introduction   419
   2.2 Object-Order Ray Tracing Using the Ray Grid   421
   2.3 Algorithm   422
   2.4 Implementation   424
   2.5 Results   434
   2.6 Conclusion   436
   Bibliography   436

3 Quadtrees on the GPU   439
Jonathan Dupuy, Jean-Claude Iehl, and Pierre Poulin

   3.1 Introduction   439
   3.2 Linear Quadtrees   440
   3.3 Scalable Grids on the GPU   443
   3.4 Discussion   447
   3.5 Conclusion   449
   Bibliography   449

4 Two-Level Constraint Solver and Pipelined Local Batching for Rigid
   Body Simulation on GPUs   451
Takahiro Harada

   4.1 Introduction   451
   4.2 Rigid Body Simulation   452
   4.3 Two-Level Constraint Solver   454
   4.4 GPU Implementation   456

4.5   Comparison of Batching Methods 459

4.6   Results and Discussion 461

Bibliography 467

5   Non-separable 2D, 3D, and 4D Filtering with CUDA   469
Anders Eklund and Paul Dufort

5.1   Introduction 469

5.2   Non-separable Filters 471

5.3   Convolution vs. FFT 474

5.4   Previous Work 475

5.5   Non-separable 2D Convolution 475

5.6   Non-separable 3D Convolution 480

5.7   Non-separable 4D Convolution 481

5.8   Non-separable 3D Convolution, Revisited 482

5.9   Performance 483

5.10 Conclusions 486

Bibliography 490

About the Editors   493

About the Contributors   495

Acknowledgments

The *GPU Pro: Advanced Rendering Techniques* book series covers ready-to-use ideas and procedures that can help to solve many of your daily graphics-programming challenges.

The fifth book in the series wouldn't have been possible without the help of many people. First, I would like to thank the section editors for the fantastic job they did. The work of Wessam Bahnassi, Marius Bjørge, Carsten Dachsbacher, Michal Valient, and Christopher Oat ensured that the quality of the series meets the expectations of our readers.

The great cover screenshots were contributed by Michal Valient from Guerrilla Games. They show the game *Killzone: Shadow Fall*.

The team at CRC Press made the whole project happen. I want to thank Rick Adams, Charlotte Byrnes, Kari Budyk, and the entire production team, who took the articles and made them into a book.

Special thanks go out to our families and friends, who spent many evenings and weekends without us during the long book production cycle.

I hope you have as much fun reading the book as we had creating it.

—Wolfgang Engel

P.S. Plans for an upcoming *GPU Pro 6* are already in progress. Any comments, proposals, and suggestions are highly welcome (wolfgang.engel@gmail.com).

Web Materials

Example programs and source code to accompany some of the chapters are available on the CRC Press website: go to http://www.crcpress.com/product/isbn/ 9781482208634 and click on the "Downloads" tab.

The directory structure closely follows the book structure by using the chapter number as the name of the subdirectory.

General System Requirements

- The DirectX June 2010 SDK (the latest SDK is installed with Visual Studio 2012).

- DirectX9, DirectX 10 or even a DirectX 11 capable GPU are required to run the examples. The chapter will mention the exact requirement.

- The OS should be Microsoft Windows 7, following the requirement of DirectX 10 or 11 capable GPUs.

- Visual Studio C++ 2012 (some examples might require older versions).

- 2GB RAM or more.

- The latest GPU driver.

Updates

Updates of the example programs will be posted on the website.

Rendering

Real-time rendering is not only an integral part of this book series, it is also an exciting field where one can observe rapid evolution and advances to meet the ever-rising demands of game developers and game players. In this section we introduce new techniques that will be interesting and beneficial to both hobbyists and experts alike—and this time these techniques do not only include classical rendering topics, but also cover the use of rendering pipelines for fast physical simulations.

The first chapter in the rendering section is "Per-Pixel Lists for Single Pass A-Buffer," by Sylvain Lefebvre, Samuel Hornus and Anass Lasram. Identifying all the surfaces projecting into a pixel has many important applications in computer graphics, such as computing transparency. They often also require ordering of the fragments in each pixel. This chapter discusses a very fast and efficient approach for recording and simultaneously sorting of all fragments that fall within a pixel in a single geometry pass.

Our next chapter is "Reducing Texture Memory Usage by 2-Channel Color Encoding," by Krzysztof Kluczek. This chapter discusses a technique for compactly encoding and efficiently decoding color images using only 2-channel textures. The chapter details the estimation of the respective 2D color space and provides example shaders ready for use.

"Particle-Based Simulation of Material Aging," by Tobias Günther, Kai Rohmer, and Thorsten Grosch describes a GPU-based, interactive simulation of material aging processes. Their approach enables artists to interactively control the aging process and outputs textures encoding surface properties such as precipitate, normals and height directly usable during content creation.

Our fourth chapter, "Simple Rasterization-Based Liquids," is by Martin Guay. He describes a powerful yet simple way of simulating particle-based liquids on the GPU. These simulations typically involve sorting the particles into spatial acceleration structures to resolve inter-particle interactions. In this chapter, Martin details how this costly step can be sidestepped with splatting particles onto textures, i.e., making use of the rasterization pipeline, instead of sorting them.

—Carsten Dachsbacher

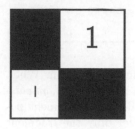

Per-Pixel Lists for Single Pass A-Buffer

Sylvain Lefebvre, Samuel Hornus, and Anass Lasram

1.1 Introduction

Real-time effects such as transparency strongly benefit interactive modeling and visualization. Some examples can be seen Figure 1.1. The rightmost image is a screenshot of our parametric Constructive Solid Geometry (CSG) modeler for 3D printing, IceSL [Lefebvre 13]. Modeled objects are rendered in real time with per-pixel boolean operations between primitives.

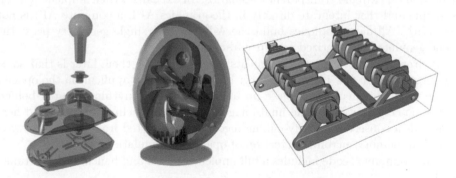

Figure 1.1. Left: Joystick model rendered with the PRE-OPEN A-buffer technique described in this chapter, on a GeForce Titan. 539236 fragments, max depth: 16, FPS: 490. Middle: Dinosaur in Egg, rendered with transparent surfaces and shadows using two A-buffers. Right: A robot body modeled with 193 solid primitives in boolean operations (CSG), rendered interactively with the PRE-OPEN A-buffer technique (modeler: IceSL). [Joystick by Srepmup (Thingiverse, 30198), Egg Dinosaur by XXRDESIGNS (Thingiverse, 38463), Spidrack by Sylefeb (Thingiverse, 103765).]

These effects have always been challenging for real-time rasterization. When the scene geometry is rasterized, each triangle generates a number of *fragments*. Each fragment corresponds to a screen pixel. It is a small surface element *potentially* visible through this pixel. In a classical rasterizer only the fragment closest to the viewer is kept: the rasterizer blindly rejects all fragments that are farther away than the current closest, using the Z-buffer algorithm. Instead, algorithms dealing with transparency or CSG have to produce ordered lists of all the fragments falling into each pixel. This is typically performed in two stages: First, a list of fragments is gathered for each pixel. Second, the lists are sorted by depth and rendering is performed by traversing the lists, either accumulating opacity and colors (for transparency effects), or applying boolean operations to determine which fragment is visible (for rendering a CSG model). The data structure is recreated at every frame, and therefore has to be extremely efficient and integrate well with the rasterizer.

A large body of work has been dedicated to this problem. Most techniques for fragment accumulation implement a form of A-buffer [Carpenter 84]. The A-buffer stores in each pixel the list of fragments that cover that pixel. The fragments are sorted by depth and the size of the list is called the *depth-complexity*, as visualized in Figure 1.3 (top-right). For a review of A-buffer techniques for transparency we refer the reader to the survey by Maule et al. [Maule et al. 11].

In this chapter we introduce and compare four different techniques to build and render from an A-buffer in real time. One of these techniques is well known while the others are, to the best of our knowledge, novel. We focus on scenes with moderate or sparse depth complexity; the techniques presented here will not scale well on extreme transparency scenarios. In exchange, their implementation is simple and they integrate directly in the graphics API; a compute API is not necessary. All our techniques build the A-buffer in a single geometry pass: the scene geometry is rasterized once per frame.

A drawback of storing the fragments first and sorting them later is that some fragments may in fact be unnecessary: in a transparency application the opacity of the fragments may accumulate up to a point where anything located behind makes no contribution to the final image. Two of the techniques proposed here afford for a conservative early-culling mechanism: inserted fragments are always sorted in memory, enabling detection of opaque accumulation.

The companion code includes a full implementation and benchmarking framework.

1.1.1 Overview

An A-buffer stores a list of fragments for each pixel. Sorting them by increasing or decreasing depth are both possible. However, the sorting technique that we describe in Section 1.3 is easier to explain and implement for decreasing values as we walk along the list. Adding to that, early culling of negligible fragments is possible for transparency rendering only when the fragments are sorted front-to-back. In order to meet both requirements for the described techniques, we consistently sort in decreasing order and obtain a front-to-back ordering by inverting the usual depth value of a fragment: if the depth z of a fragment is a `float` in the range $[-1, 1]$, we transform it in the pixel shader into the integer $\lfloor S(1-z)/2 \rfloor$, where S is a scaling factor (typically $2^{32} - 1$ or $2^{24} - 1$).

Our techniques rely on a buffer in which all the fragments are stored. We call it the *main buffer*. Each fragment is associated with a cell in the main buffer where its information is recorded. Our techniques comprise three passes: a CLEAR pass is used to initialize memory, then a BUILD pass assembles a list of fragments for each pixel and finally a RENDER pass accumulates the contribution of the fragments and writes colors to the framebuffer.

The four techniques differ along two axes. The first axis is the scheduling of the sort: when do we spend time on depth-sorting the fragments associated with each pixel? The second axis is the memory allocation strategy used for incrementally building the per-pixel lists of fragments. We now describe these two axes in more detail.

1.1.2 Sort Strategies

We examine two strategies for sorting the fragments according to their depth. The first one, POST-SORT, stores all the fragments during the BUILD pass and sorts them only just prior to accumulation in the RENDER pass: the GLSL shader copies the pixel fragments in local memory, sorts them in place, and performs in-order accumulation to obtain the final color.

The second strategy, PRE-SORT, implements an insertion-sort during the BUILD pass, as the geometric primitives are rasterized. At any time during the rasterization, it is possible to traverse the fragments associated with a given pixel in depth order.

Both strategies are summarized in Table 1.1.

Each has pros and cons: In the PRE-SORT method, insertion-sort is done in the slower global memory, but the method affords for early culling of almost invisible fragments. It is also faster when several RENDER passes are required on the same A-buffer, since the sort is done only once. This is for instance the case when CSG models are sliced for 3D printing [Lefebvre 13].

Pass	Rasterized geometry	POST-SORT	PRE-SORT
CLEAR	fullscreen quad	clear	clear
BUILD	scene triangles	insert	insertion-sort
RENDER	fullscreen quad	sort, accumulate	accumulate

Table 1.1. Summary of the POST-SORT and PRE-SORT sorting strategies.

In the POST-SORT method, sorting happens in local memory, which is faster but limits the maximum number of fragments associated with a pixel to a few hundred. Allocating more local memory for sorting more fragments increases register pressure and reduces parallelism and performance.

1.1.3 Allocation Strategies

In addition to the scheduling of the sort, we examine two strategies for allocating cells containing fragment information in the main buffer. The first one, LIN-ALLOC, stores fragments in per-pixel linked-lists and allocates fresh cells linearly from the start of the buffer to its end. Since many allocations are done concurrently, the address of a fresh cell is obtained by atomically incrementing a global counter. Additional memory is necessary to store the address of the first cell (head) of the list of fragments of each pixel. Section 1.2 details the LIN-ALLOC strategy.

The second strategy that we examine, OPEN-ALLOC, is randomized and somewhat more involved. To each pixel p we associate a pseudo-random sequence of cell positions in the main buffer: $(h(p, i))_{i \geq 1}$, for i ranging over the integers. In the spirit of the "open addressing" techniques for hash tables, the cells at positions $h(p, i)$ are examined by increasing value of i until an empty one is found. A non-empty cell in this sequence may store another fragment associated with pixel p or with a different pixel q. Such a *collision* between fragments must be detected and handled correctly. Section 1.3 details the OPEN-ALLOC strategy.

The combination of two allocation strategies (LIN-ALLOC and OPEN-ALLOC) with two schedules for sorting (POST-SORT and PRE-SORT) gives us four variations for building an A-buffer: POST-LIN (Sections 1.2.1 and 1.2.2), PRE-LIN (Section 1.2.3), POST-OPEN (Section 1.3.2) and PRE-OPEN (Section 1.3.3).

Section 1.4.1 details how fragments are sorted in local memory in the RENDER pass of the POST-SORT method. Some memory management issues, including buffer resizing, are addressed in Section 1.5, and information about our implementation is given in Section 1.6. In Section 1.7, we compare these four variations, as implemented on a GeForce 480 and a GeForce Titan.

1.2 Linked Lists with Pointers (LIN-ALLOC)

The first two approaches we describe construct linked lists in each pixel, allocating data for new fragments linearly in the main buffer. A single cell contains the depth of the fragment and the index of the next cell in the list. Since no cell is ever removed from a list, there is no need for managing a free list: allocating a new cell simply amounts to incrementing a global counter `firstFreeCell` that stores the index of the first free cell in the buffer. The counter `firstFreeCell` is initialized to zero. The increment is done atomically to guarantee that every thread allocating new cells concurrently does obtain a unique memory address. A second array, called `heads`, is necessary to store the address of the head cell of the linked list of each pixel.

Having a lot of threads increment a single global counter would be a bottleneck in a generic programing setting (compute API). Fortunately, GLSL fragment shaders feature dedicated counters for this task, via the `ARB_shader_atomic_counters` extension. If these are not available, it is possible to relieve some of the contention on the counter by allocating K cells at once for a list (typically $K = 4$). To obtain such a paged allocation scheme, the thread atomically increases the global counter by K and uses a single bit in each head pointer as a local mutex when inserting fragments in this page of K cells. The technique is described in full detail by Crassin [Crassin 10], and is implemented in the accompanying code (see `implementations.fp`, function `allocate_paged`). In our tests, the dedicated counters always outperformed the paging mechanism. However, if a generic atomic increment is used instead then the paging mechanism is faster. We use a single dedicated atomic counter in all our performance tests (Section 1.7).

We now describe the two techniques based on the LIN-ALLOC cell allocation strategy: POST-LIN and PRE-LIN.

1.2.1 Building Unsorted Lists (POST-LIN)

The simplest approach to building an unsorted list of fragments is to insert new fragments at the head of the pixel list. A sample implementation is provided in Listing 1.1.

In line 7, a cell position `fresh` is reserved and the counter is incremented. The operation must be done atomically so that no two threads reserve the same position in the buffer. It is then safe to fill the cell with relevant fragment data in lines 8 and 9. Finally, indices are exchanged so that the cell `buffer[fresh]` becomes the new head of the list.

Later, in Section 1.4.1, we describe how the fragments associated with each pixel are gathered in a thread's local memory and sorted before rendering.

```
1  const int gScreenSize       = gScreenW * gScreenH;
2  atomic_uint firstFreeCell = 0;
3  int heads[gScreenSize];
4  LinkedListCell_t buffer[gBufferSize];
5
6  void insertFront(x, y, float depth, Data data) {
7    const int fresh = atomicCounterIncrement(firstFreeCell);
8    buffer[fresh].depth = depth;
9    buffer[fresh].data  = data;
10   buffer[fresh].next  = atomicExchange(&heads[x+y*gScreenW], fresh);
11 }
```

Listing 1.1. Insertion at the head of a linked list.

```
1  atomic_uint firstFreeCell = gScreenSize;
2  Data     databuf[gBufferSize];
3  uint64_t buffer[gBufferSize + gScreenSize];
4
5  uint64_t pack(uint32_t depth, uint32_t next) {
6   return ((uint64_t)depth << 32) | next;
7  }
8
9  void insertFrontPack(x, y, uint32_t depth, data) {
10   const int fresh = atomicCounterIncrement(firstFreeCell);
11   databuf[fresh-gScreenSize] = data;
12   buffer[fresh] = atomicExchange(buffer+x+y*gScreenW,
13                                  pack(depth, fresh));
14 }
```

Listing 1.2. Insertion at the head of a linked list with packing.

1.2.2 Packing depth and next Together

In order to facilitate the understanding of later sections and render the exposition more uniform with Section 1.3, this section introduces specific changes to the buffer layout. We illustrate this new layout by describing an alternative way to build unsorted linked-lists.

The following changes are done: First, all fragment data except depth are segregated in a specific data buffer, that we call databuf. Second, the depth and the next fields are packed in a single 64-bits word. Third, the main buffer is enlarged with as many cells as pixels on screen. These additional cells at the beginning of the buffer are used just like the heads array in Listing 1.1.

Listing 1.2 shows the new insertion procedure. Two observations should be kept in mind:

- We must follow the next index $n - 1$ times to access the depth of the nth fragment, and n times to access its other data.

- Notice the new initial value of firstFreeCell and the offset needed when accessing the fragment data.

We keep this buffer layout throughout the remainder of the chapter.

The following diagram illustrates the position of four fragments $f_i, i = 1, 2, 3, 4$, inserted in this order, with depth z_i and data d_i, associated with a pixel with coordinates (x, y). Observe how each cell of the main buffer packs the depth z_i of a fragment and the index n_i of the next item in the list. Note that with this layout the index n_i of the fragment following f_i never changes.

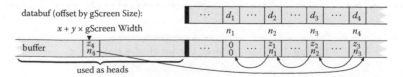

```
1  uint_32_t getNext(uint64_t cell) {
2    return cell; // extract least significant 32 bits
3  }
4
5  void insertSorted(x, y, uint32_t depth, Data data) {
6    const int fresh = atomicCounterIncrement(firstFreeCell);
7    buffer[fresh]  = 0; // 64-bits zero
8    memoryBarrier(); // make sure init is visible
9    databuf[fresh] = data;
10   uint64_t record = pack(depth,fresh), old, pos;
11   pos = gScreenW * y + x; // start of the search
12   while((old=atomicMax64(buffer+pos, record)) > 0) {
13     if( old > record ) { // go to next
14       pos = getNext(old);
15     } else { // inserted! update record itself
16       pos = getNext(record);
17       record = old;
18  } } }
```

Listing 1.3. Insertion-sort in a linked list.

1.2.3 Building Sorted Lists with Insertion-Sort (PRE-LIN)

It is also possible to perform parallel insertions at any position inside a linked list, and therefore, to implement a parallel version of "insertion-sort." General solutions to this problem have been proposed. In particular, our approach is inspired by that of Harris [Harris 01], albeit in a simplified setting since there is no deletion of single items. A sample implementation is provided in Listing 1.3.

The idea is to walk along the linked list until we find the proper place to insert the fragment. Contrary to the implementation of Harris, which relies on an atomic compare-and-swap, we use an atomic max operation on the cells of the main buffer at each step of the walk (line 12). Since the depth is packed in the most significant bits of a cell (line 10), the atomicMax operation will overwrite the fragment stored in the buffer if and only if the new fragment depth is larger. In all cases the value in the buffer prior to the max is returned in the variable old.

If the new fragment has smaller depth (line 13) then the buffer has not changed and the new fragment has to be inserted further down the list: we advance to the next cell (line 14).

If the new fragment has a larger depth (line 15) then it has been inserted by the atomicMax. At this point the new fragment has been inserted, but the remainder of the list has been cut out: the new fragment has no follower (line 7). We therefore restart the walk (line 16), this time trying to insert old as the next element of record (line 17). That walk will often succeed immediately: the atomicMax operation will be applied at the end of the first part of the list and will return zero (line 12). This single operation will merge back both parts of the list. However there is an exception: another thread may have concurrently inserted more elements, in which case the walk will continue until all elements have

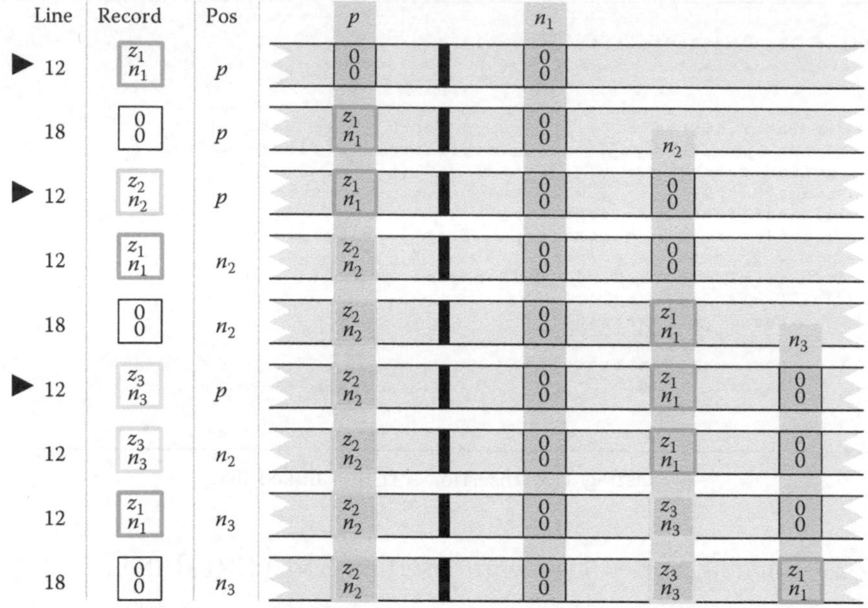

Figure 1.2. Insertion of three fragments into the list of pixel p. Their respective depths are z_1, z_2 and z_3 with $z_2 > z_3 > z_1$. The triangles on the left indicate the start of the insertion of a new fragment. Each line is a snapshot of the variables and main buffer state at each iteration of the **while** loop at lines 12 or 18 of Listing 1.3.

been properly re-inserted. Figure 1.2 illustrates the insertion of three fragments associated with a single pixel p.

Compared to the approach of [Harris 01] based on a 32-bit atomic compare and swap, our technique has the advantage of compactness and does not require synchronization in the main loop. In particular the loop in Listing 1.3 can be rewritten as follows:

```
1    while((old=atomicMax64(buffer+pos, record)) > 0) {
2        pos    = getNext( max(old,record) );
3        record = min(old,record);
4    }
```

Please refer to the accompanying source code for an implementation of both approaches (file **implementations.fp**, functions **insert_prelin_max64** and **insert_prelin_cas32**).

1.3 Lists with Open Addressing (OPEN-ALLOC)

In the previous section, a cell was allocated by incrementing a global counter, and each cell in a list had to store the index of the next cell in that list. This is the traditional linked-list data structure.

In this section, we describe a different way to allocate cells in the main buffer and traverse the list of fragments associated with a given pixel. This technique frees us from storing the index of the next cell, allowing more fragments to fit in the same amount of memory. It does come with some disadvantages as well, in particular the inability to store more that 32 bits of data per fragment.

We start with a general introduction of this allocation strategy and then introduce the two techniques based on it, POST-OPEN and PRE-OPEN.

1.3.1 Insertion

For each pixel p, we fix a sequence of cell positions in the main buffer, $(h(p,i))_{i \geq 1}$ and call it a *probe sequence*. The function h is defined as

$$h(p,i) = p + o_i \mod H,$$

or, in C speak,   `(p + offsets[i]) % gBufferSize`.

where $H = $ `gBufferSize` is the size of the main buffer. The sequence $(o_i)_{i \geq 1}$ should ideally be a random permutation of the set of integers $[0..H-1]$, so that the probe sequence $(h(p,i))_{i \geq 1}$ covers all the cells of the main buffer. We call $(o_i)_{i \geq 1}$ the *sequence of offsets*. In practice this sequence is represented with a fixed-length array of random integers, which we regenerate before each frame. The fragments associated with pixel p are stored in the main buffer at locations indicated by the probe sequence. When a fragment covering pixel p is stored at position $h(p,i)$, we say that it has *age* i, or that i is the age of this stored fragment.

There are two interesting consequences to using the probe sequence defined by function h. First, note that the sequence of offsets is independent of the pixel position p. This means that the probe sequence for pixel q is a translation of the probe sequence for pixel p by the vector $q - p$. During the rasterization, neighboring threads handle neighboring pixels and in turn access neighboring memory locations as each is traversing the probe sequence of its corresponding pixel. This *coherence* in the memory access pattern eases the stress of the GPU memory bus and increases memory bandwidth utilization. It was already exploited by García et al. for fast spatial hashing [García et al. 11].

Second, assuming that H is greater than the total number of screen pixels, then the function h becomes invertible in the sense that knowing $h(p,i)$ and i is enough to recover p as

$$p = h(p, i) - o_i \mod H,$$

or, in C speak,   (hVal + gBufferSize - offsets[i]) % gBufferSize.

Let us define $h^{-1}(v, i) = v - o_i \mod H$. The function h^{-1} lets us recover the pixel p, which is covered by a fragment of age i stored in cell v of the main buffer: $p = h^{-1}(v, i)$. In order to compute this inverse given v, the age of a fragment stored in the main buffer must be available. Hence, we reserve a few bits (typically 8) to store that age in the buffer, together with the depth and data of the fragment.

When inserting the fragments, we should strive to minimize the age of the oldest fragment, i.e., the fragment with the largest age. This is particularly important to ensure that when walking along lists of fragments for several pixels in parallel, the slowest thread—accessing old fragments—does not penalize the other threads too much. This maximal-age minimization is achieved during insertion: old fragments are inserted with a higher priority, while young fragments must continue the search of a cell in which to be written.

We define the *load-factor* of the main buffer as the ratio of the number of fragments inserted to the total size of the main buffer.

Collisions. A collision happens when a thread tries to insert a fragment in a cell that already contains a fragment. Collisions can happen since the probe sequence that we follow is essentially random. When the main buffer is almost empty (the load-factor is low), collisions rarely happen. But as the load-factor increases, the chance of collisions increases as well. The open addressing scheme that we have just described works remarkably well even when the load-factor is as high as 0.95.

A collision happens when a thread tries to insert a fragment f_p covering pixel p at position $h(p, i)$ for some i, but the cell at that position already contains a fragment f_q for some other pixel q. We then have $h(p, i) = h(q, j)$ and solve the collision depending on the value of i and j:

- If $j = i$, then $q = p$. The fragment f_q covers the same pixel p; we keep it there and try to insert fragment f_p at the next position $h(p, i+1)$. Alternatively, as in Section 1.3.3, we might compare the depths of both fragments to decide which one to keep at that position and which one to move.

- If $j \neq i$, then pixels p and q are different pixels. In that case, we store the fragment with the largest age in that cell and continue along the probe sequence of the other fragment. More precisely, if $i > j$ then the older fragment f_p replaces f_q in the main buffer and the insertion of the younger fragment f_q is restarted at age $j + 1$, i.e., at position $h(q, j + 1)$ in the main buffer. Note that the value q is not known in advance and must be computed as $q = h^{-1}(h(p, i), j)$. If $i < j$, then fragment f_q does not move and the search for a free cell for f_p proceeds at age $i + 1$ in the probe sequence of pixel p.

This *eviction* mechanism, whereby an "old" fragment evicts a younger fragment, has been demonstrated to effectively reduce the maximum age of the fragments stored in the main buffer, over all pixels. This property was discovered by Celis and Munro in their technique called *Robin Hood Hashing* [Celis et al. 85].

1.3.2 Building Unsorted Lists (POST-OPEN)

In this section, we give the full details of the construction of unsorted lists of fragments using the allocation scheme described above.

In the rest of this chapter, we assume that a cell of the main buffer occupies 64 bits, which lets us use atomic operations on a cell, and that the age of a fragment is stored in the most significant bits of the cell:

| MSB | age: 8 bits | empty: 24 bits | data: 32 bits | LSB |

In this way, the eviction mechanism described above can be safely accomplished using a single call to `atomicMax`.

We use an auxiliary 2D table A that stores, for each pixel p, the age of the oldest fragment associated with p in the main buffer. Thus, $A[p]$ indicates the end of the list of p's fragments; from which we can start the search for an empty cell for the new fragment f_p to be inserted.

The insertion procedure is shown in Listing 1.4. It increments a counter `age` starting from $A[p] + 1$ (line 2) until it finds an empty cell at position $h(p, \texttt{age})$

```
1  void insertBackOA (p, depth, data) {
2    uint       age   = A[p] + 1;
3    uint64_t record = OA_PACK(age,depth,data);
4    int        iter = 0;
5    while (iter++ < MAX_ITER) {
6      uvec2    h    = ( p + offsets[age] ) % gBufSz;
7      uint64_t old = atomicMax(&buffer[h], record);
8      if (old < record) {
9        atomicMax(&A[p], age);
10       if (old == 0) break;
11       uint32_t oage = OA_GET_AGE(old);
12       p    = (h + gBufSz - offsets[oage]) % gBufSz;
13       age  = A[p];
14       record = OA_WRITE_AGE(old, age);
15     }
16     ++age;
17     record = record + OA_INC_AGE;
18 } }
```

Listing 1.4. Insertion in a list with open addressing.

in which the `record` is successfully inserted (line 10). The `record` is tentatively inserted in the buffer at line 7. If the insertion fails, the insertion proceeds in the next cell along the probe sequence (lines 16 and 17). If it succeeds, the table A is updated and if another fragment f' was evicted (`old != 0`), the pixel q covered by f' is computed from the age of f' (line 11) and function h^{-1} (line 12). The insertion of f' continues from the end of the list of fragments for pixel q, given by $A[q] + 1$.

The macro `OA_PACK` packs the age, depth and data of a fragment in a 64-bits word. The age occupies the 8 most significant bits. The macro `OA_WRITE_AGE` updates the 8 most significant bits without touching the rest of the word. Finally, the constant `OA_INC_AGE = ((uint64_t)1<<56)` is used to increment the age in the packed `record`.

1.3.3 Building Sorted Lists with Insertion-Sort (Pre-Open)

In this section, we modify the construction algorithm above so as to keep the list of fragments sorted by depth, by transforming it into an insertion-sort algorithm.

Let f_p be the fragment, associated with pixel p, that we are inserting in the main buffer. When a collision occurs at age i with a stored fragment f'_p associated with the *same* pixel p, we know that both fragments currently have the same age. Therefore, the `atomicMax` operation will compare the cell bits that are lower than the bits used for storing the age. If the higher bits, among these lower bits, encode the depth of the fragment then we ensure that the fragment with largest depth is stored in the main buffer after the atomic operation:

MSB	age: 8 bits	depth: 24 bits	data: 32 bits	LSB

Further, it is possible to show that during the insertion of fragment f_p at age i, if a collision occurs with a fragment f_q with $h(q,j) = h(p,i)$, then $i \leq j$. Thus, the insertion procedure will skip over all stored fragments that are not associated with pixel p (since $i \neq j \Rightarrow q \neq p$) and will correctly keep the fragments associated with p sorted by decreasing depth along the probe sequence of p. The interested reader will find more detail and a proof of correctness of the insertion-sort with open addressing in our technical report [Lefebvre and Hornus 13].

Thus, we obtain an insertion-sort with open addressing simply by packing the depth of the fragment right after its age and always starting the insertion of a fragment at the beginning of the probe sequence. A sample implementation is given in Listing 1.5.

1.4 Post-sort and Pre-sort

In this section we discuss details depending on the choice of scheduling for the sort. We discuss the sort in local memory required for Post-Lin and Post-Open, as well as how to perform early culling with Pre-Lin and Pre-Open.

```
1 void insertSortedOA(p, depth, data) {
2   uint     age  = 1;
3   uint64_t record = OA_PACK(age,depth,data);
4   int      iter = 0;
5   while (iter++ < MAX_ITER) {
6     uvec2    h   = ( p + offsets[age] ) % gBufSz;
7     uint64_t old = atomicMax(&buffer[h], record);
8     if (old < record) {
9       atomicMax(&A[p], age);
10      if (old == 0) break;
11      age = OA_GET_AGE(old);
12      p   = (h + gBufSz - offsets[age]) % gBufSz;
13      record = old;
14    }
15    ++age;
16    record = record + OA_INC_AGE;
17 } }
```

Listing 1.5. Insertion-sort with open addressing.

1.4.1   POST-SORT: Sorting in Local Memory

In the POST-SORT method, the BUILD pass accumulates the fragments of each pixel in a list, without sorting them. The RENDER pass should then sort the fragments prior to accumulating their contributions. This is done in a pixel shader invoked by rasterizing a fullscreen quad. The shader for a given pixel p first gathers all the fragments associated with p in a small array allocated in local memory. The array is then sorted using bubble-sort, in a manner similar to [Crassin 10]. Insertion-sort could also be used and benefit cases where the transparent fragments are rasterized roughly in back-to-front order.

In contrast to the POST-SORT techniques, the PRE-SORT approaches perform sorting during the BUILD pass. This allows for early culling of unnecessary fragments, as described in the next section.

1.4.2   PRE-SORT: Early Culling

The PRE-SORT method has the unique advantage of keeping the fragments sorted at all times. In a transparency application, when a fragment is inserted in a sorted list it is possible to accumulate the opacity of the fragments in front of it in the list. If this opacity reaches a given threshold, we know that the color of fragment f will contribute little to the final image and we can decide to simply discard it. This early culling mechanism is possible only when the lists of fragments are always sorted, and it provides an important performance improvement as illustrated in Section 1.7.

1.5   Memory Management

All four techniques use the main buffer for storing fragments. We discuss in
Section 1.5.1 how to initialize the buffer at each new frame. All implementations
assumed so far that the buffer is large enough to hold all incoming fragments.
This may not be true depending on the selected viewpoint, and we therefore
discuss how to manage memory and deal with an overflow of the main buffer in
Section 1.5.2.

1.5.1   The CLEAR Pass

With the LIN-ALLOC strategy, the beginning of the main buffer that stores the
heads of the lists has to be zeroed. This is implemented by rasterizing a fullscreen
quad. The global counter for cell allocation has to be initially set to `gScreenSize`.
In addition, when using the paged allocation scheme with the PRE-LIN method,
an additional array containing for each pixel the free cell index in its last page
has to be cleared as well.

With the OPEN-ALLOC strategy the entire main buffer has to be cleared: the
correctness of the insertion algorithm relies on reading a zero value to recognize
a free cell. The array A used to store the per-pixel maximal age has to be cleared
as well.

Figure 1.3 shows a breakout of the timings of each pass. As can be seen, the
CLEAR pass is only visible for the OPEN-ALLOC techniques, but remains a small
percentage of the overall frame time.

1.5.2   Buffer Overflow

None of the techniques we have discussed require us to count the number of
fragments before the BUILD pass. Therefore, it is possible for the main buffer
to overflow when too many fragments are inserted within a frame. Our current
strategy is to detect overflow *during* frame rendering, so that rendering can be
interrupted. When the interruption is detected by the host application, the main
buffer size is increased, following a typical size-doubling strategy, and the frame
rendering is restarted from scratch.

When using linked lists we conveniently detect an overflow by testing if the
global allocation counter exceeds the size of the main buffer. In such a case, the
fragment shader discards all subsequent fragments.

The use of open addressing requires a slightly different strategy. We similarly
keep track of the number of inserted fragments by incrementing a global counter.
We increment this counter *at the end* of the insertion loop, which largely hides
the cost of the atomic increment. With open addressing, the cost of the insertion
grows very fast as the load-factor of the main buffer nears one (Figure 1.4). For
this reason, we interrupt the BUILD pass when the load-factor gets higher than
10/16.

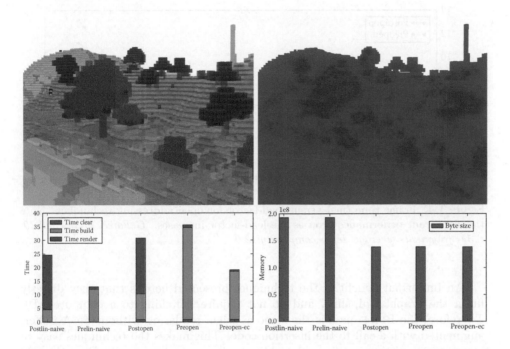

Figure 1.3. The lost empire scene, modeled with Minecraft by Morgan McGuire. The top row (left) shows the textured rendering, with 0.5 opacity (alpha from textures is ignored). The trees appear solid due to a large number of quads. The top row (right) shows a color coded image of the depth complexity. Full red corresponds to 64 fragments (average: 10.3, maximum: 46). The left chart gives the timing breakout for each pass and each technique. The CLEAR pass (red) is negligible for LIN-ALLOC techniques. POST-SORT techniques are characterized by a faster BUILD (green) but a significantly longer RENDER (blue) due to the sort. **preopen-ec** uses early culling, strongly reducing the cost of BUILD (threshold set to 0.95 cumulated opacity). The right chart shows the memory cost of each technique, assuming the most compact implementation. *Load-factor: 0.4.*

1.6 Implementation

We implement all techniques in GLSL fragment programs, using the extension `NV_shader_buffer_store` on NVIDIA hardware to access GPU memory via pointers. We tested our code on both a GeForce GTX 480 (Fermi) and a GeForce Titan (Kepler), using NVIDIA drivers 320.49. We designed our implementation to allow for easy swapping of techniques: each different approach is compiled as a separate DLL. Applications using the A-buffer use a common interface abstracting the A-buffer implementation (see `abuffer.h`).

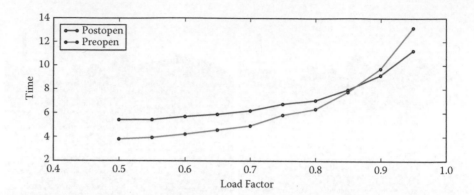

Figure 1.4. Frame time (ms) versus load-factor for open addressing techniques. Note the significant performance drop as the load-factor increases. *GeForce Titan, 320.49, 2.5M fragments, average depth complexity: 2.9.*

An important benefit of the techniques presented here is that they directly fit in the graphics pipeline, and do not require switching to a compute API. Therefore, the BUILD pass is the same as when rendering without an A-buffer, augmented with a call to the insertion code. This makes the techniques easy to integrate in existing pipelines. In addition all approaches require fewer than 30 lines of GLSL code.

Unfortunately implementation on current hardware is not as straightforward as it could be, for two reasons: First, the hardware available to us does not natively support `atomicMax` on 64 bits in GLSL (Kepler supports it natively on CUDA). Fortunately the `atomicMax` 64 bits can be emulated via an `atomicCompSwap` instruction in a loop. We estimated the performance impact to approximately 30% by emulating a 32 bits `atomicMax` with a 32 bits `atomicCompSwap` (on a GeForce GTX480). The second issue is related to the use of atomic operations in loops, inside GLSL shaders. The current compiler seems to generate code leading to race conditions that prevent the loops from operating properly. Our current implementation circumvents this by inserting additional atomic operations having no effect on the algorithm result. This, however, incurs in some algorithms a penalty that is difficult to quantify.

1.7   Experimental Comparisons

We now compare each of the four versions and discuss their performance.

1.7.1   3D Scene Rendering

We developed a first application for rendering transparent, textured scenes. It is included in the companion source code (`bin/seethrough.exe`). Figure 1.3 shows a 3D rendering of a large scene with textures and transparency. It gives the timings breakout for each pass and each technique, as well as their memory cost.

1.7.2   Benchmarking

For benchmarking we developed an application rendering transparent, front facing quads in orthographic projection. The position and depth of the quads are randomized and change every frame. All measures are averaged over six seconds of running time. We control the size and number of quads, as well as their opacity. We use the `ARB_timer_query` extension to measure the time to render a frame. This includes the CLEAR, BUILD, and RENDER passes as well as checking for the main buffer overflow. All tests are performed on a GeForce GTX480 and a GeForce Titan using drivers 320.49. We expect these performance numbers to change with future driver revisions due to issues mentioned in Section 1.6. Nevertheless, our current implementation exhibits performance levels consistent across all techniques as well as between Fermi and Kepler.

   The benchmarking framework is included in the companion source code (`bin/benchmark.exe`). The python script `runall.py` launches all benchmarks.

Number of fragments. For a fixed depth complexity, the per-frame time is expected to be linear in the number of fragments. This is verified by all implementations as illustrated Figure 1.5. We measure this by rendering a number of quads perfectly aligned on top of each other, in randomized depth order. The number of quads controls the depth complexity. We adjust the size of the quads to vary the number of fragments only.

Depth complexity. In this experiment we compare the overall performance for a fixed number of fragments but a varying depth complexity. As the size of the per-pixel lists increases, we expect a quadratic increase in frame rendering time. This is verified Figure 1.6. The technique PRE-OPEN is the most severely impacted by the increase in depth complexity. The main reason is that the sort occurs in global memory, and each added fragment leads to a full traversal of the list via the eviction mechanism.

Early culling. In scenes with a mix of transparent and opaque objects, early culling fortunately limits the depth complexity per pixel. The techniques PRE-OPEN and PRE-LIN both afford for early culling (see Section 1.4.2). Figure 1.7 demonstrates the benefit of early culling. The threshold is set up to ignore all fragments after an opacity of 0.95 is reached (1 being fully opaque).

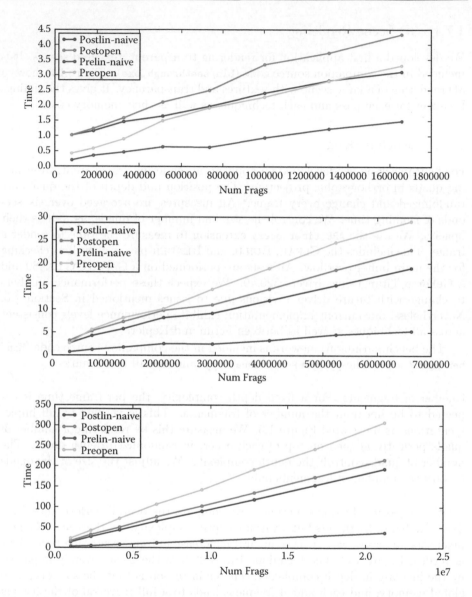

Figure 1.5. Frame time (ms) versus number of fragments. From top to bottom, the depth complexity is 5, 20, and 63 in all pixels covered by the quads. Increase in frame time is linear in number of fragments.

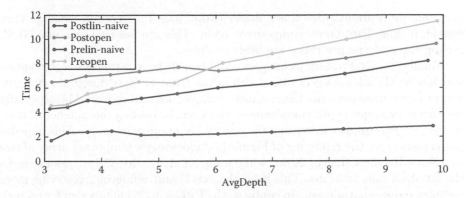

Figure 1.6. Frame time (ms) versus average depth complexity. *GeForce Titan, driver 320.49, load-factor: 0.5, 2.5M fragments.*

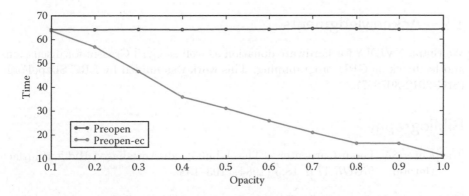

Figure 1.7. Frame time versus opacity for PRE-OPEN with and without early culling. Early culling (green) quickly improves performance when opacity increases. *GeForce Titan, driver 320.49, load-factor: 0.5, 9.8M fragments*

1.8 Conclusion

Our tests indicate that PRE-LIN has a significant advantage over other techniques, while the OPEN-ALLOC cell allocation strategy falls behind. This is, however, not a strong conclusion. Indeed, all of these methods, with the exception of POST-LIN, are penalized by the emulation of the atomic max 64 bits. More importantly, the implementation of the OPEN-ALLOC techniques currently suffers from unnecessary atomic operations introduced to avoid race conditions.

The LIN-ALLOC cell allocation strategy strongly benefits from the dedicated increment atomic counters. Our tests indicate that without these, the BUILD performance is about three times slower (using paged allocation, which is then faster), making PRE-OPEN competitive again. This implies that in a non-GLSL setting the performance ratios are likely to differ.

Finally, the POST-SORT techniques could benefit from a smarter sort, bubble-sort having the advantage of fitting well in the RENDER pass due to its straight-forward execution pattern. Using a more complex algorithm would be especially beneficial for larger depth complexities. However, increasing the number of fragments per-pixel implies increasing the reserved temporary memory. This impedes performance: for the rendering of Figure 1.3, allocating a temporary array of size 64 gives a RENDER time of 20 ms, while using an array with 256 entries increases the RENDER time to 57 ms. This is for the exact same rendering: reserving more memory reduces parallelism. In contrast, the PRE-SORT techniques suffer no such limitations and support early fragment culling.

For updates on code and results please visit http://www.antexel.com/research/gpupro5.

1.9 Acknowledgments

We thank NVIDIA for hardware donation as well as Cyril Crassin for discussions and feedback on GPU programming. This work was funded by ERC ShapeForge (StG-2012-307877).

Bibliography

[Carpenter 84] Loren Carpenter. "The A-buffer, an Antialiased Hidden Surface Method." *SIGGRAPH* 18:3 (1984), 103–108.

[Celis et al. 85] Pedro Celis, Per-Åke Larson, and J. Ian Munro. "Robin Hood Hashing (Preliminary Report)." In *Proceedings of the 25th Annual Symposium on Foundations of Computer Science*, pp. 281–288. Washington, DC: IEEE, 1985.

[Crassin 10] Cyril Crassin. "OpenGL 4.0+ A-buffer V2.0: Linked lists of fragment pages." http://blog.icare3d.org/2010/07/opengl-40-abuffer-v20-linked-lists-of.html, 2010.

[García et al. 11] Ismael García, Sylvain Lefebvre, Samuel Hornus, and Anass Lasram. "Coherent Parallel Hashing." *ACM Transactions on Graphics* 30:6 (2011), Article no. 161.

[Harris 01] Timothy L. Harris. "A Pragmatic Implementation of Non-blocking Linked-Lists." In *Proceedings of the 15th International Conference on Distributed Computing, DISC '01*, pp. 300–314. London: Springer-Verlag, 2001.

[Lefebvre and Hornus 13] Sylvain Lefebvre and Samuel Hornus. "HA-Buffer: Coherent Hashing for Single-Pass A-buffer." Technical Report 8282, Inria, 2013.

[Lefebvre 13] Sylvain Lefebvre. "IceSL: A GPU Accelerated Modeler and Slicer."
In *Distributed Computing: 15th International Conference, DISC 2001, Lis-
bon, Portugal, October 3–5, 2001, Proceedings, Lecture Notes in Computer
Science 2180*, pp. 300–314. Berlin: Springer-Verlag, 2013.

[Maule et al. 11] Marilena Maule, João Luiz Dihl Comba, Rafael P. Torchelsen,
and Rui Bastos. "A Survey of Raster-Based Transparency Techniques."
Computers & Graphics 35:6 (2011), 1023–1034.

Reducing Texture Memory Usage by 2-Channel Color Encoding
Krzysztof Kluczek

2.1 Introduction

In modern games, textures are the primary means of storing information about the appearance of materials. While often a single texture is applied to an entire 3D mesh containing all materials, they equally often represent individual materials, e.g., textures of walls, terrain, vegetation, debris, and simple objects. These single-material textures often do not exhibit large color variety and contain a limited range of hues, while using a full range of brightness resulting from highlights and dark (e.g., shadowed), regions within the material surface. These observations, along with web articles noticing very limited color variety in Hollywood movies [Miro 10] and next-gen games, coming as far as the proposal of using only two color channels for the whole framebuffer [Mitton 09], were the motivation for the technique presented in this chapter.

The method presented here follows these observations and aims to encode any given texture into two channels: one channel preserving full luminance information and the other one dedicated to hue/saturation encoding.

2.2 Texture Encoding Algorithm

Figure 2.1 presents the well-known RGB color space depicted as a unit cube. Each source texel color corresponds to one point in this cube. Approximating this space with two channels effectively means that we have to find a surface (two-dimensional manifold) embedded within this unit cube that lies as close as possible to the set of texels from the source texture. To simplify the decoding algorithm, we can use a simple planar surface or, strictly speaking, the intersection of a plane with the RGB unit cube (right image of Figure 2.1). Because we have already decided that *luminance* information should be *encoded losslessly* in a separate channel, the color plane should pass through the RGB space's origin

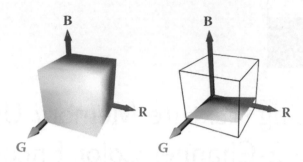

Figure 2.1. RGB color space as unit cube (left) and its intersection with a plane (right).

of zero luminance (black). Therefore, the simplified color space for the 2-channel compression is defined by a single three-dimensional vector—the plane normal.

2.2.1   Color Plane Estimation

Fitting a plane to approximate a set of 3D points is a common task and various algorithms exist. In order to find the best plane for color simplification we have to take the following preparatory steps.

First, we have to remember that RGB pixel color values in most image file formats do not represent linear base color contribution. For the purpose of this algorithm, we want to operate in the linear RGB color space. Most common file formats provide values in sRGB space [Stokes 96]. While being internally more complex, this representation can be approximated with gamma 2.2, i.e., after raising RGB values to power of 2.2 we obtain approximately linear light stimuli for red, green, and blue. We can approximate this with a gamma value of 2, which allows a simple use of multiplication and square root for conversion between sRGB and approximate linear RGB spaces. Strictly speaking, we will then be operating in a RGB space with a gamma of 1.1. While this slight nonlinearity will have only a minor impact on the estimation and the encoding, it is important to use the same simplified gamma value of 2 during the conversion back to the sRGB space after decoding for the final presentation to avoid change in the luminance levels.

After (approximately) converting color values to the linear RGB space, the other thing we have to remember is the fact that the hue perception is a result of the relation between the RGB components and is not linear. To correctly match hues as closely as possible, we could ideally use a perceptually linear color space (e.g., L*a*b*, explained in [Hoffmann 03]). However, this results in a much more costly decoding stage and thus we will limit ourselves to the linear RGB color space, accepting potential minor hue errors. Still, to minimize the impact of not operating in a perceptually correct linear RGB space, we can apply nonuniform scaling to the space before estimating the plane. This affects the error distribution across the RGB channels, allowing some hues to be represented more closely at the cost of others. The result of this non-uniform scaling is that as RGB components shrink, their influence on the color plane shrinks, because distances along the shrunk axis are shortened. Due to the hue perception's nonlinearity, it is not easy to define the scaling factors once for all potential textures, and in our tests they were set experimentally based on the sample texture set. First we tried the RGB component weights used in the luminance computation (putting most importance on G and barely any on B), but experiments showed that some material textures are better represented when the estimation is done with more balanced weighting. To achieve acceptable results for various textures, we used an experimentally chosen weight set of 1/2 for red, 1 for green and 1/4 for blue, which lies between the classic luminance component weights and the equally weighted component average. Fortunately, the perceived difference in pixel hues after the encoding changes is barely noticeable with these scaling factors. Still, the scaling factors may be used to improve texture representation by fine tuning them separately for each texture.

With the two above operations, the whole initial pixel color processing can be expressed as

$$r'_i = r_i^\gamma w_r,$$
$$g'_i = g_i^\gamma w_g,$$
$$b'_i = b_i^\gamma w_b,$$

where γ is the gamma value used to transition from the input color space to the linear color space, and w_r, w_g and w_b are the color component importance weights.

Having taken into account the above considerations, the color of every texel represents a single point in 3D space. The optimal approximating color plane will be the plane that minimizes the sum of squared distances between the plane and each point. Because the plane is assumed to be passing by the point (0,0,0), we can express it by its normal. In effect, the point-plane distance computation reduces to a dot product. Note that since we are using the RGB space, the vector components are labeled r, g, and b instead of the usual x, y, and z:

$$d_i = N \cdot P_i = n_r r'_i + n_g g'_i + n_b b'_i.$$

The optimal plane normal vector is the vector, which minimizes the point-plane distances. Such problems can be solved using least squared fit method that aims to minimize sum of squared distances. The approximation error we want to minimize is expressed as

$$err = \sum_i d_i^2 = \sum_i \left(N \cdot P_i\right)^2 = \sum_i \left(n_r r'_i + n_g g'_i + n_b b'_i\right)^2,$$

which after simple transformations becomes

$$err = n_r^2 \left(\sum_i r_i'^2 \right) + n_g^2 \left(\sum_i g_i'^2 \right) + n_b^2 \left(\sum_i b_i'^2 \right)$$
$$+ 2n_r n_g \left(\sum_i r_i' g_i' \right) + 2n_r n_b \left(\sum_i r_i' b_i' \right) + 2n_g n_b \left(\sum_i g_i' b_i' \right).$$

For minimalistic implementation, we can use the above equation to compute all six partial sums depending only on the texel colors. Then we can use a brute force approach to test a predefined set of potential normal vectors to find the one minimizing the total approximation error. Because each test is carried out in linear time, costing only several multiplications and additions, this approach is still tolerably fast.

The final step after finding the optimal color plane is to revert the color space distortion caused by the color component weighting by scaling using the reciprocal weights. Because the plane normal is a surface normal vector, the usual rule of non-uniform space scaling for normals applies and we have to multiply the normal by the inverse transpose of the matrix we would use otherwise. While the transposition does not affect the scaling matrix, the matrix inversion does and the final scaling operation is using non-reciprocal weights again:

$$N' = N \left(\begin{bmatrix} 1/w_r & 0 & 0 \\ 0 & 1/w_g & 0 \\ 0 & 0 & 1/w_b \end{bmatrix}^{-1} \right)^T = N \begin{bmatrix} w_r & 0 & 0 \\ 0 & w_g & 0 \\ 0 & 0 & w_b \end{bmatrix}.$$

As all subsequent computation is typically done in the linear RGB space, we do not have to convert into sRGB (which would be nonlinear transform anyway).

2.2.2 Computing Base Colors

The important parameters for the encoding and the decoding process are the two base colors. The color plane cutting through the RGB unit cube forms a triangle or a quadrilateral, with one of the corners placed at the point (0,0,0). The two corners neighboring the point (0,0,0) in this shape are defined as the base colors for the planar color space, as shown on Figure 2.2. Every other color available on the plane lies within the angle formed by the point (0,0,0) and the two base color points. Because the color plane starts at (0,0,0) and enters the unit cube, the base color points will always lie on the silhouette of the unit cube, as seen from the point (0,0,0). To find the base colors, we can simply compute the plane intersection with the silhouette edges, resulting in the desired pair of points. We have to bear in mind that the plane can slice through the silhouette vertices, or even embed a pair of silhouette edges. Therefore, to compute the points we can

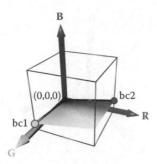

Figure 2.2. Base colors on the color plane.

use an algorithm, which walks around the silhouette computing the two points in which the silhouette crosses the plane.

The key observation now is that we can represent a hue value as the angle to the vectors spanning the plane or, alternatively, using a linear interpolation between the two base colors. In order to compute the final color, we only have to adjust the luminance and perform any required final color space conversions.

2.2.3 Luminance Encoding

The luminance of the color being encoded is stored directly. After colors have been transformed into the linear RGB space, we can use a classic equation for obtaining perceived luminance value derived from the sRGB to XYZ color space transformation in [Stokes 96]:

$$L = 0.2126 \cdot R + 0.7152 \cdot G + 0.0722 \cdot B.$$

Because the weighting coefficients sum up to 1, the luminance value ranges from zero to one. Since the luminance has its own dedicated channel in the 2-channel format, it can now be stored directly. However, as luminance perception is not linear, we are using a gamma value of 2 for the luminance storage. This is close enough to the standard gamma 2.2 and gives the same benefits—dark colors have improved luminance resolution at the cost of unnoticeably reduced quality of highlights. Also the gamma value of 2 means that luminance can simply have its square root computed while encoding and will simply be squared while decoding.

2.2.4 Hue Estimation and Encoding

To encode the hue of the color, we have to find the closest suitable color on the approximating plane and then find the proportion with which we should mix the base colors to obtain the proper hue. The hue encoding process is demonstrated

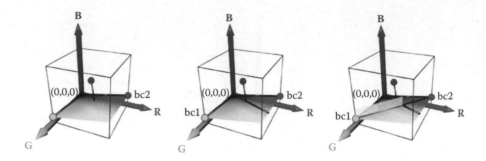

Figure 2.3. Hue encoding process

in Figure 2.3 and can be outlined as follows:

1. Project the color point in the linear RGB space onto the color plane.

2. Compute the 2D coordinates of the point on the plane.

3. Find a 2D line on plane passing through (0,0,0) and the point.

4. Find the proportion in which the line crosses the 2D line between the base color points, i.e., determine the blend factor for the base colors.

The first step is a simple geometric operation. From the second step on, we have to perform geometric operations on 2D coordinates embedded within the plane. Having the two base color points A and B, we can compute the 2D coordinate frame of the plane as

$$F_x = \frac{A}{\|A\|} \quad F_y = \frac{B - (F_x \cdot B)F_x}{\|B - (F_x \cdot B)F_x\|}$$

and then compute 2D coordinates of any point within the plane using the dot product:

$$(x_i, y_i) = (P_i \cdot F_x, P_i \cdot F_y).$$

Please note that we do not actually need the explicit RGB coordinates of the point on the plane nearest to the color being encoded, but only its 2D coordinates within the plane, x_i and y_i. As both the original point and the point projected onto the plane will have the same 2D coordinates, we can skip step 1 in the outlined algorithm completely. The projection onto the plane is a side effect of the reduction to only two dimensions.

The problem of computing the base color blend factor for hue, when considering the points embedded within the color plane, is now reduced to the problem of intersection of two lines: a line connecting both base color points and a line

```
float3 texture_decode( float2 data, float3 bc1, float3 bc2 )
{
    float3 color = lerp( bc1, bc2, data.y );
    float color_lum = dot( color, float3(0.2126,0.7152,0.0722) );
    float target_lum = data.x * data.x;

    color *= target_lum / color_lum;
    return color;
}
```

Listing 2.1. Two-channel texture decoding algorithm.

passing through the origin and the point on the plane being encoded. This gives us the following line-line intersection equation:

$$A + t(B - A) = sP.$$

Solving this linear equation for t gives us the result—the base color blend factor resulting in a hue most closely matching the hue of the encoded point. This blend factor is then simply stored directly in the second channel, completing the 2-channel encoding process.

2.3   Decoding Algorithm

The decoding algorithm is simple and best described by the actual decoding shader code in Listing 2.1.

First, the base colors bc1 and bc2, which are passed as constant data, are blended with a blend factor coming from the second channel of data, resulting in a color having the desired hue, but wrong luminance. This luminance is computed as color_lum. Next, we compute the desired luminance target_lum as a value of first channel of data squared (because we stored the luminance with gamma 2). As the resulting color is in a linear color space, we can adjust the luminance by simply dividing the color by the current luminance and then multiplying it by the desired one. If needed, we can of course convert the computed color to a nonlinear color space for presentation purposes.

2.4   Encoded Image Quality

Figures 2.4, 2.5, and 2.6 show examples of the encoding and decoding process. The example textures are taken from the CGTextures texture library and were selected because of their relatively rich content and variety.

Figure 2.4 presents a 2-channel approximation result of a dirt texture with grass patches. Both dirt and grass are reproduced with slight, but mostly unnoticeable differences in color. As the method is designed with limited-color material

Figure 2.4. Grass and dirt texture example. Original image (left) and result after the encoding/decoding process (right).

textures in mind, the color probe added on the image is of course severely degraded, but clearly shows that the estimation algorithm picked the green-purple color plane as fitting the image best. These extreme colors may not be used directly on the texture, but we should remember that all colors resulting from blending green and purple are available at this stage and this includes colors with reduced saturation in the transition zone. Because of the separate treatment of pixel luminance, the luminance values are unaffected except for processing and storage rounding errors.

Figures 2.5 and 2.6 show two examples of textures with mixed materials. This time, the estimation process has chosen a blue-yellow for the first and a

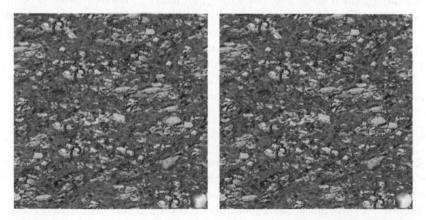

Figure 2.5. Rock and stone texture example. Original image (left) and result after the encoding/decoding process (right).

Figure 2.6. Sand, dead grass, and rocks texture example. Original image (left) and the decoded result after 2-channel compression (right).

teal-orange plane for the second image. While the stone and grass texture mostly remains unaffected, the sand, grass, and stones texture required finding a compromise resulting in some grass discoloration and smaller off-color elements changing color completely.

2.5 Conclusion

The encoding and decoding methods presented in this chapter allow storing textures with low color variety using only two texture channels. Apart from the obvious savings, this opens additional possibilities. For example, considering that most texture sampler implementations support 4-channel textures, the two remaining channels can be used for other purposes, e.g., storing x and y components of the material normal map, resulting in a compact material representation with just a single texture image. Even if not using this feature, the fact that the proposed 2-channel color encoding relies on a luminance-hue decomposition allows custom texture compression algorithms. We can assign higher priority to luminance information during texture compression, accumulating most of the compression error in hue, to changes to which the human eye is less sensitive, increasing the overall compressed image quality. We should also note that the proposed encoding scheme can be used directly with existing mip-mapping solutions, because averaging luminance-values and hue-blend factors is a good approximation of averaging color values. We should only be aware that the luminance values are stored with a gamma of 2 and may require a custom mip-map chain generation if we require fully linear color processing in the whole lighting pipeline.

Bibliography

[Hoffmann 03] Gernot Hoffmann. *CIELab Color Space*. http://docs-hoffmann.de/
cielab03022003.pdf, 2003.

[Miro 10] Todd   Miro.   *Teal   and   Orange—Hollywood,   Please   Stop   the
Madness.*   http://theabyssgazes.blogspot.com/2010/03/teal-and-orange
-hollywood-please-stop.html, 2010.

[Mitton 09] Richard Mitton. *Two-Channel Framebuffers for Next-Gen Color
Schemes.* http://www.codersnotes.com/notes/two-channel, 2009.

[Stokes 96] Michael Stokes, Matthew Anderson, Srinivasan Chandrasekar, and
Ricardo Motta. *A Standard Default Color Space for the Internet—sRGB.* http:
//www.w3.org/Graphics/Color/sRGB, 1996.

Particle-Based Simulation of Material Aging
Tobias Günther, Kai Rohmer, and Thorsten Grosch

3.1 Introduction

The composition of detailed textures, facilitating weathered and aged looks, is an everyday task for content artists in game and movie production. Examples of aged scenes are shown in Figure 3.1. In the process of meticulously editing textures, each inaccuracy or later change in the scenery can cause implausibility and quickly break the immersion. Therefore, interactively steerable, automatic simulations that favor the plausibility of aging effects, caused by interacting objects, e.g., dripping of rust, are vitally needed. This chapter describes implementation details of a GPU-assisted material aging simulation, which is based on customizable aging rules and material transport through particles. The chapter is based on

Figure 3.1. Interactively aged scene, exported and rendered in a DCC tool.

our paper [Günther et al. 12], where further results and discussions can be found. The simulation machinery is partly CUDA-based and partly rasterization-based to exploit the advantages of both sides. In fact, it is driven by an interplay of a number of modern GPU features, including GPU ray tracing, dynamic shader linkage, tessellation, geometry shaders, rasterization-based splatting and transform feedback, which are described in the following.

3.2   Overview

Our simulation of weathering effects is based on material transporting particles— so-called gammatons, introduced in [Chen et al. 05]. Gammatons are emitted from sources, such as clouds or roof gutters, to drip and distribute material, as shown in Figure 3.2. On impact, material is deposited or taken away, and the gammaton either bounces, floats, or is absorbed (see Figure 3.3). Eventually, resting material is subject to aging rules, for instance, turning metal into rust or spreading lichen growth. For this, the resting material is stored in a texture atlas, which we call *material atlas*; see later in Section 3.3.1 for a detailed discription of its content.

The simulation pipeline is illustrated in Figure 3.4. The particle movement and collision detection are done in CUDA, using Nvidia's ray tracing engine Op-tiX [Parker et al. 10]. Thus, in the *simulation step* a CUDA kernel is called, which emits and traces gammatons (elaborated in Section 3.3.2). In the following two stages, the *surface update* and the *gammaton update*, the material is transferred

Figure 3.2. Patina and dirt being transported by gammatons. A subset of the gammatons are rendered as spheres. *[Appeared in [Günther et al. 12] and reproduced by kind permission of the Eurographics Association.]*

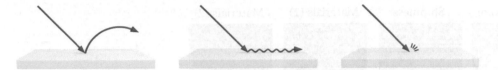

Figure 3.3. Depiction of collision responses, left to right: bounce, float, absorb. *[Appeared in [Günther et al. 12] and reproduced by kind permission of the Eurographics Association.]*

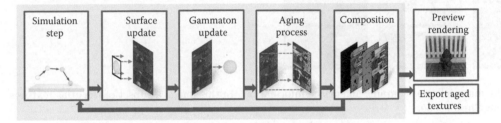

Figure 3.4. Illustration of the simulation pipeline. *[Appeared in [Günther et al. 12] and reproduced by kind permission of the Eurographics Association.]*

between the gammatons and the hit surfaces (detailed in Section 3.3.3). This happens in two consecutive steps: a rasterization pass to drop material into the *material atlas* and a transform feedback pass to update the gammaton material. Moreover, we determine the subsequent behavior of the gammatons by Russian Roulette (e.g., float, bounce, or absorb) and specify their velocity for the next iteration. In the following stage, the *aging process*, aging rules are applied, e.g., rusting in the presence of water and metal. To select the rule set, we use dynamic shader linkage, further explained in Section 3.3.4. Based on the material stored in the *material atlas* (Section 3.3.1) we compose texture maps for the aged diffuse color, shininess, surface normal, and height in the *composition stage* (Section 3.3.5). These maps can be used for preview rendering (Section 3.4) and can be exported (alongside all additional material atlas data), for instance, for external use in game engines or DCC tools.

3.3 Simulation

3.3.1 The Material Atlas

In order to decouple the weathering operations from the scene complexity, we maintain all simulation-relevant material, surface, and normalization data in a texture atlas, which we refer to as *material atlas*, depicted in Figure 3.5. Thereby, the amount of material carried by gammatons or resting on a surface—the latter is

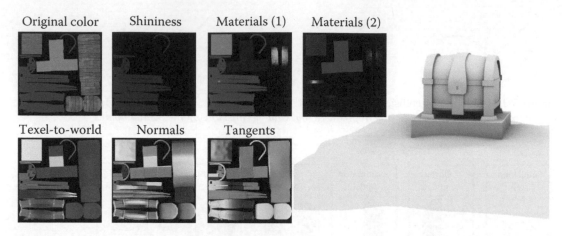

Figure 3.5. The material atlas contains all surface information. In this image a subset of the atlas textures is shown for the Chest scene.

stored in texels of the atlas—is assignable to eight available slots. In our examples, we needed only seven slots for water, dirt, metal, wood, organic, rust, and stone. All in all, the material atlas contains color + shininess (RGBA8), geometric normals and tangents (2 × RGB16F), shading normals (RGB16F), original and current height (2 × R16F), eight material amounts (ping-pong of 2 × RGBA8), eight original material amounts (2 × RGBA8), and a texture-to-world scale (RG16F), used later for equally-sized splatting. Thus, a parameterization is required for a one-to-one relation between surface points and respective atlas coordinates, which we obtain semi-automatically using standard DCC tools. For this, UV maps already present in game and movie production can be reused.

The atlas resolution is the dominant factor in trading visual quality for performance. To decrease the memory consumption, we reduced the amounts of our materials to 256 discrete steps each, thus 2 × RGBA8 textures are used for storage.

3.3.2   Gammaton Transport—The Simulation Step

To attain interactive frame rates, we only compute a fixed number of simulation steps each frame. Gammatons that are midair are marked as such and do not yet participate in material transport. The data stored for the gammatons is shown in Listing 3.1, including the payload carried by a gammaton during ray tracing, which is later passed into CUDA kernels as prd = payload record data, and the persistent data stored on the OptiX side alone (position) or shared with D3D (atlas texture coordinates of hit, material, etc.).

```
// Information a gammaton carries during tracing
struct GammaPayload
{
  uint ray_index;   // index in the hit buffers
  uint ray_depth;   // number of ray indirections
  float speed;      // speed (multiplied with direction)
};

// Hit buffer data that is used by OptiX only.
struct GammaHitOptix
{
  float3 position;  // position of the gammaton
};

// Hit buffer data that is shared between DirectX and OptiX
struct GammaHitShared
{
  float3 velocity;       // velocity vector
  int flags;             // midair (yes/no), active (yes/no)
  float2 texcoord;       // atlas coord at last hit surface
  uint2 carriedMaterial; // 8 bytes = 8 material slots
  int randomSeed;        // seed for random number generation
};
```

Listing 3.1. Data stored for the gammatons.

Recursive ray tracing. The CUDA entry program that launches the gammatons is shown in Listing 3.2 and works as follows: If a gammaton is active, i.e., it is currently midair or received a new direction in response to a collision, we continue the tracing from its last known position. Otherwise a gammaton is not active, i.e., it left the simulation domain, came to a halt on a nearly horizontal surface, or was absorbed. In that case, a new gammaton is emitted. This entry program is executed for each gammaton source in turn, using customizable emission parameters, e.g., position, direction, speed, and distribution. For the subsequent parallel processing of all gammatons, we assign each source an exclusive range of memory of a shared gammaton stream. Therefore, we set for each source a start offset g_SourceRayIndexOffset, as shown in Figure 3.6. The gammaton trajectory is traced as a recursive series of linear steps, each reporting a hit or miss. In OptiX, kernels are called for the respective events, as shown in Listings 3.3 and 3.4. In each step, we add gravity according to the traveled distance, which results in parabolic trajectories. For floating particles, gravity is acting tangentially. We trace a fixed number of linear steps per iteration until either a surface got hit, the gammaton left the domain, or the maximum recurrence depth is reached. In the latter case, we mark the gammaton as midair (flag). The material transport that is issued on impact of a gammaton is described later in Section 3.3.3. The collision response is selected by Russian Roulette on the events bouncing, floating, and absorbing (see Figure 3.3), according to their associated probabilities. Bouncing and floating particles are reflected by the tangent plane orthogonal to

```
void gammaton_entry_program ()
{
  // initialize payload
  Ray ray;  GammaPayload prd;
  prd.ray_index = launch_index + g_SourceRayIndexOffset;
  prd.ray_depth = 0;  // counts recursions

  // get gammaton data (ping pong)
  GammaHitShared& hitshared_i = HitShared_In [prd.ray_index];
  GammaHitShared& hitshared_o = HitShared_Out[prd.ray_index];

  // if gammaton is alive, continue the ray
  if (IS_ALIVE(hitshared_i.flags))
  {
    // continue from last position
    ray.origin = HitOptix[prd.ray_index].position;
    ray.direction = normalize(hitshared_i.velocity);
    prd.speed = length(hitshared_i.velocity);
    hitshared_o.carriedMaterial = hitshared_i.carriedMaterial;
  }
  else // else emit a new ray
  {
    ray.origin = generateRandomPosition();
    ray.direction = generateRandomDirection()
    prd.speed = g_InitialVelocity;
    hitshared_o.carriedMaterial = g_StartMaterial;
  }

  SET_ALIVE(hitshared_o.flags)  // set alive
  SET_BOUNCE(hitshared_o.flags) // flying freely
  hitshared_o.randomSeed = hitshared_i.randomSeed; // pass seed
  float maxDist = prd.speed * g_IntegrationStepSize;
  optixTraceGammaton(ray, prd, maxDist);          // launch ray
}
```

Listing 3.2. OptiX/CUDA entry program for gammaton emission and continue.

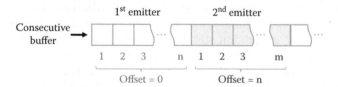

Figure 3.6. All gammaton emitters share an output gammaton stream. For each emitter a contiguous memory block is reserved to store the respective particles (here, n and m). Each gammaton keeps its address, even when inactive.

the estimated surface normal (see Section 3.3.5), and the outgoing direction is randomized by Phong lobe sampling for spreading material. For floating particles the resulting velocity vector is projected back into the tangent plane.

```
void gammaton_closest_hit ()
{
  GammaHitShared& hitshared = HitShared_Out [prd.ray_index];

  float3 v = ray.direction * prd.speed;   // velocity
  float3 phit = ray.origin + t_hit * ray.direction:
  float3 pnew = phit + attr_normal * EPSILON;   // move up

  // pick up velocity by fallen distance
  float  s = length(pnew - ray.origin);
  float dt = s / prd.speed;  // time = distance / speed
  v += dt * gravity;

  if (isTooSlow(v))                // too slow?
    SET_DEAD(hitshared.flags);     // set inactive
  SET_HIT(hitshared.flags);        // we hit a surface

  hitshared.texcoord = attr_texcoord;
  hitshared.velocity = normalize(v) * prd.speed;

  // Remember position until next launch
  GammaHitOptix& gammaState = GammaHitOptixMap [prd.ray_index];
  gammaState.position = pnew;

  // plant with probability (explained later).
  plantletPlacement (hitshared.randomSeed, pnew, attr_texcoord);
}
```

Listing 3.3.   OptiX/CUDA gammmaton closest hit program.   Attributes, e.g., `attr_normal` and `attr_texcoord`, are passed by the intersection test program.

Numerical considerations of floating particles.   We apply a numerical offset ϵ to the gammaton's position to avoid a self-intersection at the launch position. Since a floating particle moves tangentially to the surface, it virtually hovers above the surface. To create an intersection in the next iteration we let the ray aim at the surface by pulling the ray direction along the negated normal by the amount h (see Figure 3.7). The resulting speed of the floating gammatons depends on both

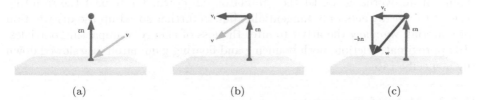

    (a)   (b)   (c)

Figure 3.7.   (a) Apply offset ϵ in normal direction to the hit position.   (b) Project the velocity $\mathbf{v}$ (•) into the tangential plane giving $\mathbf{v_t}$. (c) Pull $\mathbf{v_t}$ in negated normal direction by the amount of h, which yields a new direction $\mathbf{w}$ (•). *[Appeared in [Günther et al. 12] and reproduced by kind permission of the Eurographics Association.]*

```
void gammaton_miss()
{
  // compute position of gammaton
  float dt = g_IntegrationStepSize;
  float3 vold = ray.direction * prd.speed;

  float3 pnew = ray.origin + dt * vold;
  float3 vnew = vold + dt * gravity;

  GammaHitShared& hitshared = HitShared_Out[prd.ray_index];

  if (leftDomain(pnew)) {  // if outside bounding box
    SET_DEAD(hitshared.flags);
    return;
  }

  // Floating particle moved over edge
  if (IS_FLOAT(hitshared.flags)) {  // float
    vnew = make_float3(0,0,0);          // let gammaton fall
    SET_BOUNCE(hitshared.flags);     // free fall
  }

  // gammaton still alive after maximum depth
  prd.ray_depth++;
  if (prd.ray_depth >= MAX__GAMMATON__DEPTH) {
    HitOptix[prd.ray_index].position = pnew;
    hitshared.velocity = vnew;
    SET_ALIVE(hitshared.flags);
    SET_MIDAIR(hitshared.flags);
    return;
  }

  prd.speed = length(vnew);
  Ray ray(pnew, normalize(vnew));
  float maxDist = dt * prd.speed;
  optixTraceGammaton(ray, prd, maxDist);  // launch ray
}
```

Listing 3.4. OptiX/CUDA gammaton miss program.

the numerical offset ϵ as well as h. Floating particles can flow bottom up and around overhangs (see Figure 3.8). If a bounce event occurs or no intersection is found at an overhang, we let the gammaton fall down. On impact the resulting velocity typically acts only tangentially, but to further speed up the distribution of material, we allow the artist to alter the loss of energy of impacting particles. To approximate friction, both bouncing and floating gammatons are slowed down by a specific rate.

3.3.3   Material Transport

Our approach is based on the transport of materials by floating and bouncing gammatons. Thus, we let gammatons that hit a surface issue material transfer, for which both the material on the surface as well as the material carried by the

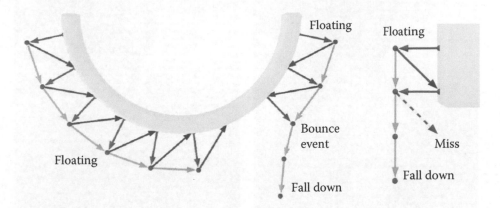

Figure 3.8. The visible course (•) of a gammaton floating around an overhang (left) and when dripping off a cliff (right). In the first, the gammaton on the right falls due to a bounce event. In the latter, the blue dashed ray misses and in response the gammaton falls down.

gammaton are sequentially updated. First, the gammatons are splatted into the material atlas to deposit material. Afterwards, a separate transform feedback pass is executed to update the material of the gammatons. (Modern graphics APIs allow for unordered access from all shader stages, making it possible to implement both update procedures in one pass. Legacy implementations require two separate steps.)

Determining transfer rates. The amount of material that is picked up depends first on the material type, for instance, to accommodate that water is more volatile than stone, and second on the material already present on the surface. The initial material on the surfaces is assigned by presets. The coefficients required for modeling volatileness `g_volatileness` are stored per material and can be part of an asset library. They are set once prior to the simulation for each material and can be stored and reused in other scenes. At runtime one degree of freedom remains: the pick-up ratio `g_pickUpRatio` between the amount of material picked up from the surface and added to the gammaton (and vice versa). A ratio of zero means that material is only picked up, whereas a ratio of one means all is dropped. Naturally, we obtain material preservation if this ratio is 1:1. Exposing this ratio to the artist allows both to speed up the aging process and to reverse it by washing away material, i.e., picking up more material than depositing (see Figure 3.9).

The amount of material to transfer is determined by the method in Listing 3.5.

Figure 3.9. Picking up more material than despositing allows for washing away material (left: before, right: after). *[Appeared in [Günther et al. 12] and reproduced by kind permission of the Eurographics Association.]*

```
float4 transferRate(float4 surfaceMat , float4 gammaMat)
{
   float4 delta =  surfaceMat * (1-g_pickUpRatio)
                 - gammaMat *     g_pickUpRatio;
   return delta * g_volatileness;
}
```

Listing 3.5. Determination of transfer rates for four materials at once.

Transport from gammaton to atlas. In order to transfer material from the gammatons into the atlas, we expand all gammatons that hit a surface to quads and splat the transferred material into the material atlas textures, using multiple render targets. The procedure is outlined in Listing 3.6. An issue to deal with is the varying area covered by texels of the atlas texture, since more space is reserved for detailed areas. To ensure that splats are equally sized in world space, we scale the quads in the geometry shader by the aforementioned, precomputed *texel-to-world scale*. Note that the clamping to the original material (last line in Listing 3.6) preserves the original material on the surface. This prevents the material from being washed away completely and thus continuously provides material input to the aging simulation.

Transport from atlas to gammaton. The gammaton material is updated afterwards in a separate transform feedback pass by feeding the gammatons into the ren-

```
void PS_SurfaceUpdate(
  in  float4 gammaPos : SV_Position,   // atlas pos of gammaton
  in  float4 gammaMat : MATERIAL,      // material of gammaton
  out float4 newMat   : SV_Target0)    // new surface material
{
  // get current and initial material on surface
  float4 curMat = g_TexMatCur.Load(gammaPos);
  float4 orgMat = g_TexMatOrg.Load(gammaPos);

  // calculate transfer rates and update material
  newMat = curMat - transferRate(curMat, gammaMat);
  newMat = max(orgMat, newMat); // clamp
}
```

Listing 3.6. Gammatons are expanded to quads in a geometry shader and are splatted into the atlas. This pixel shader removes material from the surface. Here, four material slots are updated at once.

dering pipeline as point list. In a geometry shader the material to transfer is calculated again and is added to the gammatons. Additionally, we chose this shader to handle collisions, i.e., to compute new bounce and float directions for the gammatons. Doing this in OptiX is possible as well. The respective geometry shader is outlined in Listing 3.7. We decided to keep inactive gammatons in the stream, as it eases launching of new gammatons.

3.3.4 Aging Rules

Aside from the transport of material by gammatons, the actual aging process is the other key aspect of our system. The idea is to model the temporal aging phenomena that take place if certain materials co-occur, by a set of generic rules. In our system, rules are implementations of a shader interface that alter a material set. In the simulation, we assign the chosen rule permutation by *dynamic shader linkage*. This concept is an advance from uber-shaders, for which registers are always allocated for the worst case branch, and sets of specialized shader files, which are hard to maintain due to their combinatorial growth. Dynamic shader linkage draws a profit from inlining selected functions (e.g., chosen rules) at bind time, thus enabling an optimal register allocation, while providing object-oriented aspects for the definition of rules. We chose to apply the rules to every material atlas texel by rendering a fullscreen quad, i.e., by using a pixel shader. The parameters of the rules are again stored in presets and are fetched at runtime from a single constant buffer. The interface, a sample implementation and the respective pixel shader are outlined in Listing 3.8. Practice showed that for many involved processes plausible approximations can be found by means of simple rules, as described next.

```
[maxvertexcount(1)]
void GS_GammatonUpdate( point GammaHitShared input[1],
   inout PointStream<GammaHitShared> PntStream )
{
   GammaHitShared output = input[0];
   if (IS_MIDAIR(input[0].Flags) || IS_DEAD(input[0].Flags)) {
      PntStream.Append(output);   // no need to act
      return;
   }
   // get material at surface and gammaton
   float4 surfMat = g_TexMatCur.SampleLevel(
                      g_Linear, gammaton.texcoord, 0);
   float4 gammaMat = unpackFromUint(gammaton.carriedMaterial);
   // calculate transfer rates and update material
   gammaMat += transferRate(surfMat, gammaMat);
   gammaMat = saturate(gammaMat);   // clamp
   gammaton.carriedMaterial = packToUint(gammaMat);

   float roulette = rnd(output.Seed);   // random value in [0..1]
   if (roulette < g_BounceProbability) {
      SET_BOUNCE(output.Flags);   // set bounce
      PhongLobeBounce(output);    // handles bounce
   }
   else if (roulette < g_BounceProbability+g_FloatProbability) {
      SET_FLOAT(output.Flags);    // set float
      PhongLobeBounce(output);    // handles float
   }
   else SET_DEAD(output.Flags);   // absorb

   PntStream.Append(output);
}
```

Listing 3.7. Geometry shader, used in the transform feedback loop to update both the gammaton material and the rebound direction. For simplicity, this listing shows the update of four materials. Note that both bouncing and floating gammatons are handled by the PhongLobeBounce method, depending on the value of output.Flags.

Rust. The first rule corrodes metal in the presence of water. We limit the corrosion speed by the rarer material. Therefore, we set the strength of the rust generation to the minimum of the amount of water and metal, as shown in Listing 3.8. An additional speed parameter provides user control to adjust aging processes relative to one another, e.g., to accommodate that corrosion is slower than lichen growth. Finally, the created amount of rust is added to the already existing rust on the surface.

Decay. The second rule is used to produce organic material and dirt. Here, the amount of created material depends on the currently present water and wood. The implementation is similar to the previous rule, with the difference that two materials are generated instead of one.

Evaporation. We added an additional rule that evaporates water over time; in part to model the phenomenon but also for a practical reason: as a gammaton

```
struct RuleParams {
  float Chance;
  float Speed;
  /* optional: further parameters */
};

interface IRule {
  MatProperty Apply(MatProperty mat, RuleParams p);
};

class IRust : IRule {
  MatProperty Apply(MatProperty mat, RuleParams p);
  {
    mat.Rust += min(mat.Water, mat.Metal) * p.Speed;
    return mat;
  }
};
IRust pRust;

/* other rules */

IRule pRules[NUM_RULES] = {pRust, /* other instances */ }

OUTPUT PS_AgingProcess(int3 atlasCoord)
{
  MatProperty mat = READ_SURFACE_MATERIAL(atlasCoord);
  uint seed = READ_RANDOM_SEED(atlasCoord);

  for(int r=0; r<NUM_RULES; r++)
    if (rnd(seed) < g_RuleParameters[r].Chance)
      mat = pRules[r].Apply(mat, g_RuleParameters[r]);

  OUTPUT.Material = mat;
  OUTPUT.RandomSeed = seed;
}
```

Listing 3.8. Aging rules are implementations of an interface and are bound using dynamic shader linkage. Rules are applied at a customizable probability.

source constantly emits water, we want to keep the amount of water in the scene limited to better control where aging takes place.

Since our material amounts are discretized to 256 steps each, we invoke the aging rules at a customizable probability to allow for slow corrosion speeds as well. The therefore required random numbers are generated by a linear congruence generator, thus the modified random seed is written on output to be input to the next iteration.

3.3.5 Composition

The composition stage is used to produce aged textures and is implemented in two subsequent rasterization passes. In the first pass, aged colors, shininess, and the height map are computed based on the amount of material resting on the ground. In the second pass, we estimate normals based on the height (see Figure 3.10).

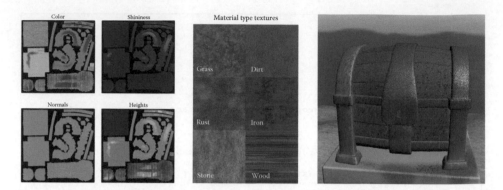

Figure 3.10. Composed textures (left), textures associated with the material types (center), composed aged chest (right). While the left side of the model is aged only slightly the amount of rust, dirt, and organic material increases to the right.

Depending on the needs of the artists or production standards, the composition processes might need to be adapted and further material information might need to be exported. For preview rendering purposes, we used the Phong reflection model and used the same output textures for a high-quality rendering in a DCC tool (see Figure 3.1). The initial material on the surface is already visually represented in the original diffuse texture. Thus, for compositing we only need to consider the amount of newly added material by taking the difference between the currently present material $\mathbf{m}_{curr}$ and the initial material $\mathbf{m}_{init}$. To assemble the resulting diffuse color, we blend the original surface texture with color textures $\mathbf{s}_i$ representing the individual material types (see Figure 3.10, center). The appearance pattern of the deposited material color $\mathbf{c}_{deposit}$ is controlled by a base strength b_i and a random variation v_i:

$$\mathbf{c}_{deposit} = \sum_i \max(0, \mathbf{m}_{curr,i} - \mathbf{m}_{init,i}) \cdot \mathbf{s}_i \cdot (b_i + v_i \cdot \xi_i),$$

whereas ξ_i denotes a uniformly destributed random number. This allows modeling a wider range of appearances, including homogeneous patina of copper or noisy rust stains on iron surfaces.

The resulting diffuse color is computed by the weighted sum of the deposited colors of all material types:

$$\mathbf{c}_{diffuse} = \mathrm{lerp}\left(\mathbf{c}_{org}, \mathbf{c}_{deposit}, \mathrm{saturate}\left(\sum_i (b_i + v_i \cdot \xi_i) \right) \right).$$

The shininess is estimated similarly, leaving out the color textures. The height map is computed based on the amount of material resting on the surface, which is then used in a second pass to estimate surface normals from neighboring texels. The parameters of the composition can be changed during or after the simulation.

3.4   Preview Rendering

Once the weathered textures are composed, we can start with the preview rendering, which serves two purposes: First, it is a preview for the eventually employed
renderer, thus needs to resemble it closely. Ideally, the simulation system should
be integrated into a content creation system, running on top of the eventually
used rendering engine. For our demo, we render the scene with forward shading
and apply the output textures from the composition stage, i.e., the aged color,
normals, height, and shininess. Second, the preview rendering needs to make the
amounts of material visible to give the content artist feedback. Therefore, we use
distance-dependent tessellation and displacement mapping to display the height
and place billboards to visualize lichen growth.

```
float dtf(float3 pos)   // distance-dependent tess factor
{
  return lerp(g_MinTessFactor, g_MaxTessFactor,
    smoothstep(g_MinTessDist, g_MaxTessDist, dist(g_Eye, pos)));
}

HS__CONSTANT__DATA ConstantHS(in InputPatch<float3, 3> Pos,
  out float Edges[3]  : SV_TessFactor,
  out float Inside[1] : SV_InsideTessFactor)
{
  HS__CONSTANT__DATA output;
  // compute tessellation factors for each vertex
  float3 tess = float3(dtf(Pos[0]), dtf(Pos[1]), dtf(Pos[2]));

  // set factors for the edges and the interior
  Edges[0] = max(tess.y, tess.z);
  Edges[1] = max(tess.x, tess.z);
  Edges[2] = max(tess.x, tess.y);
  Inside[0] = max(tess.x, Edges[0]);
}

[domain("tri")]
PS_INPUT DomainShader( HS__CONSTANT__DATA input,
  float3 UV : SV_DomainLocation,
  const OutputPatch<DS_INPUT, 3> controlPnt )
{
  // Barycentric interpolation of control points
  float3 outPos = controlPnt[0].Pos * UV.x
                + controlPnt[1].Pos * UV.y
                + controlPnt[2].Pos * UV.z;

  /* Barycentric interpolation of normal, tangents, ... */
  /* Displace surface point outPos in normal direction ... */

  return PS_INPUT(outPos, normal, tangents, ...);
}
```

Listing 3.9. We employ distance-dependent tessellation in the preview rendering to
display the amount of material on the surface by displacement mapping.

3.4.1 Displaying Height

Tessellation shaders allow for adaptive subdivision of the surface geometry by introducing two new shader stages after the vertex shader: a hull and a domain shader. The hull shader is typically used to perform calculations for each control point of a surface patch. In our case, both the vertex and hull shader by-pass positions, normals, and texture coordinates. The function `ConstantHS` in Listing 3.9 is executed once per control patch to compute the distance-dependent tessellation factors. Based on these factors, a fixed-function tessellation engine subdivides the patches. The domain shader is executed for each vertex of the refined mesh and is used to interpolate properties from the control points, i.e., positions, normals, tangents, and so on. Additionally, we apply a vertex displacement by the value in the height map, which originates in the amount of material on the surface. Eventually, the pixel shader shades the surface using normal mapping.

3.4.2 Displaying Lichen

To visualize the spread of lichen, we place and scale plantlet billboards according to the concentration of organic material, shown in Figure 3.11. To maintain a constant number of plantlets we randomly reseed them to adapt to the current organic distribution in the scene. Thereby, each gammaton is responsible for one plantlet, see function `plantletPlacement` in Listing 3.10, as called from the closest hit program in Listing 3.3. For the billboards we expand the quads in view space using a geometry shader.

Figure 3.11. Depictions of the intermediate output. Left: plantlets distributed in regions of high lichen growth. Right: Distance-dependent tessellation with displacement mapping, depending on the amount of rust and organic material. *[Appeared in [Günther et al. 12] and reproduced by kind permission of the Eurographics Association.]*

```
// Data stored per plantlet (shared between DirectX and OptiX)
struct PlantletShared {
    float3 Position;      // Position of the plantlet.
    uint RayIndex;        // Used to select texture.
    float2 AtlasCoord;    // Atlas coordinate of the plantlet.
};

void plantletPlacement(int rndSeed, float3 pos, float2 texcoord)
{
    if (rnd(rndSeed) < g_SeedProbability) {
        PlantletShared& plantlet = PlantletShared[prd.ray_index];
        plantlet.Position = pos;
        plantlet.RayIndex = prd.ray_index;
        plantlet.AtlasCoord = texcoord;
    }
}
```

Listing 3.10. CUDA device function for placing plantlets.

3.5 Results

The polishing of textures to attain weathered looks is a building brick in most content creation pipelines, one that was previously subject to manual processing alone. In Figure 3.12, we show a time series of our aging simulation and for Figure 3.1 we exported the composed textures and rendered the scenes in a standard DCC tool.

Our system presents intermediate output and allows for interactive modification of parameters (simulation, aging rules, composition, etc.) and the interactive movement of gammaton sources. Timing results are given in Table 3.1 for an Intel Core i7-2600K CPU and an Nvidia GeForce GTX 560 Ti GPU. The composition is the slowest component, though optional to the simulation pipeline. It may be broken down, to be carried out over a span of multiple frames in order to adjust to the narrow time budget of real-time applications, e.g., modern games.

Step	Chest	Hydrant	Otto
Simulation Step	2.57	1.72	2.25
Surface Update	0.03	0.03	0.03
Gammaton Update	0.03	0.03	0.03
Aging Process	0.25	0.25	0.25
Composition	7.19	7.11	7.01
Preview Rendering	2.32	2.08	1.82
Total Time	12.39	11.22	11.39

Table 3.1. Timing breakdown in milliseconds for the pipeline stages at an atlas resolution of 1K × 1K, 5K gammatons per iteration and a screen resolution of 800 × 800 pixels.

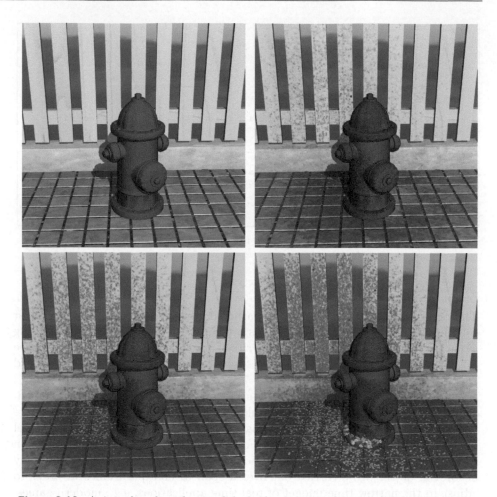

Figure 3.12. Aging of a selected part of the hydrant scene, shown at different time steps. *[Appeared in [Günther et al. 12] and reproduced by kind permission of the Eurographics Association.]*

Further discussions on user interface decisions, the impact of the atlas resolution on memory consumption and visual quality, as well as texture seam handling can be found in our paper [Günther et al. 12].

3.6   Conclusions

In this chapter, we presented an interactive material aging simulation based on gammaton tracing on the GPU. We used a simple yet powerful set of rules to obtain the most common aging effects, including dirt, rust, organic, and water precipitate, and displayed those in a few seconds in which the scene progressively and visibly ages. Open for further investigation is the simulation on large scenes. For now, our approach is limited to a few objects chosen by the content artist as a region of interest, since the memory consumption limits the material atlas size and thus the visual quality. A number of extensions to our approach are imaginable. If more memory was available, e.g., by compression, it would be possible to add multiple layers of material, not only one as we do now. Related to this is the gradual peeling of layers [Paquette et al. 02], possibly initiating a more distinctive deformation of the surface, which could go beyond the capabilities of a single-pass tessellation shader. Another direction to look into is the implementation of a more detailed temporal aging behavior, since many materials are subject to a nonlinear aging process [Gu et al. 06]. On the GPU, discrete time steps could be easily encoded in a 3D texture, whereas the third dimension is time.

Bibliography

[Chen et al. 05] Yanyun Chen, Lin Xia, Tien-Tsin Wong, Xin Tong, Hujun Bao, Baining Guo, and Heung-Yeung Shum. "Visual Simulation of Weathering by Gammaton tracing." *ACM Transactions on Graphics* 24:3 (2005), 1127–1133.

[Gu et al. 06] Jinwei Gu, Chien-I Tu, Ravi Ramamoorthi, Peter Belhumeur, Wojciech Matusik, and Shree Nayar. "Time-varying Surface Appearance: Acquisition, Modeling and Rendering." *ACM Transactions on Graphics* 25:3 (2006), 762–771.

[Günther et al. 12] Tobias Günther, Kai Rohmer, and Thorsten Grosch. "GPU-Accelerated Interactive Material Aging." In *Proceedings of the Vision, Modeling and Visualization Workshop 2012*, pp. 63–70. Genevea: Eurographics Association, 2012.

[Paquette et al. 02] Eric Paquette, Pierre Poulin, and George Drettakis. "The Simulation of Paint Cracking and Peeling." In *Graphics Interface 2002*, pp. 59–68. Natick, MA: Canadian Human-Computer Communications Society and A K Peters, Ltd., 2002.

[Parker et al. 10] Steven G Parker, James Bigler, Andreas Dietrich, Heiko Friedrich, Jared Hoberock, David Luebke, David McAllister, and Martin Stich. "OptiX: A General Purpose Ray Tracing Engine." *ACM Transactions on Graphics* 29:4 (2010), 1–13.

Simple Rasterization-Based Liquids
Martin Guay

4.1 Overview

Rasterization pipelines are ubiquitous today. They can be found in most of our personal computers as well as in smaller, hand-held devices—like smart phones—with lower-end hardware. However, simulating particle-based liquids requires sorting the particles, which is cumbersome when using a rasterization pipeline.

In this chapter, we describe a method to simulate liquids *without* having to sort the particles. Our method was specifically designed for these architectures and low shader model specifications (starting from shader model 3 for 3D liquids). Instead of sorting the particles, we splat them onto a grid (i.e., a 3D or 2D texture) and solve the inter-particle dynamics *directly* on the grid. Splatting is simple to perform in a rasterization pipeline, but can also be costly. Thanks to the simplified pass on the grid, we only need to splat the particles once.

The grid also provides additional benefits: we can easily add artificial obstacles for the particles to interact with, we can ray cast the grid directly to render the liquid surface, and we can even gain a speed up over sort-based liquid solvers—such as the optimized solver found in the DirectX 11 SDK.

4.2 Introduction

Simulating liquids requires dealing with two phases of *fluid*—the liquid and the air—which can be tricky to model as special care may be required for the interface between the two phases depending on the fluid model. In computer graphics, there are mainly two popular formulations for *fluids*: strongly incompressible and weakly incompressible.

The strong formulation is usually more complex as it requires a hard constraint (e.g., solving a Poisson equation), but it is more accurate and therefore more visually pleasing. Because it is more complex, it is often used along simple, regular *grid* discretizations [Stam 99]. For liquids, several intermediate steps are required for the surface to behave adequately [Enright et al. 02]. Implementing these steps using rasterization APIs is challenging. For instance, [Crane et al. 07] only partially implements them and the fluid behaves more like a single phase fluid. Furthermore, the strong formulation requires a surface representation like a *level-set* density field, which requires its own set of specificities (re-initialization). Again, in [Crane et al. 07] the level-set method is only partially implemented and had to be hacked into staying at a certain height; preventing them from generating such scenarios as the water jet shown in Figure 4.3.

The weak formulation on the other hand, requires only a simple soft constraint to keep the fluid from compressing. It is much simpler, but also less accurate. It is often used along particle discretizations and *mesh-free* numerical schemes like *Smooth Particles Hydrodynamics* (SPH) [Desbrun and Cani 96]. The advantage of the weak formulation along particles is really for liquids. This combination allowed reproducing the behavior of liquids without computing any surface boundary conditions similar to [Enright et al. 02]. Additionally, the particles can be used directly to render the liquid surface and there is no need for a level-set. The drawback however, is that particles require finding their neighbors, in order to compute forces ensuring they keep at a minimal distance. Typically buckets or other spacial sorting algorithms are used to cluster the particles into groups [Amada et al. 04, Rozen et al. 08, Bayraktar et al. 08], which can be cumbersome to implement using rasterization APIs.

Instead of sorting the particles, our method makes use of rasterization capabilities. First, we rasterize, or splat, the particle density onto a grid. Then, we use simple finite difference to compute all the interacting forces—including the soft incompressibility constraint—on the grid, in a single pass. Some have considered splatting before [Kolb and Cuntz 05] but had to splat for each force (*pressure and viscosity*), while we only need to splat once—for all the forces. Finally, the particles are corrected and moved by sampling the grid—which in turn can also be used *directly* to render the liquid surface by ray casting the splatted *density*. Overall, our method allows treating each particle independently while making sure they automatically repulse one another and avoid rigid obstacles in the domain.

4.3 Simple Liquid Model

Our liquid model is best described as follows: particles are allowed to move freely in the domain while their mass and kinetic energy remains conserved. For instance, if we add gravity it should translate into velocity $\mathbf{u}$. To keep the particles from interpenetrating, we add a soft incompressibility constraint P derived from the density ρ of particles and the resulting force is the negative gradient of P:

$$\frac{D\rho}{Dt} = 0,$$

$$\frac{D\mathbf{u}}{Dt} = -\nabla P + \mathbf{g} + \mathbf{f}_{\text{ext}}, \tag{4.1}$$

where $\mathbf{g}$ gravity and $\mathbf{f}_{\text{ext}}$ accounts for external forces such as user interactions. The terms $\frac{D\rho}{Dt}$ and $\frac{D\mathbf{u}}{Dt}$ account for the transport of density and velocity. There is never any density added nor removed, it is only transported and held by the particles leading to $\frac{D\rho}{Dt} = 0$. Energy added to the velocity—like gravity—needs to be conserved as well, resulting in equation (4.1). Next we define the incompressibility constraint P and how to compute the density of particles ρ.

4.3.1 Pressure Constraint

To keep the fluid from compressing and the particles from inter-penetrating, we penalize high density: $P = k\rho$ [Desbrun and Cani 96], where k is a stiffness parameter that makes the particles repulse one another more strongly (but can also make the simulation unstable if too large). Hence, by minimizing the density, the particles will move in the direction that reduces density the most and thereby avoid each other. At the same time, gravity and boundary conditions, like the walls, will act to keep the particles from simply flying away.

Keeping the particles from inter-penetrating is crucial in particle-based liquid simulations. To give strict response to the particles that are close to colliding, we can make the density nonlinear leading to the pressure constraint [Becker and Teschner 07]: $P = k \left(\frac{\rho}{\rho_0} \right)^{\gamma}$, where γ is an integer (5 in our case). Dividing by the initial density ρ_0 comes in handy for stability; it becomes easier to control the magnitude of the force through the parameter k and thereby keep the simulation stable.

Setting the initial ρ_0 can be tricky. It should be a proportional evaluation of ρ at an initial rest configuration, i.e., with a uniform distribution of particles. In practice, however, we can set it manually. We approximate ρ by performing a convolution, which we pre-compute on a texture by rasterizing, or splatting the kernels of each particle.

4.4 Splatting

To evaluate the density of particles smoothly, we perform a convolution: the density is the weighted average of the surrounding discrete samples, in this case the particles. The weight is given by a kernel function, which falls off exponentially with distance, as shown in Figure 4.1. Instead of sampling the nearby particles,

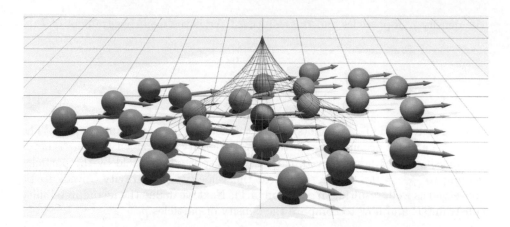

Figure 4.1. Splatting consists in *rasterizing* the smooth kernel function, the 2D case shown here in red. In Figure 4.2, we see the sum of all the kernel functions; a scalar field representing the density of particles.

Figure 4.2. Illustrating the scalar density field used to define the pressure constraint. The pressure force is proportional to the density gradient pushing the particles toward minimum density. For simplicity, we show the idea in 2D with density shown as a height field—which can also be used as the liquid surface in *Shallow Water* simulations (see Figure 4.4).

we rasterize the kernel function centered at each particle. The final result is a smooth density grid (texture)—like the one shown in Figure 4.2—that is equivalent to a convolution evaluation at each point on the texture. We could say also that we now have a virtual particle on each grid cell.

4.4.1 Rasterizing Kernel Functions

To update the velocity on the grid, we need to transfer both the density of the particles—to compute pressure—and their velocity. Hence, the first step in our algorithm is to rasterize the smooth kernel function (red in Figure 4.1) and the weighted velocity of each particle. We render the particles as points and create quad slices—spanning a cube—in the geometry shader. For each corner vertex $\mathbf{x}_i$, we write the distance $d = \|\mathbf{x}_i - \mathbf{x}_p\|$ to the center of the particle $\mathbf{x}_p$, and let the rasterizer perform the interpolation between vertices. Then, in a pixel shader, we render the smooth kernel value $w(d, r)$ to the alpha channel, and the weighted velocity $w(d, r)\mathbf{u}_p$ to the other three channels—in an additive fashion. Finally, the density on the grid can be sampled by multiplying the sum of kernel weights by the mass, and the velocity by dividing the sum of weighted velocities by the sum of weights:

$$\rho(\mathbf{x}_i) = m_i \sum_p w\left(\|\mathbf{x}_i - \mathbf{x}_p\|, r\right), \qquad \mathbf{u}(\mathbf{x}_i) = \frac{\sum_p w\left(\|\mathbf{x}_i - \mathbf{x}_p\|, r\right) \mathbf{u}_p}{\sum_p w\left(\|\mathbf{x}_i - \mathbf{x}_p\|, r\right)},$$

where i denotes texture indices, p particle indices, and r the kernel radius. We used the following convolution kernel:

$$w(d, r) = \left(1 - \frac{d^2}{r^2}\right)^3.$$

Next we update the velocity field on the grid to make the particles move in a direction that keeps them from compressing, by computing a pressure force from the density of particles and adding it to the velocity.

4.5 Grid Pass

In the grid pass, we update the splatted velocity field with the pressure force, gravity, and artificial pressure for obstacles (see Section 4.7). We compute the pressure gradient using a finite difference approximation and add forces to the velocity field using forward Euler integration:

$$\mathbf{u}^{n+1} = \mathbf{u}^n - \Delta t \left(\frac{P(x_{i+1}) - P(x_{i-1})}{\Delta x}, \frac{P(x_{j+1}) - P(x_{j-1})}{\Delta y}\right),$$

where Δt is the time step, Δx the spatial resolution of grid, and n the temporal state of the simulation.

While we update the velocity, we set the velocity on the boundary cells of the grid to a no-slip boundary condition by setting the component of the velocity that is normal to the boundary to 0. This is a simple boundary test; before writing the final velocity value, we check if the neighbor is a boundary and set the component of the velocity in that direction to 0.

4.6   Particle Update

We update the position and velocity of particles following the Particle-In-Cell (PIC) and Fluid-In-Particle (FLIP) approaches that mix particles and grids [Zhu and Bridson 05]. The main idea with these numerical schemes is that instead of sampling the grid to assign new values (e.g., velocities) to the particles, we can recover only the differences to their original values.

4.6.1   Particle Velocity

In PIC, the particle's velocity is taken directly from the grid, which tends to be very dissipative, viscous and leads to damped flow. For more lively features and better energy conservation, FLIP assigns only the *difference* in velocities; the difference between the splatted velocity and the updated splatted velocity discussed in Section 4.5.

By combining both PIC and FLIP, the liquid can be made very viscous like melting wax, or it can be made very energetic like water. A parameter r lets the user control the amount of each:

$$\mathbf{u}_p = r\mathbf{u}^{n+1}(\mathbf{x}_p) + (1-r)(\mathbf{u}_p - \Delta\mathbf{u}), \quad \text{with} \quad \Delta\mathbf{u} = \mathbf{u}^n(\mathbf{x}_p) - \mathbf{u}^{n+1}(\mathbf{x}_p),$$

where $\mathbf{u}^n$ and $\mathbf{u}^{n+1}$ are grid velocities before and after the velocity update in Section 4.5, and $\mathbf{x}_p, \mathbf{u}_p$ are the particle's position and velocity. Using a bit of PIC ($r = 0.05$) is useful in stabilizing the simulation performed with explicit Euler integration, which can become unstable if the time step is too large.

4.6.2   Particle Position

While we update the particle velocity, we also update the particle positions. We integrate the particle position using two intermediate steps of Runge-Kutta 2 (RK2), each time sampling the velocity on the grid. The second-order scheme is only approximate in our case because the velocity field on the grid is kept constant during integration. At each intermediate step, we keep the particles from leaving the domain by clamping their positions near the box boundaries:

$$\mathbf{x}_p^{n+1} = \Delta t \mathbf{u}^{n+1}(\mathbf{x}_p^{n+\frac{1}{2}}), \quad \text{with} \quad \mathbf{x}_p^{n+\frac{1}{2}} = 0.5\Delta t \mathbf{u}^{n+1}(\mathbf{x}_p^n).$$

Note that we never modify the density value of the particles.

4.7   Rigid Obstacles

We can prevent the particles from penetrating rigid obstacles in the domain by adding an artificial pressure constraint where the objects are. This follows the same logic as with the particle density. We define a smooth distance field to the surface of the object, which can also be viewed as a density field. We can use analytical functions for primitives like spheres to approximate the shape of the objects. This avoids rasterizing volumes or voxelizing meshes on the GPU. Alternatively, one could approximate shapes using *Metaballs* [Blinn 82] and implicit surfaces that naturally provide a distance field. No matter which approach we choose, the gradient of these distance fields ρ_{Obstacle} can be computed analytically or numerically and plugged into the velocity update formula covered in Section 4.5.

When looking at the Shallow Water Equations (SWE), we find similarities with the equations outlined in this chapter. In fact, by looking at the density field as the height field of a liquid surface, we can imagine using our method directly for height field simulations shown in Figure 4.4. On the other hand, there is usually a ground height term in the SWE. This in turn can be interpreted in 3D as a distance field for rigid objects as we mentioned above.

4.8 Examples

We show a few simulation examples implemented with HLSL, compiled as level 4 shaders. They include a 3D liquid with rigid objects in the domain, a 2D shallow water height field simulation, and a 2D simulation comparing with the optimized Direct Compute implementation of SPH available in the DirectX 11 SDK. Measures include both simulation and rendering. We splat particles with a radius of 3 cells on 16-bit floating point textures without any significant loss in visual quality. In general we used a grid size close to $\sqrt[d]{N_P}$ texels per axis, where d is the domain dimension (2 or 3) and N_P is the total number of particles.

In Figure 4.3, we rendered the fluid surface by raycasting the density directly. We perform a fixed number of steps and finish with an FXAA antialiasing pass (framebuffer size 1024×768). We used 125k particles on a 96^3 texture and the

Figure 4.3. A 3D liquid simulation with obstacles in the domain implemented using the rasterization pipeline. The simulation runs at 35 FPS using 125k particles on a Quadro 2000M graphics card.

Figure 4.4. The shallow water equations describe the evolution of water height over time. By looking at the height as the density of a 2D fluid, we see the equations becoming similar. Hence, our method can be used directly to simulate height fields. This figure shows a SWE simulation with 42k particles using our method.

simulation performs at 35 frames per second (FPS) on a Quadro 2000M graphics card.

In Figure 4.4, we see a shallow water simulation using 42k particles on a 256^2 grid. The simulation and rendering together run at 130 FPS using the same graphics card.

We compared our solver *qualitatively* with the SPH GPU implementation in the DirectX 11 SDK (Figure 4.5). Their solver is implemented using the Direct Compute API, has shared memory optimizations and particle neighbor search acceleration. Ours uses HLSL shaders only. In Table 4.1, we compare the performance of both methods with different particle quantities. We can see that our method scales better with the number of particles involved for a given grid size and splatting radius on the hardware we used.

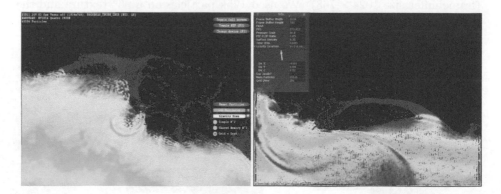

Figure 4.5. Comparison between an optimized SPH solver implemented with Compute Shaders on the left and our method implemented with rasterization APIs. Our method performs at 296 FPS using while the optimized SPH solver runs at 169 FPS.

Particle Amount	Grid Size Dim(ϕ, u)		Our Method (FPS)		DX SDK 11 (FPS)		Speedup Ratio
64,000	256^2		296		169		1.75
32,000	256^2		510		325		1.55
16,000	256^2		830		567		1.45

Table 4.1. Comparison between our method and the optimized SPH solver found in the DirectX 11 SDK.

4.9 Conclusion

In *GPU Pro 2*, we described the $1 fluid solver: by combining the simplicity of weakly incompressible fluids with the simplicity of grids, we could simulate a single phase fluid (smoke or fire) in a single pass [Guay et al. 11]. In this chapter, we described the $1 liquid solver for rasterization APIs by combining the simplicity of the particles for dealing with liquids with the simplicity of the grids to compute the forces. This is useful in getting a liquid solver running quickly on platforms that do not necessarily implement compute APIs.

Bibliography

[Amada et al. 04] T. Amada, M. Imura, Y. Yasumoto, Y. Yamabe, and K. Chihara. "Particle-Based Fluid Simulation on GPU." In *ACM Workshop on General-Purpose Computing on Graphics Processors*, pp. 228–235. New York: ACM, 2004.

[Bayraktar et al. 08] S. Bayraktar, U. Güdükbay, and B. Özgüç. "GPU-Based Neighbor-Search Algorithm for Particle Simulations." *Journal of Graphics, GPU, and Game Tools* 14:1 (2008), 31–42.

[Becker and Teschner 07] M. Becker and M. Teschner. "Weakly compressible SPH for free surface flows." In *Proceedings of the 2007 ACM SIGGRAPH/Eurographics Symposium on Computer Animation*, pp. 209–218. Aire-la-Ville, Switzerland: Eurographics Association, 2007.

[Blinn 82] J. F. Blinn. "A Generalization of Algebraic Surface Drawing." *ACM Transactions on Graphics (TOG)* 1:3 (1982), 235–256.

[Crane et al. 07] K. Crane, I. Llamas, and S. Tariq. "Real-Time Simulation and Rendering of 3D Fluids." In *GPU Gems 3*, edited by Hubert Nguyen. Upper Saddle River, NJ: Addison-Wesley, 2007.

[Desbrun and Cani 96] M. Desbrun and M.P. Cani. "Smoothed Particles: A New Paradigm for Animating Highly Deformable Bodies." In *Proceedings of*

Eurographics Workshop on Computer Animation and Simulation, pp. 61–76. New York: Springer, 1996.

[Enright et al. 02] D. Enright, S. Marschner, and R. Fedkiw. "Animation and Rendering of Complex Water Surfaces." In *Proceedings of the 29th Annual Conference on Computer Graphics and Interactive Techniques (SIGGRAPH '02)*, pp. 736–744. New York: ACM, 2002.

[Guay et al. 11] M. Guay, F. Colin, and R. Egli. "Simple and Fast Fluids." In *GPU Pro 2*, edited by Wolfgang Engel, pp. 433–444. Natick, MA: A K Peters, Ltd., 2011.

[Kolb and Cuntz 05] A. Kolb and N. Cuntz. "Dynamic Particle Coupling for GPU-Based Fluid Simulation." Presentation, Symposium on Simulation Technique, Wuppertal, Germany, March, 2005.

[Rozen et al. 08] T. Rozen, K. Boryczko, and W. Alda. "GPU Bucket Sort Algorithm with Applications to Nearest-Neighbour Search." *Journal of the 16th Int. Conf. in Central Europe on Computer Graphics, Visualization and Computer Vision* 16:1-3 (2008), 161–167.

[Stam 99] J. Stam. "Stable Fluids." In *Proceedings of the 26th ACM SIGGRAPH Conference*, pp. 121–128. New York: ACM Press, 1999.

[Zhu and Bridson 05] Y. Zhu and R. Bridson. "Animating Sand as a Fluid." In *Proceedings of ACM SIGGRAPH 2005*, pp. 965–972. New York: ACM, 2005.

Lighting and Shading

We've seen a great jump in the quality of game lighting in recent years. In a natural progression from per-vertex shaded triangles through simple per-pixel Phong of the first GPUs we entered the era of highly customized energy preserving lighting models. The new lighting models offer greater realism expected from the games on the new generation consoles, while allowing the artists much simpler control, enabling them to effectively produce the incredible amount of assets required for the new games.

The chapter "Physically Based Area Lights" by Michal Drobot discusses the lighting approach used in the Playstation 4 exclusive launch title *Killzone: Shadow Fall* from Guerrilla Games. We went beyond the energy preserving model implementation and focused on accurate area light representation needed, for example, for realistic specular reflections of the Sun. Area lights are almost a necessity for effective work with the new energy preserving lighting models, as these don't allow artists to fake bright and wide specular lobes any more.

The section also includes two chapters about volumetric lighting. "High Performance Outdoor Light Scattering Using Epipolar Sampling" by Egor Yusov describes the efficient solution for rendering large scale Sun-lit atmosphere. The author uses epipolar sampling and 1D min-max shadow maps to accelerate the rendering process.

"Volumetric Light Effects in *Killzone: Shadow Fall*" by Nathan Vos focuses on the practical solutions to the in-game rendering of volumetrics from both local lights and sunlight. He offers several methods for both speed and quality improvements of the volumetrics as well as solutions for combining volumetric effects with other transparencies in the scene.

The next chapter, "Hi-Z Screen-Space Cone-Traced Reflections," by Yasin Uludag describes the fast screen-space real-time reflections system used in the new *Mirror's Edge* game. Yasin uses ideas from cone tracing to produce plausible reflections for any surface roughness as well as hierarchical Z-buffer to accelerate the ray marching pass.

"TressFX: Advanced Real-Time Hair Rendering" by Timothy Martin, Wolfgang Engel, Nicolas Thibieroz, Jason Yang, and Jason Lacroix discusses techniques used for hair rendering in the *Tomb Raider*. The authors cover individual conservative hair rasterization and antialiasing, transparency sorting using linked lists, as well as lighting and shadowing of the hair volume.

The last chapter in this section is "Wire Antialiasing" by Emil Persson. This chapter focuses on the very specific problem of antialiasing and lighting of wire meshes (such as telephone cables).

I would like to thank all authors for sharing their ideas and for all the hard work they put into their chapters.

—Michal Valient

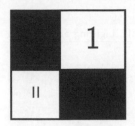

Physically Based Area Lights
Michal Drobot

1.1 Overview

This chapter presents the physically based area lighting system used in *Killzone: Shadow Fall*, developed by Guerrilla Games for Playstation 4 (see Figure 1.1).

We present a novel, real-time, analytical model for area lights, capable of supporting multiple light shapes. Each shape can be represented by simple 3D or 2D functions on a plane. Discussed applications include the following light shapes: sphere, disk, and rectangle.

The model supports diffuse and specular lighting. BRDF (bidirectional reflectance distribution function) implementation in *Killzone: Shadow Fall* rendering engine explicitly splits the material reflectance model from the lighting model itself. This allows a separation between different surface simulation algorithms and light types, which supply the former with required light quantities. To achieve this, we use the importance sampling principle to approximate nonfinite or computationally expensive integrals in the material reflectance part of the BRDF. This chapter focuses only on the derivation of the proposed framework and actual light modeling part.

All lights in the rendering engine are physically based area lights, described by radiometric quantities such as light intensity in lumens, dimensions in meters, world orientation, and light shape type. We introduce a specialized description of surface roughness that is shared or adapted to match various surface reflectance models. The light model uses light description and surface roughness, at the point being shaded, to deliver light quantity arriving at the point—split between the light model and the surface reflectance model.

In addition we discuss integration of the proposed model into deferred renderer and how it was used as a principle for environmental probe generation and dynamic analytical texture-based area lights.

Figure 1.1. Usage of area lights in *Killzone: Shadow Fall.*

1.2   Introduction

The current game industry standard for lighting models is Blinn-Phong BRDF or models directly based on it. In recent years we have seen multiple advances extending the model to support more varied materials, surface properties, and physically based properties [McAuley et al. 13] or ways to tackle aliasing problems [Baker and Hill 12]. The result of this technological push is widespread access to an efficient, predictable, well-known lighting model, capable of capturing most material properties that we might observe in common scenarios. Most research focused on refining material interactions, including well-known geometric and fresnel terms proposed in the Cook-Torrance lighting model [Cook and Torrance 81]. However, a very basic constraint of the model still exists, as it can only simulate point-based lights. In almost every scenario, the source of light has a physical size, which in real life is reflected by the correct shape of specular reflection and diffuse lighting response. Using Blinn-Phong point lighting for dynamic lights proves inadequate in many situations, creating a visual disjoint between visible lights in the scene and lighting result (see Figures 1.2 and 1.3).

Several methods exist to tackle this issue. Some of them include pre-computing "light cards" or billboard reflections and raytracing them at runtime to simulate accurate specular reflections [Mittring and Dudash 11]. Unfortunately, this system is an addition on top of standard analytical, dynamic lighting that is point based. Moreover, it doesn't provide a solution for area-based diffuse lighting.

Figure 1.2. Visual disparity between the light shape and Blinn-Phong specular reflection.

Figure 1.3. Specular reflection matches the light shape using the proposed model.

Another way of solving the problem involves switching to global illumination–based solutions. Several systems were already implemented in commercial engines, mostly voxel based [Mittring 12]; however, they can't fully substitute for analytical lights, due to stability, resolution, or quality difference.

During our research on a new iteration of the *Killzone* engine for next generation platform, we wanted to leverage current knowledge about lighting models and extend it to cover non-point-based lights. A unified way to deal with art production was also our priority. With our transition to physically based material modeling, we also wanted to have physically based lights, using real-world radiometric quantities, thus achieving a predictable shading model.

We decided to utilize existing BRDFs to model surface reaction to light and remodel the way lighting information is actually provided to those models. Standard BRDFs assume light incoming from only one direction with intensity given as a per-light set quantity. When dealing with an area-based light source, we would have to solve an integral of the lighting model over all points of the light shape. This can be achieved numerically, but unfortunately that proves unfeasible performance-wise in real-time applications. However, parts of that integral can be calculated analytically using radiometric integrals, while the rest can be efficiently approximated.

1.3 Area Lighting Model

1.3.1 Radiometric Integrals and BRDF Definition

In this section we introduce basic radiometric quantities such as light intensity, irradiance, and radiance [Pharr and Humphreys 04]. Then, we define radiometric integrals essential to solving area lighting models.

Let *intensity* be defined as the light flux density per solid angle:

$$I = \frac{d\phi}{d\omega},$$

where $d\phi$ is the light flux differential and $d\omega$ is the solid angle differential. Intensity is meaningful only for a point light source.

Irradiance defines the total amount of light flux per area:

$$E = \frac{d\phi}{dA},$$

where dA is the differential area receiving light flux.

Radiance describes the light flux density per unit area, per unit solid angle:

$$L = \frac{d\phi}{d\omega dA^\perp},$$

where $dA^\perp$ is the projected area of dA on a hypothetical surface perpendicular to the solid angle.

We also define radiance emitted $L_o(p, \omega)$ and incoming $L_i(p, \omega)$ to a point on a surface as a function of the point and direction.

Irradiance at point p with normal vector n would be defined as

$$E(p, n) = \int_{\mathcal{H}^2(n)} L_i(p, \omega) \cos\theta d\omega,$$

where $\cos\theta d\omega$ is the projected solid angle $d\omega^\perp$, with θ the angle between ω and the surface normal n. This term comes from the definition of radiance. In other words, this equation integrates incoming light from all directions on a hemisphere, around a point of integration with a given normal, with respect to the projected solid angle.

A *bidirectional reflectance distribution function* (BRDF) defines a ratio of the light reflecting from a surface point, in the viewer's direction, and the amount of light incoming to a surface from a specific direction. Therefore, a basic definition of BRDF is

$$f_r(p, \omega_o, \omega_i) = \frac{dL_o(p, \omega_o)}{dE(p, \omega_i)}.$$

In the case of real-time graphics, we are interested in finding the integral of $L_o(p, \omega_o)$ over the whole hemisphere $\mathcal{H}$ set around point p with surface normal vector n. Therefore, we are looking for

$$L_o(p, \omega_o) = \int_{\mathcal{H}^2} f_r(p, \omega_o, \omega_i) L d\omega_i.$$

Using the definition of radiance L,

$$L_o(p, \omega_o) = \int_{\mathcal{H}^2} f_r(p, \omega_o, \omega_i) L_i(p, \omega_i) \cos\theta_i d\omega_i. \tag{1.1}$$

During rendering we evaluate a finite number of lights. Therefore, we are interested in expressing integrals over area. In the case of irradiance over area A, we can define

$$E(p, n) = \int_A L_i(p, \omega_i) \cos\theta_i d\omega_i.$$

In the simplified case of n contributing lights, we can express the integral from equation (1.1) as a sum of integrals over all area lights that are visible from point p:

$$L_o(p, \omega_o) = \sum_{1..n} \int_{A(n)} f_r(p, \omega_o, \omega_i) L_i(p, \omega_i) \cos\theta_i d\omega_{i(n)}. \tag{1.2}$$

Equation (1.2), our main lighting equation, will be the basis of all derivations.

For simplicity we can assume that the light source has uniform light flux distribution so $L(p, w)$ is constant and denoted L; therefore,

$$L_o(p, \omega_o) = \sum_{1..n} L_n \int_{A(n)} f_r(p, \omega_o, \omega_i) \cos\theta_i d\omega_{i(n)}.$$

The differential solid angle is also in relation with the differential area.

In the case of a light source defined on a quadrilateral, the differential solid angle can be expressed as a function of differential area of light:

$$d\omega = \frac{dA cos\theta_o}{r^2}, \tag{1.3}$$

where r is the distance from point p on the surface to point p' on dA and θ_o is the angle between surface normal dA at point p' and $\overrightarrow{p'p}$ (see Figure 1.4).

It is worth noting that the solid angle is well defined for multiple primitives that can be used as a light source shape, such as a disk and a rectangle.

To finalize, radiance at a point per single light is defined as

$$L_o(p, \omega_o) = \sum_{1..n} L_n \int_{A(n)} f_r(p, \omega_o, \omega_i) cos\theta_i \frac{dA cos\theta_o}{r^2}. \tag{1.4}$$

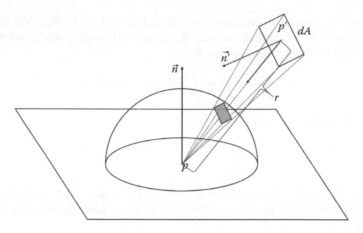

Figure 1.4. Solid angle of quadrilateral as visible from point p.

1.3.2 Material and Lighting Models

After deriving the principal integral (equation (1.4)) for light rendering, we assume that the light area is well defined and therefore possible to integrate. For simplification we restrict our reasoning to simple shapes—a sphere, a disk, and a rectangle—which are relatively easy to integrate and compute.

Our light is defined by the following parameters:

- position,

- orientation,

- outgoing light radiance in lumens,

- shape type (sphere, disk, rectangle),

- dimensions.

With those parameters we can instantly calculate L in lumens. We need to find a way to solve or approximate the integral from equation (1.4). To simplify the problem, let us look at the generalized physically based BRDF combining diffuse and specular reflectance models:

$$f_r\left(p, \omega_o, \omega_i\right) = k_d + k_s, \tag{1.5}$$

where k_d is the diffuse light model and k_s is the specular model.

We also need to set additional requirements to make this BRDF physically based:

$$f_r(p, \omega_o, \omega_i) \geq 0,$$
$$f_r(p, \omega_o, \omega_i) = f_r(p, \omega_i, \omega_o),$$
$$\bigvee_{\omega_o} \int_{\mathcal{H}^2} f_r(p, \omega_o, \omega_i) \cos\theta_i d\omega_i \leq 1. \tag{1.6}$$

For our k_d we can use the standard Lambertian diffuse model [Lambert 60]. When expressed as a part of $f_r(p, \omega_o, \omega_i)$, it takes a very simple form:

$$k_d = C_d, \tag{1.7}$$

where C_d defines the surface diffusion color.

We choose the generalized Cook-Torrance BRDF [Cook and Torrance 81] for a base of our microfacet specular model:

$$k_s(p, \omega_o, \omega_i) = \frac{D(\vec{h})F(\omega_o, \vec{h})G(\omega_i, \omega_o, \vec{h})}{4(cos\theta_i)(cos\theta_o)}, \tag{1.8}$$

where $D(\vec{h})$ is the distribution of micro-facets around surface normal n'', $F(\omega_o, \vec{h})$ is the Fresnel reflectance function, and $G(\omega_i, \omega_o, \vec{h})$ is the geometric function. As previously defined, θ_i is the angle between $\vec{n}$ and ω_i, and θ_o is the angle between $\vec{n}$ and ω_o. Generally, $\vec{h}$ is called the *half vector*, defined as

$$\vec{h} = \frac{\omega_o + \omega_i}{\|\omega_o + \omega_i\|}. \tag{1.9}$$

We are interested in finding radiance in the direction of the viewer, per light, described as follows:

$$L_o(p, \omega_o) = \int_{A(n)} f_r(p, \omega_o, \omega_i) L_i(p, \omega_i) \cos\theta_i d\omega_{i(n)}.$$

For now, we can assume, as in equation (1.2), that $L_i(p, \omega_i)$ is constant over light:

$$L_o(p, \omega_o) = L_n \int_{A(n)} f_r(p, \omega_o, \omega_i) \cos\theta_i d\omega_{i(n)}. \tag{1.10}$$

Now substitute parts of equation (1.10) with equations (1.5), (1.7), and (1.8):

$$L_o(p, \omega_o) = L_n \int_{A(n)} \left(C_d + \frac{D(\vec{h})F(\omega_o, \vec{h})G(\omega_i, \omega_o, \vec{h})}{4(cos\theta_i)(cos\theta_o)} \right) cos\theta_i d\omega_{i(n)}.$$

In the end we can define two integrals:

$$Diffuse\,(p, \omega_o) = L_n \int\limits_{A(n)} C_d \cos\theta_i d\omega_{i(n)}, \tag{1.11}$$

$$Specular\,(p, \omega_o) = L_n \int\limits_{A(n)} \frac{D(\vec{h})F(\omega_o, \vec{h})G(\omega_i, \omega_o, \vec{h})}{4(cos\theta_o)} d\omega_{i(n)}. \tag{1.12}$$

To get the final form of specular integral, we need to choose functions DFG. There are multiple sources available that discuss the best choice for a specific use scenario [Burley 12].

Unfortunately, independent of the chosen function, the integrals from equations (1.11) and (1.12) are not easily solvable for shapes other than a sphere. Therefore, we will focus on finding a suitable approximation for light shapes that can be expressed as a 2D function on a quadrilateral.

1.3.3   Approximating Diffuse Integral

Monte Carlo methods and importance sampling. One of the known ways to solve an integral is numerical integration by discretized parts. There are multiple ways and techniques to accelerate this process. A particularly interesting one for us is the Monte Carlo technique, which in general can be described in the following steps:

1. Define a domain of possible inputs.

2. Generate inputs randomly from a probability distribution over the domain.

3. Calculate the function being integrated for given inputs.

4. Aggregate the results.

With a given probability distribution, the expected variance is also known as well as the estimator for minimal acceptable error. This process can be significantly sped up using importance sampling techniques [Pharr and Humphreys 04].

The principle of *importance sampling* is to prioritize samples that would have maximum impact on the final outcome. We can find such samples using spatial heuristics. Another solution is to run an initial pass of Monte Carlo integration with a low number of samples to estimate the result variance and therefore decide which regions of integration would use more important samples.

Importance sampling is an actively researched subject with multiple different solutions. The takeaway for our reasoning is that, in any integration, there are samples more important than others, therefore minimizing the error estimator for a given amount of samples.

Application to diffuse integral. We would like to apply the Monte Carlo method to our diffuse integral. In order to simplify that process, we assume that the light shape has uniform surface normal n. Another assumption is that dA does not change for integrated points, meaning the whole shape is always visible. Therefore, we can conceptually move $dA cos\theta_o$ out of our integral and compute it once for the entire domain:

$$dA cos\theta_o \int\limits_A \frac{cos\theta_i}{r^2}. \qquad (1.13)$$

The integrated function is dependent only on the distance and cosine between the surface normal and the directions subtended by the light shape. Those are continuous and well-defined functions.

Immediately we can see that the global minimum and maximum of the integrated function are inside the sampling domain defined by the light shape. Therefore, there is a single point, on the light shape, that is able to represent the integral, thus minimizing the error estimator.

If we could find this point, we could essentially solve the integral by approximation using importance sampling with one point of highest importance. We would just need to evaluate the function once for that specific point. However, we are only interested in points that are easy to find at GPU program runtime. The ideal candidate would be given by a function of light parameters, the position of point p, and the normal n. We need to find a function that returns a point minimizing the error estimator. We also need to minimize the function complexity, to maintain runtime performance. To simplify the problem's domain, we prefer to work in the 2D space of a light quadrilateral.

Our function of interest is bounded by the light shape and defined as

$$\frac{cos\theta_i}{r^2}. \qquad (1.14)$$

We know that the function integral over area is bounded by local minima and maxima in limits of given area. The function from equation (1.14) has one global maximum and one global minimum at the shape bounds. Therefore, we know that a single point best representing the integral can be found on a segment between the maximum and minimum. In order to find it, we would have to calculate the global minimum and maximum, which we deemed to be too computationally expensive.

Instead, we decided to find an approximate important point in the proximity of the global maximum, accepting the risk of overestimation. In order to do so, we need to set boundary conditions for our search. The function from equation (1.14) is a component-wise multiplication of two functions. The maximum of their products can be found along a segment connecting their local maximums.

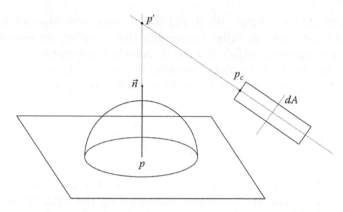

Figure 1.5. Geometric construction of point p_c.

We can easily find $cos\theta_o$ maximum on A geometrically by casting a ray from point p in the direction of the normal n of the surface, creating point p', intersecting with the light plane and finding the closest location on the shape to p', called p_c (see Figure 1.5). It is worth noting that in the case when the light plane is pointing away from the surface normal (i.e., $n \cdot n' > 0$), vector $\overline{pp'}$ should be skewed in the direction of the light plane in order to obtain intersection (see Figure 1.5).

A maximum of $\frac{1}{r^2}$ can be found by projecting point p on the light plane, creating point p_p, finding the closest point on positive hemisphere to p_p, called p'', and finally finding a closest point on the light shape to p_r (see Figures 1.6 and 1.7).

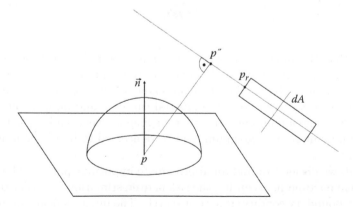

Figure 1.6. Geometric construction of point p_r when the light plane is pointing toward the surface.

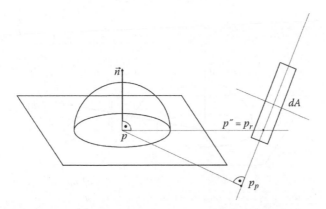

Figure 1.7. Geometric construction of point p_r when the light plane is pointing away from the surface.

As previously discussed, we were searching for the most important sample of the integral on a segment between points p_r and p_c representing component-wise local maximums (see Figure 1.8).

With those conditions set, we used a computational software package to numerically find a point on line $\overline{p_c p_r}$ that approximates the most important point as much as possible. We worked on a data set of several hundred area lights randomly generated as disk or rectangle light shapes. For every light shape we found a point on the plane that best resembles the full integral. Then, we computed the end points of our line between p_c and p_r (as if it would be calculated at runtime). Then, we numerically checked the points along the line, computing the lighting equation and comparing against a reference, using the least squares method to find point p_d, which would most accurately represent the integral.

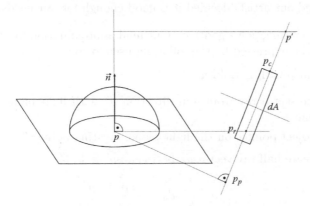

Figure 1.8. Geometric construction of line $\overline{p_c p_r}$.

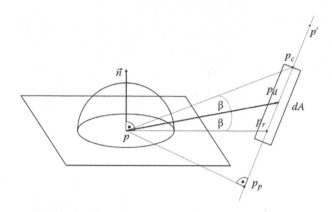

Figure 1.9. Geometric construction of point p_d.

After evaluating many test cases and several functions of various complexity, we noticed that intersecting a simple halfway vector between $\overrightarrow{pp_c}$ and $\overrightarrow{pp_r}$ with the light plane to create p_d (see Figure 1.9) works reasonably well in the majority of our cases, having a statistical error less than 0.05 against best-point approximating the integral.

After visual assessment we decided it works well enough in our use case (see Figure 1.10) and is visually indifferent from the raytaced solution (see Figure 1.11). It also proves simple enough for real-time per-pixel calculation on modern GPUs.

As another level of simplification, we used the halfway vector between $\overrightarrow{pp'}$ and $\overrightarrow{pp''}$. It allowed the important optimization of skipping the closest point to the shape calculation. Unfortunately, it yields a statistical error of more than 0.15. However, the disparity is mostly visible in an edge case scenario, where the light shape is pointing away from surface normal. There are no visual artifacts noticeable, and our artists decided it is good enough for our needs.

Area diffuse approximation algorithm. Our final approximation for diffuse integral can therefore be expressed by the following pseudo code:

- For point p with normal n:

    ○ Intersect a ray from p in direction n'' with light plane, creating new point p'.

    ○ Project point p on the light plane, creating point p''.

    ○ Create halfway vector $\overrightarrow{d_h}$ between $\overrightarrow{pp'}$ and $\overrightarrow{pp''}$:

$$\overrightarrow{d_h} = \frac{\overrightarrow{pp'} + \overrightarrow{pp''}}{\|\overrightarrow{pp'} + \overrightarrow{pp''}\|}.$$

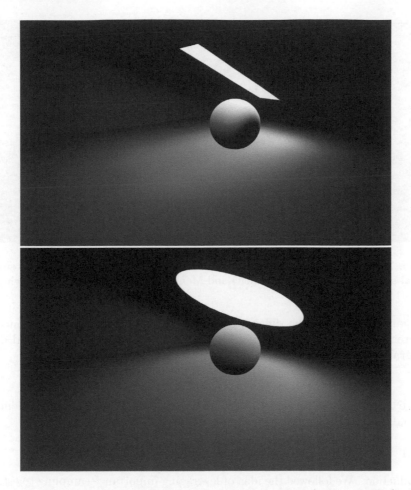

Figure 1.10. Correct wrapped diffuse lighting from rectangular (top) and disk (bottom) area light.

- Intersect a ray from p in direction $\vec{h}$ with the light plane creating point p_d. This is the most important point in terms of importance sampling.
- Treat vector $\overrightarrow{pp_d}$ as a light vector for the diffuse equation, effectively approximating the diffuse integral from equation (1.11):

$$\textit{Diffuse}\,(p, \omega_o) = L_n \int\limits_{A(n)} C_d \cos\theta \, d\omega_{i(n)} \sim L_n C_d \cos\theta_{\overrightarrow{pp_d}} \, d\omega_{\overrightarrow{pp_d}}. \quad (1.15)$$

In equation (1.15) we assume that L_n is constant for the whole area of the light. The angle between the new light vector $\overrightarrow{pp_d}$ and surface normal n is $\theta_{\overrightarrow{pp_d}}$.

Figure 1.11. Comparison between Monte Carlo raytraced reference and proposed analytical solution: proposed model (left) and Monte Carlo sampled reference (right).

We can also express the differential solid angle as a function of distance and differential area using equation (1.3). Therefore, our final approximated diffuse integral is

$$Diffuse\,(p, \omega_o) \sim L_n C_d \cos \theta_{\overrightarrow{pp_d}} \frac{dA cos\theta_o}{r^2}, \tag{1.16}$$

where θ_o is the angle between the surface normal n and the light plane orientation normal n_l and dA is given by the light shape.

1.3.4 Approximating Specular Integral

Introduction. We followed the idea of leveraging importance sampling to estimate the specular integral. First we analyzed the behavior of typical specular lighting models relying on probability distribution functions (PDFs). This led us to the definition of a specular cone of importance sampling, used to find the most important point for the specular integral and the actual integration area.

Specular in importance sampling. If we were to render specular reflection using Monte Carlo methods, we would cast a ray in every direction around the point being shaded and evaluate specular BRDF for given functions DFG from equation (1.12). Also, every PDF used to model D depends on some kind of surface-roughness parameter, denoted g. This parameter describes how focused lighting remains after reflecting off the surface.

In the case of specular reflection, we can define a vector created by reflecting in the viewer's direction ω_o against the surface normal n. Such a vector is called the reflection vector $\vec{r}$.

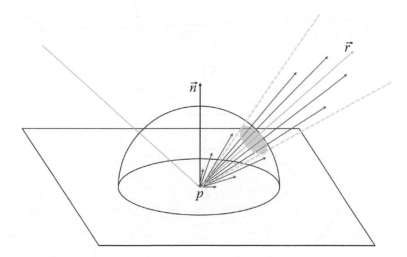

Figure 1.12. Visualization of reflection ray spread due to surface roughness.

Due to the nature of specular reflection, most samples that have meaningful weights would focus around $\vec{r}$. Their weights toward a final solution would be directly correlated to the angular distance of the ray being integrated to $\vec{r}$. They would also relate directly to material parameter g. Therefore, we can define a specular cone of importance sampling, centered around $\vec{r}$, encompassing all important ray samples (see Figure 1.12).

By the term *important*, we mean every ray that has absolute weight greater than a threshold σ (assuming that a ray shot in the direction of $\vec{r}$ would have a weight of 1.0). We can easily see that, with a constant σ, the cone apex angle α depends only on the surface glossiness factor g (see Figure 1.13). Therefore, we are interested in finding a function that calculates the specular cone angle from the surface glossiness, with a given specular model and constant σ.

As an example, we can apply this reasoning to find such a function for the Phong specular model:

$$k_{Phong} = (r \cdot n)^g. \tag{1.17}$$

We prepare data containing the specular cone angles α, at which $k_{Phong} > \sigma$. Then, for a given dataset, we find an approximation function. From possible candidates we pick a function with the lowest computational cost. In our case the function of choice is

$$\alpha\left(g\right) = 2\sqrt{\frac{2}{g+2}}. \tag{1.18}$$

It coincides with the Beckmann distribution definition of roughness m [Beckmann and Spizzichino 63], where m is given as the root mean square of the specular cone slope.

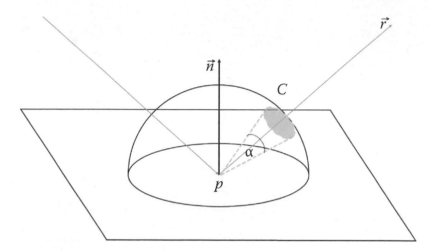

Figure 1.13. Visualization of cone of specular importance sampling.

We successfully applied this method to various specular models such as Phong, Blinn-Phong, Beckmann and GGX [Walter et al. 07]. However, it is worth noting that a cone shape is a relaxed bound on the actual distribution 3D shape, the complexity of which varies over different BRDF. Therefore, the cone shape is only approximate. In the case of Phong, the cone is actually a perfect match. However, in the case of Blinn-Phong, due to the use of the half vector, a pyramid with an ellipse base or even more complex shape would provide tighter, more accurate bounds.

Now we have an approximation model for the most important samples of our specular function. In the case of a single area light source, we would be interested in calculating the integral of our specular function over the portion of area of the light subtending the cone—defining integration limits. We can approximate the final solution by applying reasoning and methodology similar to Section 1.3.3. Again, a varied database was prepared, an integral numerically calculated, and the most important points estimated. In the end we found out that the geometric center of the integration limits area is a good point to estimate the unbounded specular integral. Let's call it p_{sc}. Therefore, to obtain the final result, we must calculate $Specular\,(p, \omega_o)$ for a single point light at p_{sc} and normalize the result by the integration limits area (see Figure 1.14).

To simplify our problem, we move to the light space (see Figure 1.15) by projecting our specular cone onto the light plane. In that case we are looking at a 2D problem, of finding the area of intersection between an ellipsoid (projected specular cone) and a given light shape (in our case a disk or rectangle, as spheres prove to be easily solvable working exclusively with solid angles).

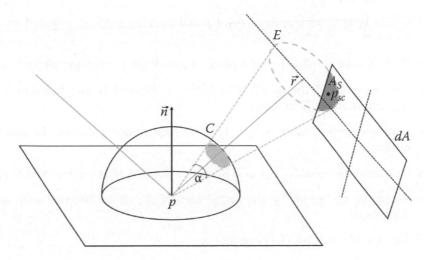

Figure 1.14. Construction of point p_{sc} and computing the intersection area A_S.

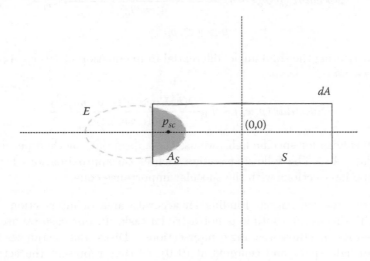

Figure 1.15. Situation from Figure 1.14 visible in 2D on the light plane.

Area specular approximation algorithm. Here is pseudo code of the algorithm to approximate area specular integral (see Figures 1.14 and 1.15 for reference):

- For every shaded point p, find reflection vector r.

- Calculate the specular importance cone apex angle $\alpha_{BRDF}(g)$ from point p and glossiness g, where $\alpha_{BRDF}(g)$ is defined per the BRDF used to model specular lighting.

- Create cone C with apex at point p and opening angle α, oriented around vector r.

- Project cone C onto the light plane of area light L, creating ellipsoid E.

- Find area A_S of the intersection between ellipsoid E and function S describing specular light shape.

- Find geometric center p_{sc} of A_S—the importance point of the specular integral.

- Calculate $Specular\,(p, \omega_o)$ as if p_{sc} was a point light, therefore vector $\overrightarrow{pp_{sc}}$.

- Normalize the result by the actual area of A_S as an effective solid angle differential.

Applying this to equation (1.12) results in

$$Specular\,(p, \omega_o) \sim L_n \frac{D(\vec{h})F(\omega_o, \vec{h})G(\omega_i, \overrightarrow{pp_{sc}}\vec{h})}{4(cos\theta_o)} d\omega_{\overrightarrow{pp_{sc}}}, \qquad (1.19)$$
$$\vec{h} = \|\omega_o, \overrightarrow{pp_{sc}}\|.$$

After substituting the solid angle differential from equation (1.19) by A_S normalization, we get

$$Specular\,(p, \omega_o) \sim L_n \frac{D(\vec{h})F(\omega_o, \vec{h})G(\omega_i, \overrightarrow{pp_{sc}}\vec{h})}{4(cos\theta_o)A_S}. \qquad (1.20)$$

When solving for specific light, we use the appropriate method per light type to calculate A_S. The following section focuses on approximations for various light-shape intersections with the specular importance cone.

Intersection area calculation. Finding an accurate area of intersection, between various 2D shapes, at runtime is not a trivial task. In our case we are looking at ellipse-disk or ellipse-rectangle intersections. Disks and rectangles are axis aligned in light space and centered at $(0,0)$, as they represent the actual light shape. Ellipses can be rotated. See Figures 1.14 and 1.15 for reference. To minimize shader complexity, we decided to approximate an ellipsoid by a simple disk. Calculating the area of intersection of two disks, or an axis-aligned box and a disk, is a reasonably easy problem to solve. In the case of a disk-disk intersection, we use the known smooth step approximation proposed by [Oat 06]:

$$A_{D0D1} = A_{min}smoothstep\left(0, 1, 1 - \|c0 - c1\| - \frac{|r0 - r1|}{r0 + r1 - |r0 - r1|}\right), \quad (1.21)$$

where $c0$, $r0$, $c1$, and $r1$ are the center and radius of disks $D0$ and $D1$, respectively (see Figure 1.16).

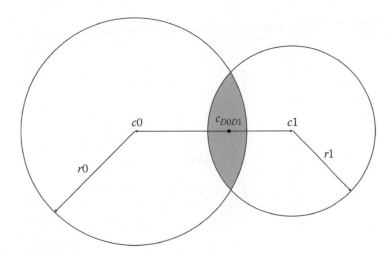

Figure 1.16. Finding area and center of intersection of disks.

The geometric center of intersection (if intersection exists) is given by

$$c_{D0D1} = c0 + (c1 - c0)\left(\frac{r0 - r1}{2\|c0 - c1\|} + 0.5\right). \tag{1.22}$$

Both equations (1.21) and (1.22) simplify under the assumption that $c0$ is at $(0,0)$.

In the case of a rectangle-disk intersection, we treat the disk as a square adjusted to have the same area as the original disk. Therefore, we can resort to simple axis-aligned rectangle-rectangle intersection mathematics. A_{R0R1} and c_{R0R1} are given by

$$tl = \max\left(c0 - \frac{d0}{2}, c1 - \frac{d1}{2}\right),$$

$$br = \min\left(c0 + \frac{d0}{2}, c1 + \frac{d1}{2}\right), \tag{1.23}$$

$$A_{R0R1} = \max\left(tl.x - br.x, 0\right)\max(tl.y - br.y, 0),$$

$$c_{R0R1} = \frac{tl + br}{2},$$

where $c0$, $d0$, $c1$, and $d1$ are the center points and dimensions of rectangles $R0$ and $R1$, respectively, and tl and br are top left and bottom right intersection corners, respectively (assuming Euclidian space with inverse y; see Figure 1.17).

It is worth noting that accurate results can only be achieved for models based on radially symmetrical PDFs. If we strip away the projection part, by substituting the projected ellipse with a disk during our intersection tests and further

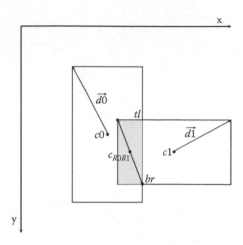

Figure 1.17. Finding the area and center of the intersection of rectangles.

integral calculation, we not only approximate the final result, but we also limit the model to radially symmetric PDFs. In the case of most microfacet BRDFs based on half vectors (equation (1.9)), the initial shape of the specular cone would be similar to an elliptical base, which would result in an ellipse shape on the light plane—thus an integral over an ellipse.

This is a rather crude approximation; however, it proved good enough in visual assessment of final results, when tested with Phong, Blinn-Phong, and GGX, using radially symmetrical light shapes (see Figures 1.18 and 1.19).

1.3.5   Nonuniform Light Sources

Up to this point we were only considering light sources with constant $L_i(p, \omega_i)$. We will now change this assumption and for simplicity assume that light intensity I is constant over the light and that $L_i(p, \omega_i)$ returns a normalized, wavelength dependent value. Looking at integrals from equations (1.11) and (1.12) and following intuitions from Sections 1.3.3 and 1.3.4, we can see that in order to acquire the correct result, we could pre-integrate equations (1.11) and (1.12) with varying $L_i(p, \omega_i)$ over the light source and then normalize by the source area. Assuming we can approximate diffuse and specular integrals at runtime, due to equations (1.16) and (1.20), we would just need to multiply those results by the pre-integrated, normalized full integral from equations (1.11) and (1.12) at our most important points for diffuse and specular integrals, respectively.

In the case of a diffuse (equations (1.11) and (1.16)), we need to integrate

$$Diffuse_{Lookup}(p_d, r) = \int\limits_{A} L_i(p_d + rn_l, \omega_i)\, d\omega_i,$$

Figure 1.18. Disk area light fit to Phong distribution.

where p_d is a point on the light plane with normal n_l and r is the distance away from the light.

To simplify, we assume that occlusion does not influence the result. Then the integral can be pre-computed in a 3D lookup table indexed by $p_d.xy$ coordinates in the light space and by distance r between points p and p_d. The distance can be normalized against the maximum distance at which computing the integral still makes a visual difference. Such a distance maximum can be calculated by solving the light shape's solid angle (equation (1.3)) for r, irrespective of $cos\theta_o$, where σ sets the boundary importance of the solid angle weight:

$$r_{max} > \sqrt{\frac{dA}{\sigma}}.$$

For distances larger than r_{max}, the solid angle would be too small and, as a result, the integral would not further change visually.

Every Z layer of the lookup table would contain the diffuse integral for point p_d, set on coordinates $p_d.xy$ in the light space, $\max(r/r_{max}, 1)$ away from the light plane. Finally, the full diffuse integral approximation is

$$Diffuse\,(p, \omega_o) \sim IC_d \cos\theta_{\overrightarrow{pp_d}} \frac{dA cos\theta_o}{r^2} Diffuse_{Lookup}\,(p_d, r)\,. \tag{1.24}$$

Figure 1.19. Disk area light fit to GGX distribution.

In the case of specular (equation (1.12)), we need to integrate

$$Specular_{Lookup}(\overrightarrow{p}\,p_{sc}, g) = \int_A L_i\,(p, \omega_i) \frac{D(\vec{h}, g)F(\omega_o, \vec{h})G(\omega_i, \omega_o, \vec{h})}{4(cos\theta_o)} d\omega_i, \quad (1.25)$$

where p is the point being shaded and p_{sc} is the most important point of the specular integral with g defined as surface roughness. Unfortunately, such a representation would require a 4D lookup table. We would like to free ourselves from knowledge of point p. According to reasoning from Section 1.3.4, we know that the integral will effectively depend on the projected cone of importance sampling radius. We also know how to create functions to calculate the specular importance cone apex angle from the surface roughness for given BRDFs (equations (1.17) and (1.18)). The projected importance cone radius depends on distance r to the light and the cone opening angle α (see Figure 1.20). Therefore, we can calculate the integral from equation (1.25) for point p_{sc} and the new roughness g', where

$$g' = f_{BRDF}(g, r). \quad (1.26)$$

To make this assumption viable, we have to restrict only to radially symmetrical PDFs:

$$Specular_{Lookup}(p_{sc}, g') = \int_A L_i\,(p, \omega_i) \frac{D(\vec{h}, g')F(\omega_o, \vec{h})G(\omega_i, \omega_o, \vec{h})}{4(cos\theta_o)} d\omega_i, \quad (1.27)$$

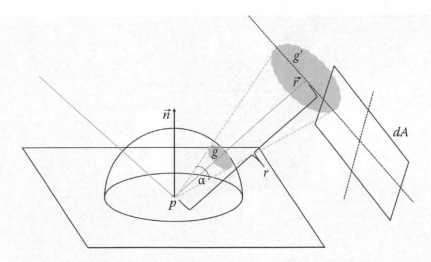

Figure 1.20. Relationship between cone angle, projected cone, and roughness.

where $\vec{h}$ is orthogonal to view direction ω_o. This effectively forces us to use Phong as our D function.

With these assumptions we can calculate equation (1.27) as a 3D lookup table indexed by $p_{sc}.xy$ coordinates in the light space and g' calculated using equation (1.26) derived for the used BRDF.

Finally, the full specular integral approximation is

$$Specular\,(p, \omega_o, g) \sim L_n \frac{D(\vec{h},)F(\omega_o, \vec{h})G(\omega_i, \overrightarrow{pp_{sc}}, \vec{h})}{4(cos\theta_o)A_S} Specular_{Lookup}(p_{sc}, g').$$

$$(1.28)$$

It is worth noting that, based on choice, functions DFG might depend on g or other surface parameters. Every additional parameter, apart from already included g, would add one more dimension to our lookup table or would have to be factored out. This is entirely based on the final choices for the specular model.

1.3.6 Solving Area Light BRDF

We presented a framework for efficient derivation of area-based lighting models based on currently known and well-researched BRDFs. The final lighting model should follow all procedures from Section 1.3, with the choice of particular DFG functions and appropriate derivation of additional parameters based directly on them. Then, diffuse and specular lighting per point can be approximated for various light types (equations (1.16) and (1.20)), including colored, non-uniform lights (equations (1.24) and (1.28)). See Figures 1.21, 1.22, and 1.23.

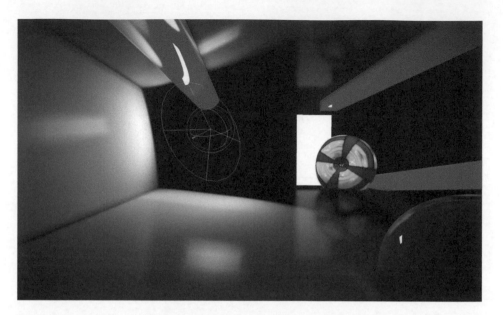

Figure 1.21. Rectangular area light.

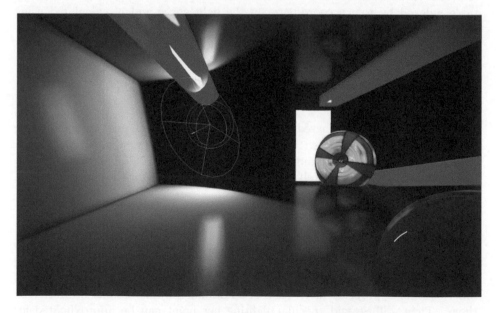

Figure 1.22. Rotated rectangular area light.

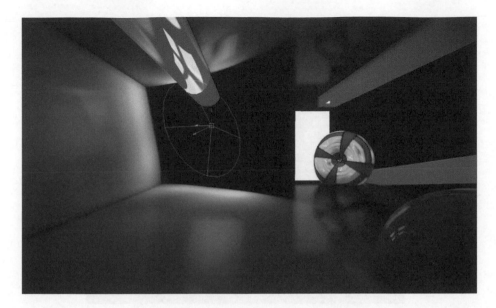

Figure 1.23. Textured rectangular area light.

1.4 Implementation

1.4.1 Introduction

Multiple ideas from this chapter were combined and used as the basis of the lighting model in *Killzone: Shadow Fall*. The light rendering engine relies heavily on real-time screen-space reflections and localized environmental reflection probes. Both solutions could efficiently support only radially symmetrical distribution-based specular (Phong). One of the dynamic texture-based lights requirements was to blend perfectly with existing image-based systems. Essentially we wanted a capability to swap dynamic area light, with image-based light card, with cube-map reflection at a distance without visual artifacts. We also wanted to support analytical shape lights allowing the highest visual quality and advanced material reflectance models.

1.4.2 Motivation

We used Cook-Torrance BRDF as the basis for our reflectance model. Normalized Blinn-Phong was used as the distribution function. Fresnel and geometric terms were calculated according to Smith-Schlick approximations [Schlick 94], matched and normalized to Blinn-Phong. We also prepared a radially symmetrical version of this BRDF. It was refitted to use Phong as the base, normalized and matched as closely as possible to reference solution.

Figure 1.24. Pre-integrated integral of environmental cube-map.

All lights use the same diffuse integral approximation reasoning shown in Section 1.3.3. Every light, depending on the light shape function, implements equation (1.16) or equation (1.24) in the case of a textured light source, to approximate the diffuse integral. That includes sunlight, omnidirectional lights, and spot lights with sphere, disk, or rectangular light shapes.

Standard analytical dynamic lights, depending on the light shape function, implement equation (1.20) to approximate the specular integral. In the case of textured area lights, we support only rectangular lights with Phong-based BRDF.

Phong-based Cook-Torrance was also used for image-based lighting convolutions and texture-based area lights. Similar to already-known methods for cube map generation [Lazarov 11], we build our kernel based on our Phong-based BRDF and generate multiple mip-map levels of cube-maps for different specular cone widths (see Figure 1.24). Similar reasoning, described mathematically in Section 1.3.5, was applied to generate image-based light cards used with textured rectangular area.

Different light shape implementation. The *Killzone* renderer supports the following light shapes: sphere, rectangle, and disk. All lights follow the framework set by the disk light implementation. They require only minor changes to the code responsible for the closest point to the shape or normalized solid angle. Therefore, we were able to efficiently share code between different light shapes.

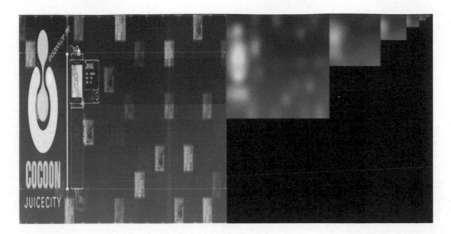

Figure 1.25. Pre-integrated specular integral of light card used with texture area lights.

It is also worth noting that sphere shape diffuse integral implementation can be vastly simplified by analytically integrating the integral as it has a closed form dependent only on the light position and radius. The sphere specular integral can also be optimized by working exclusively with the solid angle differential. There is no need to project computation into the light space, as the sphere shape is easily defined in 3D. Also, the projected solid angle is equal to the solid angle, as a sphere always subtends the same solid angle, independent of viewing direction and orientation.

Nonuniform light source implementation. We support texture-based lights using a rectangle shape as the base. We apply reasoning from Section 1.3.5 to directly compute and store pre-computed data in mip-maps of a 2D texture. Initial light intensity is provided by the texture generated by the in-game impostor rendering system or hand-painted by artists. Computed values are normalized and stored in two compressed RGB8 format textures (see Figures 1.25 and 1.26). At runtime, the rectangle light evaluates diffuse and specular integral, and multiplies the result by pre-computed partial integral from textures indexed in a similar fashion as described in Section 1.3.5

1.5   Results Discussion

Using area lights exclusively during the production of *Killzone: Shadow Fall* proved to be an important pillar of the physically based rendering pipeline. Due to the proposed model, we were able to unify lighting incoming from different sources—analytical or image based—keeping a similar response and quality. Our art production pipeline was able to produce assets in a hermetic review environ-

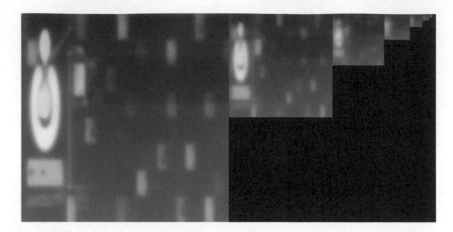

Figure 1.26. Pre-integrated diffuse integral of light card used with texture area lights.

ment, prepared as HDR pre-integrated BRDF cube-maps, and expect similar, high-quality results in game (see Figures 1.27 and 1.28).

Also due to the implicit split of material and lighting handling, teams could efficiently work on level assets, without interference between lighting and environmental departments. Previously, that kind of clash was unavoidable, as environmental artists had a tendency to tweak assets to simulate physically larger lights (i.e., by changing roughness). This habit resulted many times in duplicated assets per different in-game scenarios.

Figure 1.27. Typical usage of analytical area lights.

Figure 1.28. Typical usage of textured area lights.

The area lighting model proved to be efficient on the next generation console Playstation 4 GPU. The model itself is heavy on ALU operations (see Table 1.1), which in our case helped to amortize waiting time for multiple texture fetches from bandwidth intensive G-buffer and shadow maps. Therefore, we did not experience a noticeable slowdown in comparison with more standard point-based light models such as Blinn-Phong.

Unfortunately, several shortcuts we took during the model derivation resulted in artifacts, under certain circumstances, when using Blinn-Phong–based BRDF rectangular area lights. Due to those cases, we decided to use the rectangle shape exclusively with Phong-based BRDF, which is a better fit for the used approximations in the case of nonradially symmetrical light shapes.

Blinn-Phong Lights	Scalar ALU	% Against Base
Point	222	0%
Sphere	252	+13%
Disk	361	+62%
Rectangle	382	+72%
Texture Rectangle	405	+82%

Table 1.1. Comparision of Different light shaders assembly. Counts includes full deferred shadowed light code.

Figure 1.29. Square light shape using Phong distribution.

1.6 Further Research

In the near future we would like to focus on enhancing the normalization part of
the specular integral, which currently, due to disk approximation (Section 1.3.4),
is lacking in visual quality when compared to the reference solution. We would
be especially interested in pursuing a good approximation for Blinn-Phong and
therefore other microfacet distributions with a similar base such as the recently
popular GGX.

In order to do so, we would need to find an efficient way of finding intersections
between rotated ellipses and disks or rectangles.

We also feel that the rectangular lights specular approximation, when using
nonradially symmetrical PDFs, needs more research. As of now, the current algorithm for the most important point might result in severe artifacts at a rotation
angle of light that is orthogonal to the anisotropy direction of the PDF. A proper
search algorithm would require taking anisotropy direction into account. It is
worth noting that even in its current form, artifacts might be visually bearable
for rectangular shapes close to square (see Figures 1.29 and 1.30).

One proposed heuristic would be to treat the projected specular cone as an
elongated rectangle, oriented and extending in the direction of anisotropy. Such
shape change could be dynamic, calculated for specific BRDFs. Then, the most
important point for specular sampling would be the geometric center of the intersection between the specular rectangle and the light shape. The intersection
area could also be used as A_s for normalization (see equation (1.20)).

Figure 1.30. Square light shape using GGX distribution exhibiting minor visual artifacts.

We prototyped this approach, for rectangular lights, by analytically finding a polygon representing the light shape and the projected specular cone intersection. To find the intersection at runtime, we used a GPU-optimized version of the Liang-Barsky clipping algorithm [Liang and Barsky 84]. A light shape rectangle was treated as the clipping window, then a polygon representing the projected specular cone was clipped against it. The end result was an array of vertices representing a planar, non-self-intersecting polygon. In order to find the polygon's area, we used the Gauss formula for arbitrary polygon area.

Unfortunately, a busy production schedule has prevented further research in that promising direction. Figure 1.31 shows the proposed idea geometrically with reference shader-based solution results (Figure 1.32).

Another proposed area of research includes nonradially symmetrical PDFs support for texture-based area lights. We experimented with multisampling approaches and approximating the PDF at runtime; however, it proved to be too expensive for our real-time budgets.

1.7   Conclusion

We provided a tested framework for developing various physically based, area-based lighting models using currently researched BRDFs as the starting point. Implementation proved to be robust and efficient enough for the rendering engine of *Killzone: Shadow Fall*, a launch title for Playstation 4.

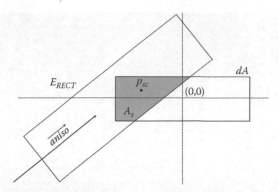

Figure 1.31. Geometric construction of point p_{sc} respecting distribution anisotropy direction. A_S due to Liang-Barsky clipping algorithm.

Figure 1.32. Runtime shader results using method from Figure 1.31.

We hope that the proposed ideas will provide other researchers and developers with tools to tackle problems of area lights and further extend the concept. In future, we hope that area-based lighting will become the de facto standard in modern video games, providing unified, predictable lighting solutions supplementing physically based material reflectance models.

Bibliography

[Baker and Hill 12] D. Baker and S. Hill "Rock-Solid Shading." SIGGRAPH 2012, Advances in Real-Time Rendering in 3D Graphics and Games Course, Los Angeles, CA, August 8, 2012.

[Beckmann and Spizzichino 63] Petr Beckmann and André Spizzichino. *The Scattering of Electromagnetic Waves from Rough Surfaces.* Oxford, UK: Pergamon Press, 1963. (Republished by Artech House in 1987.)

[Burley 12] B. Burley. "Physically-Based Shading at Disney." SIGGRAPH 2012, Practical Physically Based Shading in Film and Game Prduction Course, Los Angeles, CA, August 8, 2012.

[Cook and Torrance 81] R. Cook and K. Torrance. "A Reflectance Model for Computer Graphics." *Computer Graphics (Siggraph 1981 Proceedings)* 15:3 (1981), 301–316.

[Lambert 60] Johann Heinrich Lambert. *Photometria, sive De mensura et gradibus luminus, colorum et umbrae.* Augsburg, 1760.

[Lazarov 11] D. Lazarov. "Physically-Based Lighting in *Call of Duty: Black Ops.*" SIGGRAPH 2011, Advances in Real-Time Rendering in 3D Graphics and Games Course, Vancouver, Canada, August, 2011.

[Liang and Barsky 84] Y.D. Liang and B. Barsky. "A New Concept and Method for Line Clipping," *ACM Transactions on Graphics* 3:1 (1984), 1–22.

[Mittring and Dudash 11] M. Mittring and B. Dudash. "The Technology Behind the DirectX 11 Unreal Engine 'Samaritian' Demo." Presentation, Game Developers Conference 2011, San Francisco, CA, March, 2011.

[Mittring 12] M. Mittring. "The Technology Behind the 'Unreal Engine 4 Elemental Demo'." SIGGRAPH 2012, Advances in Real-Time Rendering in 3D Graphics and Games Course, Los Angeles, CA, August, 2012.

[Oat 06] C. Oat. "Aperture Ambient Lighting." *ACM Siggraph 2006 Courses,* pp. 143–152. New York: ACM, 2006.

[Pharr and Humphreys 04] M. Pharr and G. Humphreys. *Physically Based Rendering: From Theory to Implementation.* San Francisco, CA: Morgan Kaufman, 2004.

[Schlick 94] C. Schlick. "An Inexpensive BRDF Model for Physically-Based Rendering." *Proc. Eurographics '94, Computer Graphics Forum* 13:3 (1994), 233–246.

[McAuley et al. 13] S. McAuley et al. "Physically Based Shading in Theory and Practice." In *ACM SIGGRAPH 2013 Courses*, Article no. 22. New York: ACM, 2013.

[Walter et al. 07] B. Walter, S.R. Marschner, H. Li, and K.E. Torrance. "Microfacet Models for Refraction through Rough Surfaces." In *Proceedings of the 18th Eurographics Conference on Rendering Techniques*, pp. 195–206. Aire-la-Ville, Switzerland: Eurographics Association, 2007.

High Performance Outdoor Light Scattering Using Epipolar Sampling

Egor Yusov

2.1 Introduction

Light scattering effects in the atmosphere are crucial for creating realistic images of outdoor scenes. These effects generate the blue color in a clear sky as well as the spectrum of colors painting the horizon at sunset or sunrise. Light shafts, or god rays, are also produced by the same physical phenomenon when some sunlight is blocked by terrain features, such as mountains. Due to the complexity and numerous computations required to accurately evaluate the airlight integral, only rudimentary sky models are usually used in real-time rendering, which have a number of limitations. For example, simple models cannot handle daytime changes, restrict the camera to ground level, etc. Using screen-space imitation is a common technique to render god rays.

This chapter presents a new high performance, physically based method for computing outdoor light scattering effects while taking shadowing into account. The method combines two key concepts: epipolar sampling, which significantly reduces the number of samples for which expensive ray marching is performed, and 1D minimum/maximum binary trees, which accelerate ray marching procedure. The method is fully dynamic, and requires only a little pre-computation. It renders scattering effects for all times of day and for all camera locations, from ground views to outer space. The method is integrated with cascaded shadow maps, which are commonly used to handle large outdoor environments.

2.2 Previous Work

There were a lot of methods for rendering scattering in the Earth's atmosphere, starting with the work by Klassen [Klassen 87]. Early real-time approaches used very simple models due to hardware limitations of the time. Assuming flat Earth, constant density atmosphere and constant light intensity, Hoffman and Preetham derived a fully analytical solution for the airlight integral [Hoffman and Preetham 02]. The resulting model produces reasonable results, but only for ground views. Still, the sky looks unnatural, especially near the horizon. A more accurate model was proposed by Riley et al. [Riley et al. 04]. They also assumed Earth was flat, but the density of the atmosphere in their model decreased exponentially. To obtain a closed form solution for airlight integral, they ignored scattering on aerosols. Some attempts were made to approximate complex effects in the atmosphere with analytic functions [Preetham et al. 99]. Mitchell simulated light shafts using screen-space radial blur [Mitchell 08].

More physically accurate approaches perform numerical integration of the scattering integral with either slicing [Dobashi et al. 02] or ray marching [O'Neil 04, Schüler 12]. To accelerate numerical integration, different techniques were proposed related basically to the way optical depth is computed inside the integral. Nishita et al. [Nishita et al. 93], Dobashi et al. [Dobashi et al. 02] and O'Neil [O'Neil 04] used different pre-computed lookup tables. In his later work, O'Neil replaced the lookup table with a combination of ad hoc analytic functions [O'Neil 05]. Schüler presented sufficiently accurate analytical expression based on the approximation to the Chapman function [Schüler 12].

Some researchers tried to pre-compute the scattering integral as much as possible. While generally it depends on four variables, Schafhitzel et al. dropped one parameter and stored the integral using 3D texture [Schafhitzel et al. 07]. Bruneton and Neyret elaborated on this idea and used complete 4D parameterization [Bruneton and Neyret 08]. Their algorithm also approximates multiple scattering, and accounts for Earth surface reflection. It uses an array of 3D textures to store the resulting data; manual interpolation for the fourth coordinate is also required. To render light shafts, they used shadow volumes to compute the total length of the illuminated portion of the ray. Then they computed inscattering, assuming that the illuminated part of the ray is continuous and starts directly from the camera.

Engelhardt and Dachsbacher developed an elegant and efficient algorithm for rendering scattering effects in a homogeneous participating medium [Engelhardt and Dachsbacher 10]. They noticed in-scattered light intensity varies smoothly along the epipolar lines emanating from the position of the light source on the screen. To account for this, they proposed a technique that distributes ray marching samples sparsely along these lines and interpolates between samples where adequate. It preserves high-frequency details by placing additional samples at depth discontinuities.

Chen et al. also took advantage of epipolar geometry [Chen et al. 11]. They noticed that they could accelerate the ray marching process by using a 1D min/-max binary tree constructed for each epipolar slice. Their algorithm is rather sophisticated. It relies upon a singular value decomposition of the scattering term, and requires special care of the area near the epipole.

In this chapter we apply our previous approach [Yusov 13] to rendering scattering effects in the Earth's atmosphere. We reduce the number of samples for which the airlight integral is numerically integrated with the epipolar sampling and exploit 1D min/max binary trees to accelerate ray marching. We also discuss practical details, like integration with cascaded shadow maps [Engel 07].

2.3 Algorithm Overview

The following is a high-level overview of our algorithm. The remaining sections provide details on each step. The algorithm can be summarized as follows:

1. Generate epipolar sampling.

    (a) Compute entry and exit points of each epipolar line on the screen.

    (b) Distribute samples.

2. Select ray marching samples.

    (a) Compute coarse in-scattering for each sample.

    (b) Sparsely locate initial ray marching samples along epipolar lines.

    (c) Place additional samples where coarse in-scattering varies notably.

3. Construct 1D min/max binary tree for each epipolar slice.

4. Perform ray marching.

5. Interpolate in-scattering radiance for the rest of the samples from ray marching samples.

6. Transform scattering from epipolar coordinates to screen space and combine with the attenuated back buffer.

2.4 Light Transport Theory

Since our method ultimately boils down to efficiently solving the airlight integral, it requires an introduction. We will start with the key concepts of the light transport theory.

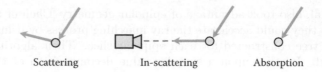

Scattering   In-scattering   Absorption

Figure 2.1. Types of interaction of light with particles.

2.4.1   Physical Model of the Air

Sunlight interacts with the particles distributed in the air as it propagates through the atmosphere. Two types of interaction are important: scattering (Figure 2.1, left), which changes the light direction, and absorption (Figure 2.1, right), which transforms the energy into other forms. Scattering in the view direction is called *in-scattering* (Figure 2.1, center). The amount of light energy per unit length scattered at point x is expressed by the total scattering coefficient $\beta^s(x)$. The angular distribution of the scattered light is described by the phase function $p(\theta)$ where θ is the angle between incident and outgoing directions.[1] The total losses of energy per unit length caused by absorption and both absorption and scattering are given by the absorption and extinction coefficients $\beta^a(x)$ and $\beta^e(x) = \beta^s(x) + \beta^a(x)$, respectively.

Air is usually modeled as a mix of two types of particles: air molecules and aerosols. Scattering by air molecules is accurately described by the Rayleigh theory. It is considerably wavelength-dependent, and almost isotropic with the following phase function: $p_R(\theta) = \frac{3}{16\pi}(1 + \cos^2(\theta))$. Precise derivation of scattering coefficients is irrelevant for this paper and can be found for instance in [Nishita et al. 93, Preetham et al. 99]. As in previous works [Riley et al. 04, Bruneton and Neyret 08], we use the following values for Rayleigh scattering coefficient at sea level: $\beta_R^s.rgb = (5.8, 13.5, 33.1)10^{-6}m^{-1}$.

Scattering by aerosols is described by the Mie theory. Cornette-Shanks function is commonly used as an approximation to the phase function of Mie particles [Nishita et al. 93, Riley et al. 04]:

$$p_M(\theta) = \frac{1}{4\pi} \frac{3(1-g^2)}{2(2+g^2)} \frac{(1+\cos^2(\theta))}{(1+g^2-2g\cos(\theta))^{3/2}}.$$

As in [Bruneton and Neyret 08], we use $g = 0.76$ and $\beta_M^s.rgb = (2,2,2)10^{-5}m^{-1}$. For aerosols we also assume slight absorption with $\beta_M^a = 0.1\beta_M^s$.

In the model of the atmosphere it is assumed that the particle density decreases exponentially with the altitude h: $\rho = \rho_0 e^{-h/H}$, where ρ_0 is the density at sea level and H is the particle scale height (which is the height of the atmosphere if the density was uniform). We use the following scale heights for Rayleigh and

---

[1] We assume that the phase function is normalized to unity such that $\int_\Omega p(\theta)d\omega = 1$ where integration is performed over the whole set of directions Ω.

Mie particles: $H_R = 7994m$, $H_M = 1200m$ [Nishita et al. 93]. Both scattering and absorption are proportional to the particle density, thus scattering/absorption coefficient at altitude h is given by scaling the appropriate coefficient at sea level with the factor $e^{-h/H}$.

2.4.2 Scattering Integral and Aerial Perspective

In our derivation of the airlight integral, we will follow a single scattering model that assumes that sunlight can only be scattered once before it reaches the camera. This is a reasonable approximation for day time. During twilight, multiple scattering becomes more important and should be considered in the production of realistic images [Haber et al. 05]. Still, a single scattering model produces reasonably convincing results. As we understand it, the only real-time method that approximates multiple scattering was proposed by Bruneton and Neyret [Bruneton and Neyret 08]. It requires a 4D lookup table with nonlinear parameterization. Performing multiple lookups into the table at runtime is quite expensive.

Consider some point P on the view ray starting at camera location C and terminating at point O (Figure 2.2). If the ray does not hit Earth or the camera is located outside the atmosphere, then either O or C is assumed to be the corresponding intersection of the ray with the top of the atmosphere. The amount of light that reaches P after attenuation by air molecules and aerosols can be expressed as $L_{Sun} \cdot e^{-T(A \to P)}$, where L_{Sun} is the sunlight radiance before entering the atmosphere, and A is the point on the top of the atmosphere through which the light reached P. The $T(A \to B)$ term is called optical depth along the path from point A to point B. It is essentially the integral of the total extinction

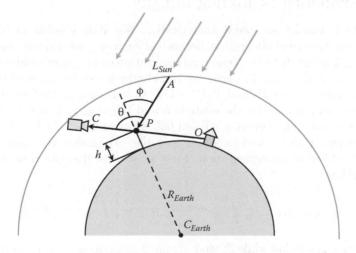

Figure 2.2. Scattering in the atmosphere.

coefficient over the path, which is given by the following equation:

$$T(A \to B) = \int_A^B (\beta_R^e e^{-h(t)/H_R} + \beta_M^e e^{-h(t)/H_M}) dt. \qquad (2.1)$$

Scattering by molecules and aerosols happens independently and is proportional to the corresponding scattering coefficient ($\beta_{R/M}^s$) at sea level and to the particle density scale factor ($e^{-h/H_{R/M}}$) at P. The fraction of scattered light going in the view direction is given by the phase function $p_{R/M}(\theta)$ for each type. Light in-scattered at P is attenuated on the way to the camera by a factor of $e^{-T(P \to C)}$. Finally, to account for shadowing, we also need to introduce a visibility term $V(P)$, which equals 1 if P is visible from light and 0 otherwise. Total in-scattering along the view ray is thus given by the following integral:

$$L_{In} = \int_C^O L_{Sun} \cdot e^{-T(A(s) \to P(s))} \cdot e^{-T(P(s) \to C)} \cdot V(P(s))$$

$$\cdot \left(\beta_R^s e^{-h(s)/H_R} p_R(\theta) + \beta_M^s e^{-h(s)/H_M} p_M(\theta) \right) ds. \qquad (2.2)$$

Initial object radiance L_O is attenuated in the atmosphere before it reaches the camera by a factor of $e^{-T(O \to C)}$. The final radiance measured at the camera is a sum of the attenuated object radiance and in-scattered light, which stands for a phenomenon called *aerial perspective*:

$$L = L_O \cdot e^{-T(O \to C)} + L_{In}. \qquad (2.3)$$

2.5   Computing Scattering Integral

Integral (2.2) cannot be solved analytically. Nor it is feasible to compute it directly with numerical integration, because at each step we will have to solve two optical depth integrals (2.1). Numerical integration can be significantly optimized using a number of tricks. To begin, we can eliminate computation of the optical depth integrals $T(A \to P)$ and $T(P \to C)$. O'Neil noticed that equation (2.1) depends on two parameters: the altitude h and the angle φ between the vertical direction and the light direction [O'Neil 04]. Optical depth $T(A \to P)$ can thus be pre-computed and stored in a lookup table. We follow the same idea, but use slightly different implementation. First we rewrite the optical depth integral (2.1) as follows:

$$T(A \to B) = \beta_R^e \int_A^B e^{-h(t)/H_R} dt + \beta_M^e \int_A^B e^{-h(t)/H_M} dt. \qquad (2.4)$$

Now one can see that while β_R^e and β_M^e are 3-component vectors, both integrals in equation (2.4) are scalar. We can use a two-channel lookup table storing total

Rayleigh and Mie particle densities up to the top of the atmosphere. With the help of this lookup table, optical depth to the top of the atmosphere $T(A \rightarrow P)$ can be computed as follows:

$$T_{A \rightarrow P} = \beta_R^e.\text{xyz} * D[h, \cos(\varphi)].\text{x} + \beta_M^e.\text{xyz} * D[h, \cos(\varphi)].\text{y}.$$

If the ray hits the Earth, the corresponding table entry should contain a large number to account for occlusion. To eliminate interpolation artifacts, in our practical implementation we avoid discontinuities in the table by allowing the altitude to become negative. This provides fast but continuous growth of the total particle density.

We also tried using the analytical expression based on an approximation to the Chapman function as proposed by Schüler [Schüler 12]. However, we found that it is quite complex and the lookup table works significantly faster.

Optical depth $T(P \rightarrow C)$ is computed by maintaining net particle densities from the camera to the current point during the numerical integration process. Finally, we can observe that angle θ does not vary across the ray, and both phase functions $p_R(\theta)$ and $p_M(\theta)$ can be evaluated outside the integral. To implement this, we integrate Rayleigh and Mie in-scattering separately and apply corresponding phase functions at the end. Pseudo-shader for the numerical integration procedure is given in Listing 2.1.

```
// Compute integration step
dP.xyz = (O.xyz−C.xyz) / N_Steps;
ds = ||dP||;

// Initialize integration variables
D_P→C.xy = 0; // Net density from camera to integration point
L_Rlgh.rgb = 0; // Rayleigh in−scattering
L_Mie.rgb = 0; // Mie in−scattering

for(float s = 0.5f; s < N_Steps; s += 1.f)
{
    // Compute position of the current point
    P.xyz = C.xyz + dP.xyz * s;
    // Compute altitude and normal to the Earth surface
    h = ||P − C_Earth|| − R_Earth;
    N_Earth.xyz = (P.xyz − C_Earth.xyz)/||P.xyz − C_Earth.xyz||;
    // Compute Rayleigh and Mie particle density scale at P
    ρ_RM.xy = e^{−h/H_RM.xy};
    // Compute cos(φ) and look−up for the net particle
    // density from P to the top of the atmosphere
    cosφ = (N_Earth, −l); // l is the light direction
    D_A→P.xy = D[h, cosφ];

    // Accumulate net particle density from the camera
    D_P→C.xy += ρ_RM.xy * ds;

    // Compute total particle density from the top of the
    // atmosphere through the integration point to camera
```

```
DA→P→C.xy = DA→P.xy + DP→C.xy;

// Compute optical depth for Rayleigh and Mie particles
TR.xyz = DA→P→C.x * βᵉR.xyz;
TM.xyz = DA→P→C.y * βᵉM.xyz;

// Compute extinction for the current integration point
ER+M.rgb = e^−(TR.xyz+TM.xyz);

// Compute differential amounts of in−scattering
dLRlgh.rgb = ρRM.x * βˢR.rgb * ER+M.rgb * ds;
dLMie.rgb = ρRM.y * βˢM.rgb * ER+M.rgb * ds;

// Compute visibility V

// Update Rayleigh and Mie integrals
LRlgh.rgb += dLRlgh.rgb * V;
LMie.rgb += dLMie.rgb * V;
}

// Apply Rayleigh and Mie phase functions
cosθ = (−v⃗, l⃗); // v⃗ is the view direction
ApplyPhaseFunctions(LRlgh.xyz, LMie.xyz, cosθ);

// Compute in−scattering and extinction from the camera
LIn.rgb = (LRlgh.rgb + LMie.rgb) * LSun;
Ext.rgb = e^−(DP→C.x*βᵉR.xyz + DP→C.y*βᵉM.xyz);
```

Listing 2.1. Numerical integration of the in-scattering integral.

2.6   Epipolar Sampling

Although the integration procedure presented in Section 2.5 is much faster than the straightforward numerical integration of equation (2.2), it is still too expensive to perform it for every screen pixel at real-time frame rates. The number of computations can be dramatically reduced with epipolar sampling, which smartly distributes expensive ray marching samples along the epipolar lines on the screen. We perform sample generation using the method described in Engelhardt and Dachsbacher's paper [Engelhardt and Dachsbacher 10] with some improvements. Epipolar lines are obtained by connecting the light source projected position with a user-defined number of points equidistantly placed along the border of the screen (Figure 2.3). Note that border coordinates should correspond to the centers of the outermost pixels, which are biased by 0.5 pixel size inward. In projection space, this defines the following rectangle: $[-1 + 1/W, 1 - 1/W] \times [-1 + 1/H, 1 - 1/H]$, where W and H are width and height of the viewport.

If the sun is on the screen, the entry point for each line is its position (Figure 2.3, left). If the sun is outside the screen, the entry point for each line is placed at the intersection of the line with the screen boundary (Figure 2.3, right). Lines that are completely behind the screen (shown in gray in Figure 2.3, right) are invalid and discarded from further processing. Then, a predefined num-

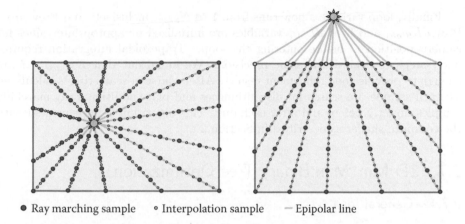

● Ray marching sample   ○ Interpolation sample   — Epipolar line

Figure 2.3. Distributing ray marching and interpolation samples along epipolar lines.

ber of samples are evenly distributed between the entry and exit points of each line. Every Nth sample is then flagged as an initial ray marching sample (in our experiments we use $N = 16$). Entry and exit points are always ray marching samples. To eliminate oversampling for short lines, which occurs when the light source is close to the screen boundary, we elongate such lines, striving to provide 1:1 correspondence between samples on the line and screen pixels.

Sample refinement in the original algorithm [Engelhardt and Dachsbacher 10] was performed by searching for depth discontinuities. We found out this is not an optimal strategy since what we really need are discontinuities in light intensity. In our method, we first compute coarse unshadowed ($V = 1$) in-scattering for each epipolar sample. For this, we perform trapezoidal integration, which can be obtained by a couple of modifications to the algorithm in Listing 2.1. We store particle density in previous point and update total density from the camera as follows:

```
D_{P→C}.xy += (ρ_{RM}.xy + Prev_ρ_{RM}.xy)/2 * ds;
Prev_ρ_{RM}.xy = ρ_{RM}.xy;
```

Rayleigh and Mie in-scattering are updated in the same way:

```
L_{Rlgh}.rgb += (dL_{Rlgh}.rgb + Prev_dL_{Rlgh}.rgb) / 2;
L_{Mie}.rgb += (dL_{Mie}.rgb + Prev_dL_{Mie}.rgb) / 2;
Prev_dL_{Rlgh}.rgb = dL_{Rlgh}.rgb;
Prev_dL_{Mie}.rgb = dL_{Mie}.rgb;
```

Finally, loop variable s now runs from 1 to N_{Steps} inclusively and Prev_ρ_{RM}, Prev_dL_{Rlgh}, and Prev_dL_{Mie} variables are initialized by appropriate values for camera position C before entering the loop. Trapezoidal integration requires fewer steps to achieve the same precision. We found out that $N_{Steps} = 7$ are enough to provide good refinement results. After coarse in-scattering is calculated for each sample, we search for discontinuities and place additional ray marching samples directly before and after each one. This algorithm is implemented with the compute shader as described in Section 2.8.

2.7 1D Min/Max Binary Tree Optimization

2.7.1 General Idea

At this point we have selected a number of ray marching samples on each epipolar line and need to compute the in-scattering integral for each one taking shadowing into account. For each sample, we cast a ray, then transform its start and end positions into the light projection space and perform ray marching in shadow map space (Figure 2.4).

Stepping through each shadow map texel would be too expensive, especially for a high-resolution shadow map. Using a fixed number of samples can cause undersampling and result in banding artifacts. We took advantage of epipolar geometry to improve performance without sacrificing visual quality. Consider camera rays casted through ray marching samples on some epipolar line (Figure 2.5). The rays clearly lie in the same plane, which we will call epipolar slice. The most important property of the slice is that the light direction also belongs to it.

The intersection of an epipolar slice with the light projection plane is a line. All camera rays in the slice project to this line and differ only in the end point.

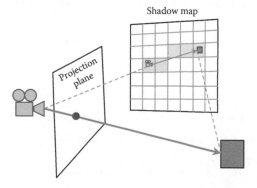

Figure 2.4. Projecting the view ray onto the shadow map.

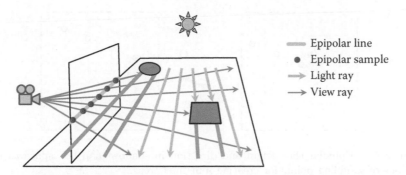

Figure 2.5. Epipolar geometry: camera rays casted through the samples on an epipolar line and light rays lie in the same plane.

Taking shadow map samples along this line results in a one-dimensional height map, which is the same for all camera rays in the slice. To perform a visibility test $V(P)$ in equation (2.2) and Listing 2.1, we essentially need to check if the current position on the view ray is under this height map or above it (Figure 2.6). It is clear that if there is a long consecutive lit or shadowed section on the ray, we can process it right away without stepping through all the underlying shadow map samples. To detect such sections, a one-dimensional minimum/maximum binary tree can be used as suggested by Chen et al. [Chen et al. 11]. Note that in contrast to their method, we do not perform rectification of the shadow map, which makes our algorithm significantly simpler. If the maximum value of depths of the ray section end points is less than the minimum depth value stored in the tree node, then the section is fully in light (such as AB in Figure 2.6). On the other hand, if the minimum of depths is greater than the node's maximum value, then the section is in shadow (CD in Figure 2.6).

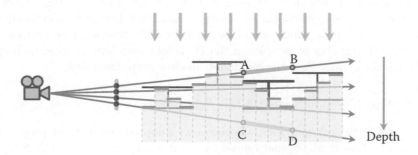

Figure 2.6. Detecting long lit and shadowed ray sections with 1D min/max binary tree.

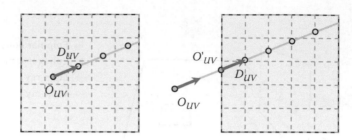

Figure 2.7.   Epipolar slice origin and direction in shadow map UV space as well as locations of sampling points for creating min/max trees.

2.7.2   Constructing Min/Max Trees

To construct a binary tree for the slice, we need to define the intersection of the slice with the shadow map. Since all camera rays in the slice project onto this line, this can be done by taking any two points on the ray and transforming them into the shadow map UV space. In our implementation, we use camera location as the first point. Its projected position O_{UV} gives us the zeroth sample in the 1D height map. To compute the direction $\vec{D}_{UV}$, we take the termination point of the ray casted through the slice exit point, transform it into the UV space and compute direction from O_{UV} to the resulting point. Then we normalize $\vec{D}_{UV}$ so that the maximum of its projections on u and v axes equals 1. If O_{UV} falls outside the shadow map boundary $[0,1] \times [0,1]$ (which is a very common case in multi-cascade set-up), we continue the line along the $\vec{D}_{UV}$ and move the origin to the first intersection with the boundary (Figure 2.7, right).

Now when we know the location O_{UV} of the zeroth sample in the 1D height map and direction $\vec{D}_{UV}$, we can determine the location of ith sample as $O_{UV} + i \cdot \vec{D}_{UV}$. The first level of the tree can be constructed by computing the min/max of every $2i$th and $(2i+1)$th samples. All the coarser levels can be built by propagating these min/max values upwards. As Figure 2.7 shows, the locations of the original samples on the shadow map do not fall in texel centers. To obtain correct results, we compute the conservative min/max bound by considering the nearest four samples, which would be used for PCF filtering (see Section 2.8). Note that the number of samples in the 1D height map built as described above is always not greater than the maximum shadow map dimension.

2.7.3   Ray Marching with 1D Min/Max Trees

In our optimized ray marching algorithm we adopted the method proposed by Tevs et al. [Tevs et al. 08] and reused by Chen et al. [Chen et al. 11]. Min/max tree traversal is implemented without recursion in this method. Transitions to coarser levels are performed one at a time so that the transition from level l to the next coarser level $l + 1$ can be performed when the sample index is divisible by 2^{l+1}. Transitions to the finer levels are done when a section is neither fully lit nor shadowed. We incorporate min/max tree traversal into the base procedure (presented in Listing 2.1). The optimized algorithm keeps track of the current min/max level l, increasing or decreasing it as necessary. When Rayleigh and Mie in-scattering integrals are updated, current section length ds is scaled by a factor of 2^l. Section 2.8 shows the shader code for the optimized algorithm.

Strictly speaking, computing the scattering contribution from a single ray section having a length of $2^l \cdot ds$ samples does not yield the same result as stepping through all the samples because the integral is nonlinear. For a point light source, we solved this problem by pre-computing the in-scattering integral and storing it in a 2D lookup table [Yusov 13]. An air-light integral for outdoor light scattering requires a 4D lookup table as shown in [Bruneton and Neyret 08] to be pre-computed. Performing lookups into this table at each step would be prohibitively expensive as the table has nonlinear parameterization. The manual interpolation for the fourth coordinate is necessary (in their work, the authors estimate the total lit length and then only perform two lookups in the table assuming lit section starts at the camera). Fortunately, integrand function varies slowly, thus even stair-step integration yields quite accurate results. We also attempted to use trapezoidal integration, but did not observe any notable quality improvement while performance plummeted. Note that in contrast to computation of the coarse in-scattering integral, which is done using only seven steps, many more steps are performed during the actual ray marching.

2.8 Implementation

We used DirectX 11 to implement our algorithm. The full source code can be found in the book's supplemental materials. It is also available on Intel Developer Zone (http://software.intel.com/en-us/blogs/2013/09/19/otdoor-light-scattering-sample-update) and GitHub (https://github.com/GameTechDev/OutdoorLightScattering). Some important implementation details follow.

2.8.1 Algorithm Workflow

The algorithm goes through the following steps:

1. Render the camera-space z coordinate to a screen-size texture `tex2DCamSpaceZ` ($W_{Scr} \times H_{Scr}$, $R32F$) by inverting the depths from the depth buffer `tex2DDepthBuffer` ($W_{Scr} \times H_{Scr}$, $D32F$).

2. Compute the screen-space coordinates of the end points of each epipolar line (Section 2.6) and render them to a $N_{Slices} \times 1$ auxiliary texture `tex2DSliceEndPoints` ($RGBA32F$).

3. Render coordinate texture `tex2DCoordinates` ($N_{Samples} \times N_{Slices}$, $RG32F$), epipolar camera-space z texture `tex2DEpipolarCamSpaceZ` ($N_{Samples} \times N_{Slices}$, $R32F$) and set up stencil buffer `tex2DEpipolarStencil` ($N_{Samples} \times N_{Slices}$, $D24US8$).

   (a) The screen-space coordinates of each epipolar sample on the line are computed by interpolating the line end points loaded from the `tex2D SliceEndPoints` texture (Section 2.6).

   (b) To compute the camera-space z coordinate for the sample, `tex2DCam SpaceZ` texture is linearly filtered at the sample location.

   (c) Stencil buffer `tex2DEpipolarStencil` is set up to mark only these samples that are located on the screen. This is implemented by setting up increment stencil function and discarding those samples that fall outside the screen.

4. For each valid epipolar sample, compute the coarse in-scattering integral as described in Section 2.6 and store it in the `tex2DInitialInsctr` texture ($N_{Samples} \times N_{Slices}$, $RGBA16F$).

   (a) Stencil `tex2DEpipolarStencil` is used to cull all invalid samples.

   (b) Trapezoidal integration with $N_{Steps} = 7$ provides a good trade-off between accuracy and performance.

   (c) Here we also render extinction texture `tex2DEpipolarExtinction` ($N_{Samples} \times N_{Slices}$, $RGBA8U$), which will be used to attenuate background.

5. Next, coarse in-scattering stored in the `tex2DInitialInsctr` texture is used to refine sampling and compute interpolation source texture `tex2DInterpol ationSource` ($N_{Samples} \times N_{Slices}$, $RG16U$). Details follow in Section 2.8.2.

6. After that, determine the slice origin and direction for each epipolar slice in each shadow cascade as described in Section 2.7.2, and store them in another auxiliary texture `tex2DSliceUVDirAndOrigin` ($N_{Slices} \times N_{Cascades}$, $RGBA32F$).

7. Min/max binary trees are then constructed as described in Section 2.7.2 and stored in the `tex2DMinMaxDepth` ($SM_{Dim} \times (N_{Slices} \cdot N_{Cascades})$, $RG16U$) texture. Details follow in Section 2.8.3.

   (a) `tex2DSliceUVDirAndOrigin` texture is used to fetch zeroth sample and direction, compute locations of the required samples, and build the first level.

   (b) All coarse levels are then rendered.

8. Next, use interpolation source texture `tex2DInterpolationSource` to update the stencil `tex2DEpipolarStencil` and mark these samples, for which we will execute ray marching. For all these samples, the interpolation source indices are the same, which is how they can be detected. Note that all culled samples are not processed.

9. Perform ray marching for all the marked samples. The resulting in-scattering is rendered to `tex2DInitialInsctr` texture (which previously contained coarse in-scattering and is now reused). Details can be found in Section 2.8.4.

10. Next, the initial in-scattering `tex2DInitialInsctr` is interpolated on all eipolar samples using interpolation source texture `tex2DInterpolationSource` and is rendered to `tex2DEpipolarInscattering`.

11. Finally, in-scattering from `tex2DEpipolarInscattering` is transformed from epipolar space back to rectangular and added to the attenuated back buffer (Section 2.8.5).

Important details of the stages are presented in the following subsections.

2.8.2 Sample Refinement

The sample refinement stage generates the interpolation source texture `tex2DInterpolationSource`, which stores the indices of the two samples on the same line, from which the sample will be interpolated. This stage is implemented with a compute shader and consists of two steps. On the first step, a shared-memory array is populated with 1-bit flags indicating if there is significant difference in coarse in-scattering (loaded from `tex2DInitialInsctr`) between each two adjacent samples in this segment. Flags are computed as follows:

```
float3 f3MaxI = max(max(f3I0, f3I1), 1e−2);
bool NoBreak = all( (abs(f3I0 − f3I1)/f3MaxI) < Threshold );
```

The flags are packed as 32 bit uints using `InterlockedOr()`. On the second step, the interpolation source samples are identified using `firstbitlow()` and `firstbithigh()` intrinsic functions. They return the bit position of the first nonzero bit starting from the lowest-order bit and the highest-order bit, respectively.

2.8.3 1D Min/Max Binary Tree Construction

We store min/max binary trees as a $SM_{Dim} \times (N_{Slices} \cdot N_{Cascades})$ `RG_16UNORM` texture `tex2DMinMaxDepth`, which contains all trees for all slices in all shadow cascades. As discussed in Section 2.7.2, each 1D height map cannot contain more than SM_{Dim} samples. It is not necessary to store the height map itself, so all coarser levels can be packed into $SM_{Dim} - 1$ samples (in case the shadow map dimension is a power of two). We pack data so that level 1 starts at column $x = 0$, level 2 starts at column $x = SM_{Dim}/2$ and so on. The data for the ith cascade begins at row $y = N_{Slices} \cdot i$.

The first tree level is obtained by reading the slice origin O_{UV} and direction $\vec{D}_{UV}$ from the `tex2DSliceUVDirAndOrigin` texture, computing the locations of the two required samples on the shadow map ($O_{UV} + 2i \cdot \vec{D}_{UV}$ and $O_{UV} + (2i+1) \cdot \vec{D}_{UV}$) and the min/max depth. To obtain conservative bounds, we use the `Gather()` instruction to fetch four depths, which would be used if PCF filtering was performed, for each location. We use the 16-bit unorm texture to save memory and bandwidth. Since conversion from 32-bit float to 16-bit uint can lose precision, we have to be careful with proper rounding, as shown in the following snippet:

```
const float  R16U_PRECISION = 1.f / (float)(1<<16);
fMinDepth = floor(fMinDepth/R16U_PRECISION)*R16U_PRECISION;
fMaxDepth =  ceil(fMaxDepth/R16U_PRECISION)*R16U_PRECISION;
```

Coarser levels are computed by reading min/max bounds from the two finer level nodes and taking minimum/maximum of these values. To implement this, we use two textures, setting them alternately as a source and destination. Since it is unlikely that very coarse tree levels could be reached, we limit the coarsest level step by 1/16 of the shadow map resolution. Rendering to low-resolution textures is inefficient on modern GPUs and numerical integration is less accurate when performing very long steps.

2.8.4 Ray Marching Shader

Ray marching shader implements the algorithm described in Section 2.7.3. `tex2D InitialInsctr` texture is set as the render target, while stencil `tex2DEpipolar Stencil` is used to execute the shader only for the marked ray marching samples. The shader full code is too long to be presented here, and Listing 2.2 contains only the most important lines, mentioning the remaining parts in comments.

We tried three strategies to process cascades. The first strategy renders each cascade in a single draw call and accumulates in-scattering in `tex2DInitialInsctr` texture using alpha blending. The second strategy uses instancing to perform this in a single draw call. The third strategy (shown in the listing) goes through all cascades in the shader. The last method works slightly better because common computations, like intersection with top of the atmosphere, are not duplicated, but the GPU is still fully utilized.

```
// Compute ray termination point, full ray length and view
// direction; truncate the ray against the top of the atmosphere
float3 f3RlghIn = 0;
float3 f3MieIn = 0;
float2 f2NetDensFromCam = 0;

for(uint Cascade=g_StartCscd; Cascade<g_NumCascades; ++Cascade)
{
   // Truncate view ray against min/max z range for the current
   // cascade, project onto the shadow map

   // Load slice origin and direction, compute integration
   // step f3UVAndDepthStep in shadow map space and in world
   // space, set up current position f3CurrUVAndDepth

   // Compute initial sample location in 1D height/map
   uint uiSamplePos =
     length(f2StartUV.xy - f2SliceOriginUV.xy)/fUVStepLen + 0.5;
   uint uiLevel = 0;
   int iDataOffset = -g_iSMDim; // Level 0 is not stored
   float fMarchedDist = 0;
   uint uiMinMaxTexYInd =
     uiSliceInd + (Cascade - g_StartCscd) * g_NumSlices;
   float fStep = 1.f;
   while( fMarchedDist < fRayLength )
   {
     IsInLight = 0;

     // If the sample is located at the appropriate position,
     // advance to the next coarser level
     if( (uiSamplePos & ((2<<uiLevel)-1)) == 0 )
     {
       iDataOffset += g_iSMDim >> uiLevel;
       uiLevel++;
       fStep *= 2.f;
     }

     while(uiLevel > 0)
     {
       // Compute depths at the ends of the current ray section
       float2 f2StartEndDepth;
       f2StartEndDepth.x = f3CurrUVAndDepth.z;
       f2StartEndDepth.y = f3CurrUVAndDepth.z +
                           f3UVAndDepthStep.z * (fStep-1);

       // Load min/max depths for the node
       float2 f2MinMaxDepth = g_tex2DMinMaxDepth.Load(
           uint3( (uiSamplePos>>uiLevel) + iDataOffset,
                  uiMinMaxTexYInd,
                  0) );

       IsInShadow = all( f2StartEndDepth >= f2MinMaxDepth.yy );
       IsInLight  = all( f2StartEndDepth <  f2MinMaxDepth.xx );

       if( IsInLight || IsInShadow )
           break; // If the ray section is fully lit or shadowed,
                  // we can break the loop
       // If the ray section is neither fully lit, nor
       // shadowed, we have to go to the finer level
       uiLevel--;
       iDataOffset -= g_iSMDim>>uiLevel;
       fStep /= 2.f;
     };
```

```
    [branch]
    if( uiLevel == 0 )
    {
        // If we are at the finest level, sample the shadow
        // map with PCF at location f3CurrUVAndDepth.xy
        IsInLight = ...
    }

    // Execute body of the loop from Algorithm 1, using
    // fStep as the scaler for the step length ds,
    // update f3RlghIn, f3MieIn, f2NetDensFromCam
    ...

    f3CurrUVAndDepth += f3UVAndDepthStep * fStep;
    uiSamplePos += 1 << uiLevel;
    fMarchedDist += fRayStepLengthWS * fStep;
    }//while( fMarchedDist < fRayLength )

}//for(uint Cascade...)

// Add contribution from the ray section behind the shadow map

// Apply Rayleigh and Mie phase functions
```

Listing 2.2. Shader code for the optimized ray marching algorithm.

To improve performance, we skip one or two of the smallest cascades (global variable `g_StartCscd` stores index of the first cascade to process). Since light scattering effects are only visible at a large scale, this has negligible visual impact. We also limit maximum distance that is covered by shadow cascades to 300 km. Therefore we need to account for the scattering from the part of the ray behind the largest cascade, which is accomplished by trapezoidal integration in the end of the shader.

To distribute cascades, we use mixed logarithmic/linear partitioning. Note that shadow cascades must cover all the view frustum, because visibility is queried not only on surfaces, but in the whole visible volume. Optimized cascade distribution techniques, like those based on determining minimum/maximum extents of the visible geometry, should be used with care. Note also that the first cascade used for ray marching must cover camera.

2.8.5 Unwarping

The final stage of the algorithm transforms the interpolated radiance stored in the `ptex2DEpipolarInscattering` texture from epipolar to rectangular space. We perform this by finding the two closest epipolar lines and projecting the sample onto them. Then we use `Gather()` instruction to fetch camera-space z coordinates from `tex2DEpipolarCamSpaceZ` texture for the two closest samples on each line and compute bilateral weights by comparing them with z coordinate of the target screen pixel (loaded from `tex2DCamSpaceZ`). Using these bilateral weights, we tweak filtering locations to obtain weighted sums of in-scattering values on each epipolar line using `Sample()` instruction.

At the final step, we combine the in-scattering value with the attenuated back buffer according to equation (2.3). Calculating extinction factor $T(O \rightarrow C)$ also requires some attention. One way to do this is to use a lookup table for the optical depth to the top of the atmosphere. Unfortunately, this method produces very noticeable artifacts near the horizon due to the limited precision of 32-bit float values and interpolation issues. Numerically integrating optical thickness (equation (2.1)) is also not an option. We use another method. When computing coarse in-scattering required to refine sampling, we also compute extinction anyway. So we store it in `tex2DEpipolarExtinction` texture and then transform it back to rectangular coordinates in the same manner as in-scattering. The resulting extinction is then used to attenuate background.

Since in-scattering is computed in high dynamic range, we perform simple tone mapping to convert the final color to low dynamic range using the following expression: `1.0 - exp(-fExposure * f3Color)`.

2.9 Results and Discussion

Figure 2.8 shows different images produced by our algorithm for various times of day and camera locations. Our technique is suitable for a wide range of graphics hardware, as it has a number of different parameters, such as $N_{Samples}$ and N_{Slices}, which enable trading quality for performance. We conducted our experiments on two different platforms. The first platform was a desktop workstation equipped with the Intel Core i7 CPU and NVidia GeForce GTX 680 high-end discrete GPU (195W TDP). The second platform was an ultrabook powered by Intel Core i5 processor and Intel HD graphics 5000 integrated GPU (15W TDP

Figure 2.8. Visual results generated by our algorithm.

Profile	SM Res $\times N_{Cscd}$	First cascade	N_{Slices}	$N_{Samples}$	Time, ms	Mem, MB
Brute force	$2048^2 \times 6$	1			304	
High qual	$2048^2 \times 6$	1	2048	1024	9.14	160
Balanced	$1024^2 \times 5$	1	1024	1024	3.45	56
High perf	$1024^2 \times 4$	2	1024	512	2.73	28

Table 2.1. Profile settings for NVidia GeForce GTX 680 (2560×1600 resolution).

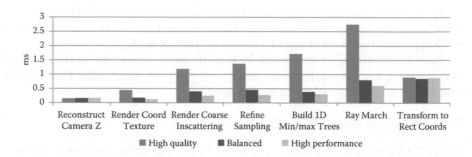

Figure 2.9. Performance of different stages of the algorithm on NVidia GeForce GTX 680 (2560×1600 resolution).

shared between CPU and GPU). On each platform, we rendered the scattering effects using brute force ray marching (which is run for every screen pixel and does not exploit 1D min/max trees) and three different quality profiles: high quality, balanced, and high performance. Results for the first test platform (images rendered at resolution of 2560×1600) can be found in Table 2.1 and Figure 2.9. Table 2.2 and Figure 2.10 show results for the second platform (images rendered at resolution of 1280×720). Initial epipolar line sampling step was set to 16 in all the experiments.

On both platforms, the results in the high quality profile are visually identical to the image generated by the brute force ray marching. At the same time, the performance improvement over brute force algorithm is more than $33\times$ and $8.8\times$ on NVidia and Intel platforms correspondingly. The balanced quality profile generates an image that is only slightly different from high quality and brute force ray marching, but it gives an additional performance advantage of $2.6\times$ and $2.3\times$ on our test platforms. On NVidia GTX 680, less than 3.5 ms are required to render the artifacts-free image at 2560×1600 resolution. The high performance profile reduces the computation times further, but image quality suffers. It must be noted that even in high performance profile, the rendered image still looks very convincing, as Figure 2.11 shows. The image does not exhibit aliasing artifacts, like stair-step patterns. Some temporal artifacts could be visible, but these are caused by low shadow map resolution, which generally affects shadow quality.

Profile	SM Res $\times N_{Cscd}$	First cascade	N_{Slices}	$N_{Samples}$	Time, ms	Mem, MB
Brute force	$1024^2 \times 6$	1			209.6	
High qual	$1024^2 \times 6$	1	1024	1024	23.6	60
Balanced	$1024^2 \times 5$	1	512	512	10.35	18
High perf	$512^2 \times 4$	2	512	256	6.19	7

Table 2.2. Quality settings for Intel HD Graphics 5000 (1280×720 resolution).

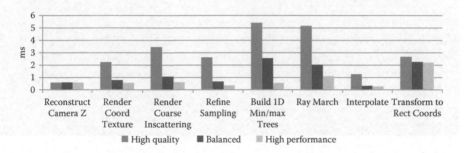

Figure 2.10. Performance of different stages of the algorithm on Intel HD Graphics 5000 (1280×720 resolution).

Memory requirements shown in the tables reflect only the amount of memory required to store algorithm-specific resources. They do not take into account shadow map size, back buffer size or camera-space z coordinate texture. The memory requirements may seem to be high, but if we take into account the fact that 16-bit float color buffer and 32-bit depth buffer at 2560×1600 resolution occupy 49 MB, memory consumption starts to look reasonable. Besides, 56 MB required for balanced profile is less than 3% of 2GB video memory available on GTX 680.

Timings for the individual steps of the algorithm are given in Figures 2.9 and 2.10. Some minor steps are not shown on the charts. The algorithmic complexity of the first and last steps does not depend on the quality settings and so is almost constant. Slight variations are caused by different sizes of textures being accessed from the shaders. Transformation from epipolar to rectangular coordinates takes ~ 0.9 ms on NVidia hardware. The ray marching step dominates in the high quality profile, while in the balanced profile it takes about the same time as final un-warping. In the high performance profile, the time of the last step dominates, so decreasing quality settings even further will not give noticeable speed-up (but will save some memory).

On Intel HD graphics 5000 hardware, the picture differs because this GPU has lower relative memory bandwidth. As a result, constructing 1D min/max binary trees, a purely bandwidth-limited step, takes more time than ray marching for

Figure 2.11. In-scattering only rendered on Intel HD graphics 5000 in high performance profile.

high-resolution shadow maps. Even when taking this time into account, the optimized algorithm is always faster.

Table 2.3 shows performance speed-ups obtained by using 1D min/max binary trees for different quality profiles for both test platforms. The RM column displays the performance improvement to the ray marching algorithm alone; the RM+MMT column shows the speed-up of the two steps: ray marching and constructing 1D min/max tees. The third column shows the performance improvement of the whole algorithm.

As Table 2.3 shows, using 1D min/max trees significantly reduces the execution times of the ray marching step. The performance gain is higher for high-resolution shadow maps (high quality profiles) as longer ray sections in shadow map space can be efficiently processed. This results in a speed-up of up to 8.6× on NVidia and up to 5.3× on the Intel platform. Taking the tree construction

	NVidia GTX 680			Intel HD graphics 5000		
Profile	RM	RM+MMT	Total	RM	RM+MMT	Total
High qual	8.6	5.3	3.8	5.3	2.6	1.7
Balanced	3.6	2.5	1.5	4.0	1.8	1.3
High perf	2.7	1.8	1.3	1.6	1.1	1.1

Table 2.3. Performance gains obtained by using 1D min/max trees.

time into account, up to 5.3× and up to 2.6× speedup is observed. Even in the high performance profile when a low-resolution shadow map is used, the ray marching still benefits from using 1D min/max binary trees.

In our algorithm, we exploited a simple strategy to place $N_{Slices}/4$ exit points on each boundary of the screen, primarily for the sake of simplicity. Therefore, the maximum distance between the two closest epipolar lines is always less than $\Delta_{Slice} = 4 \cdot \max(H_{Scr}, W_{Scr})/N_{Slices}$ pixels. Maximum distance between two samples on one epipolar line does not exceed

$$\Delta_{Sample} = \frac{\sqrt{H_{Scr}^2 + W_{Scr}^2}}{N_{Samples} - 1}.$$

Thus maximum screen-space distance from any pixel to the closest epipolar sample is bounded by the

$$0.5\sqrt{\Delta_{Slice}^2 + \Delta_{Sample}^2}.$$

For our first test platform this formula gives us 2.9, 5.2 and 5.8 pixels of maximum error for the high quality, balanced and high performance profiles, respectively. For our second platform, it gives 2.6, 5.2 and 5.7 pixels of maximum error. Since this analysis accounts for the worst case scenario, in practice the error is always much smaller than this estimation. Therefore, bilateral filtering can be performed accurately for the majority of pixels, producing convincing visual results even in the high performance profile. Note that a more sophisticated slice distribution method could be used to guarantee a predefined maximum screen-space error [Baran et al. 10].

Our algorithm can be extended to support MSAA. Most steps are performed in epipolar space and will thus be the same. The only step that requires modification is the transformation from epipolar to rectangular space. It could be broken into two sub-passes: pixel pass and sample pass. The pixel pass will be identical to the one described in Section 2.8.5 and will render to non-MSAA buffer. The per-sample pass will execute over the MSAA buffer. It will use an antialiasing mask (which is usually available when MSAA-enabled post-processing is performed) to distinguish between pixels that do not require antialiasing and those that require it. For pixels from the first group, the algorithm would read in-scattering from the non-MSAA back buffer and store it in all samples. For these pixels, which require antialiasing, the shader performs the same unwarping steps, but for each particular sample. To improve performance, the last two sub-passes can be split using stencil masking.

It is also relatively easy to extend our algorithm to approximate multiple scattering by pre-computing the secondary and higher-order scatterings and storing them in a lookup table (refer to [Bruneton and Neyret 08]). After completing ray marching, two lookups into the table will be required to approximate the effects of higher-order scattering along the ray. The average light occlusion along the ray could also be easily estimated and accounted for. While having only subtle impact during the day time, multiple scattering will improve appearance of twilight sky notably.

2.10   Conclusion and Future Work

We presented a high-performance technique for rendering light scattering effects in the Earth's atmosphere. This technique exploits epipolar sampling to efficiently reduce the number of times expensive ray marching is executed. The 1D min/max binary trees accelerate in-scattering integral calculation, and integration with cascaded shadow maps allows rendering large outdoor environments. Thanks to the number of different parameters that trade quality for performance, the technique scales from high-end discrete GPUs to low-power integrated graphics solutions. We plan on adding support for rendering dynamic clouds in the future.

Bibliography

[Baran et al. 10] Ilya Baran, Jiawen Chen, Jonathan Ragan-Kelley, Frédo Durand, and Jaakko Lehtinen. "A Hierarchical Volumetric Shadow Algorithm for Single Scattering." *ACM Transactions on Graphics* 29:6 (2010), 178:1–178:9.

[Bruneton and Neyret 08] Éric Bruneton and Fabrice Neyret. "Precomputed Atmospheric Scattering." *Special Issue: Proceedings of the 19th Eurographics Symposium on Rendering 2008, Computer Graphics Forum* 27:4 (2008), 1079–1086.

[Chen et al. 11] J. Chen, I. Baran, F. Durand, and W. Jarosz. "Real-Time Volumetric Shadows Using 1D Min-max Mip-maps." In *Proceedings of the Symposium on Interactive 3D Graphics and Games*, pp. 39–46. New York: ACM, 2011.

[Dobashi et al. 02] Y. Dobashi, T. Yamamoto, and T. Nishita. "Interactive Rendering of Atmospheric Scattering Effects Using Graphics Hardware." In *Graphics Hardware 2002*, pp. 99–107. Aire-la-Ville, Switzerland: Eurographics Association, 2002.

[Engel 07] Wolfgang Engel. "Cascaded Shadow Maps." In *ShaderX5: Advanced Rendering Techniques*, edited by Wolfgang Engel, pp. 197–206. Hingham, MA: Charles River Media, 2007.

[Engelhardt and Dachsbacher 10] T. Engelhardt and C. Dachsbacher. "Epipolar Sampling for Shadows and Crepuscular Rays in Participating Media with Single Scattering." In *ACM SIGGRAPH Symposium on Interactive 3D Graphics and Games*, pp. 119–125. New York: ACM, 2010.

[Haber et al. 05] Jörg Haber, Marcus Magnor, and Hans-Peter Seidel. "Physically-Based Simulation of Twilight Phenomena." *ACM Transactions on Graphics* 24:4 (2005), 1353–1373.

[Hoffman and Preetham 02] N. Hoffman and A. J. Preetham. "Rendering Outdoor Light Scattering in Real Time." Presentation, Game Developers Conference 2002, San Jose, CA, March, 2002.

[Klassen 87] R. Victor Klassen. "Modeling the Effect of the Atmosphere on Light." *ACM Transactions on Graphics* 6:3 (1987), 215–237.

[Mitchell 08] Kenny Mitchell. "Volumetric Light Scattering as a Post-Process." In *GPU Gems 3*, edited by Hubert Nguyen, pp. 275–285. Upper Saddle River, NJ: Addison-Wesley, 2008.

[Nishita et al. 93] Tomoyuki Nishita, Takao Sirai, Katsumi Tadamura, and Eihachiro Nakamae. "Display of the Earth Taking into Account Atmospheric Scattering." In *Proceedings of the 20st Annual Conference on Computer Graphics and Interactive Techniques, SIGGRAPH 1993*, pp. 175–182. New York: ACM, 1993.

[O'Neil 04] Sean O'Neil. "Real-Time Atmospheric Scattering." *GameDev.net*, http://www.gamedev.net/page/resources/_/technical/graphics-programming-and-theory/real-time-atmospheric-scattering-r2093, 2004.

[O'Neil 05] Sean O'Neil. "Accurate Atmospheric Scattering." In *GPU Gems 2*, edited by Matt Pharr. Upper Saddle River, NJ: Addison-Wesley, 2005.

[Preetham et al. 99] A. J. Preetham, P. Shirley, and B. Smits. "A Practical Analytic Model for Daylight." In *Proceedings of ACM SIGGRAPH*, pp. 91–100. New York: ACM, 1999.

[Riley et al. 04] Kirk Riley, David S. Ebert, Martin Kraus, Jerry Tessendorf, and Charles D. Hansen. "Efficient Rendering of Atmospheric Phenomena." In *Rendering Techniques*, edited by Alexander Keller and Henrik Wann Jensen, pp. 374–386. Aire-la-Ville, Switzerland: Eurographics Association, 2004.

[Schafhitzel et al. 07] Tobias Schafhitzel, Martin Falk, and Thomas Ertl. "Real-Time Rendering of Planets with Atmospheres." *Journal of WSCG* 15:1–3 (2007), 91–98.

[Schüler 12] Christian Schüler. "An Approximation to the Chapman Grazing-Incidence Function for Atmospheric Scattering." In *GPU Pro 3*, edited by Wolfgang Engel, pp. 105–118. Natick, MA: A K Peters, 2012.

[Tevs et al. 08] A. Tevs, I. Ihrke, and H.-P. Seidel. "Maximum Mip-maps for Fast, Accurate, and Scalable Dynamic Height Field Rendering." In *Proceedings of the 2008 Symposium on Interactive 3D Graphics and Games*, pp. 183–190. New York: ACM, 2008.

[Yusov 13] Egor Yusov. "Practical Implementation of Light Scattering Effects Using Epipolar Sampling and 1D Min/Max Binary Trees." Presentation, Game Developers Conference 2013, San Francisco, CA, March, 2013. Available online (http://gdcvault.com/play/1018227/Practical-Implementation-of-Light-Scattering).

Volumetric Light Effects in
Killzone: Shadow Fall
Nathan Vos

3.1 Introduction

Volumetric light effects are caused by light being scattered in humid, dusty, or smoky environments (as in Figure 3.1). It's an amazing looking natural phenomenon. It can be used to create great-looking images and add a lot of atmosphere to the environment.

Many articles have been written about light scattering and volumetric light effects. Most of them focus on techniques that improve rendering performance and image quality. However, most of them don't address the challenges that need to be overcome when implementing the effect in a real-life game scenario.

In this chapter we will talk about how we managed to take our engine to the next level by introducing volumetric light effects in *Killzone: Shadow Fall* and how we dealt with the problems we encountered during the development process.

Figure 3.1. Examples of volumetric light effects.

One of the major challenges we faced was to find a way to give artists full control to define where and how much volumetric light should be visible in the scene. We also wanted to add the possibility of animating the intensity of the volumetric light to create more natural-looking effects. In this chapter we will describe how we used particle effects and a special 3D scattering amount lookup texture to make this possible.

We also needed to find a way to deal with transparent objects in our scenes. The problem here is that transparent objects are either rendered before or after the volumetric light effects. If the transparent objects are drawn first, the volumetric light effects will occlude them. If the volumetric light effects are drawn first, the transparent objects will occlude the volumetric light. We will show how we store the intensity of the volumetric light in another 3D texture and how we use this data to composite the transparent objects into the scene.

Our render engine uses deferred rendering [Valient 09]. This means that the scene is rendered in multiple phases. In the first phase all information of the scene's geometry is gathered in the so-called geometry buffer (G-buffer). The G-buffer contains all information needed to light the scene, such as surface normal, albedo color, roughness, reflective color, etc. In the second phase all lights are rendered into the lighting accumulation buffer. For each light a polygonal shape is rendered that will cover all pixels that will be illuminated by the light. The shape is rendered using a shader that will sample all information from the G-buffer and perform the proper lighting calculations for each pixel. All light shapes are rendered additively to the lighting accumulation buffer to form an image of the lit scene. All techniques described in this chapter are applicable to any type of rendering method; however, some implementation details will only be relevant to deferred rendering engines.

3.2   Basic Algorithm

To render the volumetric light effects, we start by rendering a shape for each light that represents the light's volume. For point lights we will render a sphere and for spot lights a cone. For the sunlight we will render a fullscreen quad, as the volume of the sunlight covers the entire scene. We render each shape with a special volumetric light shader. For each pixel the shader will calculate the line segment of the view ray that intersects the light's volume. We then enter the ray-march loop, which takes multiple light contribution samples across this line segment. Artists can define the number of ray-march steps we take on a per-light basis. For each ray-march step the sample position is calculated, and the sample is lit using the same code we would normally use to light the geometry. When performing the lighting calculations, we assume we are lighting a completely diffuse white surface that is facing the light direction to get the maximum contribution of the light at the sample's position. Because we use the same code that is used to calculate the lighting for a regular surface, we automatically support all light features we have, such as shadow mapping, fall-off ranges, textures to define the light's color, etc. To improve rendering performance, we disabled all shadow filtering features. We found that taking a simple point sample from the shadow map for each ray-march step is sufficient to create good looking results so we save a lot of GPU cycles by not doing any advanced shadow filtering.

The lit sample color will be scaled by the ray-march step size and by the scattering factor, which determines the intensity of the volumetric light. In Section 3.2.3 we will describe how the scattering factor is calculated. Finally, all ray-march samples are added together, and the effect is rendered additively to the scene.

3.2.1 Omni-lights and Spotlights

In the volumetric light shader for omni- and spotlights, we start by defining a ray that travels from the camera position to the world position of the pixel on the screen (Figure 3.2(a)). The world position is calculated by taking the pixel's depth value from the depth buffer and projecting it back to world space using the inversed view-projection matrix. The next step is to find the intersection points of where the ray enters and exists the sphere or cone. Based on these intersection points a line segment is defined that represents the segment that travels through the light's volume (Figure 3.2(b)). The volumetric light shader will take multiple samples across this line segment to render the volumetric light effect (Figure 3.2(c)). We render the omni- and spotlight shapes with depth-test enabled to make sure that pixels that are occluded by the scene's geometry will be discarded. Figure 3.3 shows an example scene of a volumetric point light placed within a shadow-casting sphere with holes. This example scene will be used as a reference throughout.

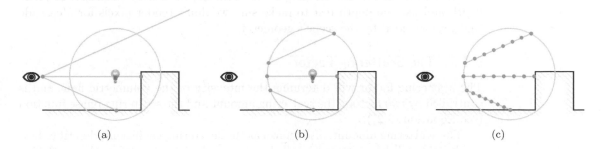

| (a) | (b) | (c) |

Figure 3.2. (a) Initial rays for omni-light. (b) Line segments after light volume intersection test. (c) Ray-march samples.

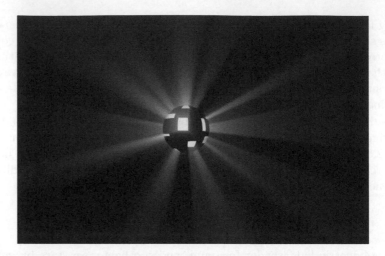

Figure 3.3. Example scene showing a volumetric shadow casting point light placed within a shadow-casting sphere with holes.

3.2.2 Sunlight

For the sunlight we use cascaded shadow mapping [Valient 09]. Because we use deferred rendering, we can render each cascade of the sunlight separately. This method is very useful because we can re-use the same shadow map for each cascade and therefore save a lot of render buffer memory.

To render the volumetric light effect for the sunlight, we draw a fullscreen quad after each sunlight cascade using a special sunlight volumetric light shader. For each pixel the shader will march from the cascade's near depth to the cascade's far depth along the view ray (Figure 3.4(a) and 3.4(b)). When our ray-march sample depth turns out to be deeper than the value in the depth buffer, we will break out of the ray-march loop (Figure 3.4(b)).

We render each fullscreen quad at the same depth as the cascade's near plane depth and use the depth test to make sure we don't render pixels for a cascade that are occluded by the scene's geometry.

3.2.3 The Scattering Factor

The scattering factor will determine the intensity of the volumetric light and is controlled by two factors, the scattering amount and the scattering phase function (see Equation (3.2)).

The scattering amount, also known as the scattering coefficient, describes how much light will be scattered in all directions. Artists can define the scattering amount on a per-light basis. For the sunlight we also gave them the possibility of setting fade ranges for the scattering amount based on height and view distance.

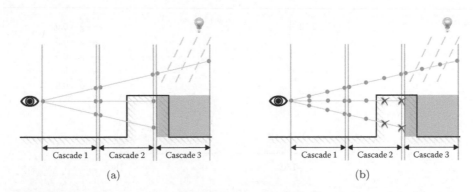

(a) (b)

Figure 3.4. (a) Initial rays for each sunlight cascade. Red shows where the cascade is not being rendered due to depth test failure. (b) Ray march samples for each sunlight cascade. Red crosses show where we break out of the ray-march loop.

In Section 3.5 we will describe how we extended the system by using a 3D lookup texture to control the scattering amount more accurately and more dynamically.

The scattering phase function defines the angular distribution of the scattered light. The phase function can be used to determine how much of the total scattered light is scattered toward the camera. For the volumetric light effects in *Killzone: Shadow Fall*, we want to simulate the scattering of light by aerosols like dust, mist, and smoke. The way light is scattered by aerosols is described by Mie-scattering. Mie-scattering shows that light will scatter more in the forward direction when scattered by bigger particles in the atmosphere (Figure 3.5). To approximate the Mie-scattering phase function, we use the Henyey-Greenstein phase function [Henyey and Greenstein 41]:

$$f_{HG}(\theta) = \frac{(1-g)^2}{4\pi \cdot (1 + g^2 - 2g \cdot cos(\theta))^{3/2}}. \qquad (3.1)$$

The *g* value in Equation (3.1) controls how much light will scatter in the forward direction (Figure 3.6). This value should actually be based on the type of particles

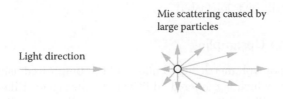

Figure 3.5. Mie-scattering: light scatters more in the forward direction when scattered by bigger particles.

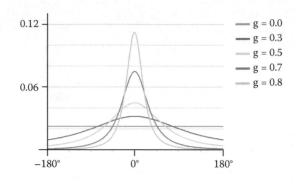

Figure 3.6. Henyey-Greenstein phase function result for different values of g.

in the atmosphere that cause the light to scatter, but for practical reasons we use a constant value for it which can be tweaked by artists.

Then, we calculate the scattering factor f_{SF} for a certain view angle as

$$f_{SF}(\theta) = f_{HG}(\theta) \cdot \text{scattering amount.} \tag{3.2}$$

3.3 Low-Resolution Rendering

The straightforward ray-marching approach we use is nice because it's relatively simple to implement. However, the drawback is that we need quite a lot of samples to make it look good. The more samples we take, the more expensive the volumetric light shader will be.

To improve the rendering performance, we decided to render the effect at a lower resolution. We have tried to render at quarter resolution but found that the loss of quality was too big, so we decided to render the effect to a half-resolution buffer we call the *volumetric light buffer*. To be able to render at lower resolution we also need to downscale the depth buffer accordingly so we can still use the depth test when rendering the volumetric light. Another advantage of this is that sampling from a half-resolution depth buffer when reconstructing the pixel's world position will be a lot faster.

3.3.1 Bilateral Upsampling

The half-resolution volumetric light buffer will be composited using a bilateral upsampling shader, which is rendered additively to the scene. Bilateral upsampling [Sloan et al. 07] will make sure that we can composite the half-resolution buffer nicely without causing blurry artifacts on object edges in the high-resolution image (Figure 3.7(a)).

(a)   (b)   (c)

Figure 3.7. (a) Upsampling using regular bilinear filter causes blurry edges. (b) Up-sampling using bilateral filter to preserve sharp edges. (c) Image after being processed by MSAA antialiasing filter.

For each full-resolution pixel we will sample the depth and color of the four nearest half-resolution pixels. For each of the four samples, a weight is calculated to account for regular bilinear filtering. Each weight is then scaled down based on the difference between the high-resolution depth and the sample's half-resolution depth. The bigger the difference in depth, the smaller the weight of the half-resolution sample. All weights are divided by their total sum to make sure they are normalized. The four samples are scaled by their weight and added together to form the final resulting color (Figure 3.7(b) and 3.7(c)) [Shopf 09].

3.4 Dithered Ray Marching

In order to improve the rendering performance even more, we decided to reduce the number of ray-march steps we were taking. Lowering the number of ray-march steps will cause banding artifacts in the volumetric light (Figure 3.10(a) and (b)). This is caused by the fact that each sample will have more influence on the final image and the error caused by undersampling gets worse.

To reduce the artifacts, we added a small grayscale dither pattern texture (Figure 3.9(a)), which is tiled across the screen. For each fragment that is being rendered, we sample this texture and use the grayscale value to offset the ray-march sample positions over depth. The values in the texture range from 0.0 to 1.0, where 1.0 defines an offset as big as the distance between two ray-march samples (Figure 3.8(b)).

The dither texture (Figure 3.9(a)) is 4×4 pixels in size. The distribution of the ray-march offsets within the dither texture is based on the Bayer matrix [Bayer 73]. The offsets are arranged such that each successive offset has the biggest possible 2D distance within the texture considering the texture will be tiled (Figure 3.9(b)). Because each volumetric light pixel within a 4×4 boundary will get a different offset, we get a nicely dithered result (Figure 3.10(c)).

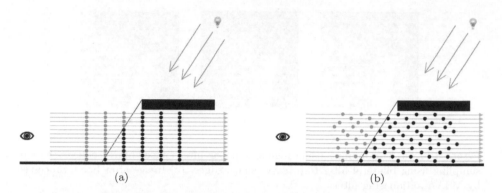

Figure 3.8. (a) Ray-march samples without dithered offset. (b) Ray-march samples with dithered offset.

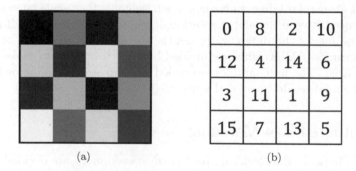

Figure 3.9. (a) 4×4 pixel dither pattern texture. (b) Sample offsets. Values in the texture are 1/16th of the values shown.

3.4.1 Bilateral Gaussian Blur

Using a bilateral Gaussian blur filter we can filter the dither pattern, which will result in a smooth looking image (Figure 3.10(d)). The bilateral Gaussian blur is performed in two passes [Pham and van Vliet 05]. In the first pass the filter will blur the image horizontally. Using a shader we will copy the dithered image to another buffer. The shader will sample the source pixel and three pixels on either side of it. For each sample a weight is calculated based on the Gaussian distribution function. Each weight is then scaled based on the difference in depth of the sample compared to the depth of the source pixel. A bigger difference in depth results in a lower weight (Figure 3.11). We will normalize the weights by dividing them by their total sum. The final shader output color is calculated by adding all weighted samples together (Figure 3.12(b)).

(a)   (b)

(c)   (d)

Figure 3.10. (a) Volumetric light being cast from an omni-light, placed in a shadow-casting sphere, rendered using 256 ray-march steps. (b) Reducing the step count to 32 steps causes bad-looking artifacts. (c) Volumetric light rendered using 32 steps and the dither pattern to offset the ray-march sample positions. (d) Final result after applying the bilateral Gaussian blur filter.

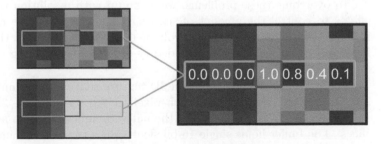

Figure 3.11. Horizontal bilateral Gaussian blur pass. The current pixel being processed is marked red. The left shows the color (top) and depth (bottom) input samples. The right shows the un-normalized weights of the samples based on Gaussian distribution and depth difference.

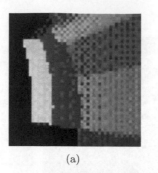 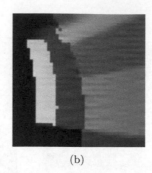 

(a)   (b)   (c)

Figure 3.12. (a) Dithered source image. (b) Result after applying horizontal bilateral Gaussian blur pass. (c) Final result after applying vertical bilateral Gaussian blur pass.

In the second pass we copy the image back using the same technique but now we will sample three pixels above and three pixels below the current pixel to get a vertical blur. The final result is a smooth looking image in which the sharp object edges are still preserved (Figure 3.12(c)).

3.5   Controlling the Amount of Scattering

Till now our implementation gave us some nice looking volumetric light effects. However, the effect looked too uniform and too static. It lacked a dusty or smoky feel to it. We also didn't have enough control to define where, when, and how much volumetric light should be visible in certain areas of the scene. We needed a way to control the amount of volumetric light more accurately and more dynamically.

To overcome these problems, we came up with a solution that uses particle effects to control the amount of scatting. The reason to use particle effects is because they allow us to define a volume in a very flexible way, they're integrated in all our other game systems, and they are ideal for creating animated smoke- and dust-like effects.

The particles are rendered to a 3D texture that will hold multiple scattering amount values over depth for each pixel on the screen. The 3D texture has a width and height that is 1/8th of the native render resolution and has 16 depth slices. The buffer holds single 16-bit float values to store the amount values and will be used to store the amounts for depths up to 128 meters. To increase the depth resolution close to the camera we distribute the depth slices using the following equation:

$$d(i) = \left(\frac{i}{(N-1)} \right)^C * R. \tag{3.3}$$

Slice index	Depth in meters
0	0.0
1	0.57
2	2.28
3	5.12
...	...
13	96.14
14	111.50
15	128.0

Table 3.1. Depths for depth slices.

The equation calculates the depth (d) for each slice index (i). N defines the number of depth slices and R defines the depth range we want to cover. C defines the curvature of the function. $C = 1.0$ will result in depth slices evenly distributed across the entire depth range. A higher value of C will move slices near the camera closer to each other and will spread distant slices farther apart. We use $C = 2.0$ in our implementation to get a nice distribution. Table 3.1 and Figure 3.13 show the depth slice distribution when using 16 depth slices and a depth range of 128 meters.

To calculate the 3D texture lookup depth coordinate for a given view-space depth, we use the following equation:

$$\text{lookup\_depth} = \left(\frac{\text{view\_space\_depth}}{R} \right)^{(1/C)} \tag{3.4}$$

As shown in the equation, we divide the view-space depth by the depth range R. We then raise it to the power of $(1.0/C)$, which is the inverse of the power of the curvature constant C. This will give us the normalized depth coordinate that we can use to sample the 3D texture. The code used to calculate the 3D texture lookup depth coordinate is shown in Listing 3.1.

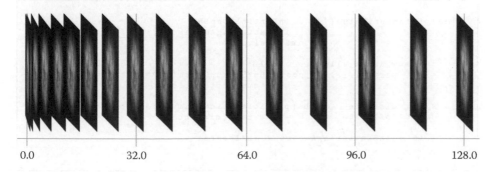

| 0.0 | 32.0 | 64.0 | 96.0 | 128.0 |

Figure 3.13. Depth slice distribution when $N = 16$, $C = 2.0$, and $R = 128.0$.

```
float GetLookupDepth(float inViewSpaceDepth)
{
  float depth_range     = 128.0;      //< Depth range R
  float inv_curve_power = 1.0/2.0;    //< Inv. power (1.0 / C)

  return pow((inViewSpaceDepth / depth_range), inv_curve_power);
}
```

Listing 3.1. Calculating the 3D texture lookup depth coordinate for a given view-space depth.

We render the particles as traditional camera-facing billboards. The particle's alpha channel will be used to define the scattering amount. To calculate the influence a particle has on each depth slice, we use the code shown in Listing 3.2. In the function we first calculate the 3D texture lookup depth coordinate. We then scale the value up to a 0.0 to 15.0 range to map it within the range of our depth slice indices. The resulting value `particle_slice_pos` defines the position of the particle between the slices. The influence a particle has on each depth slice is based on the absolute value of the difference between `particle_slice_pos` and each slice index. We refer to this value as `distance` because it describes the distance of the particle to the depth slice in texture space.

If the distance is 0.0, the particle is located at the same depth as the depth slice and the particle influence should be 1.0. A distance equal to or greater than 1.0 means the particle is more than one slice away and the influence will be 0.0. For distances ranging between 0.0 and 1.0, the influence will be equal to the reversed value of `distance`. For any slice index the influence can be easily calculated by clamping the `distance` value to a 0.0 to 1.0 range and reversing the result to a 1.0 to 0.0 range using $f(x) = 1 - x$.

```
float GetAmountValue(float inParticleDepth,
                     float inScatteringAmount,
                     int   inSliceIndex)
{
    int   num_depth_slices   = 16; //< Number of depth slices
    float particle_slice_pos = GetLookupDepth(inParticleDepth) *
                               (num_depth_slices - 1);

    float distance  = abs(particle_slice_pos - inSliceIndex);
    float influence = 1.0 - saturate(distance);

    return inScatteringAmount * influence;
}
```

Listing 3.2. Calculating the particle's scattering amount value for a single depth slice.

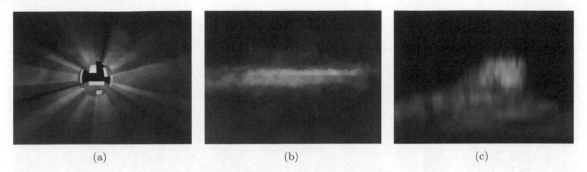

(a)   (b)   (c)

Figure 3.14. (a) Scene using 3D scattering amount lookup. (b) Front view of the scattering amount 3D texture. (c) Top view of the middle scan-line of the 3D texture. Bottom of the image is close to the camera.

The amount value of each depth slice will be incremented by the value the `GetAmountValue` function returns. When all particles have been rendered, we end up having a 3D lookup texture that gives us an approximation of the scattering amount for each pixel on the screen over depth. In the ray-march loop we sample the 3D texture for each ray-march step at the proper view-space depth using the function from Listing 3.1 to get the scattering amount. The scattering amount is then scaled by the world-space distance traveled by each ray-march step. Although the depth representation of the amount of scattering is not very accurate, it does give us a lot of control over the amount of volumetric light at different locations in the scene. The slight variations in the intensity make the effect look much more natural (Figures 3.14–3.17).

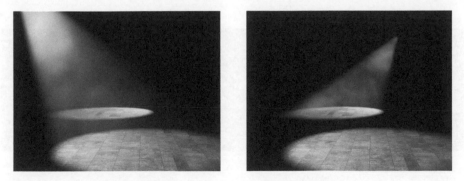

Figure 3.15. Test scene that shows how a particle effect can be used to cause light scattering in different locations in the scene. In the left image a particle effect is placed close to the camera to cause the light of the nearest spotlight to scatter. In the right image the same particle effect is moved farther away from the camera to cause light scattering for the spotlight in the back.

(a)

(b)   (c)   (d)

Figure 3.16. (a) Volumetric light scattering controlled by particle effects placed in the scene. Notice the sunlight only being scattered close to the trees. (b) Volumetric light buffer. (c) Top view of the middle scan-line of the scattering amount buffer showing scattering amount over depth. Bottom of the image is close to the camera. (d) Single depth slice of the scattering amount buffer.

Figure 3.17. (a) Forest scene. Particle effects are used to only cause light scattering between the trees. (b) Volumetric light buffer. (c) Top view of the middle scan-line of the amount buffer. Bottom of the image is near the camera. (d) Single slice of the scattering amount buffer showing the particles that control the scattering amount.

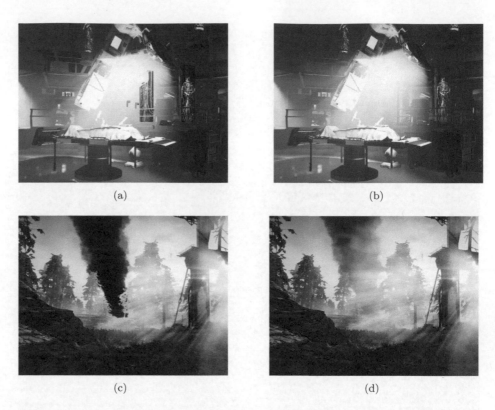

Figure 3.18. (a) Scene with volumetric light effects and transparent objects. Notice the dark transparent objects in the background not being properly composited with the volumetric light. (b) The same scene now using the volume light intensity buffer to properly blend volumetric light with the transparent objects. (c) A smoke particle effect not blending properly with the volumetric light effect. (d) Result after using the volume light intensity buffer to properly blend the smoke with the volumetric light effect.

3.6   Transparent Objects

The way we render our volumetric lights and composite them to the scene causes problems when rendering transparent objects that use alpha blending (Figure 3.18(a)). Especially alpha-blended particle effects didn't blend properly with the volumetric lighting effects (Figure 3.18(c)). Depending on the rendering order, either the volumetric light is drawn in front of all transparent objects, or the transparent objects occlude the volumetric light effects.

In order to solve this issue, we had to find a way to make the transparent shaders aware of the existence of the volumetric light. If we know how much volumetric light is in front of a transparent surface, we can blend the volumetric light properly with the transparent objects (Figure 3.18(b) and (d)).

```
float GetSliceIntensity(float inSampleDepth,
                        float inIntensity,
                        float inSliceIndex)
{
    int num_depth_slices = 8; //< Number of depth slices

    float sample_slice_pos = GetLookupDepth(inSampleDepth) *
                             (num_depth_slices - 1);

    float sample_distance = sample_slice_pos - inSliceIndex;
    float sample_influence = 1.0 - saturate(sample_distance);

    return inIntensity * sample_influence;
}
```

Listing 3.3. Calculating the volume light intensity value for a single depth slice.

The solution we came up with is similar to the technique we used earlier to control the amount of scattering. Instead of storing the amount of scattering at certain depths, we will store the accumulated intensity of volumetric light over depth in another 3D texture, which we call the *volume light intensity buffer*.

For each ray-march step we will calculate the luminance of the ray-march sample color. We will then use the view-space depth of the sample to determine the influence of the sample on each depth slice of the 3D texture. The intensity value of each depth slice is then incremented by the sample's luminance scaled by the influence.

We use the function shown in Listing 3.3 to calculate the intensity values for the 3D texture slices. The influence the ray-march sample intensity has on a depth slice is calculated such that the first slice closer in depth will get a linear interpolated influence based on the difference of the slice index and `sample_slice_pos`. All slices further in depth will get an influence of 1.0, and all slices closer in depth will get an influence of 0.0.

Because the volumetric light shader is rendered in half-resolution rather than the 1/8th resolution, we needed to reduce the number of depth slices of the volume light intensity buffer to 8 and reduce the effective distance to 64 meters for performance reasons. When all lights have been rendered, the volume light intensity buffer will approximate the volumetric light intensity of all volumetric lights occluding the scene over depth (Figure 3.19(b)).

All transparent objects rendered after the volumetric light buffer has been composited will sample the volume light intensity buffer at the proper view-space depth to find out how much volumetric light is in front of them. We use the same function as shown in Listing 3.1 to calculate the 3D texture lookup depth coordinate, but with an adjusted value for `depth_range` to account for the reduced depth range. For the `inViewSpaceDepth` parameter we pass the view-space depth of the transparent surface. The result of the 3D texture lookup will represent the intensity of the volumetric light in front of the transparent surface.

(a)   (b)

Figure 3.19. (a) Sphere example scene. (b) Top down view of one scan-line of the volumetric intensity buffer.

Equation (3.5) shows how we calculate a new surface color for the transparent shader:

$$NewColor = OrgColor + VLBufferColor \cdot \frac{SampledIntensity}{VLBufferIntensity}. \qquad (3.5)$$

`OrgColor` is the original output color of the shader. `VLBufferColor` is the color sampled from the volumetric light buffer, and its luminance is referred to as `VLBufferIntensity`. The `SampledIntensity` variable refers to the intensity sampled from the volume light intensity buffer as described earlier. The fraction of volumetric light that occludes the surface is calculated by dividing `SampledIntensity` by `VLBufferIntensity`. The `VLBufferColor` is scaled by the fraction and added to the original surface color.

3.7 Limitations

Due to the low depth resolution of our 3D lookup textures, the sampled scattering amount and light intensity values aren't very accurate. Although we got some good looking results from the current implementation, there are some limitations and artifacts that should be mentioned. Most of them could be solved by increasing the depth resolution of the 3D textures or using a different way to store the values over depth as discussed in Section 3.8.1.

3.7.1 Scattering Amount Buffer

Artifacts can be seen when lights, especially at larger distances, pick up wrong scattering amount values. When moving the camera back and forth through the scene, the volume light intensity of certain lights could fade in and out because of this. To keep these artifacts to a minimum, we only use the particles to roughly define scattering for larger areas. We also make sure we render enough particles over depth to keep the scattering amount over depth as smooth as possible and make sure to keep the amount values subtle and natural looking.

3.7.2 Compositing Transparent Objects

Our solution to composite transparent objects to the scene works well for transparent objects close to the camera. However, when volumetric light effects are close to transparent objects and being viewed at larger distances, the intensity curve is not accurate enough to correctly determine the amount of volumetric light in front of the transparent surface. In these cases transparent objects can look darker or lighter than they should. The fading artifact described earlier can also be seen on transparent objects when moving the camera back or forth. However, the integration of transparent objects in the scene is still better than when not accounting for volumetric light at all. Better algorithms to store the values over depth and/or increasing the depth resolution of our 3D textures can reduce these artifacts.

Also, the technique cannot distinguish different volumetric light sources, which can cause problems. If we would have a red, green, and blue volumetric light behind each other, then the final volumetric-light-buffer color would be white. The transparent objects will blend with the final volumetric-light-buffer color and thus blend with the white color, while they should actually be aware of different colors at different depths. This causes artifacts where transparent objects placed within a volumetric light can show strange color differences caused by other volumetric lights at larger distances, which shouldn't affect the transparent object at all. Storing the red, green, and blue intensities separately in the intensity buffer could potentially solve this; however, due to our performance and memory limitations, we did not investigate this subject further. As long as the light colors within a scene don't vary too much, the artifact is hardly noticeable.

3.8   Future Improvements

3.8.1   Curve Compression Methods

The accuracy and range of the scattering amount and volume light intensity buffers could be improved by storing the values over depth differently using some form of curve compression algorithm instead of storing the values directly in a 3D texture.

Other articles related to rendering of transparent shadow casting objects propose other alternatives to store values over depth [Lokovic and Veach 00, Salvi et al. 11]. They describe how to store a light transmittance function over depth. Our solution could benefit from this research. Alternatively the use of discreet cosine transforms (DCT) or fast fourier transforms (FFT) to store the amount of scattering and volume light intensity could also be valuable subjects to research.

Unfortunately, due to our tight release schedule, we didn't have time to find a better solution that both improves quality and maintains acceptable performance.

3.8.2 Epipolar Sampling

To improve our rendering performance, we have reduced the amount of ray-march samples by lowering the resolution of our volumetric light buffer. Epipolar sampling [Yusov 14] also dramatically reduces the number of ray-march samples. However, instead of lowering the resolution in screen space, it reduces the resolution across the epipolar lines from the light source relative to the viewer's position. Lowering the resolution across these lines is far less noticeable. By using epipolar sampling we should be able to reduce the amount of pixels for which we execute the ray-march loop even more without losing or maybe even improving quality.

3.9 Conclusion

We have shown a practical implementation of volumetric lighting effects as being used in *Killzone: Shadow Fall*. Using half-resolution buffers and dithered ray-march offsets, we have improved performance and maintained good image quality.

We managed to give the artist full control over the intensity of volumetric light in our scenes by using particles to render a 3D texture that defines the amount of light scattering.

By rendering another 3D lookup texture that defines the intensity of volumetric light over depth, we solved most of the compositing problems related to transparent objects.

Although there are limitations to our approach, it does show a solution that deals with the problems we have found during the development of the volumetric light effects in *Killzone: Shadow Fall*.

Bibliography

[Bayer 73] Bryce Bayer. "An Optimum Method for Two-Level Rendition of Continuous-Tone Pictures." *IEEE International Conference on Communications* 1 (1973): 11–15.

[Henyey and Greenstein 41] L. G. Henyey and J. L. Greenstein. "Diffuse Reflection in the Galaxy." *Astrophysical Journal* 93 (1941), 70–83.

[Lokovic and Veach 00] Tom Lokovic and Eric Veach. "Deep Shadow Maps." In *Proceedings of ACM SIGGRAPH 2000, Computer Graphics Proceedings, ACS*, pp. 385–392. New York: ACM, 2000.

[Pham and van Vliet 05] Tuan Q. Pham and Lucas J. van Vliet. "Separable Bilateral Filtering For Fast Video Preprocessing." In *Proceedings of the IEEE International Conference on Multimedia and Expo*, Article no. 1521458. Washington, DC: IEEE Computer Society, 2005.

[Salvi et al. 11] Marco Salvi, Kiril Vidimèe, Andrew Lauritzen, Aaron Lefohn, and Matt Pharr. "Adaptive Volume Shadow Maps." In *GPU Pro 2*, edited by Wolfgang Engel, pp. 225–241. Wellesley, MA: A K Peters, Ltd., 2011.

[Shopf 09] Jeremy Shopf. "Mixed Resolution Rendering." Presentation, Game Developers Conference 2009, San Francisco, CA, March, 2009. (Available at http://developer.amd.com/wordpress/media/2012/10/ShopfMixedResolutionRendering.pdf.)

[Sloan et al. 07] Peter-Pike Sloan, Naga K. Govindaraju, Derek Nowrouzezahrai, and John Snyder. "Image-Based Proxy Accumulation for Real-Time Soft Global Illumination." In *Proceedings of the 15th Pacific Conference on Computer Graphics and Applications*, pp. 97–105. Washington, DC: IEEE Computer Society, 2007.

[Valient 09] Michal Valient. "The Rendering Technology of *Killzone 2*." Presentation, Game Developers Conference 2009, San Francisco, CA, March, 2009. (Available at http://www.guerrilla-games.com/publications.)

[Yusov 14] Egor Yusov. "High Performance Outdoor Light Scattering Using Epipolar Sampling." In *GPU Pro 5*, edited by Wolfgang Engel, pp. 101–124. Boca Raton, FL: A K Peters/CRC Press, 2014.

Hi-Z Screen-Space Cone-Traced Reflections

Yasin Uludag

4.1 Overview

This chapter will introduce a novel approach for calculating reflections on dynamic 3D scenes, one that works on arbitrary shaped surfaces. Algorithms and techniques that were researched during the early development of *Mirror's Edge* are presented and shared.

The methods we will look into outperform any other methods both in terms of performance and image quality, as can be seen in Section 4.8, "Performance," and Section 4.9, "Results."

We will take a look into the latest work done in the area of real-time reflections, analyze their pros and cons and where they fail to deliver. Then we'll look into a new approach for calculating reflections in real time at game interactive frame rates.

First we will present the algorithm itself, which uses a screen-space aligned quad tree we call *Hierarchical-Z* (Hi-Z) buffer to accelerate the ray tracing. The hierarchy is stored in the MIP channels of the Hi-Z texture. This acceleration structure is used for empty space skipping to efficiently arrive at the intersection point. We will further discuss all the pre-computation passes needed for glossy reflections and how they can be constructed. We will also look into a technique called screen-space cone tracing for approximating rough surfaces, which produce blurred reflections. Moreover, performance and optimization for the algorithm are discussed. Then extensions to the algorithm are shown for improving and stabilizing the result. One such extension is temporal filtering, which allows us to accumulate the reflection results of several previous frames to stabilize the output result of the current frame by re-projecting the previous images even when the camera moves. The ability to approximate multiple ray bounces for reflections within reflections comes for free when doing temporal filtering because the previous frames already contain the reflections. Research and development techniques currently being developed will be mentioned, such as packet tracing for grouping several rays together into a packet and then refining/subdividing and shooting smaller ray packets once a coarse intersection is found. Another direction for future research that will be mentioned is screen-space tile-based tracing where if an entire tile contains mostly rough surfaces we know we can shoot fewer rays because the result will most likely be blurred, thereby gaining major performance, which gives us more room for other types of calculations for producing better images.

Finally timers will be shown for PCs. For the PC we will use both NVIDIA- and AMD-based graphics cards. Before we conclude the chapter, we will also mention some future ideas and thoughts that are being currently researched and developed.

This novel and production-proven approach (used in *Mirror's Edge*), proposed in this chapter guarantees maximum quality, stability, and good performance for computing local reflections, especially when it is used in conjunction with the already available methods in the game industry such as local cube-maps [Bjorke 07, Behc 10]. Specific attention is given to calculating physically accurate glossy/rough reflections matching how the stretching and spreading of the reflections behave in real life from different angles, a phenomenon caused by micro fractures.

4.2 Introduction

Let's start with the actual definition of a reflection:

> *Reflection* is the change in direction of a wave, such as a light or sound wave, away from a boundary the wave encounters. Reflected waves remain in their original medium rather than entering the medium they encounter. According to the *law of reflection*, the angle of reflection of a reflected wave is equal to its angle of incidence (Figure 4.1).

Reflections are an essential part of lighting; everything the human eye perceives is a reflection, whether it's a specular (mirror), glossy (rough), or diffusive

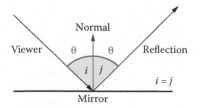

Figure 4.1. Law of reflection states that incident angle i equals reflection angle j.

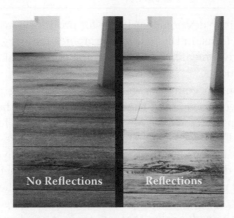

Figure 4.2. Impact of reflections toward the goal of achieving photorealism. Notice the reflection occlusion near the contact points of the floor and the door blocking the incident light.

reflection (matte). It's an important part of achieving realism in materials and lighting. Reflection occlusion also helps out with grounding the object being reflected into the scene at the contact points, as we can see in Figures 4.2 and 4.3. It's an important part of our visual understanding of reality and it shouldn't be taken lightly, as it can make a big difference in achieving realism.

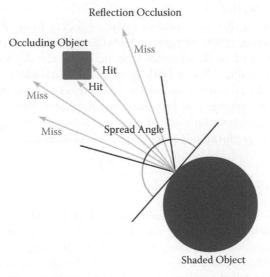

Figure 4.3. Illustration showing reflection occlusion where the hit rays block the light just like the door blocks the white light in Figure 4.2.

There has been little development lately for producing accurate reflections, especially glossy reflections, in the real-time graphics industry at high performance game frame-rate levels, meaning an algorithm has to run at a fraction of our per frame millisecond budget.

Solving reflections in computer games has been a big challenge due to the high performance requirements of the computations. We have a limited budget of milliseconds to spare for each frame, 16.6 milliseconds for 60 FPS and 33.33 milliseconds for 30 FPS, to recalculate everything and present an image to the user. This includes everything from game simulation, physics, graphics, AI to Network, etc. If we don't keep the performance level at such small fractions of a second, the user will not experience feedback in real time when giving input to the game. Now imagine that a fraction of those milliseconds needs to go to reflections only. Coming up with an algorithm that runs as fast as a few milliseconds and still keeps the quality level at maximum is hard using rasterization-based techniques that GPU hardware runs on.

Though game developers have been able to produce fake reflections for a very long time on simple cases, there is no solution that fixes every issue up to an acceptable level of realism with the performance levels required. For planar surfaces, meaning walls and floors, it's easy to flip the camera and re-render the entire scene and project the resulting image onto the planar surface to achieve what we today call planar reflections. This works for planar surfaces such as floors and walls but it's a completely different story for arbitrarily shaped surfaces that can reflect toward any direction per pixel. Re-rendering the entire scene and re-calculating all the lightings per plane is also an expensive operation and can quickly become a bottleneck.

The only solution that gives perfect results existing today is what we call ray tracing. But, tracing reflected rays and mathematically intersecting geometric primitives (a bunch of small triangles that make up the 3D world) is computationally and also memory heavy both in terms of bandwidth and size, because the rays could really go anywhere and we would need to keep the entire 3D scene in memory in a traversable and fast-to-access data structure. Even today, with the most optimized algorithms and data structures, ray tracing is still not fast enough in terms of performance to be deployed on games.

4.3 Previous Work

Generating 100% accurate and efficient reflections is difficult if not impossible with rasterization-based hardware used in GPUs today. Though we have moved on toward more general computing architectures allowing us more freedom, it's still not efficient enough to use a real ray tracer. For this reason game developers have for a long time relied on planar reflections where you re-render the scene from a mirrored camera for each plane, such as floors or walls, and project the image

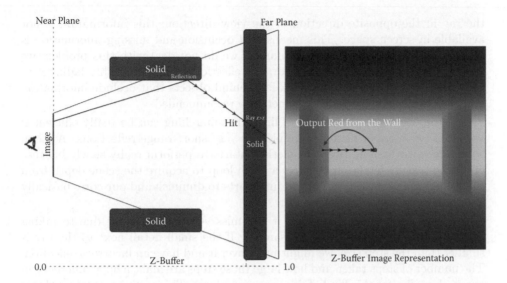

Figure 4.4. Ray marching by taking small steps in screen space using the Z-buffer (depth buffer, an image representing scene depth in floating point numbers) until the ray depth is below the surface. Once it is below the surface, we can stop the ray marching and use the new coordinates to acquire the reflection color and apply it on the pixel we started the marching from.

to create a planar reflection. Another technique that has been relied upon for a very long time is cube-maps, six images capturing 360 degrees of the surrounding environment from a single point with a 90-degree field of view for each side, hence these reflections are only valid from that specific point only.

A new idea called screen-space local reflections was first showed by [Graham 10] at Beyond3D forums and then later introduced into Crysis 2 DX11 patch by Crytek [Tiago et al. 12]. They both proposed a simple ray marching algorithm in screen space. Screen space means that we do everything in 2D framebuffer objects, images, as a post-processing effect.

It's a fairly simple idea; you just compute a screen-space reflection vector using the scene normal buffer and ray-march through the pixels at a certain step size until the ray depth falls below the scene depth stored in what we call a depth buffer. Once the ray depth is below the scene depth, we detect a hit and use the new screen-space coordinate to read the scene color, which is used as reflection for the pixel we started the ray-marching from. This technique is illustrated in Figure 4.4.

However since this computation is performed in screen space, there are limitations that need to be taken care of. A built-in problem with this kind of technique is that not all of the information is available to us. Imagine a mirror reflecting the ray in the opposite direction of the view direction; this information is not available in screen space. This means that occlusion and missing information is a huge challenge for this technique and if we do not deal with this problem we will have artifacts and produce incorrect reflection colors. Smoothly fading rays that fall outside the screen borders, fall behind objects that occlude information and rays that point toward the camera are recommended.

On the other hand this type of linear ray marching can be really efficient if you do a low number of steps/samples for very short range reflections. As soon as you have really long rays this method starts to perform really slowly because of all the texture fetches it requires at each loop to acquire the scene depth from the Z-buffer. Due to this latency hiding starts to diminish and our cores basically stall, doing nothing.

It's also error prone such that it can miss very small details due to taking a fixed constant step size at each sample. If the small detail next to the ray is smaller than the step size, we might jump over it and have an incorrect reflection. The number of steps taken and how large those steps are make a huge difference in terms of quality for this kind of linear ray marching. This technique also produces staircase artifacts, for which you have to employ some form of a refinement once an intersection point is found. This refinement would be between the previous ray-march position and the ray-march intersection point to converge into a much more refined intersection. A low number of binary search steps or a single secant search is usually enough to deal with the staircase artifacts for pure specular rays. (See Figure 4.5.) Crytek employs ray length jittering at each iteration step to hide the staircase artifacts.

A simple linear ray-marching algorithm that traverses the depth buffer can be written with fewer than 15 lines of code, as we can see in Listing 4.1.

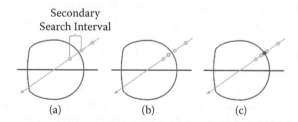

Secondary
Search Interval

(a)   (b)   (c)

Figure 4.5. Binary search illustration between the intersection position and the last position of the ray. Basically it takes the middle point of the two and checks if it's still intersecting; if true it does it again until it can resurface, which is a refined position. We can also visualize the constant step sizes linear ray marching takes and end up in the wrong coordinate, which results in staircase artifacts, so we need some form of a refinement. Binary search and secant search are popular ones. [Original image courtesy of [Risser 07].]

```
#define LINEAR_MARCH_COUNT 32
for(int i = 0; i < LINEAR_MARCH_COUNT; ++i)
{
    // Read scene depth with current ray.
    float d = depthBuffer.SampleLevel( pointSampler, ray.xy, 0 );

    // Check if ray is greater than the scene, it means we
    // intersected something so end.
    if( ray.z > d )
        break;

    // Else advance the ray by a small step and continue the
    // loop. Step is a vector in screen space.
    ray += step;
}
```

Listing 4.1. A simple linear ray marching to illustrate the concept of walking a depth buffer until an intersection is found. We can quickly see that this technique is fetch bound. The ALU units are not doing a lot of work as there are too few ALU instructions to hide the latency of the global memory fetches the shader has to wait to complete.

So let's take a close look at some major problems for this kind of a technique.

1. It takes small-sized steps, it conducts many fetches, and latency starts to bottleneck quickly.

2. It can miss small details in the case that the step it takes is larger than the small detail next to the ray.

3. It produces staircase artifacts and needs a refinement such as a secant or binary search.

4. It is only fast for short travels; ray-marching an entire scene will stall the cores and result in slow performance.

Our goal is to introduce an algorithm that can solve all four points.

All of those points can be solved by introducing an acceleration structure, which can then be used to accelerate our rays, basically traversing as much distance as the ray can possibly take without risking missing any details at all. This acceleration structure will allow the ray to take arbitrary length steps, and especially large ones as well whenever it can. It's also going to conduct fewer fetches and thereby perform faster. The acceleration structure is going to produce great results without needing an extra refinement pass, although it doesn't hurt to do a final secant search between the previous pixel and the current pixel because an acceleration structure is usually a discrete set of data. Since we gain major speedups by using an acceleration structure, we will also be able to travel longer and ray-march an entire scene with much better performance.

The algorithm called Hi-Z Screen-Space Cone Tracing proposed in this chapter can reflect an entire scene with quick convergence and performs orders of magnitude faster than the linear constant step-based ray-marching algorithm.

4.4 Algorithm

The proposed algorithm can be divided into five distinct steps:

1. Hi-Z pass,

2. pre-integration pass,

3. ray-tracing pass,

4. pre-convolution pass,

5. cone-tracing pass.

We will go through each step by step now.

4.4.1 Hi-Z Pass

The *Hierarchical-Z buffer*, also known as the Hi-Z buffer, is constructed by taking the minimum or maximum of the four neighboring values in the original Z-buffer and storing it in a smaller buffer at half the size. In our case for this chapter, we will go with the minimum version.

The Z-buffer holds the depth values of the 3D scene in a buffer such as a texture/image. The figure below represents the minimum value version of how a Hi-Z construction works:

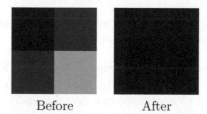

Before   After

The result is a coarse representation of the original buffer. We do this consecutively on the resulting buffers until we arrive at a buffer with the size of 1, where we no longer can go smaller. We store the computed values in the mip-channels of a texture. This is represented in Figure 4.6.

The result is what we call a Hi-Z buffer, because it represents the Z values (also known as scene depth values) in a hierarchical fashion.

This buffer is the heart of the algorithm. It's essentially a screen/image aligned quad tree that allows us to accelerate the ray-tracing algorithm by noticing and

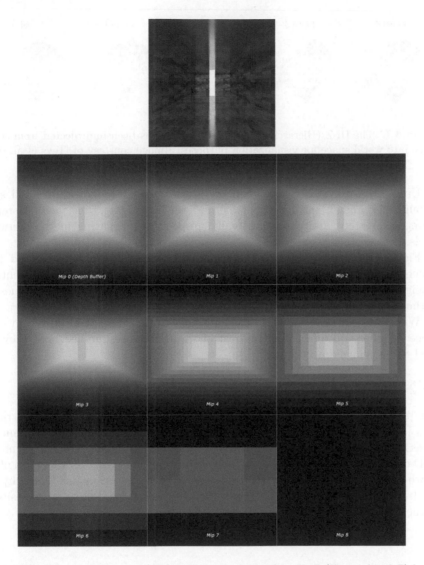

Figure 4.6. The original scene (top) and the corresponding Hi-Z (Hierarchical-Z) buffer (bottom) where the 2×2 minimum depths have been used successively to construct it. It serves as an acceleration structure for our rays in screen space. Mip 0 is our depth buffer that represents the scene depth per pixel. At each level we take the minimum of 2×2 pixels and produce this hierarchical representation of the depth values.

skipping empty space in the scene to efficiently and quickly arrive at our desired intersection point/coordinate by navigating in the different hierarchy levels. Empty space in our case is the tiles we see in the image, the quads.

Level 4   Level 3   Level 2   Level 1   Level 0

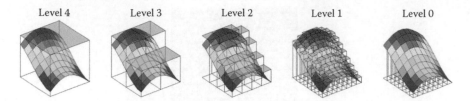

Figure 4.7. The Hi-Z (Hierarchical-Z) buffer, which has been unprojected from screen space into world space for visualization purposes. [Image courtesy of [Tevs et al. 08].]

Unlike the previously developed methods, which take constant small steps through the image, the marching method we investigate runs much faster by taking large steps and converges really quickly by navigating in the hierarchy levels.

Figure 4.7 shows a simple Hierarchical-Z representation unprojected from screen space back into world space for visualization purposes. It's essentially a height field where dark values are close to the camera and bright values are farther away from the camera.

Whether you construct this pass on a post-projected depth buffer or a view-space Z-buffer will affect how the rest of the passes are handled, and they will need to be changed accordingly.

4.4.2 Pre-integration Pass

The pre-integration pass calculates the scene visibility input for our cone-tracing pass in a hierarchical fashion. This pass borrows some ideas from [Crassin 11], [Crassin 12], and [Lilley et al. 12] that are applied to voxel structures and not 2.5D depth. The input for this pass is our Hi-Z buffer. At the root level all of our depth pixels are at a 100% visibility; however, as we go up in this hierarchy, the total visibility for the coarse representation of the cell has less or equal visibility to the four finer pixels:

$$\text{Visibility}_n \leq \text{Visibility}_{n-1}.$$

(See also Figure 4.8.) Think about the coarse depth cell as a volume containing the finer geometry. Our goal is to calculate how much visibility we have at the coarse level.

The cone-tracing pass will then sample this pre-integrated visibility buffer at various levels until our ray marching accumulates a visibility of 100%, which means that all the rays within this cone have hit something. This approximates the cone footprint. We are basically integrating all the glossy reflection rays. We start with a visibility of 1.0 for our ray; while we do the cone tracing, we will keep subtracting the amount we have accumulated until we reach 0.0. (See Figure 4.9.)

Figure 4.8. The area of interest between the minimum and maximum depth plane of the four pixels for which we calculate the visibility; basically, take the percentage of empty volume.

We cannot rely on only the visibility buffer, though. We must know how much our cone actually intersects the geometry as well, and for that we will utilize our Hi-Z buffer. Our final weight will be the accumulated visibility multiplied by how much our cone sphere is above, in between, or below the Hi-Z buffer.

The format for this pre-integration buffer is an 8 bit per channel texture that gives 256 values to represent our visibility. This gives 0.390625% of increments for our visibility values $(1.0/256.0)$, which is good enough precision for transparency.

Again, this pass is highly dependent on whether we have a post-projected depth Hi-Z or a view-space Hi-Z buffer.

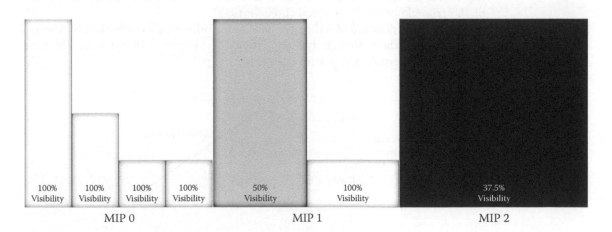

Figure 4.9. A 2D representation of the hierarchical pre-integrated visibility buffer. The percent is calculated between the minimum and maximum depths. The height is the depth and the color is the amount of visibility.

4.4.3   Ray-Tracing Pass

The following function is the reflection formula where $\vec{V}$ is the view direction and $\vec{N}$ is the surface normal direction (surface orientation) and the return value is the reflection vector:

$$Reflect(\vec{V}, \vec{N}) = 2(\vec{V} \cdot \vec{N})\vec{N} - \vec{V}.$$

The dot is the dot product, also known as the scalar product, between the two vectors. We will later use this function to calculate our reflection direction for the algorithm.

Before we continue with the ray-tracing algorithm, we have to understand what the depth buffer of a 3D scene actually contains. The depth buffer is referred to as being nonlinear, meaning that the distribution of the depth values of a 3D scene does not increase linearly with distance to the camera. We have a lot of precision close to the camera and less precision far away, which helps with determining which object is closest to the camera when drawing, because closer objects are more important than farther ones.

By definition division is a nonlinear operation and there is a division happening during perspective correction, which is where we get the nonlinearity from. A nonlinear value can't be linearly interpolated. However, while it is true that the Z-values in the depth buffer are not linearly increasing relative to the Z-distance from the camera, it is on the other hand indeed linear in screen space due to the perspective. Perspective-correct rasterization hardware requires linear interpolation across an entire triangle surface when drawing it from only three vertices. In particular the hardware interpolates 1/Z for each point that makes up the surface of the triangle using the original three vertices.

Linear interpolation of Z directly does not produce correct depth values across the triangle surface, though 1/Z does [Low 02]. Figure 4.10 explains why non-perspective interpolation is wrong.

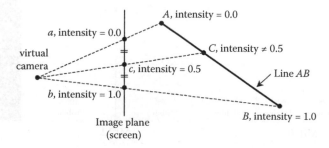

Figure 4.10. Illustration of interpolating an attribute directly in screen space giving incorrect results. One must do perspective correct interpolation as described in [Low 02]. The depth buffer value, 1/Z, is perspective correct so this allows us to interpolate it in screen space without any further computation.

We can observe the fact that the depth buffer values are linear in screen space, due to perspective, by taking the partial derivatives, gradients, of them using ddx and ddy instructions in Microsoft HLSL and outputting them as color values. For any planar surface the result is going to be a constant color, which tells us a linear rate of change the farther the planes are from the camera in screen space.

Anything that behaves linearly is also going to allow us to interpolate it, just like the hardware, which is a very powerful fact. It's also the reason we did the Hi-Z construction on the nonlinear depth buffer. Our ray tracing will happen in screen space, and we would like to exploit the fact that the depth buffer values can be interpolated correctly in screen space because they're perspective-corrected. It's like the perspective cancels out this nonlinearity of the values.

In the case that one desires to use a view-space Hi-Z buffer and not a post-projected buffer, one has to manually interpolate the Z-value just as perspective interpolation does, $1/Z$. Either case is possible and affects the rest of the passes as mentioned earlier. We will assume that we use a post-perspective Hi-Z from now on. Now that we know the depth buffer values can be interpolated in screen space, we can go back to the Hi-Z ray-tracing algorithm itself and use our Hi-Z buffer.

We can parameterize our ray-tracing algorithm to exploit the fact that depth buffer values can be interpolated. Let $\mathbf{O}$ be our starting screen coordinate, the origin, let the vector $\vec{D}$ be our reflection direction, and finally let t be our driving parameter between 0 and 1 that interpolates between the starting coordinate $\mathbf{O}$ and ending coordinate $\mathbf{O} + \vec{D}$:

$$Ray(t) = \mathbf{O} + \vec{D} * t,$$

where the vector $\vec{D}$ and point $\mathbf{O}$ are defined as

$$\vec{D} = \vec{V}_{ss}/\vec{V}_{ss_z},$$

$$\mathbf{O} = \mathbf{P}_{ss} + \vec{D} * -\mathbf{P}_{ss_z}.$$

$\vec{D}$ extends all the way to the far plane now. The division by $\vec{V}_z$ sets the Z-coordinate to 1.0, but it still points to the same direction because division by a scalar doesn't change a vector's direction. $\mathbf{O}$ is then set to the point that corresponds to a depth of 0.0, which is the near plane. We can visualize this as a line forming from the near plane to the far plane in the reflection direction crossing the point we are shading in Figure 4.11.

We can now input any value t to take us between the starting point and ending point for our ray-marching algorithm in screen space. The t value is going to be a function of our Hierarchical-Z buffer.

But we need to compute the vector $\vec{V}$ and $\mathbf{P}$ first to acquire $\mathbf{O}$ and $\vec{D}$. $\mathbf{P}$ is already available to us through the screen/texture coordinate and depth. To get $\vec{V}$ we need another screen-space point $\mathbf{P}'$, which corresponds to a point somewhere

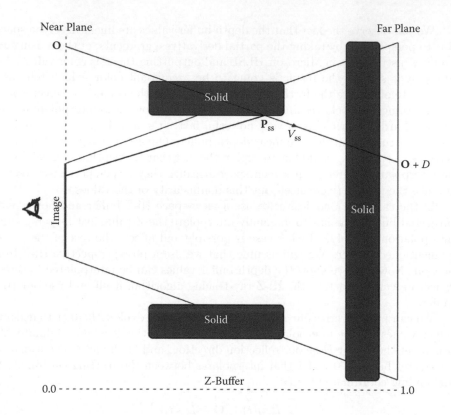

Figure 4.11. An illustration showing $\mathbf{O}$, $\vec{D}$, $\mathbf{P}$, and $\vec{V}$ variables from the equations. $\mathbf{O} + \vec{D} * t$ will take us anywhere between starting point $\mathbf{O}$ and ending point $\mathbf{O} + \vec{D}$ where t is between 0 and 1. Note that $\vec{V}$ is just a vector, direction, and has no position. It was put on the line for visualization purposes.

along the reflection direction. Taking the difference of these two will yield us a screen-space reflection vector:

$$\vec{V}_{ss} = \mathbf{P'_{ss}} - \mathbf{P_{ss}},$$

where the available $\mathbf{P}$ is defined as

$$\mathbf{P_{ss}} = \{\mathbf{texcoord_{xy}} \ \ \mathbf{depth}\}.$$

The other $\mathbf{P'}$ along the reflection direction can be computed by taking the view-space point, view-space direction, and view-space surface normal, computing a view-space reflection point, projecting it into clip space $[-1, 1]$ range, and finally converting from clip space into screen space $[0, 1]$ range, as we can see below:

$$\mathbf{P_{cs}} = (\mathbf{P_{vs}} + Reflect(\vec{V}_{vs}, \vec{N}_{vs})) * \mathbf{M_{proj}},$$

$$\mathbf{P'_{ss}} = \frac{\mathbf{P_{cs}}}{\mathbf{P_{cs_w}}} * [0.5 \quad -0.5] + [0.5 \quad 0.5].$$

Once we have a screen-space reflection vector, we can run the Hi-Z traversal to ray-march along the acceleration structure using $\mathbf{O}$, $\vec{D}$, and t.

We'll first look at the pseudo code in Listing 4.2. The algorithm uses the Hi-Z buffer we constructed earlier to accelerate the ray marching. To visualize the algorithm in Listing 4.2 step by step, follow Figure 4.12.

Once the ray-tracing algorithm has run, we have our new coordinate in screen space that is our ray intersection point. Some ideas are borrowed from displacement mapping techniques found in the literature [Hien and Lim 09, Hrkalovic and Lundgren 12, Oh et al. 06, Drobot 09, Szirmay-Kalos and Umenhoffer 06]. One major difference is that we start on the root level while displacement techniques start on the leaf level for marching a ray. Ray-marching with a view-space Z-buffer is a bit more involved because we have to manually interpolate the Z-coordinate as it is not possible to interpolate it in screen space.

```
level = 0 // starting level to traverse from

while level not below N // ray-trace until we descend below the
                        // root level defined by N, demo used 2

    minimumPlane  = getCellMinimumDepthPlane ( . . . )
    // reads from the Hi-Z texture using our ray
    boundaryPlane = getCellBoundaryDepthPlane ( . . . )
    // gets the distance to next Hi-Z cell boundary in ray
    // direction

    closestPlane  = min( minimumPlane, boundaryPlane )
    // gets closest of both planes

    ray = intersectPlane ( . . . )
    // intersects the closest plane, returns O + D * t only.

    if intersectedMinimumDepthPlane
    // if we intersected the minimum plane we should go down a
    // level and continue
        descend a level

    if intersectedBoundaryDepthPlane
    // if we intersected the boundary plane we should go up a
    // level and continue
        ascend a level

color = getReflection( ray ) // we are now done with the Hi-Z ray
                             // marching so get color from the intersection
```

Listing 4.2. Pseudo code for implementing the Hi-Z ray tracing.

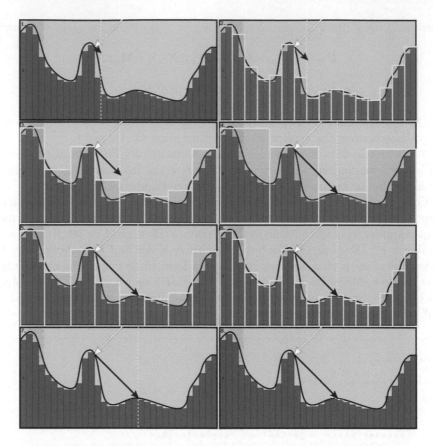

Figure 4.12. Hi-Z ray-tracing step by step going up and down in the hierarchy of the buffer to take longer jumps at each step. [Source image courtesy of [Drobot 09].]

4.4.4 Pre-convolution Pass

The pre-convolution pass is an essential pass for the algorithm for computing blurred glossy reflections emitted from microscopic rough surfaces. Just like in the Hi-Z pass, which outputs a hierarchy of images, this pass also does so, but with a different goal in mind.

We convolve the original scene color buffer to produce several different blurred versions out of it as we can see in Figure 4.13. The final result is another hierarchical representation, images at different resolutions with different levels of convolution, which is stored in the mip-map channels.

These blurred color buffers will help out with accelerating rough reflections to achieve results similar to what we can see in Figure 4.14.

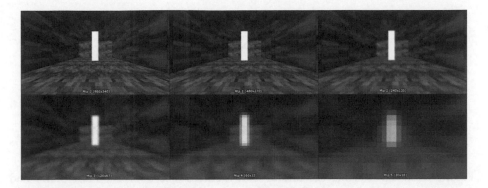

Figure 4.13. Convolved color texture of a simple scene with different level of convolution at each level. This will be later used to create our rough reflections.

Usually to simulate this kind of blurred reflections in ray-tracing-based renderers, we would shoot a lot of diverged rays defined by the cone aperture, say 32 more, and average the resulting colors together to produce a blurred reflection. (See Figures 4.15 and 4.16.)

However, this quickly becomes a very expensive operation and the performance decreases linearly with the number of rays we shoot, and even then the technique produces noisy and unacceptable results that need further processing to smooth out. One such technique is called image-space gathering [Robison and Shirley 09], which works really well even on pure mirror reflections to make them appear like rough reflections as a post-process.

Figure 4.14. Different levels of roughness on the spheres produce diverged reflection rays, which results in the viewer perceiving blurred reflections. [Image courtesy of [David 13].]

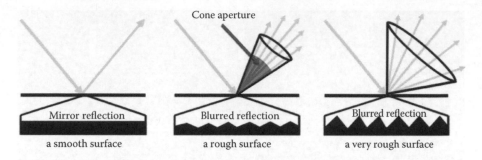

Figure 4.15. The rougher the surface is at a microscopic level, the more blurry and weaker the reflection appears. Fewer rays hit the iris of the perceivers' eye, which gives the weaker appearance. [Original image courtesy of [ScratchaPixel 12].]

Another drawback of shooting randomly jittered rays within the cone aperture is the fact that parallel computing hardware such as the GPU tends to run threads and memory transaction in groups/batches. If we introduce jittered rays we slow down the hardware because now all the memory transactions are in memory addresses far away from each other, slowing the computation by tremendous amounts because of cache-misses and global memory fetches, and bandwidth becomes a bottleneck.

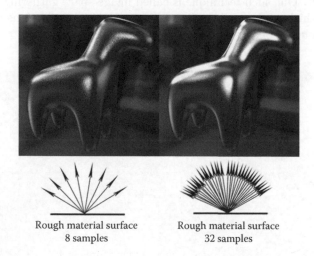

Figure 4.16. Noisy reflections produced by firing multiple diverged rays and averaging the results together for glossy reflections. Even 32 rays per pixel are not enough to create a perfectly smooth reflection and the performance decreases linearly with each additional ray. [Original images courtesy of [Autodesk 09] and [Luxion 12].]

Section 4.4.5 will propose a method that is merely an approximation but runs really fast without the need for firing multiple rays or jittering. By just navigating in the hierarchy of the blurred color images we discussed in this pass, depending on the reflection distance and roughness of the surface we are reflecting from, we can produce accurate glossy reflections.

4.4.5 Cone-Tracing Pass

The cone-tracing pass runs right after the Hi-Z ray-tracing pass finishes, and it produces the glossy reflections of the algorithm. This pass uses all our hierarchical buffers.

The output from the ray-tracing pass is our screen-space intersection coordinate as we saw earlier. With that we have all the knowledge to construct a screen-space aligned cone, which essentially becomes an isosceles triangle.

The idea is simple; Figure 4.17 shows a cone in screen space that corresponds to how much the floor diverges the reflection rays at maximum. Our goal is to accumulate all the color within that cone, basically integrate for every single ray that diverges. This integration can be approximated by sampling at the circle centers, where the size of the circle decides at which hierarchy level we read the color from our textures, as we saw in Section 4.4.3. Figure 4.18 illustrates this.

We determine whether the cone intersect our Hi-Z at all. If it does, we determine how much it intersects and multiply this weight with the pre-integrated visibility for that level and point. This final weight is accumulated until we reach 100%, and we weigh the color samples as well during the traversal. How you determine whether the cone intersects the Hi-Z for empty space is highly dependent on whether you use a post-projected Hi-Z or view-space Hi-Z.

First, we need to find the cone angle for a specific roughness level. Our reflection vector is basically the Phong reflection model because we just compute a reflection vector by reflecting the view direction on the normal. To approximate

Figure 4.17. A cone in screen space is essentially an isosceles triangle with the in-radius circles that will be able to sample/read the hierarchical buffers.

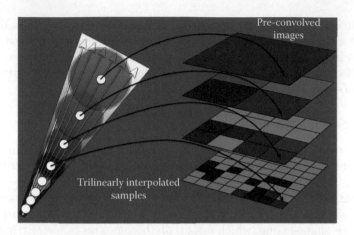

Figure 4.18. The cone integrates the rays, arrows, we see in the image by sampling, reading, at different levels in our convolved, blurred, color image depending on the distance and surface roughness. It blends both between the neighboring pixels and between the hierarchy levels, which is what we call *trilinear interpolation* for smooth transitions and blended results.

the cone angle for the Phong model, we use

$$\theta = \cos\left(\xi^{\frac{1}{\alpha+1}}\right),$$ (4.1)

where α is the specular power and ξ is hard-coded to 0.244. This is the basic formula used for importance sampling of a specular lobe; it is the inverse cumulative distribution function of the Phong distribution. Importance-sampling applications generate a bunch of uniform random variables [0–1] for ξ and use Equation 4.1 to generate random ray directions within the specular lobe in spherical coordinates [Lawrence 02]. The hard-coded value 0.244 seems to be a good number for covering a decent range of cone-angle extents. Figure 4.19 shows how well this equation maps to the cone angle extents of the Phong specular lobe in polar coordinates.

To get a perfectly mirrored ray with the Phong model, the specular power value would need to be infinity. Since that will not happen and graphics applications usually have a cap on their specular power value, we need a threshold value to support mirror reflections for the cone tracer. We can clearly see that there is not much change between a power of 1024 and 2048. So, any specular power in the range of 1024–2048 should be interpolated down to an angle of 0.

If we want another type of reflection model with more complicated distribution, we would need to pre-compute a 2D lookup table and index it with roughness as the u coordinate and $\vec{V} \cdot \vec{N}$ as the v coordinate, which would then return a local reflection direction. This local reflection direction would need to be transformed into a global reflection vector for the Hi-Z tracing pass.

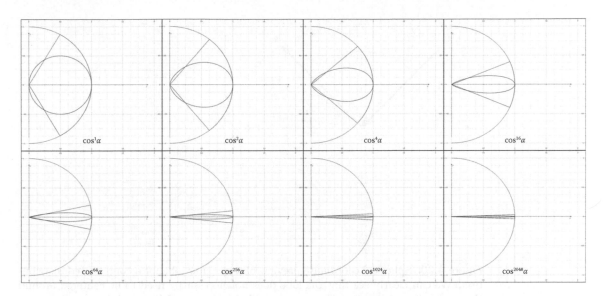

Figure 4.19. Polar coordinate plot of the specular lobe with various specular power values. The red ellipse is the specular lobe and the black isosceles triangle shows the cone angle extents using the formula presented earlier; α is the angle and $\cos\alpha$ is powered to various specular power values.

So, for any distribution model, we average at pre-computation time all the reflection vectors within the specular lobe—importance sampling using uniform random variables $[0\text{–}1]$—with a specific roughness value that gives the vector where the reflection vector is strongest, and then we store this vector in a 2D texture table. The reason we average all the reflection vectors within the lobe is the fact that complicated BRDF models often don't produce a lobe with respect to the pure specular reflection vector. They might be more vertically stretched or behave differently at grazing angles, and we are interested in finding the reflection vector that is the strongest within this specular lobe, which we can clearly see in Figure 4.20.

The RGB channel of this table would contain the local reflection vector and the alpha channel would contain either an isotropic cone-angle extent with a single value or anisotropic cone-angle extents with two values for achieving vertically stretched reflections, which we revisit later.

For this chapter, we just assume that we use a Phong model. We need to construct an isosceles triangle for the cone-tracing pass using the newly obtained angle θ. Let $\mathbf{P_1}$ be the start coordinate of our ray in screen space and $\mathbf{P_2}$ be the end coordinate of our ray, again in screen space. Then the length l is defined as

$$l = \|\triangle_\mathbf{P}\| = \|\mathbf{P_2} - \mathbf{P_1}\|.$$

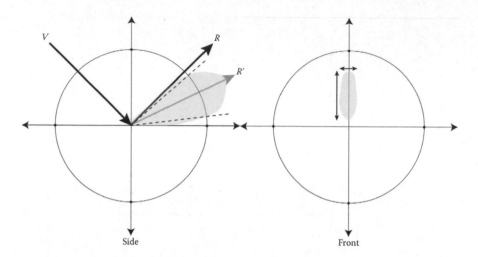

Figure 4.20. Spherical coordinate preview of a specular lobe for a complicated distribution. We can clearly see that the lobe does not necessarily need to be centered around the pure reflection vector. If we average all the vectors within the lobe, we get a new reflection vector $\vec{R}'$ that represents our reflection direction more precisely.

Once we have the length for our intersection, we can assume that it's the adjacent side of our isosceles triangle. With some simple trigonometry we can calculate the opposite side as well. Trigonometry says that the tangent of θ is the opposite side over the adjacent side:

$$\tan(\theta) = \frac{opp}{adj}.$$

Using some simple algebra we discover that the opposite side that we are looking for is the tangent of θ multiplied by the adjacent side:

$$opp = \tan(\theta)adj.$$

However, this is only true for right triangles. If we look at an isosceles triangle, we discover that it's actually two right triangles fused over the adjacent side where one is flipped. This means the opposite is actually twice the opposite of the right triangle:

$$opp = 2\tan(\theta)adj \tag{4.2}$$

Once we have both the adjacent side and the opposite side, we have all the data we need to calculate the sampling points for the cone-tracing pass. (See Figure 4.21.)

To calculate the in-radius (circle radius touching all three sides) of an isosceles triangle, this equation can be used:

$$r = \frac{a(\sqrt{a^2 + 4h^2} - a)}{4h},$$

where a is the base of the isosceles triangle, h is the height of the isosceles triangle, and r is the resulting in-radius. Recall that the height of the isosceles triangle is

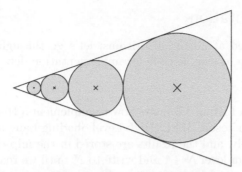

Sample ponts from ray start →ray finish

Figure 4.21. The isosceles triangle with the sampling points for the cone-tracing pass in screen space. To find the sample points of our cone in screen space, we have to use some geometry and calculate the in-radius of this isosceles triangle. Note that this is an approximation and we are not fully integrating the entire cone.

the length of our intersection we calculated before and the base of our isosceles triangle is the opposite side. Using this formula we find the radius of the in-radius circle. Once we have the in-radius of the isosceles triangle, we can take the adjacent side and subtract the in-radius from it to find the sampling point we are interested in. We can now read the color from the correct coordinate in screen space.

To calculate the rest of the sampling points, all we have to do is subtract the in-radius another time to reach the leftmost side of the circle and then recalculate the opposite side with this new adjacent side using equation 4.2, and then rerun the in-radius formula to get the next smaller circle. We do this successively for as many samples as we want to take.

We accumulate the correct color by using a trilinear filtering scheme (smoothly filtering between the neighboring pixels and between the hierarchy levels). We also weigh the color with the transparency buffer and by how much our cone-sphere intersects the coarse depth cells. This is done in front-to-back order, so it is basically a linear search algorithm. The larger the cone is, the faster it runs. The weight is accumulated to know how much visibility is integrated. One might want to take smaller offsets between the circles to achieve smoother results; however, that gets more expensive. If the cone tracer doesn't accumulate a visibility of 100%, we can blend in the rest of the visibility using, say, cube-maps with the same roughness.

Again depending on the format of the Hi-Z buffer, if we use a view-space Z version, then how we determine whether the cone-sphere intersects the Hi-Z buffer—as well as how we calculate the sampling points on the cone—is different One can use the cone angle with the view-space Z distance to find the sphere size and then project this using perspective division into screen space, keeping aspect ratio in mind.

4.5   Implementation

We have now looked at all the algorithms; let's go through them in the same order again, looking at sample code for implementation details.

4.5.1   Hi-Z Pass

The code snippet in Listing 4.3 shows how to implement a Hi-Z construction pass in DirectX using Microsoft HLSL (High Level Shading Language). This shader is executed successively, and the results are stored in the mip-channels of the Hi-Z buffer. We read from level $N-1$ and write to N until we reach a size of 1×1 as mentioned in Section 4.4.1.

To render into the same texture that we read from in DirectX 11 terms, we will have to make sure that our `ID3D11ShaderResourceView` objects point to a single mip-channel and not the entire range of mip-channels. The same rule applies to our `ID3D11RenderTargetViews` objects.

4.5.2   Pre-integration Pass

The code snippet in Listing 4.4 shows how to implement a pre-integration pass in DirectX using Microsoft HLSL. It basically calculates the percentage of empty

```
float4 main( PS_INPUT input ) : SV_Target
{
    // Texture/image coordinates to sample/load/read the depth
    // values with.
    float2 texcoords = input.tex;

    // Sample the depth values with different offsets each time.
    // We use point sampling to ignore the hardware bilinear
    // filter. The constant prevLevel is a global that the
    // application feeds with an integer to specify which level
    // to sample the depth values from at each successive
    // execution. It corresponds to the previous level.
    float4 minDepth;

    minDepth.x = depthBuffer.SampleLevel( pointSampler,
        texcoords, prevLevel, int2(  0,  0) );
    minDepth.y = depthBuffer.SampleLevel( pointSampler,
        texcoords, prevLevel, int2(  0, -1) );
    minDepth.z = depthBuffer.SampleLevel( pointSampler,
        texcoords, prevLevel, int2( -1,  0) );
    minDepth.w = depthBuffer.SampleLevel( pointSampler,
        texcoords, prevLevel, int2( -1, -1) );

    // Take the minimum of the four depth values and return it.
    float d = min( min(minDepth.x, minDepth.y), min(minDepth.z,
        minDepth.w) );

    return d;
}
```

Listing 4.3. How to implement the Hierarchical-Z buffer taking the minimum of 2×2 depth values from the depth buffer.

space within the minimum and maximum of a depth cell and modulates with the previous transparency.

```
float4 main( PS_INPUT input ) : SV_Target
{
    // Texture/image coordinates to sample/load/read the depth
    // values with.
    float2 texcoords = input.tex;

    float4 fineZ;
    fineZ.x    = linearize( hiZBuffer.SampleLevel( pointSampler,
        texcoords, mipPrevious, int2(  0,  0) ).x );
    fineZ.y    = linearize( hiZBuffer.SampleLevel( pointSampler,
        texcoords, mipPrevious, int2(  0, -1) ).x );
    fineZ.z    = linearize( hiZBuffer.SampleLevel( pointSampler,
        texcoords, mipPrevious, int2( -1,  0) ).x );
    fineZ.w    = linearize( hiZBuffer.SampleLevel( pointSampler,
        texcoords, mipPrevious, int2( -1, -1) ).x );

    // hiZBuffer stores min in R and max in G.
    float minZ = linearize( hiZBuffer.SampleLevel( pointSampler,
        texcoords, mipCurrent ).x );
    float maxZ = linearize( hiZBuffer.SampleLevel( pointSampler,
        texcoords, mipCurrent ).y );

    // Pre-divide.
    float coarseVolume = 1.0f / (maxZ - minZ);

    // Get the previous four fine transparency values.
    float4 visibility;
    visibility.x = visibilityBuffer.SampleLevel( pointSampler,
        texcoords, mipPrevious, int2(  0,  0 ) ).x;
    visibility.y = visibilityBuffer.SampleLevel( pointSampler,
        texcoords, mipPrevious, int2(  0, -1 ) ).x;
    visibility.z = visibilityBuffer.SampleLevel( pointSampler,
        texcoords, mipPrevious, int2( -1,  0 ) ).x;
    visibility.w = visibilityBuffer.SampleLevel( pointSampler,
        texcoords, mipPrevious, int2( -1, -1 ) ).x;

    // Calculate the percentage of visibility relative to the
    // calculated coarse depth. Modulate with transparency of
    // previous mip.
    float4 integration = fineZ.xyzw * abs(coarseVolume)
        * visibility.xyzw;

    // Data-parallel add using SIMD with a weight of 0.25 because
    // we derive the transparency from four pixels.
    float coarseIntegration = dot( 0.25f, integration.xyzw );

    return coarseIntegration;
}
```

Listing 4.4. The demo uses both a minimum Hi-Z buffer and a maximum Hi-Z buffer. With them, we calculate how much empty space there is in between the hierarchy depth cells. We linearize the post-projected depth into view-space Z for the computation. We could also output a linear Z-buffer during the Hi-Z pass, but this would require some changes in the ray-tracing pass and cone-tracing pass because view-space Z cannot be interpolated in screen space by default.

4.5.3   Ray-Tracing Pass

The implementation in Listing 4.5 is the Hi-Z ray-tracing code in Microsoft HLSL. The code snippet is heavily commented and should be easy to follow once the algorithm presented in Section 4.4.3 is clear.

```
float3 hiZTrace( float3 p, float3 v )
{
    const float rootLevel = mipCount - 1.0f; // Convert to 0
                                              // based indexing

    float level        = HIZ_START_LEVEL; // HIZ_START_LEVEL was
                                           // set to 2 in the demo
    float iterations   = 0.0f;

    // Get the cell cross direction and a small offset to enter
    // the next cell when doing cell crossing.
    float2 crossStep, crossOffset;
    crossStep.x    = ( v.x >= 0 ) ? 1.f : -1.f;
    crossStep.y    = ( v.y >= 0 ) ? 1.f : -1.f;
    crossOffset.xy = crossStep.xy * HIZ_CROSS_EPSILON.xy;
    crossStep.xy   = saturate( crossStep.xy );

    // Set current ray to the original screen coordinate and
    // depth.
    float3 ray = p.xyz;

    // Scale the vector such that z is 1.0f
    // (maximum depth).
    float3 d = v.xyz /= v.z;

    // Set starting point to the point where z equals 0.0f (<-
        minimum depth).
    float3 o = intersectDepthPlane(p.xy, d.xy, -p.z);

    // Cross to next cell so that we don't get a self-
    // intersection immediately.
    float2 rayCell    = getCell(ray.xy, hiZSize.xy);
    ray               = intersectCellBoundary(o.xy, d.xy, <-
        rayCell.xy, hiZSize.xy, crossStep.xy, crossOffset.xy);

    // The algorithm loop HIZ_STOP_LEVEL was set to 2 in the
    // demo; going too high can create artifacts.
    [loop]
    while( level >= HIZ_STOP_LEVEL && iterations < MAX_ITERATIONS<-
        )
    {
        // Get the minimum depth plane in which the current ray
        // resides.
        float minZ = getMinimumDepthPlane( ray.xy, level, <-
            rootLevel );

        // Get the cell number of our current ray.
        const float2 cellCount  = getCellCount(level, rootLevel);
        const float2 oldCellIdx = getCell(ray.xy, cellCount);

        // Intersect only if ray depth is below the minimum depth
        // plane.
        float3 tmpRay            = intersectDepthPlane( o.xy, d.xy<-
            , max( ray.z, minZ) );
```

```
            // Get the new cell number as well.
            const float2 newCellIdx = getCell(tmpRay.xy, cellCount);

            // If the new cell number is different from the old cell
            // number, we know we crossed a cell.
            [branch]
            if ( crossedCellBoundary(oldCellIdx, newCellIdx) )
            {
                // So intersect the boundary of that cell instead,
                // and go up a level for taking a larger step next
                // loop.
                tmpRay = intersectCellBoundary(o, d, oldCellIdx,
                    cellCount.xy, crossStep.xy, crossOffset.xy);
                level  = min(HIZ_MAX_LEVEL, level + 2.0f);
            }

            ray.xyz = tmpRay.xyz;

            // Go down a level in the Hi-Z.
            --level;

            ++iterations;
        } // end while

        return ray;
}
```

Listing 4.5. Some of the functions are not shown because of code length. This is only a minimum tracing for the sake of simplicity. The full implementation of those functions can be seen with the demo code on the book's website. The demo uses minimum-maximum tracing, which is a bit more complicated than this. View-space Z tracing is a bit more complicated and not shown.

4.5.4 Pre-convolution Pass

The pre-convolution pass is just a simple separable blur with normalized weights so that they add up to 1.0 when summed—otherwise we would be creating more energy than what we had to begin with in the image. (See Figure 4.22.)

The filter is executed successively on the color image and at each step we reduce the image to half the size and store it in the mip-channels of the texture. Assuming that we are at half resolution, this would correspond to 960×540; when convolving level 2 (240×135), we read from level 1 (480×270) and apply the separable blur passes.

The 1D Gaussian function for calculating our horizontal and vertical blur weights is

$$G(x) = \frac{1}{\sqrt{2\pi\sigma^2}}e^{-\frac{x^2}{2\sigma^2}}.$$

So, for example, a 7×7 filter would have an inclusive range from -3 to 3 for x.

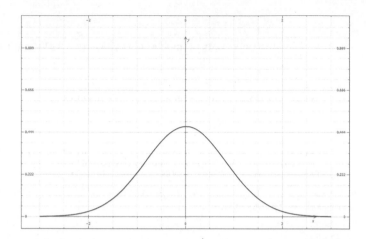

Figure 4.22. The normalized Gaussian curve used in the demo for weighting colors.

The normalized Gaussian weights then would be 0.001, 0.028, 0.233, 0.474, 0.233, 0.028, and 0.001, which when summed equal 1.0 exactly.

We don't want to produce more energy when doing the local blurring in the image, we want to keep the total energy in the image the same so the weights must equal 1.0 when summed—otherwise we are going to end up with more energy than what we started with so our image would have become brighter.

Listing 4.6 is a simple simple horizontal and vertical Gaussian blur implementation in the shading language Microsoft HLSL.

The final convolved images are produced by running the horizontal blur passes first and then the vertical blur passes successively for each level, which then are stored in the mip-channel of our color texture.

The choice of 7×7 seems to give good matching results for the needs of the demo. Using a wider kernel with a wider range of weights will cause wrong results because our transparency buffer and the colors associated with it will not match on a pixel basis anymore. Notice that our Gaussian weights take the colors mostly from the two neighboring pixels.

4.5.5 Cone-Tracing Pass

The cone-tracing pass is one of the smaller and easier-to-understand passes. In short it calculates the in-radiuses for the triangle made up from the cone and samples at different levels in our hierarchical color convolution buffer and pre-integrated visibility buffer (see Listing 4.7). Refer back to Section 4.4.5 for the algorithm explanation. The result can be seen in Figure 4.23

```
// Horizontal blur shader entry point in
// psHorizontalGaussianBlur.hlsl
float4 main( PS_INPUT input ) : SV_Target
{
    // Texture/image coordinates to sample/load the color values
    // with.
    float2 texcoords = input.tex;
    float4 color;

    // Sample the color values and weight by the pre-calculated
    // normalized Gaussian weights horizontally.
    color += colorBuffer.SampleLevel( pointSampler, texcoords,
        prevLevel, int2( -3, 0 ) ) * 0.001f;
    color += colorBuffer.SampleLevel( pointSampler, texcoords,
        prevLevel, int2( -2, 0 ) ) * 0.028f;
    color += colorBuffer.SampleLevel( pointSampler, texcoords,
        prevLevel, int2( -1, 0 ) ) * 0.233f;
    color += colorBuffer.SampleLevel( pointSampler, texcoords,
        prevLevel, int2( 0, 0 ) ) * 0.474f;
    color += colorBuffer.SampleLevel( pointSampler, texcoords,
        prevLevel, int2( 1, 0 ) ) * 0.233f;
    color += colorBuffer.SampleLevel( pointSampler, texcoords,
        prevLevel, int2( 2, 0 ) ) * 0.028f;
    color += colorBuffer.SampleLevel( pointSampler, texcoords,
        prevLevel, int2( 3, 0 ) ) * 0.001f;

    return color;
}
// Vertical blur shader entry point in
// psVerticalGaussianBlur.hlsl
float4 main( PS_INPUT input ) : SV_Target
{
    // Texture/image coordinates to sample/load the color values
    // with.
    float2 texcoords = input.tex;
    float4 color;

    // Sample the color values and weight by the pre-calculated
    // normalized Gaussian weights vertically.
    color += colorBuffer.SampleLevel( pointSampler, texcoords,
        prevLevel, int2( 0, 3 ) ) * 0.001f;
    color += colorBuffer.SampleLevel( pointSampler, texcoords,
        prevLevel, int2( 0, 2 ) ) * 0.028f;
    color += colorBuffer.SampleLevel( pointSampler, texcoords,
        prevLevel, int2( 0, 1 ) ) * * 0.233f;
    color += colorBuffer.SampleLevel( pointSampler, texcoords,
        prevLevel, int2( 0, 0 ) ) * 0.474f;
    color += colorBuffer.SampleLevel( pointSampler, texcoords,
        prevLevel, int2( 0, -1 ) ) * 0.233f;
    color += colorBuffer.SampleLevel( pointSampler, texcoords,
        prevLevel, int2( 0, -2 ) ) * 0.028f;
    color += colorBuffer.SampleLevel( pointSampler, texcoords,
        prevLevel, int2( 0, -3 ) ) * * 0.001f;

    return color;
}
```

Listing 4.6. Simple horizontal and vertical separable blur shaders, with a 7×7 kernel.

```
// Read roughness from a render target and convert to a BRDF
// specular power.
float specularPower   = roughnessToSpecularPower( roughness );

// Depending on what BRDF used, convert to cone angle. Cone
// angle is maximum extent of the specular lobe aperture.
float coneTheta       = specularPowerToConeAngle(
    specularPower );

// Cone-trace using an isosceles triangle to approximate a cone
// in screen space
for(int i = 0; i < 7; ++i)
{
    // Intersection length is the adjacent side, get the opposite
    // side using trigonometry
    float oppositeLength  = isoscelesTriangleOpposite(
        adjacentLength, coneTheta );

    // Calculate in-radius of the isosceles triangle now
    float incircleSize    = isoscelesTriangleInradius(
        adjacentLength, oppositeLength );

    // Get the sample position in screen space
    float2 samplePos      = screenPos.xy + adjacentUnit *
        (adjacentLength - incircleSize);

    // Convert the in-radius into screen size (960x540) and then
    // check what power N we have to raise 2 to reach it.
    // That power N becomes our mip level to sample from.
    float mipChannel      = log2( incircleSize *
        max(screenSize.x, screenSize.y) );

    // Read color and accumulate it using trilinear filtering
    // (blending in xy and mip direction) and weight it.
    // Uses pre-convolved image and pre-integrated transparency
    // buffer and Hi-Z buffer. It checks if cone sphere is below,
    // in between, or above the Hi-Z minimum and maxamimum and
    // weights it together with transparency.
    // Visibility is accumulated in the alpha channel.
    totalColor += coneSampleWeightedColor( samplePos, mipChannel ↩
        );

    if( totalColor.a > 1.0f )
        break;

    // Calculate next smaller triangle that approximates the cone
    // in screen space.
    adjacentLength        = isoscelesTriangleNextAdjacent(
        adjacentLength, incircleSize );
}
```

Listing 4.7. Again the full implementation of some of the functions is not shown because of code length. The demo code available online has the full implementation; the demo also comes with alternative toggle-able code for accumulating the colors such as basic averaging, distance-based weighting, and hierarchical pre-integrated visibility buffer weighting.

Figure 4.23. Cone-tracing algorithm capable of producing glossy reflections in screen space. Notice how the algorithm ensures that the further the reflection is from caster, the more spread it becomes like in the real world.

There is a conflict between the Hi-Z tracer and the cone tracer. Hi-Z tries to find a perfect specular as fast as possible while the cone tracer needs to take linear steps to integrate the total visibility in front-to-back order for correct occlusion.

This is not shown in this chapter because of complexity but the Hi-Z buffer is actually used together with the cone angle to find an early intersection at a coarse level to early exit out of the Hi-Z loop; then, we jump straight to the cone-tracing pass to continue with the linear stepping for glossy reflections. The Hi-Z functions as an empty-space determiner; once we have a coarse intersection with the cone, we can jump straight into the cone tracer to integrate the visibility and colors from that point onwards.

The more roughness we have on our surfaces, the cheaper this technique gets because we sample bigger circles and do larger jumps. Conversely, the less rough the surface is, the further the Hi-Z can travel for a perfect specular reflection so it all balances out evenly. Again, implementation is dependent on whether you use post-projected Hi-Z or view-space Hi-Z.

4.6 Extensions

4.6.1 Smoothly Fading Artifacts

We already talked about the inherent problems with screen-space local reflection in Section 4.2. Without further ado, rays traveling the opposite direction of the viewing ray and rays that fall close to the screen borders or outside the screen should be faded away due to lack of information available to us in the screen space. We can also fade rays based on ray travel distance.

A quick and simple implementation is shown in Listing 4.8. The demo ships with a more robust implementation.

One could fade away based on local occlusion as well, where a ray starts traveling behind an object and fails to find a proper intersection. One would

```
// Smoothly fade rays pointing towards the camera; screen space
// can't do mirrors (this is in view space).
float fadeOnMirror    = dot(viewReflect, viewDir);

// Smoothly fade rays that end up close to the screen edges.
float boundary        = distance(intersection.xy,
                                 float2(0.5f, 0.5f)) * 2.0f;
float fadeOnBorder = 1.0f - saturate( (boundary - FADE_START) /
   (FADE_END - FADE_START) );

// Smoothly fade rays after a certain distance (not in
// world space for simplicity but shoudl be).
float travelled   = distance(intersection.xy, startPos.xy);
float fadeOnTravel    = 1.0f - saturate( (travelled - FADE_START)
   / (FADE_END - FADE_START) );

// Fade the color now.
float3 finalColor = color * ( fadeOnBorder  * fadeOnTravel *
   fadeOnMirror );
```

Listing 4.8. Artifact removal snippet for fading the rays that have a high chance of failing and computing incorrect reflection results. FADE_START and FADE_END drive how quickly the fading should happen, where they are between 0 and 1. Though the code snippet shows the same parameters used for both the fading techniques, one should use different parameters and tweak them accordingly.

store when the ray entered such a state and then, depending on the distance traveled, fade the ray during that state to remove such unwanted artifacts.

4.6.2 Extrapolation of Surfaces

Since the ray-marching step might not find a true intersection, we could potentially extrapolate the missing information. Assuming the screen is covered with mostly rough surfaces with glossy reflections, we could run a bilateral dilation filter, which basically means take the surface normal and depth into account when extrapolating the missing color (i.e., flood-filling the holes). For any surface other than rough surfaces, the dilation filter might fail horribly because of potential high-frequency reflection colors.

One might be able to use a tile-based filter that finds good anchor points per tile and then run a clone brush filter to extrapolate the missing information for non-rough surfaces. The tile-based approach should work well for running the dilation only on the needed pixels.

4.6.3 Improving Ray-Marching Precision

If we use a nonlinear, post-projected depth buffer, most of the depth values fall very quickly into the range between 0.9 and 1.0, as we know. To improve the precision of the ray marching, we can reverse the floating-point depth buffer.

This is done by swapping the near and the far planes in the projection matrix, changing the depth testing to greater than and equal instead of lesser than and equal. Then, we could clear the depth buffer to black instead of white at each frame because 0.0 is where the far plane is now. This will turn 1.0 to the near plane in the depth buffer and 0.0 to the far plane. There are two nonlinearities here: one from the post-perspective depth and one from the floating point. Since we reversed one, they basically cancel each other out, giving us better distribution of the depth values.

Keep in mind that reversing the depth buffer affects our Hi-Z construction algorithm as well.

One should always use a 32-bit floating-point depth buffer; on AMD hardware the memory footprint of 24-bit and 32-bit depth buffers is the same, with which the fourth generation consoles are equipped also.

Another technique that can be used to improve depth precision is to actually create the Hi-Z buffer over a view-space Z depth buffer. We would need to output this in the geometry pass into a separate render target because recovering it from a post-perspective depth is not going to help the precision. This gives us uniformly distributed depth values. The only issue with a view-space Z depth buffer is that since it's not post-perspective, we can't interpolate it in screen space. To interpolate it we would have to employ the same technique as the hardware interpolator uses. We take $1/Z$ and interpolate it in screen space and then divide this interpolated value again by $1/Z$' to recover the final interpolated view-space Z. However, outputting a dedicated linear view-space Z buffer might be too costly. We should test a reversed 32-bit floating-point depth buffer first. The cone-tracing calculations are also a bit different with a view-space Z buffer. We would need to project the sphere back into screen space to find the size it covers at a particular distance. There are compromises with each technique.

4.6.4 Approximate Multiple Ray Bounces

Multiple bounces are an important factor when it comes to realistic reflections. Our brain would instantly notice that something is wrong if a reflection of a mirror didn't have reflections itself but just a flat color. We can see the effect of multiple reflections in Figure 4.24.

The algorithm presented in this chapter has the nice property of being able to have multiple reflections relatively easily. The idea is to reflect an already reflected image. In this case the already reflected image would be the previous frame. If we compute the reflection of an already reflected image, we'll accumulate multiple bounces over time. (See Figure 4.25.) But since we always delay the source image by a frame, we'll have to do a re-projection of the pixels. To achieve this re-projection, we'll basically transform the current frame's pixel into the position it belonged to in the previous frame by taking the camera movement into account [Nehab et al. 07].

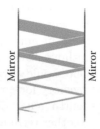

Figure 4.24. Infinite reflections when two mirrors are parallel against each other. Notice how the strength of the reflections decreases with the number of bounces we have due to absorption where the light is transferred to heat and some is reflected back again. The result is darker reflections at further ray depths. Notice the green tint as well that the ray accumulates over time from the glass as it bounces, due to iron oxide impurities in an ordinary soda-lime glass [Wikipedia 14]. The green tint is usually most noticeable on the edges of a glass. [Image courtesy of [Merry Monk 11].]

Once we know the position of where it belonged in the previous frame, we'll also need to detect if that pixel is valid or not. Some pixels might have moved outside the screen borders and some might have been blocked/occluded, etc. If the camera has moved drastically between the previous frame and the current frame, we might have to reject some of the pixels. The easiest way of doing this would be to store the previous frame's depth buffer; once we have done a re-projection of the current pixel into the previous frame, we just compare them by an epsilon and detect a fail or success. If they are not within an epsilon value we know the pixel is invalid. To get even more accurate results, one could also use the normal (surface orientation) of the previous frame and the normal of the re-projected pixel. The demo uses only the depth for rejection invalid pixels.

Mathematically speaking, we need to use the current inverted camera projection matrix and the previous camera projection matrix to take us from the current frame's pixel into the previous frame:

$$\mathbf{M}' = \mathbf{VP}_{\mathbf{curr}}^{-1}\mathbf{VP}_{\mathbf{prev}},$$

where $\mathbf{M}'$ is the concatenated re-projection matrix, $\mathbf{VP}_{\mathbf{curr}}^{-1}$ is the inverse view projection matrix from the current frame, and $\mathbf{VP}_{\mathbf{prev}}$ is the view projection matrix from the previous frame. When multiplied with a pixel $\mathbf{P}_n$ in clip space, this will take us to the corresponding pixel $\mathbf{P}_{n-1}$ in the previous frame in homoge-

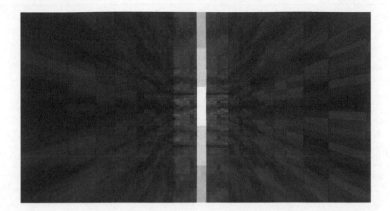

Figure 4.25. The effect of re-projecting an already reflected image and using it as a source for the current frame. This produces multiple reflections and just like in the real world the reflections lose intensity the further in reflection depth it gets.

nous space. We just need to divide the result with the w component to finally get the clip-space coordinate. Then we can just map it into screen space and start reading from the previous frame color buffer and thereby have an infinite number of reflection bounces. Figure 4.26 and Listing 4.9 show the concept of un-projecting and re-projecting a pixel into the previous camera's pixel position.

Another benefit of using the previous frame is the fact that we are taking the final lighting and all transparent object information into account as well as the possibility of including post-processing effects that have been applied to the image. If we would have used the current unfinished frame, we would lack all of those nice additions—though not all post-process effects are interesting.

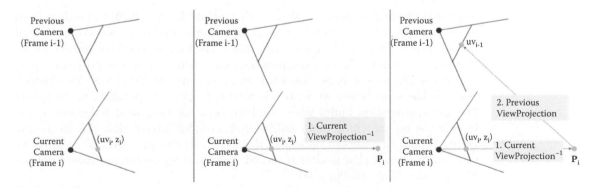

Figure 4.26. Illustration of how a pixel in screen space is transformed into its old coordinate by re-projection, which can be used to read from the previous color buffer.

```
float2 texcoords = input.tex.xy;

// Unpack clip position from texcoords and depth.
float depth         = depthBuffer.SampleLevel(pointSampler,
    texcoords, 0.0f);
float4 currClip     = unpackClipPos(texcoords, depth);

// Unpack into previous homogenous coordinates:
// inverse(view projection) * previous(view projection).
float4 prevHomogenous = mul(currClip,
    invViewProjPrevViewProjMatrix);

// Unpack homogenous coordinate into clip-space coordinate.
float4 prevClip       = float4(prevHomogenous.xyz /
    prevHomogenous.w, 1.0f);

// Unpack into screen coordinate [-1, 1] into [0, 1] range and
// flip the y coordinate.
float3 prevScreen     = float3(prevClip.xy * float2(0.5f, -0.5f)
    + float2(0.5f, 0.5f), prevClip.z);

// Return the corresponding color from the previous frame.
return prevColorBuffer.SampleLevel(linearSampler, prevScreen.xy,
    0.0f);
```

Listing 4.9. Re-projecting a pixel into its previous location in the previous frame's color image. Implementation details for rejecting pixels are omitted. Demo comes with the full code.

If you have a motion blur velocity vector pass, more specifically 2D instantaneous velocity buffer, you can use that instead of re-projecting with the code above. Using 2D instantaneous velocity is more stable but that is beyond the topic of this chapter.

4.6.5   Temporal Filtering

Temporal filtering is another enhancer that helps the algorithm to produce even more accurate and stable results by trying to recover and reuse pixels over several frames, hence the name *temporal*, over time. The idea is to have a history buffer that stores the old reflection computation, and then we run a re-projection pass over it just like we saw in Section 4.6.4, and reject any invalid pixels. This history buffer is the same buffer we write our final reflection computation to, so it acts like an accumulation buffer where we keep accumulating valid reflection colors. In case the ray-marching phase fails to find a proper intersection, due to the ray falling behind an object or outside of the screen, we can just rely on the previous re-projected result that is already stored in the history buffer and have a chance of recovering that missing pixel.

Temporal filtering helps stabilize the result because a failed pixel in frame N due to occlusion or missing information might be recovered from frame $N - 1$, which was accumulated over several frames by re-projection of pixels. Having the possibility of recovering pixels that were valid in the previous frames but invalid in the current frame is essential and is going to give much better results and stabilize the algorithm. It's also possible to get huge speedups by not running the ray-marching code if the recovery is accurate enough so that we don't need to recalculate the reflection at all.

This little enhancer walks hand in hand with Section 4.6.2, "Multiple Ray Bounces," since both rely on re-projection.

4.6.6 Travel Behind Surfaces

It is possible to travel behind objects using a Minimum and a Maximum Hi-Z buffer. In case the ray crosses a cell and ends up behind both the minimum and the maximum depth of the new cell, we can just cross that cell as well and continue with the Hi-Z traversal. This assumes that the surface has not infinitely long depth. A global small epsilon value can also be used, or a per object thickness epsilon value into a render target. Traveling behind objects is really a hard problem to solve if we do not have information on object thickness.

4.6.7 Ray Marching Toward the Camera

We've looked at the algorithm using a Minimum Hi-Z hierarchy for rays to travel away from the camera. It's also possible for mirror-like reflected rays to travel toward the camera and thereby have a chance of hitting something, though this chance is very small and would mostly benefit curved surfaces. A small change is required for the algorithm, which makes use of an additional hierarchy, the Maximum Hi-Z, for any ray that would want to travel toward the camera.

A texture format such as R32G32F would be appropriate for this change, the R channel would store the minimum and the G channel would store the maximum.

There is a very small amount of pixels that have a chance of actually hitting something, so this change might not be worth it as this would add an overhead to the entire algorithm.

4.6.8 Vertically Stretched Anisotropic Reflections

In the real world the more grazing angles we see on glossy surfaces, the more anisotropic reflections we perceive. Essentially the reflection vectors within the reflection lobe are spread more vertically than horizontally, which is the main reason why we get the vertical stretching effect.

To achieve this phenomenon with screen-space reflections, we have to use the `SampleGrad` function of our color texture during the cone-tracing accumulation pass of the reflection colors, give this sampler hardware some custom calculated vertical and horizontal partial derivatives, and let the hardware kick the anisotropic filterer to stretch the reflections for us. This is highly dependent on the BRDF used and how roughness values map to the reflection lobe.

We could also manually take multiple samples to achieve the same result. Basically, instead of sampling quads, we sample elongated rectangles at grazing angles.

We saw earlier in Section 4.4.5 that for complicated BRDF models we would need to pre-compute a 2D table of local reflection vectors and cone angles. A texture suited for this is R16G16B16A16. The RGB channels would store the local vector and the alpha channel would store either one isotropic cone-angle extent or two anisotropic vertical and horizontal cone-angle extents. These two anisotropic values for the cone would decide how many extra samples we would take vertically to approximate an elongated rectangle to stretch the reflections.

4.7 Optimizations

4.7.1 Combining Linear and Hi-Z Traversal

One drawback of the Hierarchical-Z traversal is that it is going to traverse down to lower hierarchy levels when the ray travels close to a surface. Evaluating the entire Hierarchical-Z traversal algorithm for such small steps is more expensive than doing a simple linear search with the same step size. Unfortunately the ray starts immediately close to a surface, the surface we are reflecting the original ray from. Doing a few steps of linear search in the beginning seems to be a great optimization to get the ray away from the surface and then let the Hierarchical-Z traversal algorithm do its job of taking the big steps.

In case the linear search finds intersections, we can just early-out in the shader code with a dynamic branch and skip the entire Hi-Z traversal phase. It's also worth it to end the Hi-Z traversal at a much earlier level such as 1 or 2 and then continue with another linear search in the end. The ending level could be calculated depending on the distance to the camera, since the farther away the pixel is, the less detail it needs because of perspective, so stopping much earlier is going to give a boost in performance.

4.7.2 Improving Fetch Latency

Partially unrolling dynamic loops to handle dependent texture fetches tends to improve performance with fetch/latency-bound algorithms. So, instead of handling one work per thread, we would actually pre-fetch the work for the next N loops. We can do this because we have a deterministic path on our ray. However, there is a point where pre-fetching starts to hurt performance because the register usage rises and using more registers means less buckets of threads can run in parallel. A good starting point is $N = 4$. That value was used on a regular linear tracing algorithm and a speedup of $2\times$–$3\times$ was measured on both NVIDIA and AMD hardware. The numbers appearing later in this chapter do not include these improvements because it wasn't tested on a Hi-Z tracer.

4.7.3 Interleaved Spatial Coherence and Signal Reconstruction

Because most of our rays are spatially coherent, we can shoot rays every other pixel—so-called interleaved sampling—and then apply some sort of signal reconstruction filter from sampling theory. This works very well with rough reflections since the result tends to have low frequency, which is ideal for signal reconstruction. This was tested on linear tracing-based algorithms, and a performance increase of about $3\times$–$4\times$ was achieved. The interleaving pattern was twice horizontally, twice vertically. These improvements were also not tested on a Hi-Z tracer, so the numbers presented later do not include these either.

4.7.4 Cross-Bilateral Upsampling or Temporal Super-Sampling

Since we run the ray tracing at half-resolution, we do need a smart upsampling scheme to make up for the low number of pixels. A cross-bilateral image upsampling algorithm is a perfect fit for this kind of a task [Kopf et al. 07], but a temporal super-sampling algorithm is even better: after four frames we will have full-resolution traced results using the temporal re-projection that was explained earlier.

For the cross-bilateral upsampler, The full-resolution depth buffer would be an input together with the half-resolution reflection color buffer. The algorithm would upsample the reflection color buffer to full resolution while preserving silhouettes and hard edges. It's way faster and cheaper to calculate the reflections at half-resolution than full-resolution. However, to recompose the image back to the original screen, at full-resolution, we need to scale it up while preserving the hard edges, and that's exactly what the Cross-Bilateral Upsampling algorithm is good for.

While upsampling one could also use another approach and append the pixels at depth discontinuities to an append/consume buffer and re-trace only those pixels at high resolution later for higher quality. This was not tested.

4.8 Performance

The demo runs at half-resolution, meaning 960×540, and it's running super-fast:

- 0.35–0.39 ms on NVidia GTX TITAN,

- 0.70–0.80 ms on NVidia GTX 670,

- 0.80–0.90 ms on AMD 7950.

The timers are the Hi-Z Ray-Marching and Cone-Tracing combined.

The demo is memory latency bound, and the memory unit is 80–90% active, which gives little to no room for our ALU units to work because they just sit there waiting for a fetch to complete.

According to GPU PerfStudio 2, we are having 50% cache misses because of nonlocal texture buffer accesses when traversing using the Hi-Z acceleration structure and we also suffer from noncoherent dynamic branching since a GPU executes branches in lock-step mode. If an entire bucket of threads (group of 32 threads for Nvidia called Warp, 64 for AMD called Wavefront) does not take the same branch, then we pay the penalty of stalling some threads until they converge again into the same path. This gets worse as the threads keep taking different branches for some pixels.

One optimization that was not tried, but mentioned by [Tevs et al. 08], is using a 3D texture to store the Hi-Z instead of a 2D texture. According to [Tevs et al. 08], using a 3D texture for a displacement mapping technique, where each slice represents the hierarchy levels of our Hi-Z, gives better cache hits and a performance boost of 20% due to less L2 traffic and more texture cache hits.

Since we are memory latency bound due to cache misses and incoherent texture accesses, while jumping up and down in the hierarchy, this might be a good optimization to try, though it would use much more memory.

4.9 Results

The presented algorithm works really well and produces great reflections, both specular and glossy, and it runs at easily affordable speeds for games. The most noticeable detail is the spread of reflections as they get farther away from the source, which is the selling point of the entire algorithm. (See Figures 4.27 and 4.28.)

4.10 Conclusion

In this chapter we looked at Hi-Z Screen-Space Cone Tracing to compute both specular and glossy reflections at game interactive frame rates and performance

Figure 4.27. Cone-tracing algorithm with different level of glossiness on the tile material, giving the appearance of diverged reflection rays. The reflection becomes more spread the farther away it is, and it is stretching just like the phenomena we see in the real world.

Figure 4.28. Another example of Hi-Z Screen-Space Cone Tracing producing spread reflections the farther it travels due to micro fracture simulation using material roughness.

levels. While the algorithm works well for local reflections, there are some edge cases where it may fail because of insufficient information on the screen. This algorithm can only reflect what the original input image has, as we have seen. You will not be able to look at yourself in the mirror since that information is not available to us in screen space. Hi-Z Screen-Space Cone Tracing is more of a supplementary effect for dynamic reflections in dynamic 3D scenes with the cheap glossy appearance on them, and it's recommended that you combine it with other types of reflection techniques such as local box projected [Behc 10] or sphere projected [Bjorke 07] cube-maps to take over when Hi-Z Screen-Space Cone Tracing fails as a backup plan. Hi-Z Screen-Space Cone Tracing should not be used on its own as a single solution because of the inherent problems the screen-space algorithm has, unless you have a very specific controlled scene with a specific camera angle where you can avoid the problems to begin with, such as flat walls and no mirrors, etc. The glossy reflections help hide artifacts that are otherwise visible as mirror reflections.

4.11 Future Work

The system could be extended in many ways. One idea is to take a screenshot of a 3D scene and store the color and depth information in conjunction with the camera basis. With this we could at run time re-project this local screenshot without any dynamic objects obscuring interesting information from us. The screenshots would act like local reflection probes, and we would pick the closest interesting one and do our Hi-Z traversal.

The Hi-Z Screen-Space Cone-Tracing technique could also be applied on cube-maps, where we construct a cube-mapped Hi-Z acceleration structure and ray-march within this cube volume. This would allow us to reflect anything outside the screen as well with pixel perfect ray-tracing-like results. This technique, Hi-Z Cube-Map Ray Tracing, is ongoing research and it will be published at a later time.

Another expansion could be packet tracing. This is ongoing research also and will be published at a later time. The basic idea is to group several rays together and basically shoot a packet of rays, like a frustum. As we intersect the coarse Hi-Z, we can refine/subdivide the packet and shoot several more rays. This way we can quickly intersect coarse Hi-Z levels and then do fewer operations as we travel, though this makes the implementation more complex and harder to maintain and relies heavily on compute shaders. Grouping coherent rays should give an excellent boost in performance.

One could also do tiled tracing, where each tile identifies the roughness value of the scene. In case the entire tile is very rough, we can probably get away with shooting fewer rays and extrapolating most of the pixel colors. This multi-resolution handling should also give an excellent boost in speed, though again this also relies heavily on compute shaders.

All of those topics are ongoing research and will be, as said before, published at a later time if it makes it out of the research and development phase.

4.12 Acknowledgments

I would like to give my special thanks to my co-workers who supported me at EA DICE—Mikael Uddholm, Rendering Engineer of *Mirror's Edge*, and Charles de Rousiers, Rendering Engineer of *Frostbite*—and to my leads for proofreading this chapter, also at EA DICE—Jonas Åberg, Technical Director of *Mirror's Edge*, and Daniel Johansson, Lead Software Engineer of *Mirror's Edge*.

I would also like to give my special thanks to the editors of *GPU Pro 5*—Michal Valient of Guerilla Games and Wolfgang Engel of Confetti FX—and to project editor Charlotte Byrnes of CRC Press.

Bibliography

[Autodesk 09] Autodesk. "General Utility Shaders." *mental ray Architectural and Design Visualization Shader Library*, http://download.autodesk.com/us/maya/2011help/mr/shaders/architectural/arch_util.html, 2009.

[Behc 10] Behc. "Box Projected Cubemap Environment Mapping." http://www.gamedev.net/topic/568829-box-projected-cubemap-environment-mapping/, 2010.

[Bjorke 07] Kevin Bjorke. "Image-Based Lighting." In *GPU Gems*, edited by Randima Fernando, Chapter 19. Upper Saddle River, NJ: Addison-Wesley, 2007.

[Crassin 11] Cyril Crassin. "GigaVoxels: A Voxel-Based Rendering Pipeline For Efficient Exploration of Large and Detailed Scenes." PhD thesis, Université de Grenoble, Saint-Martin-d'Hères, France, 2011.

[Crassin 12] Cyril Crassin. "Voxel Cone Tracing and Sparse Voxel Octree for Real-Time Global Illumination." http://on-demand.gputechconf.com/gtc/2012/presentations/SB134-Voxel-Cone-Tracing-Octree-Real-Time-Illumination.pdf, 2012.

[David 13] David. "The Layering Library (MILA) UI: BETA SHADERS." *Elemental Ray,* http://elementalray.wordpress.com/2013/01/22/the-layering-library-mila-ui-beta-shaders/, January 22, 2013.

[Drobot 09] Michal Drobot. "Quadtree Displacement Mapping with Height Blending." In *GPU Pro*, edited by Wolfgang Engel, pp. 117–148. Natick, MA: A K Peters, Ltd., 2009.

[Graham 10] Graham. "Screen Space Reflections." *B3D Forum,* forum.beyond3d.com/showthread.php?t=56095, January 10, 2010.

[Hien and Lim 09] Tu The Hien and Low Kok Lim. "Real-Time Rendering of Dynamic Dispalcement Maps." http://www.nus.edu.sg/nurop/2009/SoC/TuTheHien_NUROP.pdf, 2009.

[Hrkalovic and Lundgren 12] Ermin Hrkalovic and Mikael Lundgren. "Review of Displacement Mapping Techniques and Optimization." Blekinge Institute of Technology, http://www.bth.se/fou/cuppsats.nsf/all/9c1560496a915078c1257a58005115a0?OpenDocument, 2012.

[Kopf et al. 07] Johannes Kopf, Michael F. Cohen, Dani Lischinski, and Matt Uyttendaele. "Joint Bilateral Upsampling." *ACM Transactions on Graphics (Proceedings of SIGGRAPH 2007)* 26:3 (2007), Article no. 96.

[Lawrence 02] Jason Lawrence. "Importance Sampling of the Phong Reflectance Model." www.cs.virginia.edu/~jdl/importance.doc, 2002.

[Lilley et al. 12] Ian Lilley, Sean Lilley, and Nop Jiarathanakul. "Real-Time Voxel Cone Tracing." http://cis565-fall-2012.github.io/lectures/11-01-GigaVoxels-And-Sparse-Textures.pdf, 2012.

[Low 02] Kok-Lim Low. "Perspective-Correct Interpolation." http://www.gamedev.net/topic/416957-z-bufferperspective-correct-interpolation/, March 12, 2002.

[Luxion 12] Luxion Inc. "Roughness Parameter (Glossy)." *KeyShot 3 User's Manual,* http://www.keyshot.com/keyshot3/manual/material_types/glossy_samples_parameter.html, 2012.

[Merry Monk 11] The Merry Monk. "Infinite Mirror image." http://www.themerrymonk.com/wp-content/uploads/2011/05/infinite_mirror.jpg, 2011.

[Nehab et al. 07] Diego Nehab, Perdo V. Sander, Jason Lawrence, Natalya Tatarchuk, and John R. Isidoro, "Accelerating Real-Time Shading with Reverse Reprojection Caching." In *Proceedings of the 22nd ACM SIGGRAPH/EUROGRAPHICS Symposium on Graphics Hardware*, pp. 25–35. Aire-la-Ville, Switzerland: Eurographics Association, 2007.

[Oh et al. 06] Kyoungsu Oh, Hyunwoo Ki, and Cheol-Hi Lee. "Pyramidal Displacement Mapping: A GPU based Artifacts-Free Ray Tracing through an Image Pyramid." In *Proceedings of the ACM Symposium on Virtual Reality Software and Technology*, pp. 75–82. New York: ACM, 2006.

[Risser 07] Eric Risser. "True Impostors." In *GPU Gems 3*, edited by Hubert Nguyen, Chapter 21. Upper Saddle River, NJ: Addison-Wesley, 2007.

[Robison and Shirley 09] Austin Robison and Peter Shirley. "Image Space Gathering." In *Proceedings of the Conference on High Performance Graphics 2009*, pp. 91–98. New York: ACM, 2009.

[ScratchaPixel 12] ScratchaPixel.   "Material   Appearance." http://www.scratchapixel.com/lessons/3d-basic-lessons/lesson-14-interaction-light-matter/material-appearance/, 2012.

[Szirmay-Kalos and Umenhoffer 06] Laszlo Szirmay-Kalos and Tamas Umenhoffer. "Displacement Mapping on the GPU—State of the Art." http://sirkan.iit.bme.hu/~szirmay/egdis_link.htm, 2006.

[Tevs et al. 08] Art Tevs, I. Ihrke, and H.-P. Seidel. "Maximum Mipmaps for Fast, Accurate, and Scalable Dynamic Height Field Rendering." In *Proceedings of the 2008 Symposium on Interactive 3D Graphics and Games*, pp. 183–190. New York: ACM, 2008.

[Tiago et al. 12] Tiago Souse, Nickolay Kasyan, and Nicolas Schulz. "CryENGINE 3: Three Years of Work in Review." In *GPU Pro 3*, edited by Wolfgang Engel, pp. 133–168. Boca Raton, FL: A K Peters/CRC Press, 2012.

[Wikipedia 14] Wikipedia. "Glass Coloring and Color Marking." https://en.wikipedia.org/wiki/Glass_coloring_and_color_marking, 2014.

TressFX: Advanced Real-Time Hair Rendering

Timothy Martin, Wolfgang Engel, Nicolas Thibieroz, Jason Yang, and Jason Lacroix

5.1 Introduction

Hair is one of the key materials in the realm of realistic real-time character rendering that has proven to be a difficult endeavour. The conventional approach would be to author hair using "fins and shells" or a standard mesh, then use a combination of textures, noise maps, and anisotropic lighting to produce the effect of a full head of hair [Scheuermann 04]. In this chapter, we cover a real-time hair rendering technique that renders hair as individual strands and how that technique was modified and optimized to integrate into a game and run at peak performance. (See Figure 5.1.) Hair-specific topics that will be covered include geometry expansion, antialiasing, lighting, shadows, and the usage of per-pixel

Figure 5.1. Here is a comparison of hair rendered in *Tomb Raider* using a mesh with a cloth simulation applied to the ponytail in the left image versus the TressFX advanced real-time hair rendered as individual strands in the image on the right.

linked lists for order independent transparency. Lastly, we cover further ideas
that may be worthwhile to expand the use of the hair technique or advance it
further.

To look into the technology demo that this chapter follows and that was used
as a base for integration into *Tomb Raider*, download the latest TressFX demo
at http://developer.amd.com/tools-and-sdks/graphics-development/amd-radeon
-sdk/.

5.1.1 Overview

In order to cover each part of the hair rendering in the easiest way to follow, it
is best to trace through the data flow path from raw hair vertices to the final
rendered image. So, here we give a high-level overview of the chapter, outlining
what to expect in each section.

Section 5.2 covers the *geometry expansion* step. We cover how hair geometry
is expanded from line primitives into quads that properly cover the pixels on
screen to represent hair.

The next step involves lighting and shadowing, covered in separate sections. In
Section 5.3, we cover details on the hair lighting model. In the separate section on
shadows, called "Shadowing and Approximated Hair Self-Shadowing," we cover
the hair self-shadowing approximation calculations and implementation as well
as how we handle hair casting and receiving environment shadows.

Section 5.5 covers *antialiasing*. In this section, we cover how antialiasing is
specifically applied to hair and the image-based approach that was used in *Tomb
Raider*.

The next section, titled "Transparency," covers how transparency is handled
with per-pixel linked lists. The section covers the two relevant shader passes:
A-Buffer Fill and *Sort and Draw*. We also describe where each of the steps,
covered in the previous sections, occurs relative to or within the transparency
shader passes.

Section 5.7 covers integration specifics. In this section, we cover how to handle
writing hair depth, because the final rendering of hair may need to be treated
as an opaque (or partially opaque) object when dealing with other transparent
objects or depth-based effects such as depth of field.

Lastly, we have the "Conclusion" section to sum up the content of the chapter
and cover possible paths of further work or improvement.

5.2 Geometry Expansion

We represented hair geometry data as individual strands made up of line segments. The line segments are represented as successive vertices. In order to
render hair in a typical triangle rasterizing graphics pipeline, each of the line segments undergoes an expansion to a quad made up of two triangles [Yu et al. 12].

To generate these two triangles, each line segment results in six vertices. The full extent of the geometry expansion occurs in the vertex shader. Here are the two steps involved in the hair geometry expansion:

- *World-space hair fiber radius expansion:* The rasterized hair fibers end up being a sequence of view plane aligned billboards for each hair fiber segment. The individual hair fiber segments are expanded by the hair fiber radius in world space when these billboards are generated.

- *Screen-space pixel expansion:* After projecting the expanded hair fiber vertices, an additional expansion occurs to ensure that a single hair fiber covers at least one pixel width by adding $\sqrt{2}/2 \approx 0.71$ to the projected hair fiber radius.

See Listing 5.1 to see how both of these described steps are performed in the vertex shader that performs the hair geometry expansion.

```
static const uint  HairVertexSelection[] = {0, 1, 0, 1, 1, 0};
static const float OffsetDir[] =
    {-1.f, -1.f, 1.f, -1.f, 1.f, 1.f};
static const uint OffsetDirIndex[] = {0, 0, 1, 0, 1, 1};

HairPSInput HairVS( uint vertexId : SV_VertexID )
{
  HairPSInput Output = (HairPSInput)0;
  float thicknessFactor[] = ... // normalized thickness scaler
// two tangents and vertices of the hair fiber segment
  float3 t[2], v[2];
// calculate right vector for billboarding the hair fiber quad
  float3 right[] = { cross(t[0], normalize(v[0] - g_vEye)),
          cross(t[1], normalize(v[1] - g_vEye)) };
  float2 proj_right[] =
    { normalize( mul(float4(right[0], 0), g_mViewProj).xy ),
      normalize( mul(float4(right[1], 0), g_mViewProj).xy ) }

  // Setting up the indexing for calculating one of the
  // 6 verts of the 2 triangles making a quad

  // indexing vert 0 to 5
  uint localVertId = vertexId % GENERATED_VERTEX_COUNT;

  // choosing vertex in the fiber segment
  uint idx          = HairVertexSelection[localVertId];

  // choosing which direction to offset from the fiber segment
  uint offDirIndex = OffsetDirIndex[localVertId];

  float4 hairEdgePositions[2]; // 0 is negative, 1 is positive

  // World-space expansion
  hairEdgePositions[0] = float4(v[idx] +
    -1.f * right[idx] * thicknessFactor[idx] * fiberRadius, 1.f);
  hairEdgePositions[1] = float4(v[idx] +
    1.f * right[idx] * thicknessFactor[idx] * fiberRadius, 1.f);
  hairEdgePositions[0] = mul(hairEdgePositions[0], g_mViewProj);
```

```
hairEdgePositions[1] = mul(hairEdgePositions[1], g_mViewProj);

// Output after screen-space expansion
Output.Position = hairEdgePositions[offDirIndex] +
 hairEdgePositions[offDirIndex].w * OffsetDir[localVertId] *
 float4(proj_right[idx] * 0.71f / g_WinSize, 0.0f, 0.0f);
Output.Tangent  = t[idx];
Output.WorldPos = v[idx];

// Used for image-space-based antialiasing,
//   for having the nearest edge positions of
//   the hair fiber in the pixel shader
Output.p0 = hairEdgePositions[0].xy/hairEdgePositions[0].w;
Output.p1 = hairEdgePositions[1].xy/hairEdgePositions[1].w;
return Output;
}
```

Listing 5.1. The vertex shader that performs the hair geometry expansion.

5.3   Lighting

After the geometry expansion occurs in the vertex shader, lighting calculations follow as one of the first steps in the pixel shader during the hair geometry pass.

The lighting calculations for the hair stem from a fur rendering model introduced by [Kajiya and Kay 89], as well as from work done by in [Marschner et al. 03]. The lighting equation in [Kajiya and Kay 89] provides a basis for the lighting with a tangent-based diffuse and specular component. Hair lighting in [Marschner et al. 03] is based on an analytical approach and adds the concept of a dual specular highlight. The result of combining these two works can be seen in a presentation by Scheuermann, where a practical real-time lighting equation is defined for hair [Scheuermann 04].

5.3.1   Diffuse

The diffuse component is based on applying lambert diffuse lighting to a cylinder. Kajiya's paper [Kajiya and Kay 89] provides a derivation of the diffuse component, which is found by integrating along the circumference of a half cylinder and accumulating the reflected diffuse component along that circumference. The derivation ends with a simple equation for the diffuse component:

$$K_d \sin(t, l),$$

where K_d is the diffuse reflectance, t is the hair fiber tangent, and l is the light vector. Given this derivation, the diffuse component will be strongest when the light direction is perpendicular to the tangent of the hair.

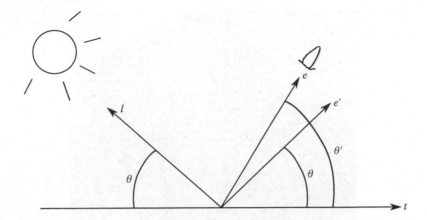

Figure 5.2. This figure serves as a visual supplement to the calculations necessary for the hair specular component. See Section 5.3.2.

5.3.2 Specular

The specular component from the hair lighting model described by [Kajiya and Kay 89] is based on the Phong specular model [Phong 73], where light is reflected off a hair strand based on the tangent direction of the hair. The tangent of the hair fiber represents the tangent of the surface that the light will reflect off of. See Figure 5.2 and the following derivation for the hair specular component:

$$K_s \cos{(e, e')}^p$$

$$K_s \cos{(\theta - \theta')}^p$$

$$K_s(\cos{(\theta)} \cos{(\theta')} + \sin{(\theta)} \sin{(\theta')})^p$$

$$K_s((t \cdot l)(t \cdot e) + \sin{(t, l)} \sin{(t, e)})^p,$$

where K_s is the specular reflectance. The eye vector is represented with e, while l is the light vector and e' is the corresponding reflection vector. the angle between the hair tangent t and the light vector l is θ, and θ' is the angle between the eye vector e and the hair fiber tangent t.

5.3.3 Practical Real-Time Hair Lighting

Given the defined diffuse and specular hair shading components and Marschner's more analytical approach, Scheuermann presents a phenomenologically derived hair lighting model [Scheuermann 04]. Figure 5.3 shows the dual specular highlights in a real-world image that the Scheuermann model attempts to reproduce.

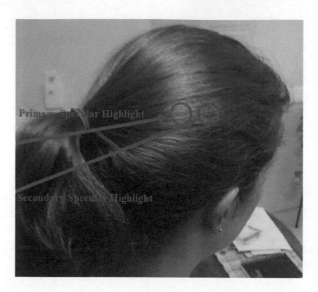

Figure 5.3. An image, found in and courtesy of [Scheuermann 04], which shows the dual specular highlights in hair that the resulting practical real-time hair lighting model attempts to produce.

Marschner's paper [Marschner et al. 03] describes a primary and secondary highlight. The primary highlight is shifted toward the hair tip, and is primarily influenced by the light color. The secondary highlight is shifted toward the hair root, and is influenced by the light color and hair color. To combine the two specular highlights, the reflection vector for the primary highlight is shifted in toward the direction of the hair tangent, pointing from root to tip, and the secondary highlight may be shifted in the opposite way, away from the direction of the hair fiber tangent (see Figure 5.4).

5.4   Shadows and Approximated Hair Self-Shadowing

In addition to lighting calculations, the hair receives environment shadows and self-shadowing. In this section, we explain what we used to handle hair receiving and casting shadows as well as hair self-shadowing in *Tomb Raider*.

We chose to approximate the self-shadowing calculation because of the comparative cost of generating and applying a deep shadow map in order to apply accurate self-shadowing effects [Lacroix 13, Engel and Hodes 13]. For the approximation, a regular shadow map may be used, which will hold the depth of the hair fibers closest to the light source. This shadow map of the hair serves as a representation of the topmost layer of the hair. Using this shadow map, an approximated *number of fibers* occluding the hair fragment can be calculated and

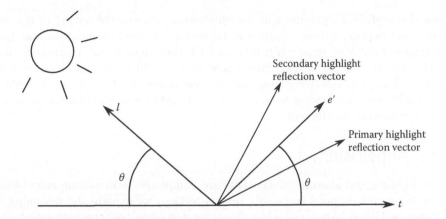

Figure 5.4. This figure shows a simple representation of the reflection vector shift that occurs to generate the dual highlights. The secondary highlight reflection vector is shifted toward the root of the hair fiber (which is against the direction of the hair fiber tangent), and the primary highlight reflection vector is shifted toward the hair fiber tip.

used to apply a volumetric self-shadowing term. The resulting effect is similar to deep shadow maps but at a much lower cost. Here is the approximated deep shadow maps calculation:

$$number\ of\ fibers = \frac{(depth\ range)}{(fiber\ spacing) * (fiber\ radius)},$$

$$hair\ shadow\ term = (1 - hair\ shadow\ alpha)^{number\ of\ fibers}.$$

In these calculations *depth range* is the distance between the hair fragment being shaded and the corresponding shadow map depth. *Fiber spacing* and *fiber radius* are artistic tweakables that help define how dense the hair is when calculating the hair self-shadowing term. *Fiber radius* is considered in the geometry expansion step (see Section 5.2), so it is best to adjust the *fiber spacing* when tuning hair self-shadowing. A larger *fiber spacing* means a lower *number of fibers* count, which leads to a lighter self-shadowing term. The *hair shadow alpha* defines how much light energy goes through each of the approximated *number of fibers*. Each fiber allows $(1 - hair\ shadow\ alpha)$ light through, so $(1 - hair\ shadow\ alpha)^{number\ of\ fibers}$ calculates the amount of light that goes through the approximated *number of fibers* and reaches the hair fragment being shadowed.

In order to take care of hair casting shadows on the environment as well as hair self-shadowing, hair was rendered into the engine's shadow maps just like any other shadow casting object. This allowed hair to cast shadows on the environment as any typical shadow mapping occurs. These shadow maps were also useful for applying hair self-shadowing. Due to the nature of the self-shadowing approximation calculation, there was no need to separate hair from the engine's shadow maps when dealing with the environment casting shadows on the hair because typically environment objects will be a large distance away from the hair. The relatively large distance will generate a large number of fibers, which will drive the shadow term to zero, as would be expected for a solid object casting a shadow on the hair.

5.5 Antialiasing

After lighting and shadow calculations are completed, antialiasing calculations occur for each hair pixel fragment. In this section, we explain the reasoning for having specialized hair antialiasing. Then we will cover how the hair antialiasing is performed. Lastly, we'll cover an alternative image-space approach we developed [Engel and Hodes 13, Lacroix 13], which we found to perform faster than the geometrically based approach proposed by [Yu et al. 12].

Rendering individual hair strands can result in heavy aliasing issues. (See Figure 5.5.) An individual hair strand will look like a jagged line once projected into screen space. Also, with a large amount of hair strands, aliasing will not only cause jagged hair strands, but there can also be noise among the final result of shading a clump of hair strands. With hair, we can take advantage of special geometry information and apply a specialized hair antialiasing to improve the overall render quality.

An additional important benefit of the specialized hair antialiasing is to simulate the thinness of individual hair strands. Previous real-time hair rendering simulations would run into issues where individual hair strands would appear too thick. Applying the specialized hair antialiasing helps soften the edges of

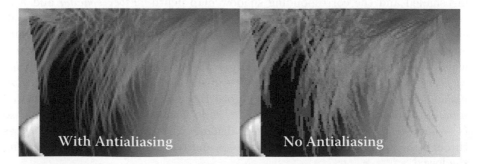

Figure 5.5. Here is a comparison of hair rendered with and without the specialized hair antialiasing. The largest noticeable difference is the jagged staircasing present in the image without antialiasing versus the softer hair edge pixels in the image with antialiasing.

individual hair strands, which is especially important when the hair strands are sub-pixel in width.

In order to apply antialiasing to the hair pixels, the strategy is to calculate the percentage of the screen pixel that is covered by the hair fiber. This percentage value is called *coverage* and this *coverage* value directly modifies the hair alpha. By using the *coverage* value to modulate the hair alpha, hair pixels become more transparent near the edges of hair strands in order to produce the antialiasing effect. One approach to antialiasing uses a ray-cone intersection of the pixel and hair fiber [Yu et al. 12]. With the ray-cone intersection approach, the area of the ray-cone cross section at the intersection with the hair fiber is determined, then the percentage of this area that is covered by the hair fiber becomes the *coverage* value for the corresponding pixel.

An alternative approach we took to apply the specialized hair antialiasing is handled in image space instead. A related generic antialiasing approach that inspired our image-space approach for hair is *geometric post-process antialiasing* (GPAA) [Persson 12], for applying antialiasing to polygon edges in a screen-space pass. Pixels that lie on polygon edges are evaluated for their distance to the actual image space projected edge locations. The distances to each polygon edge are used to generate blend weights for blending between the bordering polygons.

Our image-based hair antialiasing approach uses the location of the hair fiber edges to evaluate each hair fragment's distance with respect to these edges. The farther the pixel is outside the hair fiber, the more we decrease the *coverage* value. The farther the pixel is inside of the hair fiber, the more we increase the *coverage* value. A pixel directly on the hair fiber edge has a 0.5 *coverage* value. A hair fragment 0.5+ pixel distance outside the hair fiber edge has a *coverage* of 0. A hair fragment 0.5+ pixel distance inside the hair fiber edge has a *coverage* value of 1. See Listing 5.2 to see how the image-based hair antialiasing calculation is performed in the pixel shader.

In Figure 5.6, we see a hair fiber segment's outline after being projected onto the screen. The blue lines in the figure show the "hair fiber edge"-to-"pixel center" that is calculated for each hair fragment for the image-space-based antialiasing. The pixels are marked **A**, **B**, and **C** depending on their resulting *coverage* values. The pixels marked **A** have *coverage* values near 0 because the pixel centers are nearly a half-pixel outside the hair fiber. Pixels marked **B** are the pixels that are near the hair fiber edge, which result in *coverage* values near 0.5. **C** pixels are nearly a half-pixel distance within the hair fiber, so these pixels will have *coverage* values near 1.

5.6   Transparency

Transparency for hair rendering is important for a high-quality implementation. Working together with hair antialiasing, transparency helps to simulate the pres-

```
float ImageBasedHairAA(float2 p0, float2 p1, float2 pixelLoc)
{
    // p0, p1, pixelLoc are in d3d clip space (-1 to 1)x(-1 to 1).
    // p0 and p1 are the two nearest hair fiber edge positions
    //    to the hair fragment being shaded.

    // Scale positions so 1.f = half pixel width
    p0 *= g_WinSize.xy;
    p1 *= g_WinSize.xy;
    pixelLoc *= g_WinSize.xy;

    float p0dist = length(p0 - pixelLoc);
    float p1dist = length(p1 - pixelLoc);
    float hairWidth = length(p0 - p1);

    // will be 1.f if pixel outside hair, 0.f if pixel inside hair
    float outside = any( float2(step(hairWidth, p0dist),
                         step(hairWidth, p1dist)) );

    // if outside, set sign to -1, else set sign to 1
    float sign = outside > 0.f ? -1.f : 1.f;

    // signed distance
    //(positive if inside hair, negative if outside hair)
    float relDist = sign * saturate( min(p0dist, p1dist) );

    // returns coverage based on the relative distance
    // 0, if completely outside hair edge
    // 1, if completely inside hair edge
    return (relDist + 1.f) * 0.5f;
}
```

Listing 5.2. This is the function used to perform the image-based hair antialiasing calculation. See Listing 5.1 to see where **p0** and **p1** are calculated.

ence of thin individual hair strands. Also, where each hair fragment has its own lighting and shadowing applied separately, transparency is important for a high-quality volumetric result.

Due to the large amount of geometry and high possibility of a large number of transparent layers within a single pixel, dealing with correctly blending the many transparent layers of hair becomes a challenge. The hair transparency is handled through the use of Order Independent Transparency with per-pixel linked lists [Thibieroz 11]. For every pixel on screen that has one or more layers of hair, a linked list is generated containing each overlapping hair fragment.

The transparency for hair is handled by two separate passes. The first pass, the *A-Buffer Fill*, generates the unsorted linked lists for each pixel on screen that contains hair fragments. The second pass, *Sort and Draw*, traverses the per-pixel linked lists, sorting and blending for the final hair pixel result [Yu et al. 12]. In the rest of this section, we'll go through some of the specifics of the hair transparency passes and how that works with per-pixel linked lists.

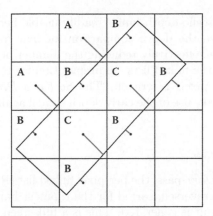

Figure 5.6. The specialized hair antialiasing calculation is performed by finding the distances between the pixels and the closest hair fiber edge. The blue segments here represent the distances that are found then used to modify the hair *coverage* value. The pixels marked **A** are nearly a half-pixel distance outside the hair fiber, so their *coverage* values will be near 0. Pixels marked **B** are pixels near the hair fiber edge, which means these pixels will have *coverage* values near 0.5. The pixels marked **C** are nearly a half-pixel distance within the hair fiber resulting in *coverage* values close to 1.

5.6.1 Hair Fragment Linked List Node

The linked list node consists of color, depth, and a next node pointer. Each component of the linked list node is stored as a 32-bit unsigned integer. The color is the final shaded hair fragment (from a single hair fiber) and includes alpha for hair transparency blending and hair antialiasing (see Section 5.5 for more information on hair antialiasing). When stored into the linked list node, color is packed into eight bits per channel (red, green, and blue) and eight bits for alpha. The hair fragment's depth relative to the camera is stored, which will be used for sorting the layers of hair fragments in the linked lists. The next node pointer points to another fragment in the linked list or no fragment if the node is at the end of the list [Yu et al. 12, Lacroix 13, Engel and Hodes 13].

5.6.2 A-Buffer Fill

During the *A-Buffer Fill* pass, the hair goes through a geometry pass and all strands are rendered (see the section on Geometry Expansion for more specifics on the geometry pass), then each individual hair fragment gets processed in the pixel shader. Each hair fragment undergoes lighting and shading. The *coverage* calculation for the specialized hair antialiasing occurs here and is applied to the hair fragment's alpha. Lastly, the fragment is stored in the linked list of the corresponding screen space pixel.

Having the main scene depth buffer readily usable here allows for the use of early depth stencil, so the depth comparison for hair fragments occurs before pixel shader execution, effectively reducing the number of pixels that need to be shaded and stored in the linked lists. In preparation for the *Sort and Draw* pass, a stencil for the hair pixels is written. The *Sort and Draw* pass is a fullscreen pass, so in order to make use of the early depth stencil again, a stencil comparison must be used.

5.6.3   Sort and Draw

During the *Sort and Draw* pass, the per-pixel linked list (PPLL) generated by the *A-buffer Fill* pass is traversed, sorted for the topmost hair pixels, then the final blended hair pixel result is generated. This is a fullscreen pass, where each pixel location is used to look up the corresponding per-pixel linked list. The topmost fragments are found and stored locally. While searching for the topmost hair fragments, the remaining hair fragments are blended out of order. The locally stored topmost layers are then blended in order.

Finding the eight topmost fragments is sufficient because of the contribution of a fragment at layer eight and beyond start to get minimal, so the out of order blending produces little to no variation in the final shaded result. The maximum influence m of a hair fragment on the final shaded result can be calculated based on the layer number n and the maximum alpha a possible for a hair fragment:

$$m = a * (1 - a)^{n-1}.$$

Given this formula, the maximum influence of a hair fragment at the eighth layer is ≈ 0.01715, meaning the influence at layer eight is barely over one percent. Layers beyond layer eight will influence the final shaded result less and less. Because of this, using the top eight layers is sufficient enough to minimize variation in the final shaded result.

The sorting is performed using the depth stored in the linked list node. To search for the to most hair fragments, the linked list is simple iterated over, while keeping a local copy of the current topmost hair fragments readily available for a simple comparison.

5.7   Integration Specifics

One thing not addressed in this chapter so far is writing depth for the hair in order for hair to work correctly with depth-based effects, such as depth of field. We cover three different ways to handle the depth write: writing a constant depth for all hair pixels, precise depth per hair pixel, and a selective depth write with precise depth per hair pixel. We chose to go with the last approach in *Tomb Raider* because it was the solution that maximized quality and was tolerant enough to deal with the large variance of camera conditions, close-ups with depth of field, and hair rendering with other transparent materials and effects [Lacroix 13, Engel and Hodes 13].

5.7.1 Constant Depth for Hair Pixels

In the same pass as the *Sort and Draw*, when the fullscreen quad is drawn, the quad may be drawn with a depth at the average depth or "hair object" position. Because the stencil is used during the *Sort and Draw* pass, the depth writes can be turned on and set to always pass and always write if the stencil comparison is successful. This is the most relaxed approach with the smallest overhead. One drawback is that depth is written for all hair pixels, even when hair is sparse, and edge hair pixels have near zero alpha, which will appear almost completely transparent. This drawback means the possibility for some noticeable visual artifacts with depth-based effects. One such example is in depth of field, where pixels that have nearly transparent hair fragments in them will not be blurred into the background far-focus, and there will be a "transparent halo" artifact around the hair. Another drawback is because of the lack of more precise depth information for all hair pixels.

5.7.2 Depth Per Hair Pixel

In order to get depth data for all hair pixels, a separate render target may be used during the *Sort and Draw* pass to capture the depth of the hair fragment in each per-pixel linked list that is closest to the viewer. A second pass is needed after this to copy the depth information collected into the depth buffer. The reason for separating this into two passes, rather than writing the more precise depth in the *Sort and Draw* pass, is because depth writes through the pixel shader are not possible when the depth result is influenced by flow control in shader code. This approach will result in more precise depth information per-pixel, but will still suffer from the "transparent halo" problem previously described in Section 5.7.1.

5.7.3 Selective Depth Write

To deal with the "transparent halo" problem, this last depth writing solution takes a conditional approach to writing depth, by evaluating final shaded hair fragments during the *Sort and Draw* pass for opaque or near-opaque final hair pixels. The criteria for evaluating pixels includes examining the number of hair fragment layers and the final alpha value being used for blending. Pixels with a large number of hair fragment layers or a large final alpha value can be marked as opaque and have their precise depth captured and written in a second pass, like the previously described depth writing solution.

Pass	Number of Draw Calls	Time (ms)
Shadow map render	16	0.7414
Shading and AA	4	2.0303
Sort and Draw	1	0.8660
Total	21	3.6377

Table 5.1. Performance numbers for the scene in Figure 5.7 for TressFX in *Tomb Raider* on an AMD Radeon HD 7970.

5.8 Conclusion

We were able to take a technology demo for hair and integrate that into a game. This chapter explains how each part of the advanced real-time hair works, and covers optimizations that we developed to improve the original hair technology demo and make it more viable for use in a game. In the rest of the conclusion, we cover details on performance and ideas for future work and improvements.

5.8.1 Performance

The performance of the hair technology is another interesting topic, because it is highly reliant on scene conditions. Given the large amount of hair geometry data and varying (but can be large) amount of hair pixels to process, the overall performance of the advanced real-time hair can vary depending on the amount of hair fragments on screen. If there are enough hair fragments on screen, then the technique becomes pixel shader limited, but if hair is far away from the screen, then the technique is vertex shader limited. Given this, pixel shader-based optimizations (such as simpler lighting calculations or the image-based hair antialiasing presented in this chapter) become effective when scene conditions cause the technique to be pixel shader limited.

Refer to Tables 5.1 and 5.2 for performance numbers for TressFX in *Tomb Raider* in two separate scenes. For these two scenes, the performance numbers vary because of the different scene conditions. The main factor to consider here is the number of hair fragments being processed. The scene used for the performance numbers in Table 5.2 (see Figure 5.8) has many more hair fragments on screen than the scene used for Table 5.1 (see Figure 5.7).

Pass	Number of Draw Calls	Time (ms)
Shadow map render	4	0.1992
Shading and AA	4	3.7104
Sort and Draw	1	3.0181
Total	9	6.9277

Table 5.2. Performance numbers for the scene in Figure 5.8 for TressFX in *Tomb Raider* on an AMD Radeon HD 7970.

Figure 5.7. The first scene used for gathering performance numbers.

Figure 5.8. The second scene used for gathering performance numbers.

5.8.2 Future Work and Improvements

An important point to explore is also where the technique can use improvements. Here are some possible improvement ideas:

- Reduce the need for random access patterns of memory in the *Sort and Draw* pass by storing or rendering a limited number of transparent hair pixel layers.

- Integrate the advanced real-time hair rendering into a deferred lighting engine. This will require storing data needed for hair lighting into the per-pixel linked lists instead of the shaded hair fragment color. AMD has an example implementation of this available in the latest TressFX sample available on the AMD website at http://developer.amd.com/tools-and-sdks/graphics -development/amd-radeon-sdk/.

- Improve the way vertex and other geometry data is utilized for geometry expansion, by reducing the amount of data to process in the hair geometry pass. It should be possible to take advantage of vertex buffers and index buffers rather than manually indexing into structured buffers in the vertex shader to perform the geometry expansion.

Bibliography

[Engel and Hodes 13] Wolfgang Engel and Stephan Hodes. "Hair Rendering in Tomb Raider: AMD's TressFX." Presentation, FMX 2013, Stuttgart, Germany, April 24, 2013.

[Kajiya and Kay 89] James T. Kajiya and T. L. Kay. "Rendering Fur with Three Dimensional Textures." In *Proceedings of the 16th Annual Conference on Computer Graphics and Interactive Techniques*, pp. 271–280. New York: ACM, 1989.

[Lacroix 13] Jason Lacroix. "A Survivor Reborn: Tomb Raider on DX11." Presentation, Game Developers Conference 2013, San Francisco, CA, April 23, 2013.

[Marschner et al. 03] Stephen R. Marschner, Henrik Wann Jensen, Mike Cammarano, Steve Worley, and Pat Hanrahan. "Light Scattering from Human Hair Fibers." *ACM Transactions on Graphics* 22:3 (2003), 780–791.

[Persson 12] Emil Persson. "Geometric Antialiasing Methods." In *GPU Pro 3*, edited by Wolfgang Engel, pp. 71–87. Natick, MA: A K Peters, Ltd., 2012.

[Phong 73] Bui Tuong Phong. "Illumination for Computer-Generated Images." Ph.D. thesis, The University of Utah, Salt Lake City, UT, 1973.

[Scheuermann 04] Thorsten Scheuermann. "Practical Real-Time Hair Rendering and Shading." In *ACM SIGGRAPH 2004 Sketches*, p. 147. New York: ACM, 2004.

[Thibieroz 11] Nicolas Thibieroz. "Order-Independent Transparency Using Per-Pixel Linked Lists." In *GPU Pro 2*, edited by Wolfgang Engel, pp. 409–431. Natick, MA: A K Peters, Ltd., 2011.

[Yu et al. 12] Xuan Yu, Jason C. Yang, Justin Hensley, Takahiro Harada, and
    Jingyi Yu. "A Framework for Rendering Complex Scattering Effects on
    Hair." In *Proceedings of the ACM SIGGRAPH Symposium on Interactive
    3D Graphics and Games, I3D '12*, pp. 111–118. New York: ACM, 2012.

Wire Antialiasing
Emil Persson

6.1 Introduction

There are many sources of aliasing in rendered images. The two most common culprits are geometric edges and shading. Historically these sources of aliasing have been resolved by Multi-Sample Antialiasing (MSAA) and mip-mapping with trilinear filtering respectively. With mip-mapping and trilinear filtering, which were supported on consumer-level hardware even way back in the 1990s, textures on surfaces were essentially free from aliasing. In the early 2000s, as consumer-level hardware gained MSAA support, the remaining problem of edge aliasing, often referred to as "jaggies," was more or less a solved problem. Games of this era could then be relatively aliasing free since the geometric detail was limited enough that MSAA effectively eliminated all geometric aliasing, and shading was typically simple and low frequency and did not introduce any additional aliasing on top of the surface texture. The main exception was alpha-tested objects, such as fences and foliage, which sorely stood out in an otherwise relatively aliasing-free environment.

As games have adopted increasingly more sophisticated lighting models and with geometric density constantly on the rise, aliasing has unfortunately made a strong comeback in modern games. Mip-mapping alone no longer fully solves the shader aliasing problem. Complex lighting introduces aliasing where the mip-mapped textures alone exhibit none. In particular the specular component tends to cause lots of aliasing. This field is poorly researched and only a few approaches exist to properly deal with the problem. The most notable work here is LEAN mapping [Olano and Baker 10]. On the geometry side we are getting increasingly denser geometry, and as geometry gets down to the sub-pixel level, MSAA is no longer sufficient.

Much research remains to be done to solve these problems once and for all. This chapter does not present a final solution to all these problems; however, it presents a technique for solving one specific, but common, subset of geometric aliasing in games, namely that of phone wires and similar long and thin objects.

While the technique has been dubbed Wire Antialiasing, it applies to any object that can be decomposed to a set of cylindrical shapes. This includes wires, pipes, poles, railings, light posts, antenna towers, many types of fences, and even grass if represented as actual geometry rather than as alpha textures. Tree trunks and branches may also be cylindrical enough to work. These are all common elements in games and frequent sources of aliasing.

6.2   Algorithm

6.2.1   Overview

The problem with very thin geometry, such as wires, is that it tends to degenerate into a set of flickering and disconnected pixels when it gets sub-pixel sized. Why is that? In technical terms, what happens is that the visibility function gets undersampled. In plain English, the wire simply misses the pixels. A pixel only gets shaded if the geometry covers the pixel center. If the wire is thinner than a pixel, chances are that at some points it will simply slide in between two pixel centers and end up not shading any of them. In this case there will be a gap. The thinner the wire gets, the worse the problem gets. However, if the geometry is wider than a pixel, we are guaranteed to have a continuous line with no gaps. The problem thus occurs when geometry goes sub-pixel sized. The idea of this technique, then, is to simply keep the wire one pixel wide or larger. To emulate a sub-pixel coverage, we simply fade away the wire by outputting the coverage to alpha and applying blending.

What about MSAA? Unfortunately, MSAA does not solve the problem. It alleviates it somewhat, but the improvement is rather marginal. With $4\times$ multisampling, the visibility function is now sampled at twice the rate horizontally and vertically. In other words, the wire can now be about half a pixel wide (depending on sample locations) without risking missing all samples somewhere. This is not much of an improvement, and all we have accomplished is to push the problem into the distance. We can now have the wire twice as far away before the problem occurs, or have a half as thin wire, but that is all. Actually, when we enable MSAA, we normally want to eliminate "jaggies." If we have a half-pixel wide wire, MSAA may keep it continuous in this case; however, it will be jagged, because it only hits a single sample per pixel. There is not enough resolution to estimate the coverage, but it simply boils down to more or less a binary on/off per pixel.

While MSAA does not by itself solve the thin geometry problem, it is still valuable for this technique. While we are guaranteeing gap-free wires, we are not producing smooth antialiased results as such. In fact, the wires will be jagged by default. So we use MSAA for what it excels at, namely removing those jaggies. So despite increased visibility function sampling rate with MSAA enabled, we still limit wires to a one pixel width and keep the additional resolution for MSAA to estimate coverage and eliminate the jaggies, just like MSAA normally does. Our technique is thus independent of the MSAA mode. It can also run without MSAA, but the wires will then look as jagged as (but not worse than) the rest of the scene.

6.2.2 Method

The wire is represented in the vertex buffer much like one might normally design a wire, with the exception that we need to be able to vary the wire's radius at runtime, so we do not store final vertex positions but instead store the center of the wire. The final vertex position will then be computed by displacing the vertex along the normal. For this we provide a wire radius, in world-space units. This would typically be a constant for wires and would be best passed in the constant buffer, but for some types of objects (such as antenna towers, light posts, and grass straws), it could make sense to store a radius value per vertex instead.

The first step is to estimate how small a radius we are allowed without violating our minimum one pixel width requirement given the current vertex position in the view frustum. This scales linearly with the w-value of the transformed vertex, depending on the field of view (FOV) angle and render-target resolution. With a projection matrix computed the usual way with a vertical FOV, a constant scale factor can be computed as in equation (6.1):

$$PixelScale = \frac{\tan(FOV/2)}{height}.$$ (6.1)

This value can be computed once and passed as a constant. The radius of a pixel-wide wire is then given by multiplying by the vertex's w-value. The w-value can be found by doing a dot product between the vertex position and the last row of the view-projection matrix (or column, depending on the matrix convention used). Once we know the radius of a pixel-wide wire, we can simply clamp our radius to this value to ensure our wire is always at least one pixel wide. The shader code for this is in Listing 6.1.

While adjusting the radius guarantees that we get gap-free wires, the result is inevitably also that the wires will appear wider and wider as they go farther into the distance if we do not also take the original unexpanded wire's pixel coverage into account. Compare Figure 6.1 and Figure 6.2 for an illustration of this effect. What we need to do is to compensate by computing the coverage of the real unexpanded wire and fading the contribution accordingly. This is what will give the wire its natural and alias-free appearance. This can be accomplished by outputting the coverage value to alpha and enabling alpha blending. As shown on the last line in Listing 6.1, the coverage fade factor is simply the original real radius of the wire divided by the expanded radius. In other words, if the radius was expanded to twice the size to cover one pixel, then the wire is half a pixel wide and the coverage consequently 0.5. As the wire gets farther into the distance, it

```
// Compute view-space w
float w = dot(ViewProj[3], float4(In.Position, 1.0f));

// Compute what radius a pixel-wide wire would have
float pixel_radius = w * PixelScale;

// Clamp radius to pixel size.
float new_radius = max(Radius, pixel_radius);

float3 position = In.Position + radius * In.Normal;

// Fade out with the reduction in radius versus original.
float fade = Radius / new_radius;
```

Listing 6.1. Computing radius and fade factor.

Figure 6.1. Original wire. Note how the wire is aliased and full of holes despite 4×
MSAA being enabled.

will now appear fainter and fainter, maintaining the appearance of a thin wire,
as illustrated in Figure 6.3. Comparing Figure 6.3 to Figure 6.1, it can be seen
that the wires look identical, except for the fact that Figure 6.3 does not suffer
from aliasing artifacts.

6.2.3   Lighting

The technique as described so far works fairly well; we have eliminated the geometric aliasing, but unfortunately thin wires also tend to suffer from shading
aliasing as the lighting function gets sampled very sparsely and pseudo-randomly.
When the wire reaches pixel size, any texture sampling would likely go down to
the lowest mip-map and get uniformly colored by default; however, the normal

Figure 6.2. Expanded wire. Note that the wire is now free from gaps and aliasing, but appears unnaturally thick in the distance.

Figure 6.3. Final wire. Wire now appears natural and alias free.

can go from pointing straight up to straight down over the course of a single pixel, potentially resulting in severe aliasing from the lighting. The simplest approach to deal with this problem is to choose a soft lighting model that results in a minimum amount of aliasing, such as Half Lambert [Valve 08]. For many wires this could be good enough as it blends fairly well into an environment otherwise lit by more physically correct models. However, even with this simple model (and even more so for more complex ones), it is crucial to enable centroid sampling on the interpolators. The error introduced from sampling outside of the wire is simply far too great.

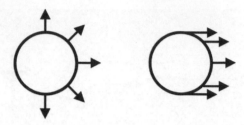

Figure 6.4. Left: Original normals. Right: Normals by the time the wire goes sub-pixel, assuming the viewer is to the right of the wire.

If sticking to Half Lambert is not enough, there are a few different approaches for dealing with this. We have tried a couple of methods that both work relatively well and can also be combined. Both involve fading over from our regular lighting model into something uniformly colored over some distance before reaching pixel size. The first method is simply computing our lighting as usual, then computing the Half Lambert as well, and then fading between these two. In our test scene a good fade range was from about 4 pixels wide and fully faded over to Half Lambert as it reached a single pixel. This is not based on any science but purely from testing various ranges and subjectively selecting what looked best for us. Depending on your lighting model and parameters, this could be tweaked differently. The advantage of this method is that it is straightforward and simple and tends to work fairly well.

The other method we tried involves flattening the normals over the distance. The thinner the wire gets, the more we are bending the normals toward the center normal from the viewer's point of view. As the wire goes down to a single pixel width, the normal will be entirely flat, and consequently result in a uniform lighting result. (See Figure 6.4.)

Since all this does is modify the input normal, this method is compatible with any lighting model, although results may vary.

6.2.4   Use with Deferred Shading

Deferred shading typically has a single global lighting model. This could make it tricky to fade between a soft light model, such as Half Lambert, and the engine's regular lighting model. The most straightforward approach is to simply render wires in a forward pass after the deferred lighting pass. The blended part of the wire (i.e., where it is smaller than a pixel wide) will have to be rendered as a translucent object anyway because of the blending. Typically wires take up a very small amount of screen space, so rendering the entire wire, including fully opaque parts, would normally have a minimal impact on performance. In the case where it is desirable to render opaque parts into the G-buffer, the normal bending approach above integrates very well as all it does is modify the input normal. The bent normal can then be written to the G-buffer and shaded as part of the regular deferred lighting pass.

6.2.5   Use with FXAA

This technique works very well together with MSAA, where MSAA takes care of all the jaggies, just like it is designed to do. But not all games use MSAA anymore; a whole bunch of filtering-based approaches to antialiasing have been used recently [Jimenez et al. 11a] and several have gone into shipping games. Arguably the most popular ones are FXAA [Lottes 09] and MLAA [Reshetov 09, Jimenez et al. 11b]. We have tested this technique in conjunction with FXAA and found that FXAA became nearly ineffective on the pixel-wide wires left by this technique. Consequently, as a workaround, the wire needs to be expanded somewhat for FXAA to take effect. Fortunately, as little as about 1.3 pixels width is enough for FXAA to pick up the edges. Somewhat wider wires do result in a somewhat lower quality overall, but not too bad. Other similar techniques, such as MLAA, may be better suited for dealing with pixel-thin wires, but the author has not verified that this is the case.

6.3   Conclusion and Future Work

A technique has been presented that effectively deals with aliasing on a specific (but frequently occurring) subset of aliasing-prone geometry. This is a welcome tool to reduce aliasing in games, but it does not solve the entire problem space of aliasing in real-time rendering. Much research is still needed. An obvious next step would be to explore ways to extend this technique to other shapes than cylinders. We believe extending it to rectangular shapes such as bricks and planks should be relatively straightforward and could work fundamentally the same, with the exception that we need to take view orientation into account for estimating size in terms of pixels. From there it may be possible to solve the staircase. Stairs are a frequent source of aliasing artifacts in games, as the top and side view of the steps tend to get lit differently, resulting in ugly Moiré patterns when the steps get down to pixel size.

Solving all these special cases may be enough for games, but ideally it would be desirable to solve the general case, where a model with any amount of fine detail and thin sub-pixel sized triangles could be rendered in an alias-free manner, without resorting to super-sampling, and preferably without a preprocessing step.

Bibliography

[Jimenez et al. 11a] Jorge Jimenez et al. "Filtering Approaches for Real-Time Antialiasing." SIGGRAPH 2011 Course, Vancouver, Canada, August, 2011. (Available at http://iryoku.com/aacourse/.)

[Jimenez et al. 11b] Jorge Jimenez, Belen Masia, Jose I. Echevarria, Fernando Navarro, and Diego Gutierrez. "Practical Morphological Antialiasing." In *GPU Pro 2*, edited by Wolfgang Engel, pp. 95–120. Natick, MA: A K Peters, Ltd., 2011. (See also http://www.iryoku.com/mlaa/.)

[Lottes 09] Timothy Lottes. "FXAA." White Paper, Nvidia, http://developer. download.nvidia.com/assets/gamedev/files/sdk/11/FXAA_WhitePaper.pdf, 2009.

[Olano and Baker 10] Marc Olano and Dan Baker. "LEAN Mapping." http:// www.csee.umbc.edu/~olano/papers/lean/, 2010.

[Reshetov 09] Alexander Reshetov. "Morphological Antialiasing." Preprint, http://visual-computing.intel-research.net/publications/papers/2009/mlaa/ mlaa.pdf, 2009.

[Valve 08] Valve Developer Community. "Half Lambert." https://developer. valvesoftware.com/wiki/Half_Lambert, 2008.

Image Space

In this part we will cover three rendering algorithms that operate primarily in image or screen space. While there are multiple reasons for working in image space, one particularly nice property is that such techniques are usually straightforward to port between different rendering engines, platforms, and architectures. Often these effects require little more than some shader code and the ability to draw a screen-aligned rectangle, thus making them easy to share with other graphics programmers and technical artists.

Our first chapter, "Screen-Space Grass" by David Pangerl, describes an efficient and unique method for drawing background grass. This technique utilizes a very fast screen space technique and presents a novel solution to the otherwise very difficult problem of drawing many thousands or even millions of grass instances.

Next, João Raza and Gustavo Nunes present "Screen-Space Deformable Meshes via CSG with Per-Pixel Linked Lists." This chapter provides a method by which ordinary geometric meshes may be cut and deformed dynamically in screen space. The chief strength of their technique is in its generality and applicability to many interesting scenarios that come up in games and other real-time applications such as damage deformation, rigid object fracture, and destruction.

Our final chapter, "Bokeh Effects on the SPU" by Serge Bernier, offers a bokeh-style depth of field rendering technique that is optimized for the PS3's SPUs. Depth of field is an important visual tool in games and other interactive media. This new technique is exciting in that it provides a "next-generation" camera lens effect on a current generation platform.

We hope that you find these techniques both useful and inspiring while developing your own image space rendering techniques!

—Christopher Oat

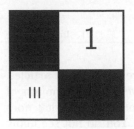

1

Screen-Space Grass
David Pangerl

1.1 Introduction

Grass is a fundamental part of any outdoor nature scene. Unfortunately, grass is also a difficult and complex thing to render realistically due to its abundance. (See, for example, Figure 1.1.)

In this chapter we present a novel technique for realistically rendering mid-ground and background grass in screen space. This technique was developed for the games *Agricultural Simulator 2013* and *Industry Giant 3*.

1.2 Motivation

The usual approach for rendering grass in the distance requires generating and processing a large amount of geometry or instances, and this consumes a lot

Figure 1.1. An example scene from *Agricultural Simulator 2013* showing Screen-Space Grass in action. Notice distant grass areas with a shivering grass effect.

of CPU and GPU resources. This approach has been covered in many articles, but its main limitation is that it is not well suited for covering vast amounts of terrain. In order to solve this problem, we considered the question: what does one actually see when they look at grass in the distance? You do not see many individual blades of grass nor any detailed grass movement. What you do see is some general noisy movement, wind patterns, and some grass blades only at boundary regions (where the grass stops and the terrain changes to some other material). From these observations we decided to implement our grass using noise in screen space.

The beauty of this technique is that it is extremely cheap, it is very realistic, it does not require any additional resources or preprocessing, it scales beautifully over an entire terrain, and it can extend to vast distances into the scene. It is also very easy to integrate into existing rendering pipelines.

This technique does not cover nearby grass rendering, where individual grass fins are actually visible. Near grass rendering is a very well covered topic, and we encourage the reader to see [Pelzer 04] and [Whatley 05].

1.3   Technique

Screen-Space Grass (SSG) is rendered in post-processing as a fullscreen quad. It requires some kind of per-pixel depth information that we get from *camera-space position*, but it could also be used for rendering pipelines without it (by reading depth information some other way or by ignoring obstruction detection).

The complete algorithm consists of two stages:

1. terrain stencil masking,

2. post-process fullscreen pass.

When rendering the terrain, we must stencil-mask it with a unique stencil value. We use a stencil mask value of 2 for terrain and 1 for everything else.

During post-process, we execute a fullscreen pass with our SSG shader. The SSG shader samples two textures: the scene's *color* buffer and a *position* texture (or a depth buffer from which a position may be derived). The *color* texture is used for color sampling and a smudge effect, and the *position* texture is used for grass scale and object obstruction detection.

SSG should be computed after the opaque rendering stage and lighting are complete, so that we have a final framebuffer color, but before edge detection, fog, and other post-processing effects.

1.3.1   Generating Realistic Grass Noise

To generate grass noise we use a simple vertical up-down smudge. It is a very simple idea that produces realistic grass noise and edge fins.

Figure 1.2. Grass smudging effect.

In reality, grass grows upward but in our case "smudging" the grass downward simplifies our stencil masking because it allows us to use our original terrain geometry to generate the stencil mask (in the same pass). To create an upward smudge, we would need to somehow extend the stencil mask upward.

For our smudge function we used a simple modulated screen-space quantization:

```
float xx=inSPos.x / TDeviceSize[0].x;
float yy=inSPos.y / TDeviceSize[0].y;

float d      =_blend( len , 0 , 500 , 100 , 500 );
float dclose=_blend( len , 0 ,  20 ,  30 ,   1 );

d*=dclose;

yy+=xx * 1000 / d;

float  yoffset=frac( yy * d ) / d;
```

The *source pixel* from `inTex0.xy - float2( 0 , yoffset )` is going to be smudged to the *target pixel* (output pixel) `inTex0.xy`, as in Figure 1.2.

With this formula we get a straight vertical grass smudge effect, as in Figure 1.3.

To break up the regular vertical lines and to add a bit of noise, we change the modulation to

```
yy+=xx * 1000
```

However, for some games straight vertical lines may actually be desirable to achieve a certain visual effect (e.g., *Industry Giant 3* uses straight lines; see Figure 1.4).

Figure 1.3. Base smudge grass noise function producing straight vertical lines.

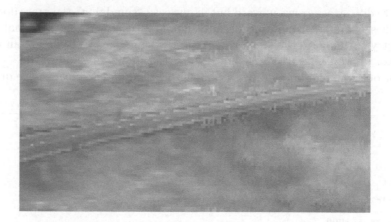

Figure 1.4. Regular terrain rendering on the left. Screen-Space Grass rendering used in *Agricultural Simulator 2013* on the right.

The terrain pixels on the upper edge of the stencil masked area are going to be smudged by pixels outside of the stencil masked space, creating the effect of grass blades on the top of terrain ridges, as in Figure 1.5.

1.3.2   Is It Really Grass?

The whole terrain is not necessarily composed of grass. We would also like to be able to render roads, dirt and sand patches, and other areas that are not covered in grass. We would also like to support objects that are rendered on top of the grassy terrain. Such objects are, of course, masked by a stencil; however, the grass smudge effect can mistake them for grass pixels (*source pixel*) even if they are just outside the stencil marked area (stencil-marked-area pixels are only guaranteed not to be the *target pixels* for the SSG effect). See Figure 1.6.

Figure 1.5. Correct grass fins on edge of stencil marked area.

Figure 1.6. Road and sign are ignored by SSG.

Regions of the stencil masked terrain that do not contain grass may be filtered out with a simple test that checks if the pixel is green. While this may seem too simplistic, we found it to work perfectly for detecting grass:

```
int     isgreen=backcolor.g > backcolor.r + 0.01f &&
                backcolor.g > backcolor.b + 0.01f;
```

This simple test for detecting green pixels is the main reason for requiring a stencil mask. If we had no stencil masking, then all green pixels on the screen would be treated as grass (e.g., all green trees and all green objects). Of course, with stencil masking, we also get a little speed optimization since only terrain pixels are processed by a SSG shader. Other games may find it more convenient

Figure 1.7. Left: fins bleed from undetected obstructed object. Right: obstructed object detection.

to mark their grass using a spare alpha channel instead of relying on pixel color to detect grass.

It is worth mentioning that a similar noise effect would also be great for simulating micro leaf movement on distant trees.

Visual artifacts can result from smudging *source pixels* that are not part of the terrain. This can happen when an object is rendered on top of the terrain (e.g., trees and other props). To detect these pixels, we must take an additional sample from the *position* texture of the *source pixel*. If the *source pixel* is closer to the camera than the target pixel, then it should not be smudged to the *target pixel* (see also Figure 1.7):

```
float4 poscs2=tex2D( Color1SamplerPoint , uvoffset );
if( poscs2.z < poscs.z ) return backcolor;
```

1.4   Performance

The SSG compiled for pixel shader model 3.0 uses approximately 51 instruction slots (4 texture and 47 arithmetic). The measured performance cost without stencil mask (SSG shader was forcefully executed on the entire framebuffer) was 0.18 milliseconds at 1920 × 1200 on our tests with a GeForce GTX 560 (drivers 320.18).

1.5 Conclusion

We presented a novel technique for post-process screen-space grass that can be applied over vast terrain areas. The technique is extremely cheap, it is very realistic, it does not require any additional resources or preprocessing, it scales efficiently over a large terrain even at vast distances, and it is very easy to integrate into an existing rendering pipeline. See the gallery of results in Figures 1.8–1.15.

Figure 1.8. SSG example 1 from *Agricultural Simulator 2013*.

Figure 1.9. SSG example 2 from *Agricultural Simulator 2013*.

Figure 1.10. SSG example 3 from *Agricultural Simulator 2013*.

Figure 1.11. SSG example 4 from *Agricultural Simulator 2013*.

1.6   Limitations and Future Work

The smudge effect is implemented to be perfectly vertical since it does not use camera tilt and is as such not convenient for a game that tilts the camera. We need to develop another smudge function for such cases.

Figure 1.12. SSG example 5 from *Agricultural Simulator 2013*.

Figure 1.13. SSG example 6 from *Agricultural Simulator 2013*.

We would also like to add realistic wind movement into the grass noise function. One very interesting effect comes from just using *target pixel* color as an additional noise modulator:

```
yy+=backcolor.g * 0.04f;
```

Figure 1.14. SSG example 7 from *Agricultural Simulator 2013*.

Figure 1.15. SSG example 8 from *Agricultural Simulator 2013*.

As mentioned before, a similar effect could also be used to simulate micro leaves noise for trees in the distance.

1.7   Screen-Space Grass Source Code

This is the source code for the SSG.fx effect.

```
float4 TDeviceSize[2]; // rtt size in TDeviceSize[0].xy
float4 TTimer[1];       // game time in TTimer[0].w

void vsmain(float3      inPos           : POSITION,
            float3      inTex           : TEXCOORD,
            //
            out float4  outPos          : POSITION,
            out float4  outTex0         : TEXCOORD0 )
{
   outPos=inPos;
   //
   outTex0=inTex;
   // half pixel offset
   outTex0.xy+=TDeviceSize[1].zw; // 0.5f / rtt size in [1].zw
}

float _blend(float val, float val0, float val1, float res0,
   float res1)
{
   if( val <= val0 ) return res0;
   if( val >= val1 ) return res1;
   //
   return res0 + (val-val0) * (res1-res0) / (val1-val0);
}

float4 psmain(float4 inTex0       : TEXCOORD0,
              float2 inSPos        : VPOS) : COLOR
{
   // get target depth
   float4    poscs=tex2D( Color1SamplerPoint,
                         inTex0.xy);
   //
   float     len=length( poscs.xyz );
   //
   float4    backcolor=tex2D( Color0SamplerPointClamp,
                             inTex0.xy );
   // check if color is green (aka grass)
   int    isgreen=backcolor.g > backcolor.r + 0.01f &&
                  backcolor.g > backcolor.b + 0.01f;
   //
   if( isgreen )
   {
       float4    color=0;
       // rtt size in TDeviceSize[0].xy
       float xx=inSPos.x / TDeviceSize[0].x;
       float yy=inSPos.y / TDeviceSize[0].y;
       //
       float d=_blend( len , 0 , 500 , 100 , 500 );
       float dclose=_blend( len , 0 , 20 , 30 , 1 );
       //
       d*=dclose;
       //
       yy+=xx * 1000;

       // add a little wind movement
       yy+=TTimer[0].w * 0.004f;
       //
       float   yoffset=frac( yy * d ) / d;
       //
       float2 uvoffset=inTex0.xy - float2(0,yoffset);
       //
       color=tex2D(Color0SamplerPointClamp,uvoffset);
```

```
        // check if obstructed
        // get source depth
        float4 poscs2=tex2D( Color1SamplerPoint ,
                             uvoffset );
        // check if source is closer to camera than target
        if ( poscs2.z < poscs.z ) return backcolor;
        // blend a bit
        return lerp ( backcolor , color ,
                      saturate ( 1-yoffset * d / 3.8 ) );
    }
    //
    return backcolor;
}

technique defaultshader
{
    pass p0
    {
        CullMode        = None;
        ZEnable         = false;
        ZWriteEnable    = false;
        //
        StencilEnable   = true;
        StencilFunc     = Equal;
        StencilPass     = Keep;
        StencilFail     = Keep;
        StencilZFail    = Keep;
        StencilRef      = 2;        // stencil mask is set to 2
        //
        VertexShader    = compile vs_3_0 vsmain();
        PixelShader     = compile ps_3_0 psmain();
    }
}
```

Bibliography

[Pelzer 04] Kurt Pelzer. "Rendering Countless Blades of Waving Grass." In *GPU Gems*, edited by Randima Fernando, Chapter 7. Upper Saddle River, NJ: Addison-Wesley, 2004.

[Whatley 05] David Whatley. "Toward Photorealism in Virtual Botany." In *GPU Gems 2*, edited by Matt Pharr, Chapter 1. Upper Saddle River, NJ: Addison-Wesley, 2005.

Screen-Space Deformable Meshes via CSG with Per-Pixel Linked Lists
João Raza and Gustavo Nunes

2.1 Introduction

In this chapter we describe a deformable mesh method that utilizes an implementation of the Constructive Solid Geometry (CSG) algorithm in real time through the usage of a per-pixel linked list data structure stored in the GPU memory. Via this method, the proposed CSG algorithm manages to have a constant number of passes. This contrasts with standard image-based CSG implementations in which the number of required rendering passes increases linearly with the scene's depth complexity.

Although the union, intersection and difference CSG operations can be rendered via this approach, this chapter focuses on the difference operation, since it yields a deformable mesh scenario. Moreover, a modification to the CSG algorithm behavior is made in a particular case to properly target the deformable mesh scenario. The solution presented here is generic, does not make any assumption on the scene's topology, and works for any concave, convex, or flat mesh.

2.2 Mesh Deformation Scenario

Games and real-time applications utilize deformable meshes as a mechanism for enhancing the user experience and providing immediate feedback to their actions. Common scenarios are for deforming car models when they hit obstacles, or altering walls as explosions impact them. Mechanisms to enable mesh deformation vary from altering the vertices in the mesh structure to utilizing parallax mapping. Although these algorithms succeed in presenting a deformable mesh to the end user, they usually are not general enough so that the deformation mechanisms are applicable in any particular scenario and/or any particular mesh. Parallax mapping does not work well with curved surfaces, while altering the vertices structure in a mesh requires a high polygon count to look smooth.

Methods to circumvent this limitation use screen-space rendering techniques to assess which pixels should be clipped. Clipping pixels in screen space to deform meshes is not in itself a new concept for games [Vlachos 10]. The Sequenced Convex Subtraction algorithm [Stewart et al. 00] and the Goldfeather algorithm [Goldfeather et al. 86, Goldfeather et al. 89] are part of this group of implementations, for example. However, these traditional CSG techniques are usually implemented on the GPU [Guha et al. 03] through some sort of depth peeling method [Everitt 01]. This has the disadvantage of relying on multiple rendering passes proportional to the scene's depth complexity.

To address these limitations, this chapter presents a solution that allows meshes to deform with a high degree of flexibility, by utilizing another mesh that acts as the deforming component. Our solution is independent of the scene's depth complexity, since it requires a constant number of passes. In addition, departing from other CSG rendering methods [Stewart et al. 02] that assume a particular scene topology, the proposed solution is generic and works for any given scene. The algorithm still works even when deforming flat meshes, which in the common use for CSG leaves a hole in the mesh, as opposed to deforming it.

2.3   Algorithm Overview

2.3.1   Creating the Per-Pixel Linked List

Initially the entire scene must be rendered using a shader that stores each incoming fragment into a per-pixel linked list. This section will give a quick overview of this concept; for a more comprehensive explanation, see [Thibieroz 11].

To create the linked list we use two unordered access view buffers (UAVs). One is the head pointer buffer, while the other is a node storage buffer of linked lists. The head pointer buffer is equivalent in dimensions to the render target. Each pixel in the render target has an equivalent pixel in the head pointer buffer. These two pixels are correlated by the pixel's (x, y) coordinate in the render target. What this means is that each pixel in the render target will have only one equivalent address in the head pointer buffer. All pixels in the head pointer buffer either point to a location in the node storage buffer or to an invalid value. If a pixel in the head pointer buffer points to a valid location in the node storage buffer, then the node it points to is considered the first node in the per-pixel linked list. Each valid node in the node storage buffer may point to another node in the node storage buffer, thus creating a linked list of nodes.

As a new pixel is rendered, a lookup is made in the head pointer buffer for its equivalent address. If it points to any valid location in the node storage buffer, then a new node is added in the node storage buffer, while adjusting the corresponding linked list to point to it. If the pixel doesn't point to any valid location in the node storage buffer, meaning this is the first pixel to be added for its equivalent render target pixel, then a new node in the node storage buffer is added. The head pointer buffer is then updated to point to that node.

Via this method, one is able to keep track of all rendered fragments for each pixel on-screen. For simplicity, we will collectively refer to these two UAV buffers throughout this chapter as a per-pixel linked list, since their end-product yields exactly that.

2.3.2   The Scene vs. Deformer Mesh

For clarification, throughout this chapter we will refer to the scene as any mesh that has to be rendered to the end user that could be deformed. In Figure 2.3, the cube would be considered the scene. Any and all pixels that were derived via rendering calls from the scene are thus referred to as pixels from the scene. For simplicity, we will also refer to pixels from the scene as M+ pixels.

In contrast, for generating the CSG algorithm, we will also utilize a deformer mesh. The deformer mesh will not appear in the final image that is displayed to the user. Its sole purpose is to have its pixels as part of the heuristics in constructing a deformed mesh to the end user in the final image. Any and all pixels that were derived via rendering calls from the deformer mesh are thus referred to as deforming pixels. For simplicity, we will also refer to pixels from deforming mesh as M− pixels.

2.3.3   Per-Pixel Linked List Node

Each node in the per-pixel linked list will contain the rendered pixel RGB color, its depth value, and a flag indicating if it is a back-facing or front-facing generated pixel, as well as a flag indicating if the pixel belongs to M+ or M−.

2.3.4   Rendering the Scene and the Deformer Mesh
into the Per-Pixel Linked List

The first step in the algorithm is to render the front-facing pixels of the entire scene plus the front-facing pixels of the deformer mesh into the per-pixel linked list. The second step is to render the back-facing pixels of the entire scene plus the back-facing pixels of the deformer mesh into the per-pixel linked list. Two constant buffer variables are used in these two rendering passes. One buffer is used to express to the shader storing the pixels into the linked list that the incoming fragments are either front facing or back facing. The other buffer provides information to the shader that the incoming fragments belong to M+ or M−. All this data is then stored in each node in the linked list.

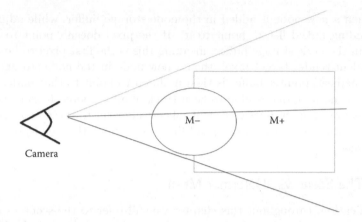

Figure 2.1. Three lines of sight from the camera. The linked list on the green line of sight will contain no nodes, the red line of sight will have [M− front, M+ front, M− back, M+ back] in its list, and the blue line of sight will have [M+ front, M+ back] in its list.

2.3.5   Sorting the Linked List

Once the linked list contains all pixel information, a shader program will sort all pixels in each of the linked lists based on their depth values. The result is that each linked list will contain a list of pixels sorted from closest to farthest depth from the camera. To help illustrate the result of this step, take as an example Figure 2.1. In it we have a camera that's positioned in world coordinates, a scene mesh (M+), and a deforming mesh (M−) that intersects the scene mesh. Both M+ and M− are inside the camera's frustum.

Look at the three lines of sight (red, green, blue) from the camera. Once sorted, the per-pixel linked list on the green line of sight will have no nodes in it. The red line of sight will have [M− front, M+ front, M− back, M+ back] in its list. The blue line of sight will have [M+ front, M+ back] in its list.

2.3.6   Determining M+ and M− Intersections

For the next set of steps, we will need to assess if M+ and M− intersected, that is, if any given M+ pixel is inside M−, as well as if any M− pixel is inside M+. To assess if any given M+ pixel is inside or outside M−, we linearly traverse the sorted per-pixel linked list starting from the closest pixel. If a front-facing M− pixel is found, then any subsequent M+ pixels are inside M− until a back-facing M− pixel is found. In addition, if the first M− pixel found on the list is a back-facing one, this means that all previously found M+ pixels were inside M−, since this is a case where the camera is inside M−. One can also determine if an M− pixel is inside M+ by utilizing the same steps described but switching the keywords of M− for M+ and vice versa.

2.3.7 Saving the Right Pixel Depth for Lookup

Once the per-pixel linked list is sorted based on depth, the algorithm needs to assess what is the correct pixel to be rendered on screen for each pixel in the list. We begin traversing the linked list from the closest pixel to the farthest one. If any front-facing pixel of M+ is found that is currently outside of M−, then that is the pixel to be rendered on screen. If any back-facing pixel of M− is found that is currently inside of M+, then that is the pixel to be rendered on screen. If there is a valid M+ and M− pixel to be rendered, whichever is closest to the camera wins. The front-facing M+ or back-facing M− pixel to render will be referred to in this chapter as the eligible rendered pixel for consistency. If we used the per-pixel linked lists exemplified in Figure 2.1 to retrieve the set of eligible rendered pixels, we would have none for the green line of sight, the first M− back-facing pixel for the red line of sight, and the first M+ front-facing pixel for the blue line of sight.

The eligible rendered pixel case described above works when M+ is a non-flat mesh (such as a cube). When M+ is a flat mesh (such as a wall), then the eligible rendered pixel is either any front-facing pixel of M+ that is outside of M−, or the first back-facing pixel of M− that lies behind a M+ front-facing pixel.

Via this heuristic, the method to communicate to the final render pass (the next step in the algorithm) the eligible rendered pixel, is by storing the eligible rendered pixel depth value in an auxiliary texture buffer. The final pass rendering step will then use that auxiliary texture buffer as a lookup table. Please see the book's website for the code that executes all of the steps outlined in this section.

2.3.8 Final Pass Render

In the final render pass, we re-render the front-facing pixels of M+, as well as the back-facing pixels of M−, with a final pass shader. This final pass shader will compare the incoming fragment's depth value with what is stored in the auxiliary texture buffer. If the fragment's depth value is equal to the one stored in the auxiliary texture buffer, then that means that the incoming fragment is the eligible rendered pixel. It then gets rendered in the render target. All other fragments are clipped. Figure 2.2 displays how Figure 2.1 would look after

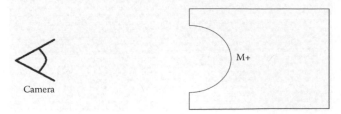

Figure 2.2. The final scene once M− is subtracted from M+.

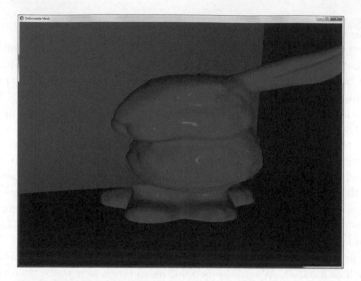

Figure 2.3. The Stanford bunny acts as M− and the cube acts as M+ (prior to the algorithm having run).

the final rendering pass. Figure 2.3 is a display of the algorithm in which the Stanford bunny acts as M− and the cube acts as M+, with the algorithm turned off. Figure 2.4 is the same point of view, but with the algorithm turned on. Figure 2.5 is a close up of Figure 2.4.

Figure 2.4. The same point of view as Figure 2.3 but with the algorithm enabled.

Figure 2.5. A zoomed-in view of the scene while the algorithm is enabled.

2.4   Optimizations

Areas of potential optimization involve knowing beforehand the topology of the rendered scene (such as if M+ and M− are colliding or not) or determining beforehand if M− is convex or not. Further, one might leverage the D3D 11.2 fixed function overlay hardware technique [Sorbo 13] to minimize the memory consumption of the GPU by having a lower dimension swap chain. This means one could use a lower dimension set of buffers to generate the per-pixel linked list. We leave these areas of optimization up to the reader, since our goal for the sample code and code snippets in this chapter was to focus on readability, as well as providing a generic framework for end developers to work on.

2.5   Conclusion

Deformable meshes are a common scenario in several contemporary games, and being able to produce a flexible environment in which artists have a greater degree of freedom is always useful. The algorithm discussed in this chapter aims to provide a solution for this space. As elaborated previously, there are several ways to optimize the proposed algorithm, but we hope this serves as a building block for whoever is interested in the deformable mesh scenario.

2.6   Acknowledgements

João Raza would like to thank his family and wife for all the support they've provided him. Gustavo Nunes would like to thank his wife and family for all their help. Special thanks goes to their friend F. F. Marmot.

Bibliography

[Everitt 01] C. Everitt. "Interactive Order-Independent Transparency." White Paper, NVIDIA Corporation, 1999.

[Goldfeather et al. 86] J. Goldfeather, J. P. M. Hultquist, and H. Fuchs. "Fast Constructive Solid Geometry Display in the Pixel-Powers Graphics System." *ACM Computer Graphics (SIGGRAPH '86 Proceedings)* 20:4 (1986), 107–116.

[Goldfeather et al. 89] J. Goldfeather, S. Molnar, G. Turk, and H. Fuchs. "Near Realtime CSG Rendering Using Tree Normalization and Geometric Pruning." *IEEE Computer Graphics and Applications* 9:3 (1989), 20–28.

[Guha et al. 03] S. Guha, S. Krishnan, K. Munagala, and S. Venkatasubramanian. "Application of the Two-Sided Depth Test to CSG Rendering." In *Proceedings of the 2003 Symposium on Interactive 3D Graphics*, pp. 177–180. New York: ACM, 2003.

[Sorbo 13] B. Sorbo. "What's New in D3D 11.2." BUILD, Microsoft, 2013.

[Stewart et al. 00] N. Stewart, G. Leach, and S. John. "A CSG Rendering Algorithm for Convex Objects." *Journal of WSCG* 8:2 (2000), 369–372.

[Stewart et al. 02] N. Stewart, G. Leach, and S. John. "Linear-Time CSG Rendering of Intersected Convex Objects." *Journal of WSCG* 10:2 (2002), 437–444.

[Thibieroz 11] N. Thibieroz. "Order-Independent Transparency Using Per-Pixel Linked Lists." In *GPU Pro 2*, edited by Wolfgang Engel, pp. 409–431. Natick, MA: A K Peters, Ltd., 2011.

[Vlachos 10] Alex Vlachos. "Rendering Wounds in Left 4 Dead 2." Presentation, Game Developers Conference 2010, San Francisco, CA, March 9, 2010. (Available at http://www.valvesoftware.com/publications/2010/gdc2010_vlachos_l4d2wounds.pdf.)

3

III

Bokeh Effects on the SPU

Serge Bernier

3.1 Introduction

Graphics programmers work hard to spend their per-frame millisecond budget wisely—by ensuring the color buffer gamma is correct, using a true high dynamic range pipeline, or trying to have the best antialiasing technique possible. Therefore it can be surprising to actually spend more milliseconds to produce a blurred image! Many games use depth of field (DOF) to focus the player's attention on a particular part of the frame, as well as to reinforce the depth illusion in the rendered image. Depth of field has a natural home in cutscenes, which typically have a more cinematographic feel, using framing and focus on a particular character or object to deliver a critical plot line for the game.

Of course, the use of depth of field is mainly driven by the artistic direction of a game, and this can differ dramatically from game to game. Typically, to create the in-game depth-of-field lens effect, we blur a copy of the framebuffer and interpolate between the blurred and non-blurred version depending on the distance of each pixel to the focal plane. For many years the blurring technique used was just a simple Gaussian blur to approximate the lens effect; however, a new technique is around the corner that allows us to achieve a much more real, filmic DOF effect. It is called *bokeh*, a Japanese word meaning "confused" or "dizzy." In our context we use it to qualify the aesthetic quality of the blur applied to the out-of-focus part of the image. Typically the bokeh effect will make highlights or light sources blur out into discs, or shapes that show the number of iris blades in the camera lens. A DirectX11 implementation was shown at GDC 2011 in the Samaritan tech demo driven by the Unreal Engine. This technique enhanced the DOF effect, giving something much closer to the look that we often see in a movie. (See Figure 3.1.) Many techniques can be found on the web to implement the bokeh effect, but in this chapter I will focus on the sprite-based approach [Pettineo 11], applied to the Playstation 3 with a *Synergistic Processing Unit* (SPU) twist! Instead of using the compute shader, geometry shader, or the `DrawInstancedIndirect` call feature in the DX11 API, this chapter will explain

Figure 3.1. Bokeh example from a real camera.

how to use the SPUs to analyze the framebuffer luminance and generate bokeh draw calls.

3.2   Bokeh Behind the Scenes

To understand what the bokeh effect is, we need to first understand depth of field. Depth of field is the distance from the focal plane in which objects appear in focus. (See Figure 3.2.)

Objects outside this region are considered out of focus and will appear blurred. In film or photography, depth of field is mainly a characteristic of the lens and focus distances. One important thing to understand is that objects don't go from

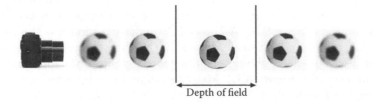

Figure 3.2. Depth of field is the distance between the nearest and farthest objects in a scene that appear acceptably sharp in an image.

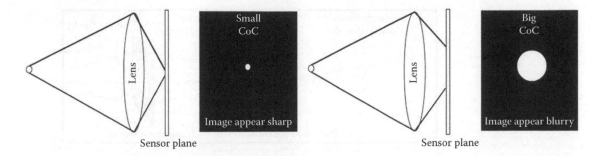

Figure 3.3. Variation of the CoC for a combination of subject distances.

sharp to unsharp abruptly. It gradually goes out of focus as it gets farther from the focal point. Since it is a gradient, we quantify the blur amount with the size of the *circle of confusion* (CoC). The bigger the CoC value for a particular pixel, the more blur you apply to it. Conversely, the smaller the CoC value, the sharper the pixel should appear. (See Figure 3.3.)

The CoC value will vary in the range $[0, 1]$ and will indicate how much in or out of focus the pixel is. The blur amount, generally in pixel size, will be multiplied by the CoC of the pixel to find the blur amount for a particular pixel in the framebuffer. The maximum blur value will be game driven and is something that artists can tweak to achieve the desired DOF effect.

So what does bokeh have to do with all this? Well, bokeh is intimately connected to the lens aperture, or more precisely, the aperture shape. On a real camera the quantity of light passing through the lens is controlled by the aperture. A set of blades mounted into the lens controls the light entering the camera, as shown in Figure 3.4.

We can now see how the lens design affects the shape of out-of-focus highlights. (See Figure 3.5.) Typically, you will have a nice circular bokeh shape with a fully opened aperture. Some lens manufacturers have iris blades with curved edges to make the aperture more closely approximate a circle rather than a polygon.

Figure 3.4. Aperture shape depending on the f-stop. We can see now where the bokeh shape is coming from!

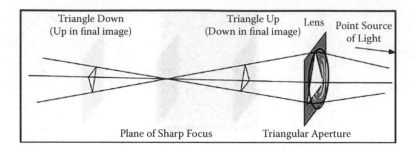

Figure 3.5. Aperture shape affecting out-of-focus detail in the image.

3.3   The Sprite-Based Approach

Sprite-based bokeh effects are pretty simple to understand and are very flexible, allowing artist modification to achieve the desired result. The main idea is to take each pixel of the framebuffer and analyze its luminance:

$$L_{i,j} = 0.2126R_{i,j} + 0.7152G_{i,j} + 0.0722B_{i,j},$$

$$\text{average pixel luminance} = \frac{\Sigma_i^m \Sigma_j^n L_{i,j}}{m \times n}.$$

To analyze each pixel of the framebuffer, you start with a filter kernel, to analyze the pixels surrounding the current pixel. The bigger the kernel size is, the more expensive the luminance calculation is. (See Figure 3.6.) In my tests I

Figure 3.6. Framebuffer example with a 5×5 pixel kernel used to compute the average luminance of the pixel.

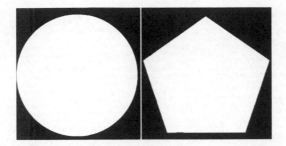

Figure 3.7. Examples of bokeh shape textures.

decided to go with a simple case, so kernel size equaled 1, with a buffer downscaled by a factor of 2. The result was quite good in performance and quality. Using the filter kernel, calculate the luminance for each pixel and simply spawn a texture sprite (see Figure 3.7) at the pixel screen space position if the luminance pixel is higher than a certain threshold. This luminance threshold value can be editable by the artist so they can adjust at which luminance value the pixel will produce a bokeh sprite when the pixel is out of focus. Performing the threshold test on each pixel will give you a list of pixels that will spawn a bokeh sprite. The last step is to calculate a proper scale for the bokeh sprite. The scale typically has a maximum size, which is also editable by artists. In this step, the depth value of the pixel is used to determine how much the pixel is out of focus. This represents the circle of confusion mentioned earlier and at its maximum value it represents a fully open aperture.

In short you need to calculate how much the pixel is out of focus and apply a pixel scale to the 1×1 bokeh sprite that you will spawn. The more the pixel is out of focus (remember that in the DOF explanation a pixel is gradually out of focus), the bigger the sprite will be on screen. If the scale value is 20 pixels, the bokeh sprite spawned at a pixel fully out of focus will be 20×20 pixels. (See Figure 3.8.)

At the end of this process you end up with a list of sprites containing

- x screen-space position of the pixel,

- y screen-space position of the pixel,

- z linear value of the pixel needed to depth test the bokeh sprite in the pixel shader,

- UV coordinates of the bokeh texture,

- CoC value of the pixel needed to adjust the blending amount to preserve energy conservation,

- color value of the pixel.

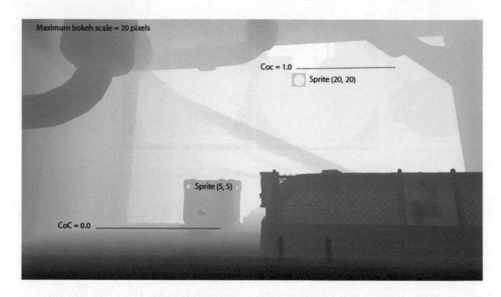

Figure 3.8. CoC across the framebuffer.

Now, depending on the platform you are developing for, this process can be done by different work units. On DX11, all this is realized in the compute shader with the color and depth buffer used as textures. On PS3, we don't have this stage available, but we do have the SPUs!

3.4   Let's SPUify This!

On PS3 the memory is split in two: main and video memory. Typical pipelines have the main color buffer placed in video memory for performance and memory footprint reasons. Since the SPUs like to work on buffers placed in main memory (read/write mode), the first step is to transfer the main color buffer into main memory. SPUs can work on buffers placed in video memory but the write speed will be slower.

After the reality synthesizer (RSX) transfers the color buffer to main memory, the SPU can start analyzing the scan lines to find each possible location where a bokeh sprite should be spawned. Basically, SPUs will write sprite information in a vertex buffer reserved in main memory that the RSX will process to display the bokeh sprites. The SPU program then patches the draw call previously reserved in the command buffer and removes the Jump To Self (JTS). During this process we calculate the average luminance of the color buffer needed in the tone mapping step, allowing us to save the Graphics Processing Unit (GPU) downscaling steps to find the average luminance of the color buffer.

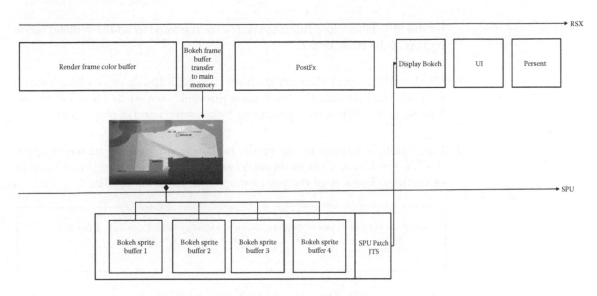

Figure 3.9. Bokeh effect timeline example.

The effect is very similar to the bokeh effect available from the DirectX 11 API, using the compute shader.

Let's detail the different steps (see also Figure 3.9):

1. Transfer the color buffer to main memory. You can transfer at full resolution or half resolution depending on the budget or quality of the bokeh effect you want.

2. Prepare (n) SPU jobs working on a sub-part of the color buffer to analyze the pixel luminance.

3. Each SPU fills a vertex buffer with the bokeh sprite information.

4. On the PPU, reserve space in the command buffer for the `SetDrawArrays`. Since the command `SetDrawArrays` has a variable size in the command buffer depending on the number of vertices, we must declare a maximum number of vertices and reserve that space in the command buffer. JTS commands are inserted before each `SetDrawArrays` so that the RSX waits until the SPUs are done.

5. On the PPU we issue (n) draw calls working on (n) vertex buffers depending on the number of SPU jobs we decided to spawn to process the framebuffer: for example, if we decided to create two SPU jobs, both jobs would work on half of the framebuffer, and we would need to issue on the PPU two draw calls each using their own vertex buffer (so two vertex buffers) and patched

by the SPU jobs. Note that the sprites are rendered in additive blend mode on top of the color buffer.

6. On the SPUs, each bokeh job analyzes the pixels and spawns a bokeh sprite for each pixel passing the luminance threshold, scaled by the CoC factor. The scale is clamped to a maximum bokeh scale size (in pixel space).

7. Each sprite is written in the vertex buffer (x, y, z position in screen space + UVs + color) and the `SetDrawArrays` is patched with the correct number of vertices. The rest of the reserved space is filled with NOPs.

```
void SetDrawArrays ( ContextData *thisContext , const uint8_t
    mode ,
const uint32_t first , const uint32_t count )
```

where `mode` = QUADS, `first` = 0, and `count` = the number of pixels that passed the luminance threshold with a valid CoC value.

8. The SPU patches the JTS so RSX can consume the graphic commands.

9. RSX draws each batch of bokeh sprites using additive blending.

10. Depth test is done in the pixel shader since we have the z position of the sprite in the vertex buffer.

11. The blend amount is adjusted to respect energy conservation for the bokeh sprite.

There are various ways to hide the luminance analysis and bokeh draw call generation steps done by the SPUs. In my case I decided to kick the RSX transfer right after the blended objects. This leaves enough time for the SPUs to analyze the framebuffer and fill the vertex buffer that the RSX will use to display the bokeh sprites on top of the framebuffer. The important thing to remember is to be careful not to stall the RSX. One nice thing about all this is that by doing the luminance computation on the SPUs you can have the total frame luminance for free! Normally, a game will have some kind of luminance/tone mapping adaptation of the framebuffer at the end of the frame. Adaptation effects usually involve the GPU by adding the work of doing a cascade of downscale passes to find the average luminance of the framebuffer. This obviously has some cost on the GPU and can be removed if you analyze the framebuffer on the SPUs.

3.5 Results

3.5.1 SPU

The present metrics are done on a half resolution 720p color buffer in main memory:

- 1 SPU working on a 640×360 buffer = **2.8ms**.

- 5 SPUs working on a 640×360 buffer = **0.65ms**!

The computations are done in a *Structure of Array* (SoA) manner, allowing the processing of four pixels at once. The SPU could certainly be more optimized by better balancing the odd/even pipes and reducing instruction latency.

3.5.2 RSX

On the RSX the cost is totally dependent on the number of bokeh sprites you decide to spawn and the screen coverage each sprite has (this is dependent on the bokeh maximum scale in pixels).

- Transfer to main memory with a draw call: 1280×720 to a 640×360 surface (untiled) = **0.44 ms**.

For the bokeh sprite draw calls, I will use a capture to show performance but remember that the number is dependent on the number of sprites per SPU job and the bokeh maximum scale.

Figure 3.10 shows a test case to analyze the cost of bokeh sprites on the RSX.

Total cost of the draw calls of the bokeh sprites = **0.56ms** for 5660 vertices with a 10 pixel maximum bokeh scale factor. (See Figure 3.11.)

Figure 3.10. Bokeh effect with a pentagon bokeh shape.

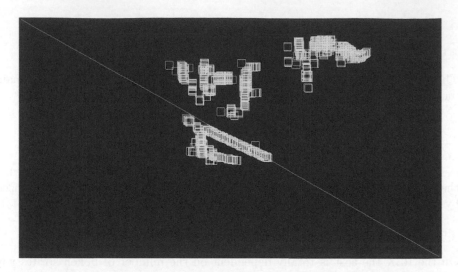

Figure 3.11. Wire frame view of the bokeh sprite draw calls.

3.6   Future Development

- Optimize SPU code by distributing the instructions evenly between the odd and even SPU pipelines.

- Since the SPU computes the luminance for each pixel we could have the total luminance of the color buffer without involving the RSX (downsampling and reading the final target on PPU). This could save the downsampling step on the RSX if you have some sort of Eye Adaptation post-process in your pipeline.

- Try to remove or push the vertex maximum number.

- Maybe spawn one SPU job working on the whole color buffer and sort the bokeh sprites to use only the brightest ones.

- Work with a bigger kernel size to generate fewer bokeh sprites.

- SPU's could write the bokeh sprite directly in the framebuffer. Instead of writing the vertex buffer, SPU's calculate for each sprite the 2D transfers representing lines contained in the Bokeh sprites. The RSX would use this buffer in additive blend mode to add it on top of the framebuffer.

Bibliography

[Pettineo 11] Matt Pettineo. "How to Fake Bokeh (And Make It Look Pretty Good)." http://mynameismjp.wordpress.com/2011/02/28/bokeh/, February 28, 2011.

Mobile Devices

Mobile devices are becoming increasingly more powerful, and with the advent of OpenGL ES 3.0, we now start seeing algorithms on mobile devices that previously weren't possible. This section covers topics ranging from real-time skin rendering to deferred shading and mobile compute.

In "Realistic Real-Time Skin Rendering on Mobile," Renaldas Zioma and Ole Ciliox share how they implemented skin rendering using physically based shading models for the Unity "The Chase" demo. Their method makes use of approximations and lookup textures in order to balance the arithmetic and texture load.

In "Deferred Rendering Techniques on Mobile Devices," Ashley Vaughan Smith explores various techniques for doing deferred rendering on mobile devices. This chapter steps through deferred shading, light pre-pass rendering and light indexed rendering, and also details extensions that allow efficient read-access to individual render targets to further improve performance.

In "Bandwidth Efficient Graphics with ARM Mali GPUs," Marius Bjørge presents new ARM Mali GPU extensions that allow applications to efficiently read and write data to the on-chip tile buffer. Applications can read the current color, depth, and stencil values as well as treat the tile buffer as a local storage with full read and write access. The chapter also contains example use-cases such as soft particles and deferred shading.

In "Efficient Morph Target Animation Using OpenGL ES 3.0," James Lewis Jones shows how OpenGL ES 3.0 can be used to do morph target animation efficiently on mobile devices. Transform feedback is used to blend a set of poses, and the chapter also describes how to batch blending of multiple poses to reduce the number of passes.

In "Tiled Deferred Blending," Ramses Ladlani describes a method for doing deferred blending. Blended primitives are first tiled to screen-space tiles, and then each tile is rendered while blending the primitives in a single fragment shader pass. The method has proven efficient on immediate mode renderers where blending involves an expensive read-modify-write operation with the framebuffer.

In "Adaptive Scalable Texture Compression," Stacy Smith presents ASTC, a new texture compression format that has been accepted as a Khronos standard. ASTC is set to pretty much replace all existing compressed texture formats. It supports bit rates ranging from 0.89 bpp up to 8 bpp for both LDR and HDR textures. This chapter explains how it works, how to use it, and how to get the most out of it.

In "Optimizing OpenCL Kernels for ARM Mali-T600 GPUs," Johan Gronqvist and Anton Lokhmotov go into the details of writing efficient OpenCL kernels for ARM Mali-T600 GPUs. This chapter introduces the ARM Mali-T600 GPU series and goes into a deep discussion of the performance characteristics of various OpenCL kernels.

Lastly, I would like to thank all the contributors of this section for their great work and excellent chapters.

—Marius Bjørge

Realistic Real-Time Skin Rendering on Mobile
Renaldas Zioma and Ole Ciliox

1.1 Introduction

Rendering realistic human skin has always been a challenge. Skin and especially faces have many subtle properties to which our brain and eyes are very well adapted. As observers we are very quick to spot discrepancies and missing details in shading of the skin—and reject them as implausible.

Despite these challenges, the task of rendering realistic skin in real time has became possible in recent years [Jimenez 12] using the power of modern GPUs and physically based shading models. In this chapter we will discuss how to adopt the most visually important aspects of skin shading—this time on mobile GPUs.

1.2 Overview

The challenge of skin rendering lies in the fact that both aspects of light reflectance—(a) subsurface scattering and (b) surface reflectance—are more complex compared to most non-organic materials like plastic or wood.

For many uniform materials [Pharr and Humphreys 04] we can approximate subsurface scattering computation with a single diffuse term and surface reflectance with a simple calculation of specular—using Blinn-Phong, for example.

Skin, however, consists of multiple layers of translucent tissue with different light reflectance and scattering properties. In order to achieve a plausible image at real time, we have to find an effective approximation of light interacting within multiple tissue layers.

1.2.1 Skin Surface Reflectance Model

When the light hits the surface of the skin, a small fraction of it is reflected from the outermost oily layer. The oil and tissue cells of the outermost layer are dielectric materials and reflect the light without coloring it, so it can be modeled with a specular reflection function.

Most of the light enters the skin, where it is absorbed, scattered, or reflected. A significant portion of the light is reflected at the interface between subsurface layers and exits the skin again. Unsurprisingly, as demonstrated by [Donner and Jensen 05], single specular lobe is not enough to simulate this complicated process. For our implementation we have followed advice from [d'Eon and Luebke 07] and adopted two separate specular reflectance lobes.

We know from practical observations that surface reflectance is very important for how we perceive skin. Modeling specular reflectance with traditional Blinn-Phong is simply not enough. For more physically accurate surface reflectance we chose a model inspired by microfacet theory.

We use (a) Beckmann as microfacet distribution function, (b), we use a very crude approximation of the geometric term, and (c) we sacrifice correctness of the Fresnel term by measuring it from per-pixel normal instead of half-vector. Overall, our model is close to the simplification of Cook-Torrance in [Kelemen and Szirmay-Kalos 01].

1.2.2   Skin Subsurface Scattering Model

Beneath the skin's surface, light quickly becomes diffuse as it scatters and acquires color as it gets partially absorbed by the tissue. To make matters more complicated, skin consists of many layers of tissue with slightly different absorption properties—an analytical solution for such a process quickly becomes unviable.

Instead of simulating complex diffusion in subsurface skin layers, incoming light can be captured in a dedicated buffer and then blurred. Both the original article [Borshukov and Lewis 03] and the high-quality real-time implementation [d'Eon and Luebke 07] suggest using multiple gaussian blurs in texture space. However, such an approach quickly becomes impractical on mobile GPU due to high-memory bandwidth requirements.

Alternatively, incoming light can be captured in a screen-space buffer [Jimenez et al. 09], and subsurface scattering can be approximated by blurring directly in screen space. This approach has significantly lower memory bandwidth requirements with relatively small quality degradation—perfect for mobile GPUs.

1.2.3   Importance of Linear Lighting

Accurate shading of skin will fall short without gamma correction; an unrealistic yellowish tint of the skin is a typical sign [d'Eon and Luebke 07]. Since albedo textures are authored and stored in sRGB gamma, we have to *uncompress* them into the same linear space where lighting equations take place and then *compress* them back to match the sRGB gamma of display.

1.3 Power of Mobile GPU

Despite recent tremendous developments and rapid performance improvements, mobile GPUs are still at least one league behind their desktop siblings. Although programmable flexibility of mobile GPUs is quickly gaining (OpenGL ES3.0 compatible GPUs have all the features of the last generation consoles and sometimes more), computational power (ALU) and memory bandwidth are lagging behind.

Let's look at important aspects of skin rendering and discuss how viable those approaches are on mobile GPUs.

1.3.1 Skin Subsurface Scattering

Although the blurring of the screen-space buffer requires an additional rendering pass, in practice the whole subsurface scattering step takes only around 5–10% of the GPU workload in our demo, and it scales very well with the numbers of skin shaded geometry. The performance-versus-quality trade-off can easily be managed by reducing the resolution of the screen-space buffer.

1.3.2 Physically Based Shading

Even the simplest energy-conserving Blinn-Phong specular lobe is still too expensive for a real-time application on mobile GPU today. It requires too many ALU operations per-pixel. If we want to achieve a physically plausible shading beyond Blinn-Phong, then we have to rely heavily on pre-computing the BRDF using 2D textures.

Final shading of skin pixels takes around 50% of GPU workload for close-up scenes in our demo. It proved crucial to optimize this part of the algorithm.

1.3.3 Per-pixel Environment Reflections

To evaluate environment reflections a per-pixel normal sampled from normal map has to be transformed from tangent to world space. That requires three additional dot products per-pixel.

We opt to sacrifice quality and sample environment reflections using per-vertex normal instead. Because we employ extremely dense geometry for the characters, visual difference was minimal in our case.

1.3.4 Linear Lighting

Although sRGB (gamma corrected) texture reads are trivial operations for the desktop GPU, in the case of OpenGL ES2.0 such reads are only available via platform-specific extensions. Even in the case of OpenGL ES3.0 where gamma correction is part of the core API, texture reads might incur different costs depending on the GPU family. The same situation applies when writing out linear values into the final sRGB framebuffer—an extension is required in the case of

OpenGL ES2.0 and varying performance can be expected in the case of OpenGL ES3.0 depending on the device.

However, we can be smart and gamma correct only when it is absolutely necessary, i.e., only for skin pixels. The rest of scene geometry can be shaded without gamma correction.

We expect this optimization to be unnecessary in the relatively close future when OpenGL ES3.0 takes over and performance differences between GPU families become smaller.

1.4   Implementation

1.4.1   Screen-Space Light Accumulation Buffer

Our approach to subsurface scattering is to use a temporary low-resolution screen-space buffer where we accumulate all incoming light, both diffuse and ambient (see Figure 1.1). By default we use quarter resolution of the screen for the light accumulation buffer.

We start by rendering all skin shaded characters in the scene, evaluating incoming light and storing results in the buffer. Note that we want to store the light as it hits the surface and disregard albedo of the skin at this step. We mark covered pixels with alpha values to distinguish them from the background for further use in the blur step.

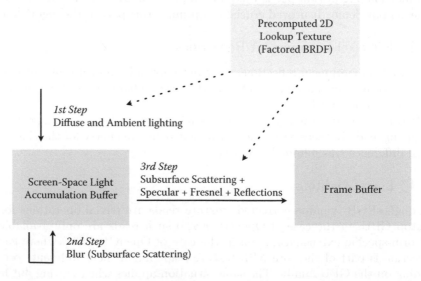

Figure 1.1. Block diagram of skin shading steps.

When rendering into the light accumulation buffer we offset geometry a little bit along normals to compensate for the low resolution of the buffer and to have more visually pleasing results on the edges of the skin shaded geometry. Possible offsets in the center of the skinned objects will be covered when we perform blur in the next step.

1.4.2   Subsurface Scattering (Screen-Space Diffusion)

As a second step, we perform a separable Gaussian blur that simulates the scattering inside the skin tissue. We use the alpha channel values to mask out the regions without skin to avoid leaking of the light. We found that one blur pass is enough to achieve visually pleasing results; however, multiple blur passes will improve the quality of the final image.

Subsequently, results of the blurred light accumulation buffer will be sampled in the final step of the skin shading to retrieve the diffuse component of the light-affecting pixels.

In practice it is rare for skin to cover a significant portion of the screen. We take advantage of that fact by generating bounding quad geometry and blurring only inside. This allows us to save on the memory bandwidth, especially when skin shaded characters are farther away.

1.4.3   Skin Layers

Many offline and online render systems model skin as a three-layer material with an oily top, an epidermal, and a subdermal layer, all employing different light absorption and scattering parameters. We, however, have opted for only a two-layer model for performance reasons. In fact we present a "fake" three-layer model to the artist because most seem more familiar with such setup (see Figure 1.2). Then we internally convert parameters to suit our two-layer model. The mixing of the layers is done in the last step of the skin shading.

1.4.4   Implementing a Physically Based Shading

As discussed earlier, we chose physically based microfacet distribution for our specular reflectance. To achieve real-time performance on mobile GPUs we pre-compute a single 2D lookup texture to capture the most intensive aspects of our BRDF calculation. We pre-compute the lookup texture by evaluating our custom BRDF before rendering of the scene starts.

Later, inside the pixel shader, we will address lookup texture using the angle between normal and half-vector ($N \cdot H$) on one dimension and the angle between normal and view vector ($N \cdot V$) on another dimension. We can store response to varying roughness parameters in the mip-chain of the lookup texture.

Figure 1.2. UI controls for multilayered skin and two specular lobes.

We use all four channels of pre-computed lookup texture separately to store different information:

- the first two channels contain $N \cdot H$ and $N \cdot V$ response for both specular lobes;

- the third channel contains a pre-computed Fresnel term for $N \cdot V$;

- the last channel contains an energy conservation term for the diffuse component, the integral of light reflected before it enters subsurface layers.

Because of the use of pre-computed lookup texture, overhead for the second specular lobe is negligible. Moreover, we achieve the energy conservation virtually for free.

1.4.5   GPU Workload Balance

We strive to split the workload between pre-computing and real-time evaluation of the parts of our lighting equation in such a way as to leverage the parallel nature of GPU arithmetic units and texture access units.

Note that finding an appropriate size of the lookup texture is a very important optimization step. An increase in the lookup texture size leads to better visual quality with less visible banding, but at the same time puts more stress on the texture cache and causes potential micro-stalls. For our demo we chose to use a 32×128 resolution for the lookup texture.

1.4.6   Alternative BRDF Factoring

There are other possible BRDF factoring approaches when working with the pre-computed lookup textures. One alternative is to use the angle between normal and half-vector ($N \cdot H$) and the angle between view and light vectors ($V \cdot L$)—ideal for storing different approximations of the Cook-Torrance model developed by [Schüler 11].

1.4.7   Selective Gamma Correction

As discussed earlier, linear lighting is an important aspect of skin shading and requires an inverse gamma correction of the input albedo textures and a gamma correction of the output. We use a couple of tricks to speed these steps on mobile GPUs.

First we use a gamma of 2.0, which allows us to use square (multiplication with self) and square root operations for *compression* and *decompression*. Multiplication and square root operations are significantly faster than calculating the power of 2.2 or 2.4.

Second we do gamma correction only on the most important pixels on the screen instead of doing it fullscreen as we would on a desktop or console. We implement the correction explicitly in the pixel shader.

1.4.8   Reflecting Environment

On top of the analytical specular reflections, we use a pre-rendered cube-map for reflecting light coming from all the surrounding environment. Reflected environment light is factored by both a Fresnel term and artist-defined reflectivity map and is mostly used for characteristic rim reflections on the skin.

1.4.9   Scattering for Eyes

Eyes were initially one of our biggest challenges. They seemed to "stick out" of the character shading. The solution we ended up with is to neglect simulation of the subsurface scattering inside the eyes. We simply do not render eyes into the light accumulation buffer. Possible issues are hidden by the typically very high amount of reflectivity when shading eyes (see Figure 1.3). For close ups, we added a small amount of parallax offset to model the eye lens refractions.

1.4.10   Skin Level of Detail

To avoid waxy and very flat-looking skin in the distance, the size of the scattering kernel needs to be decreased according to the distance from the viewer. However, using very small blur kernels with the accumulation buffer can result in a *low-resolution* look. Hence, along with decreasing the effect of blur at a distance, we also fade into a simpler single pass skin shader. A single pass skin shader

Figure 1.3. Fake "scattering" and surface reflectance of the eyes.

does a very crude approximation of the subsurface scattering by rejecting the high frequency of per-pixel normals (so-called *bent normals* from [Penner and Borshukov 11] and others) while keeping the surface reflectance part identical to the main shader. As a pleasant side effect, this makes distant skin much cheaper to render.

1.5   Results

1.5.1   Issues and Limitations

Our current skin shading approach is limited to a single per-pixel light for performance reasons. We evaluate the rest of the lights per-vertex.

A comparatively expensive aspect of our approach could be that skin shaded geometry needs to be rendered twice: first into the light accumulation buffer, next into the framebuffer. However, the first pass uses a very cheap shader and renders a relatively small amount of pixels.

Due to the limitation of the screen-space scattering approach, the backscattering phenomena (such as ears flashing up in red color when in front of a light source) are difficult to model. Reasonable quality-versus-performance results can be achieved using pre-computed thickness maps along with sampling inverted normals to approximate backscatter while rendering into the light accumulation buffer.

1.5.2   Comparison

A pre-integrated approach as described by [Penner and Borshukov 11] can be used to render skin on mobile GPUs. However, we found that determining a curvature to sample pre-integrated BRDF per-pixel can be quite expensive on mobile GPUs. Pre-computing curvature offline and storing in additional texture is possible and has to be investigated, along with the applicability of using the pre-integrated approach along with per-vertex lighting.

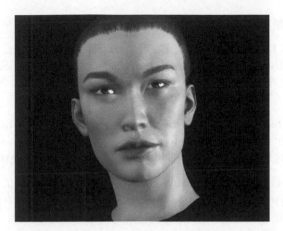

Figure 1.4. Example showing most features of the skin.

1.5.3 Shader

Our final shader (see Figure 1.4) contains four independent texture reads,

1. albedo and reflectivity map,

2. normal map,

3. environment reflection cube-map,

4. blurred irradiance texture,

and one dependent texture read for pre-calculated BRDF lookup texture. The shader executes around 40 vector operations per pixel. This amount of texture reads and arithmetic operations leads to good utilization of parallel units in modern Mobile GPU.

1.6 Summary

An average frame of our demo "The Chase" contains more than 60,000 animated polygons with the skin shaded geometry covering a significant portion of the screen. By employing the approach described in this chapter combined with optimized rendering for the rest of the scenery, we achieve smooth 30 frames per second on iPad4 at full Retina resolution (2048×1536 pixels). We achieve similar performance on a variety of modern mobile devices.

Bibliography

[Borshukov and Lewis 03] George Borshukov and J. P. Lewis. "Realistic Human Face Rendering for *The Matrix Reloaded*." In *ACM SIGGRAPH 2003 Sketches & Applications, SIGGRAPH '03*, p. Article no. 1. New York: ACM, 2003.

[d'Eon and Luebke 07] Eugene d'Eon and David Luebke. "Advanced Techniques for Realistic Real-Time Skin Rendering." In *GPU Gems 3*, edited by Hubert Nguyen, pp. 293–347. Upper Saddle River, NJ: Addison-Wesley, 2007.

[Donner and Jensen 05] Craig Donner and Henrik Wann Jensen. "Light Diffusion in Multi-layered Translucent Materials." *ACM Transactions on Graphics* 24:3 (2005), 1032–1039.

[Jimenez et al. 09] Jorge Jimenez, Veronica Sundstedt, and Diego Gutierrez. "Screen-Space Perceptual Rendering of Human Skin." *ACM Transactions on Applied Perception* 6:4 (2009), 23:1–23:15.

[Jimenez 12] Jorge Jimenez. "Practical Real-Time Strategies for Photorealistic Skin Rendering and Antialiasing." Ph.D. thesis, Universidad de Zaragoza, Zaragoza, Spain, 2012. Available online (http://diglib.eg.org/EG/DL/dissonline/doc/jimenez.pdf).

[Kelemen and Szirmay-Kalos 01] Csaba Kelemen and László Szirmay-Kalos. "A Microfacet Based Coupled Specular-Matte BRDF Model with Importance Sampling." In *Proceedings Eurographics '01*, pp. 25–34. Aire-la-Ville, Switzerland: Eurogrpahics Association, 2001.

[Penner and Borshukov 11] Eric Penner and George Borshukov. "Pre-Integrated Skin Shading." In *GPU Pro 2*, edited by Wolfgang Engel, pp. 41–55. Natick, MA: A K Peters, Ltd., 2011.

[Pharr and Humphreys 04] Matt Pharr and Greg Humphreys. *Physically Based Rendering: From Theory to Implementation.* San Francisco: Morgan Kaufmann, 2004.

[Schüler 11] Christian Schüler. "The Blinn-Phong Normalization Zoo." www.thetenthplanet.de/archives/255, 2011.

Deferred Rendering Techniques on Mobile Devices

Ashley Vaughan Smith

2.1 Introduction

With ongoing advances in GPU technology and the introduction of OpenGL ES 3.0, it has now become possible to utilize rendering techniques that were previously only usable on desktop GPUs. Applications that use dynamic lighting require a technique to shade the scene in an efficient way in real time. On mobile devices with a low power requirement, this is difficult to achieve.

This chapter discusses the available techniques for deferred rendering [Hargreaves and Harris 04] on mobile devices and implementation details that allow optimized rendering of these techniques. The purpose of this chapter is to give the reader an overview of the available deferred rendering techniques using OpenGL ES 2.0 and 3.0, but not an in-depth tutorial on implementing each technique. Readers unfamiliar with deferred rendering may wish to review previous literature about deferred rendering, e.g., [Calver 03, Thibieroz 04]. Also included are new opportunities to use OpenGL ES extensions to optimize these techniques even further.

2.2 Review

In review, there are two mainstream approaches to going about lighting a scene: forward rendering and deferred rendering. Forward rendering was common in fixed function pipelines, such as OpenGL ES 1.0, where there was no option to use deferred rendering. It is also possible to use forward rendering with programmable pipelines like OpenGL ES 2.0. An application that uses forward rendering requires information for a set number of lights that will be used to affect the geometry in the first pass. This usually requires some way of discarding lights when there are too many affecting a single piece of geometry or rendering the same piece of geometry multiple times and blending the results. Because of this, forward rendering is $O(\text{geometry} \cdot \text{lights})$ in processing complexity, meaning the complexity of rendering geometry is affected by the total number of lights in the scene.

2.2.1   Deferred Rendering

Deferred rendering [Hargreaves and Harris 04] is a technique whereby the application defers a scene's lighting calculations until all information required is available in a second pass. The technique decouples the lighting complexity from rendering the geometry and also allows the application to move these lights dynamically without needing to discard lights. This technique also helps the application to reduce the number of light calculations to a minimum by considering lighting on a per-fragment basis instead of a per piece-of-geometry basis. Deferred rendering is $O(\text{lights})$ in processing complexity, therefore this allows the application to render many more lights in the scene compared to the forward rendering approach.

Deferred rendering comes at a cost because the information to shade geometry in screen space requires that each pixel have all lighting information required available in G-buffers. With screens larger than 1920×1080 on some recent mobile devices, this can reach into tens of MBs, which needs to be written and read each frame. This increases memory usage and memory bandwidth, which could be utilized better.

2.3   Overview of Techniques

The techniques covered in this chapter are

- deferred rendering [Hargreaves and Harris 04],

- light pre-pass rendering [Engel 08],

- light indexed rendering [Treblico 09].

Also covered are how each of these techniques applies to both OpenGL ES 2.0 and OpenGL ES 3.0; as each API now has different features available and OpenGL ES extensions, these are features that are available on different mobile devices that are not present in the core OpenGL ES API. Applications can utilize these features but some mobile devices will not expose them.

2.3.1   Deferred Rendering

Deferred rendering [Hargreaves and Harris 04] is the traditional way of deferring the light calculations until a second pass. This technique involves writing out at least albedo, normals and depth to the G-buffer in one pass. Then in a separate pass, render each of the lights with geometry representing the volumes of the

```
glGenTexture ( 1, &m_uiAlbedoTexture );
glBindTexture ( GL_TEXTURE_2D, m_uiAlbedoTexture );
glTexImage2D ( GL_TEXTURE_2D, 0, GL_RGBA, 1920, 1080, 0, GL_RGBA,
 GL_UNSIGNED_BYTE, 0 );
// Create other textures

glGenFramebuffers ( 1, &m_uiGBufferFBO );
glBindFramebuffer ( GL_FRAMEBUFFER, m_uiGBufferFBO );
glFramebufferRenderbuffer ( GL_FRAMEBUFFER,
 GL_DEPTH_STENCIL_ATTACHMENT, GL_RENDERBUFFER,
 m_uiGBufferRenderBuffer );
glFramebufferTexture2D ( GL_FRAMEBUFFER, GL_COLOR_ATTACHMENT0,
 GL_TEXTURE_2D, m_uiAlbedoTexture, 0 );
glFramebufferTexture2D ( GL_FRAMEBUFFER, GL_COLOR_ATTACHMENT1,
 GL_TEXTURE_2D, m_uiNormalsTexture, 0 );
// Bind other textures to attachments

GLenum bufs [] = { GL_COLOR_ATTACHMENT0, GL_COLOR_ATTACHMENT1 };
glDrawBuffers ( 2, bufs );
```

Listing 2.1. An example of how to create a G-buffer for deferred rendering in OpenGL ES 3.0.

lights. i.e., a sphere for a point light, a fullscreen quad for a directional light. This pass reads the information from the G-buffer and additively calculates the lighting for the scene.

OpenGL ES 2.0. Deferred rendering in OpenGL ES 2.0 is not optimal because applications do not have access to multiple render targets. The application would need to render the geometry once for each render target with this technique unless the extension `GL_EXT_draw_buffers`, described later in this chapter, is used.

OpenGL ES 3.0. In OpenGL ES 3.0 deferred rendering can be used much like in desktop OpenGL (Listing 2.1).

OpenGL ES 3.0 uses out variables in the fragment shader to implement multiple render targets. Each of these may have a layout specifier that binds that fragment output to an attached texture. For example,

```
layout ( location = 0 ) out lowp vec4 albedoOutput;
layout ( location = 1 ) out lowp vec4 normalsOutput;
```

Encoding. Utilizing deferred rendering requires a way of encoding diffuse albedo color, normal information, and either depth or world position into textures. These are the minimum requirements for the G-buffer in deferred rendering. Albedo color and normals can be encoded without any further changes. However, as world position encoding requires three times the memory bandwidth of writing

```
precision highp float; // Requires highp
vec4 packFloatToVec4( const float value ) {
 vec4 bitSh = vec4( 256.0*256.0*256.0, 256.0*256.0, 256.0, 1.0 );
 vec4 bitMsk = vec4( 0.0, 1.0/256.0, 1.0/256.0, 1.0/256.0 );
 vec4 res = fract( value * bitSh );
 res -= res.xxyz * bitMsk;
 return res;
}
float unpackFloatFromVec4( const vec4 value ) {
 const vec4 bitSh = vec4( 1.0/( 256.0*256.0*256.0 ),
  1.0/( 256.0*256.0 ), 1.0/256.0 , 1.0 );
 return dot( value, bitSh );
}
```

Listing 2.2. Encoding and decoding a single floating point value into 32 bits of an RGBA8 texture.

depth only, applications that are memory bandwidth limited should consider encoding depth instead and reconstruct the world position in the light volume pass. Reconstructing the world position from depth in both OpenGL ES 2.0 and 3.0 is recommended, as these APIs do not have floating point render target support as a core feature.

To encode depth to a texture in OpenGL ES 2.0 requires the extension `GL_OES_depth_texture`. If this extension is not available, the application can instead encode the depth into 32 bits of a separate RGBA8 texture. An example of how to encode the depth into 32 bits of the texture is shown in Listing 2.2. This method may also be used to encode world position.

To reconstruct the position from this depth, the application can use the following code (Listing 2.3). This code applies when rendering the light volumes and takes the world position of the current view frustum as input uniforms to the shader.

```
gl_Position = mvpMatrix * inVertex;
vec2 textureCoord = gl_Position.xy / gl_Position.w;
textureCoord = ( textureCoord + 1.0 ) * 0.5;

// Interpolate the far frustum so that we have a point in world
// space. Multiply by w as gl will do this for us while
// interpolating varyings, noperspective is not available
farWorldPos = mix(
 mix( farFrustumBL, farFrustumTL, textureCoord.y ),
 mix( farFrustumBR, farFrustumTR, textureCoord.y ),
  textureCoord.x ) * gl_Position.w;
nearWorldPos = mix(
 mix( nearFrustumBL, nearFrustumTL, textureCoord.y ),
 mix( nearFrustumBR, nearFrustumTR, textureCoord.y ),
  textureCoord.x ) * gl_Position.w;
```

Listing 2.3. Reconstructing the world position from a linear depth.

Then in the fragment shader the world position can be acquired.

```
float depth = unpackFloatFromVec4(
  texture( depthTexture, textureCoord ) );
// Multiply by w to negate the implicit divide by w
vec3 world = mix( nearWorldPos * gl_FragCoord.w,
  farWorldPos * gl_FragCoord.w, depth );
```

In OpenGL ES 3.0 depth textures are a core feature.

As shown above, a common practice in deferred rendering is reconstructing the world position from a depth value. When using an RGBA8 texture to encode depth, the application can linearize the depth value it writes out. Therefore reconstructing world position by using a depth texture is different from using an RGBA8 texture, as the depth texture value is not linearized. Listing 2.4 [Reinheart 13] is an example that will reconstruct the world position from a depth texture and the `GL_OES_depth_texture` extension.

Utilizing deferred rendering in both OpenGL ES APIs has been described above, giving the application the flexibility to use either a depth texture or a separate render to texture to encode the depth value. Limitations with deferred rendering include the memory usage required for the G-buffers and the memory bandwidth of writing this information. This leaves the application less bandwidth to use for more detailed texturing. If the application requires more intensive texturing it can use a different technique, light pre-pass. Figure 2.1 shows the intermediate render targets for this technique.

2.3.2 Light Pre-pass Rendering

Light pre-pass rendering [Engel 08] differs from deferred rendering by storing only the lighting information per pixel instead of the geometry information. The advantage here is reduced memory required by the application and therefore reduced memory bandwidth usage. It involves rendering the (light color)·(light direction×

```
uniform vec2 pixelSize; // 1.0/viewportSize
vec3 ndcSpace = vec3( gl_FragCoord.xy * pixelSize,
  texture( depthTexture, textureCoord ).x ) * 2.0 - 1.0;

vec4 clipSpace;
clipSpace.w = projMatrix[3][2] /
  (ndcSpace.z - (projMatrix[2][2] / projMatrix[2][3]));
clipSpace.xyz = ndcSpace * clipSpace.w;

vec4 worldPos = inverseViewProjMatrix * clipSpace;
```

Listing 2.4. An example of how to reconstruct world position from a depth texture.

Figure 2.1. The render targets for deferred rendering: from left to right, final image, normals, encoded depth, and albedo color.

normal) information to a texture and then doing a second pass of geometry with the diffuse textures to produce the final image. As this technique processes the geometry twice, if the application is limited by vertex processing then this technique may not be the best option. However, if the application is limited by fragment operations, then this technique may be a good option because it uses less memory and therefore less memory bandwidth than other techniques.

OpenGL ES 2.0 and 3.0. Light pre-pass rendering can be performed in both OpenGL ES 2.0 and 3.0.

Limitations of both deferred and light pre-pass rendering include the inability to do hardware antialiasing. A technique that allows this possibility is called light indexed rendering. When using a depth texture, the application can avoid using multiple render targets. Figure 2.2 shows the intermediate render targets for this technique.

2.3.3   Light Indexed Rendering

Light indexed rendering [Treblico 09] is so-called because instead of storing the required lighting information such as normals and color per pixel, we store an index to the light affecting each pixel. We then use this index to sample separate one-dimensional textures, each with a different property, i.e., light position and light color. This acts like forward rendering; however, there is much more control

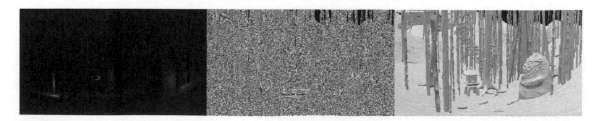

Figure 2.2. Render targets for light pre-pass rendering: lighting texture (left), encoded depth (center), and normals (right).

over how many lights can affect each pixel and the number of light sources is still decoupled from the rendering complexity.

Another advantage of light indexed rendering is that it allows the user to turn on hardware antialiasing. This is not possible with the previous two techniques because the APIs do not expose multisampled multiple render targets.

OpenGL ES 2.0 and 3.0. Light indexed rendering can be applied in both OpenGL ES 2.0 and 3.0. In this technique the application first renders the light volumes in the scene to a fullscreen texture. Each of these volumes has a unique index. This index is written to the texture in a specific channel using `glColorMask()` allowing up to four lights (one for each channel of the texture) and up to 256 different lights in the scene (the maximum index that can be stored in one channel of an RGBA8 texture). If the application determines that some pixels will be affected by more than four lights, it can render the extra light volumes to a different texture. This allows the application in reality to have any number of lights per pixel.

In the second pass the application renders the scene geometry passing in diffuse textures and information to shade the scene. It then looks up the index from the light index texture in screen space and uses that index to look up the light properties. An example of this lighting calculation is shown in Listing 2.5.

```
uniform sampler2D lightIndexTex, lightPositions,
  lightScales, lightColors, diffuseTex;

varying vec3 worldPosition;
varying vec2 diffuseTexCoord;
varying vec3 vertexWorldNormals;

vec3 doLightCalc(float lightId, vec3 worldNormal)
{
  // very simple lighting
  float lightScale = texture2D(lightScales, vec2(0.0, lightId)).x;
  vec3 lightPosition = texture2D(lightPositions, vec2(0.0,
      lightId)).rgb;
  vec3 lightColor = texture2D(lightColors, vec2(0.0,
      lightId)).rgb;

  vec3 lightDirection = normalize(lightPosition - worldPosition);
  float lightDist = distance(lightPosition, worldPosition);
  float invLightDist = max(lightScale - lightDist * 0.5, 0.0);

  float attenuation = 1.0 / lightDist;

  float ndl = clamp(dot(worldNormal, lightDirection), 0.0, 1.0);
  float attenuation2 = ndl * invLightDist * attenuation;

  return attenuation2 * lightColor;
}
```

Listing 2.5. Lighting calculations in light indexed deferred rendering.

```
void main()
{
 vec3 worldNormal = vertexWorldNormals;
 vec2 texCoord = gl_FragCoord.xy * pixelSize;

 vec3 diffuse = texture2D(diffuseTex, diffuseTexCoord).rgb;

 vec4 lightIndices = texture2D(lightIndexTex, texCoord);

 // Do a lighting calculation for each channel in the texture(s)
 // Not checking if a light index is valid means calculating some
 //   useless lighting calculations
 vec3 lightIntensity = doLightCalc(lightIndices.r, worldNormal);
 lightIntensity += doLightCalc(lightIndices.g, worldNormal);
 lightIntensity += doLightCalc(lightIndices.b, worldNormal);
 lightIntensity += doLightCalc(lightIndices.a, worldNormal);
 gl_FragColor = vec4(diffuse * lightIntensity, 0.0);
}
```

Listing 2.6. Scene rendering in light indexed deferred rendering.

The lighting is calculated for each channel in the current texture. With some GPU architectures it is often more optimal to do the lighting calculation for each channel even if it is not used. This is because branches in the shader will cause stalls in the pipeline. An example of calculating the lighting for a given pixel is shown in Listing 2.6.

Sorting lights. Light indexed rendering has a maximum number of lights per pixel that can be shown. If the number of lights per pixel exceeds this then the application needs to decide what to do. The application can have a maximum of as many lights per pixel as we can render to multiple textures. However, if this maximum is reached during execution, then lights will need to be discarded, throwing away the light influence of one or more lights from one frame to the next. In order to make this as un-noticeable as possible, the lights should be sorted so that the lights that take up the least screen space or are smallest in contribution to the final image are discarded first. There is also a possibility of joining multiple small lights into one larger one to reduce the number of lights per pixel.

This section has described how to use light indexed rendering in OpenGL ES 2.0 and 3.0; the next section describes how to optimize each of the techniques using OpenGL ES extensions.

2.4 OpenGL ES Extensions

This chapter has covered various deferred rendering techniques and how to implement them using OpenGL ES 2.0 and 3.0. Each of these APIs has various OpenGL ES extensions that may be utilized to optimize the techniques. This section describes how to utilize these extensions with some new techniques for deferred rendering. The extensions are

- GL_EXT_draw_buffers

- GL_EXT_shader_framebuffer_fetch

2.4.1 Draw Buffers

The draw buffers extension enables the ability to use multiple render targets in OpenGL ES 2.0. The API does not provide this functionality without the extension. The extension entry point `glDrawBuffersEXT()` works the same as `glDrawBuffers()` in OpenGL ES 3.0 and provides the same attachment indices. GLSL shaders that use this extension must declare so at the top of the GLSL source files:

```
#extension GL_EXT_draw_buffers : require
```

2.4.2 Framebuffer Fetch

The framebuffer fetch extension provides the contents of the framebuffer to GLSL using `gl_LastFragData[0]`, or by using the `inout` specifier when using OpenGL ES 3.0. Also named programmable blending, it allows the application to do custom blending equations to merge the incoming fragment color with the framebuffer color.

When using light indexed rendering the extension allows the application to avoid calling `glColorMask()` between rendering each set of lights. Instead, the application can perform custom blending in the fragment shader and avoid state changes.

```
gl_FragData[0] = vec4( lightIndex , gl_LastFragData[0].xyz );
```

Or, in OpenGL ES 3.0:

```
layout(location = 0) inout highp vec4 ioLightIndex;
void main() {
  ioLightIndex = vec4( lightIndex , ioLightIndex.xyz );
}
```

Technique	OpenGL ES 2.0	OpenGL ES 3.0	MSAA available
Deferred	N (Y with extensions)	Y	N
Light-pre pass	N (Y with extensions)	Y	N
Light indexed	Y	Y	Y

Table 2.1. Overview of which techniques are applicable to each API.

This is the equivalent of rendering the first set of lights in the red channel only, then the blue channel, etc. It assumes that none of the pixels rendered in each set overlap.

2.5   Conclusion and Future Work

This chapter has covered various techniques of rendering multiple, dynamic lights efficiently in OpenGL ES 2.0 and 3.0. Each technique has advantages and use-cases and this chapter has discussed the possibilities for using these techniques, allowing the reader to choose which techniques to utilize. Table 2.1 gives an overview of which techniques work with which APIs.

The framebuffer fetch extension is relatively new to the mobile graphics space. Further work on how to utilize this extension would be of use in future deferred rendering work. For example, this functionality could allow the use of alpha-blended objects in deferred rendering. There is also the possibility of using the currently unused alpha channels in both deferred and light pre-pass rendering for specular highlights.

Bibliography

[Calver 03] Dean Calver. "Photo-Realistic Deferred Lighting." White paper, http://www.beyond3d.com/content/articles/19, 2003.

[Engel 08] Wolfgang Engel. "Light Pre-Pass Renderer." http://diaryofa graphicsprogrammer.blogspot.co.uk/2008/03/light-pre-pass-renderer.html, March 16, 2008.

[Hargreaves and Harris 04] Shawn Hargreaves and Mark Harris. "Deferred Shading." Presentation, NVIDIA Developer Conference: 6800 Leagues Under the Sea, London, UK, June 29, 2004. Available online (https://developer.nvidia.com/sites/default/files/akamai/gamedev/docs/6800_Leagues_Deferred_Shading.pdf).

[Reinheart 13] Alfonse Reinheart. "Compute Eye Space from Window Space." Preprint, http://www.opengl.org/wiki/Compute_eye_space_from_window_space, 2013.

[Thibieroz 04] Nicolas Thibieroz. "Deferred Shading with Multiple Render Targets." In *ShaderX2: Shader Programming Tips & Tricks with DirectX 9*, edited by Wolfgang Engel, pp. 251–269. Plano, TX: Wordware Publishing, 2004.

[Treblico 09] Damian Treblico. "Light Indexed Deferred Rendering." In *ShaderX7: Advanced Rendering Techniques*, edited by Wolfgang Engel, Chapter 2.9. Boston: Charles River Media, 2009.

Bandwidth Efficient Graphics with ARM® Mali™ GPUs

Marius Bjørge

3.1 Introduction

GPUs in mobile devices today are becoming increasingly powerful. The biggest concern in the mobile space is battery life and one of the biggest consumers of battery is external memory access. Modern mobile games use post-processing effects in various ways and while the GPU itself is capable of doing this, the bandwidth available to the GPU is typically not.

A major strength of Mali and other tile-based architectures is that a lot of operations can be performed on-chip without having to access external memory. For an application to run efficiently on such architectures it is beneficial to try and keep the processing on-chip for as long as possible. Flushing tile-buffer data to a framebuffer that is subsequently read by sampling a texture can be expensive and consume a lot of bandwidth.

ARM have implemented extensions for OpenGL ES 2.0 and OpenGL ES 3.0 to reduce the requirement of accessing external memory for doing post-processing and other operations. This chapter introduces these extensions as well as use-cases for them.

3.2 Shader Framebuffer Fetch Extensions

The Mali-T600 series and Mali-400 series of GPUs support a fragment shader extension that allows applications to read existing framebuffer color, depth, and stencil of the current pixel being processed. Since the data is in the tile buffer, reading it is practically free and you avoid the bandwidth consuming write-read loop that otherwise would be required.

This section will introduce two extensions:

- GL_ARM_shader_framebuffer_fetch

- GL_ARM_shader_framebuffer_fetch_depth_stencil

3.2.1   GL_ARM_shader_framebuffer_fetch

This extension enables reading of the existing framebuffer color. This enables use-cases such as programmable blending and other operations that may not be possible to implement using fixed-function blending.

The extension is enabled by adding

```
#extension GL_ARM_shader_framebuffer_fetch : enable
```

to the very start of a fragment shader.

See Table 3.1 for a list of the built-in variables added by the extension and Listing 3.1 for a simple programmable blending example using the extension.

Variable	Type	Description
gl_LastFragColorARM	vec4	Reads the existing framebuffer color.

Table 3.1. New built-in variables introduced with the GL_ARM_shader_frame buffer_fetch extension.

```
#extension GL_ARM_shader_framebuffer_fetch : enable
precision mediump float;

uniform vec4 uBlend0;
uniform vec4 uBlend1;

void main(void)
{
  vec4 Color = gl_LastFragColorARM;

  Color = lerp(Color, uBlend0, Color.w * uBlend0.w);
  Color *= uBlend1;

  gl_FragColor = Color;
}
```

Listing 3.1. Programmable blending using GL_ARM_shader_framebuffer_fetch.

3.2.2 GL_ARM_shader_framebuffer_fetch_depth_stencil

This extension enables reading of the existing framebuffer depth and stencil values. This enables use-cases such as programmable depth/stencil testing, soft particles, and modulating shadows. It also offers applications a very convenient method of reconstructing 3D positions of any pixel on the screen.

The extension is enabled by adding

```
#extension GL_ARM_shader_framebuffer_fetch_depth_stencil : enable
```

to the very start of a fragment shader.

See Table 3.2 for a list of the built-in variables added by the extension and Listings 3.2 and 3.3 for example use-cases for this extension.

```glsl
#extension GL_ARM_shader_framebuffer_fetch_depth_stencil : enable
precision mediump float;

uniform float uTwoXNear;          // 2.0 * near
uniform float uFarPlusNear;       // far + near
uniform float uFarMinusNear;      // far - near
uniform float uInvParticleSize;

uniform sampler2D uParticleTexture;

varying float vLinearDepth;
varying vec2 vTexCoord;

void main(void)
{
    vec4 ParticleColor = texture2D(uParticleTexture, vTexCoord);

    // convert from exponential depth to linear
    float LinearDepth = uTwoXNear / (uFarPlusNear - ↩
        gl_LastFragDepthARM *
        uFarMinusNear);

    // compute blend weight by subtracting current fragment depth ↩
        with depth in depth buffer
    float Weight = clamp((LinearDepth - vLinearDepth) * ↩
        uInvParticleSize, 0.0, 1.0);

    // modulate with particle alpha
    ParticleColor.w *= Weight;

    gl_FragColor = ParticleColor;
}
```

Listing 3.2. Sample that uses depth read-back to render soft particles.

Variable	Type	Description
gl_LastFragDepthARM	float	Reads the existing framebuffer depth value.[a]
gl_LastFragStencilARM	int	Reads the existing framebuffer stencil value.

[a] The returned depth value is in window coordinate space.

Table 3.2. New built-in variables introduced with the GL_ARM_shader_framebuffer_fetch_depth_stencil extension.

```
#extension GL_ARM_shader_framebuffer_fetch_depth_stencil : enable
precision highp float;

uniform float uTwoXNear;      // 2.0 * near
uniform float uFarPlusNear;   // far + near
uniform float uFarMinusNear;  // far - near

vec2 pack16(float x)
{
  vec2 p;
  p.y = fract(x * 255.0);
  p.x = x - p.y / 255.0;
  return p;
}

void main(void)
{
  // convert from exponential depth to linear
  float Depth = uTwoXNear / (uFarPlusNear - gl_LastFragDepthARM *
     uFarMinusNear);

  // compute moments
  float m1 = Depth;
  float m2 = Depth * Depth;

  // store and pack for RGBA8 texture format
  gl_FragColor = vec4(pack16(m1), pack16(m2));
}
```

Listing 3.3. Sample that creates a variance shadow map [Donnelly and Lauritzen 06] in a single pass. The benefit of this approach is that there's no need to invoke the fragment shader while writing geometry to depth. This fragment shader is used as a final resolve shader to convert the depth into variance moments.

3.2.3   Limitations

These extensions have a couple of limitations:

- When multisampling is enabled the gl_LastFragColorARM, gl_LastFragDepthARM, and gl_LastFragStencilARM built-in variables will return a value that is between the minimum and maximum of the samples values.

- The GL_ARM_shader_framebuffer_fetch extension does not work with multiple render targets.

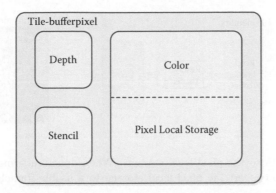

Figure 3.1. A pixel in the tile buffer. Note that color and pixel local storage are physically stored at the same location, so writing to one will overwrite the other. Also note that depth and stencil are separate from the pixel local storage data.

3.3 Shader Pixel Local Storage

The Mali-T600 series of GPUs support a fragment shader extension that can completely change how applications and games construct pixel data. The extension, which is only available for OpenGL ES 3.0, provides a mechanism for applications to pass information between fragment shader invocations covering the same pixel. This persistent data is stored in a format that is independent of the currently attached framebuffer. On the Mali-T600 series the pixel local storage size is 128 bits, which can be freely partitioned by the application. (See Figure 3.1.)

With Shader Pixel Local Storage an application can freely control the per fragment dataflow throughout the lifetime of a framebuffer. Figure 3.2 illustrates normal rendering behavior without pixel local storage.

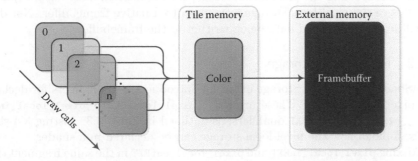

Figure 3.2. The rendered geometry overwrites the existing color value. This is what the pipeline normally looks like when rendering opaque geometry.

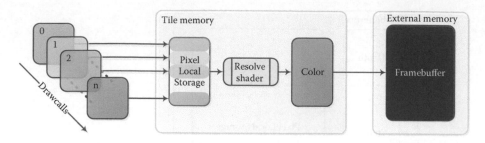

Figure 3.3. Each draw call adds data to the pixel local storage. When done rendering, the application must use a custom resolve shader to convert the pixel local storage to a usable framebuffer color. This needs to be done before end of frame.

Shader Pixel Local Storage changes this by allowing the application to store more data at each pixel fragment. With Shader Pixel Local Storage you no longer generate a pixel per fragment shader invocation. Instead, each pixel is the product of a queue of fragment shaders, which build up the result progressively, and rasterization is the means for describing the queue of fragment work. Figure 3.3 illustrates this by having multiple draw calls read and write to the pixel local storage.

3.3.1   Extension Usage

Shader Pixel Local Storage can be enabled and disabled by calling `glEnable` and `glDisable` with `GL_SHADER_PIXEL_LOCAL_STORAGE_EXT`.

The extension can be enabled in a fragment shader with

```
#extension GL_EXT_shader_pixel_local_storage : enable
```

Before disabling the pixel local storage, the application must ensure that the contents of the pixel local storage is resolved to a native framebuffer. Not doing so will lead to undefined data being written to the framebuffer.

3.3.2   Pixel Local Storage

The Shader Pixel Local Storage extension introduces new qualifiers for declaring the pixel local storage. These are the `__pixel_localEXT`, `__pixel_local_inEXT`, and `__pixel_local_outEXT` qualifiers, as outlined in Table 3.3. Listing 3.4 shows an example of how the pixel local storage can be declared in a shader.

Mixing `pixel_local_inEXT` and `pixel_local_outEXT` in the same fragment shader allows applications to process, reinterpret, and convert data between fragment shader invocations.

`__pixel_localEXT`	Storage can be read and written to.
`__pixel_local_inEXT`	Storage can be read from.
`__pixel_local_outEXT`	Storage can be written to.

Table 3.3. Qualifiers for declaring the pixel local storage.

```
__pixel_localEXT FragLocalData
{
  highp uint v0;
  highp uint v1;
  highp uint v2;
  highp uint v3;
} Storage;
```

Listing 3.4. Declaring a pixel local storage.

3.3.3 Layout Qualifiers

Layout qualifiers describe how the variable data is laid out in the underlying storage. Currently supported layout qualifiers are listed in Table 3.4. For a complete list of supported qualifiers, please see the extension specification [Khronos 14].

An implicit data conversion occurs when reading from or writing to a pixel local variable. When declaring a variable with a layout qualifier, the variable base type and number of components must match that of the qualifier; otherwise, a compiler error is produced.

Listings 3.5, 3.6, and 3.7 show some sample declarations using different data types.

Layout	Base Type
r32ui	uint (default)
r11f_g11f_b10f	vec3
r32f	float
rg16f	vec2
rgb10_a2	vec4
rgba8	vec4
rg16	vec2
rgba8i	ivec4
rg16i	ivec2
rgb10_a2ui	uvec4
rgba8ui	uvec4
rg16ui	uvec2

Table 3.4. Supported layout qualifiers.

```
__pixel_localEXT FragLocalData
{
  highp uint v0; // all of these will use the
  highp uint v1; // default r32ui layout.
  highp uint v2;
} Storage;
```

Listing 3.5. All variables will use the default **r32ui** storage layout.

```
layout(r32f) __pixel_localEXT FragLocalData
{
  highp float v0; // all of these will inherit the r32f layout
  highp float v1; // from the local storage declaration.
  highp float v2;
} Storage;
```

Listing 3.6. All variables will inherit the **r32f** storage layout.

```
__pixel_localEXT FragLocalData
{
  layout(r11f_g11f_b10f) vec3 v0;
  layout(r32ui) uint v1;
  layout(rg16) vec2 v2;
              vec2 v3; // v3 will inherit from the previously
                       // defined layout qualifier (rg16).
} Storage;
```

Listing 3.7. Multiple storage layouts used together.

3.3.4 Usage Patterns

There are multiple ways to use this extension.

Pixel local storage. This example uses the Shader Pixel Local Storage to do all the rendering.

1. Clear framebuffer to 0.

2. Call `glEnable(GL_SHADER_PIXEL_LOCAL_STORAGE_EXT)`.

3. Do operations on the pixel local storage by rendering geometry, etc.

4. Resolve from pixel local storage to one or more user-defined fragment shader outputs.

5. Call `glDisable(GL_SHADER_PIXEL_LOCAL_STORAGE_EXT)`.

6. Call `eglSwapbuffer`.

Combined rendering. This example shows how an application can combine the use of pixel local storage with a normal rendering pipeline.

1. Begin frame with normal rendering by just writing color to a user-defined fragment shader output.

2. Call `glEnable(GL_SHADER_PIXEL_LOCAL_STORAGE_EXT)`.

3. Get the current framebuffer color by using the `GL_ARM_shader_framebuffer` `_fetch` extension and store value in the pixel local storage.

4. Do more operations on the pixel local storage by rendering geometry, etc.

5. Resolve from the pixel local storage to a user-defined fragment shader output.

6. Call `glDisable(GL_SHADER_PIXEL_LOCAL_STORAGE_EXT)`.

7. Continue rendering with shaders that write to one or more user-defined fragment shader outputs. Render alpha-blended geometry, GUI, etc.

8. Call `eglSwapbuffer`.

3.3.5 Limitations

The extension has the following limitations:

- When writing to pixel local storage, the value of the framebuffer pixel covered by that fragment becomes undefined.

- When writing to any user-defined fragment output, the pixel local storage values for that fragment become undefined.

- Multiple render targets is not supported while pixel local storage is enabled.

- Multisampling is not supported.

- Blending is not supported.

3.4 Deferred Shading Example

Techniques such as deferred shading [Hargreaves and Harris 04] are typically implemented using multiple render targets by rendering the required intermediate data and then sampling from this data using textures. While flexible, this approach consumes a large amount of external memory bandwidth.

Since the deferred shading data is often only written to and read by shaders executing on the same pixel position, the Shader Pixel Local Storage extension can offer a more efficient alternative by keeping the data on-chip. This allows large amounts of data to be kept per-pixel, with zero external memory bandwidth impact.

The Shader Pixel Local Storage extension can be used to implement deferred shading in a way very similar to the classic multiple render target based approach. In this section we look at what such an implementation might look like.

The implementation can be split up into three rendering steps:

1. render geometry,

2. light accumulation,

3. resolve.

3.4.1 Step 1: Render Geometry

This step is implemented almost the same way as the classic approach using multiple render targets. The only difference is that we write everything to the pixel local storage. This means that existing code can often be easily ported to make use of this extension. (See Listing 3.8.)

```
#version 300 es
#extension GL_EXT_shader_pixel_local_storage : enable

precision mediump float;

__pixel_local_outEXT FragData
{
  layout(r11f_g11f_b10f) mediump vec3 Color;
  layout(rgb10_a2) mediump vec4 Normal;
  layout(r11f_g11f_b10f) mediump vec3 Lighting;
} gbuf;

in mediump vec2 vTexCoord;
in mediump vec3 vNormal;
uniform mediump sampler2D uDiffuse;

void main(void)
{
  // store diffuse color
  gbuf.Color = texture(uDiffuse, vTexCoord).xyz;

  // store normal vector
  gbuf.Normal = vec4(normalize(vNormal) * 0.5 + 0.5, 0.0);

  // reserve and set lighting to 0
  gbuf.Lighting = vec3(0.0);
}
```

Listing 3.8. Example code that initializes the pixel local storage with G-buffer data.

3.4.2 Step 2: Light Accumulation

This step makes use of both the Shader Pixel Local Storage extension and the depth/stencil fetch extension to compute the light contribution of each light. The lights are rendered with depth test enabled and depth writes off. (See Listing 3.9.)

```
#version 300 es
#extension GL_EXT_shader_pixel_local_storage : enable
#extension GL_ARM_shader_framebuffer_fetch_depth_stencil : enable

precision mediump float;

__pixel_localEXT FragData
{
  layout(r11f_g11f_b10f) mediump vec3 Color;
  layout(rgb10_a2) mediump vec4 Normal;
  layout(r11f_g11f_b10f) mediump vec3 Lighting;
} gbuf;

uniform mat4 uInvViewProj;
uniform vec2 uInvViewport;
uniform vec3 uLightPos;
uniform vec3 uLightColor;
uniform float uInvLightRadius;

void main(void)
{
  vec4 ClipCoord;
  ClipCoord.xy = gl_FragCoord.xy * uInvViewport;
  ClipCoord.z = gl_LastFragDepthARM;
  ClipCoord.w = 1.0;
  ClipCoord = ClipCoord * 2.0 - 1.0;

  // Transform to world space
  vec4 WorldPos = ClipCoord * uInvViewProj;
  WorldPos /= WorldPos.w;

  vec3 LightVec = WorldPos.xyz - uLightPos;
  float fDist = length(LightVec);
  LightVec /= fDist;

  // unpack normal from pixel local storage
  vec3 normal = gbuf.Normal.xyz * 2.0 - 1.0;

  // Compute light attenuation factor
  float fAtt = clamp(1.0 - fDist * uInvLightRadius, 0.0, 1.0);
  float NdotL = clamp(dot(LightVec, normal), 0.0, 1.0);

  // compute and add light value back to pixel local gbuf storage
  gbuf.Lighting += uLightColor * NdotL * fAtt;
}
```

Listing 3.9. Accumulate light contribution by rendering light geometry.

```
#version 300 es
#extension GL_EXT_shader_pixel_local_storage : enable

precision mediump float;

__pixel_local_inEXT FragData
{
  layout(r11f_g11f_b10f) mediump vec3 Color;
  layout(rgb10_a2) mediump vec4 Normal;
  layout(r11f_g11f_b10f) mediump vec3 Lighting;
} gbuf;

// Declare fragment shader output.
// Writing to it effectively clears the contents of
// the pixel local storage.
out vec4 FragColor;

void main(void)
{
  // read diffuse and lighting values from pixel local gbuf ↵
      storage
  vec3 diffuse = gbuf.Color;
  vec3 lighting = gbuf.Lighting;

  // write contents to FragColor. This will effectively write
  // the color data to the native framebuffer format of the
  // currently attached color attachment
  FragColor = diffuse * lighting;
}
```

Listing 3.10. This example code resolves the contents of the pixel local storage to the native framebuffer format. This is a very simple shader that modulates the data in the pixel local storage and writes it to a fragment shader output.

3.4.3   Step 3: Resolve Everything

This step is similar to classic deferred shading implementations we also need to resolve the pixel local storage to store the color data in the native framebuffer format. (See Listing 3.10.)

3.4.4   Bandwidth Numbers

The example deferred shading implementation has very different bandwidth usage when compared to a conventional multiple render target implementation. As Figure 3.4 shows, using the extensions saves as much as 9× total read and write bandwidth per frame. This also translates into reduced power consumption and longer battery life, which is very important in mobile devices. Table 3.5 shows a further breakdown of the graph. The multiple render target implementation is set up as follows:

- RGBA10_A2 for albedo with D24S8 depth/stencil,
- RGBA10_A2 for normals,
- RGBA10_A2 for lighting.

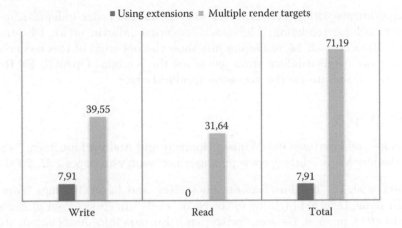

Figure 3.4. External bandwidth comparison for deferred shading implementations. Assuming 1080p resolution with 32-bit framebuffer and D24S8 depth/stencil.

	Extensions		MRT	
	Read	Write	Read	Write
Fill G-buffer	0 MB	0 MB	0 MB	23.73 MB
Light accumulation	0 MB	0 MB	15.82 MB	7.91 MB
Resolve	0 MB	7.91 MB	15.82 MB	7.91 MB
Totals	0 MB	7.91 MB	31.64 MB	39.55 MB

Table 3.5. Breakdown of graph data showing a 9× bandwidth reduction.

Note: Read data for lighting is approximated since this depends on coverage and overdraw. This is isolated to only framebuffer bandwidth and does not take into account texture lookups for diffuse and normal when filling the G-buffer. It does not take into account bandwidth consumed by vertex shader reads/writes and fragment shader varying reads since that will be similar on both implementations.

3.5 Conclusion

We introduced extensions that allow applications to reduce the need to access external memory. Reducing external memory access can not only increase performance, but also increase battery life. Use-cases such as programmable blending and reading of depth/stencil can enable applications to allow more work to be done in on-chip memory. The novel Shader Pixel Local Storage extension gives applications even more control of the per-pixel data in tile-enabling use-cases such as deferred shading.

Experiments with other use-cases such as limited order independent transparency, volume rendering, Lightstack rendering [Martin et al. 13], and Forward+ [Harada et al. 12] rendering just show the potential of this technology.

For more detailed information please see the Khronos OpenGL ES Registry [Khronos 14] website for the extension specifications.

Bibliography

[Donnelly and Lauritzen 06] William Donnelly and Andrew Lauritzen. "Variance Shadow Maps." http://www.punkuser.net/vsm/vsm_paper.pdf, 2006.

[Harada et al. 12] Takahiro Harada, Jay McKee, and Jason C. Yang. "Forward+: Bringing Deferred Lighting to the Next Level ." In *Proceedings of Eurographics 2012*, pp. 5–8. Geneva, Switzerland: Eurographics Association, 2012.

[Hargreaves and Harris 04] Shawn Hargreaves and Mark Harris. "Deferred Shading." Presentation, NVIDIA Developer Conference: 6800 Leagues Under the Sea, London, UK, June 29, 2004. Available online (http://http.download.nvidia.com/developer/presentations/2004/6800_Leagues/6800_Leagues_Deferred_Shading.pdf).

[Khronos 14] Khronos. "OpenGL ES Registry." http://www.khronos.org/registry/gles/, 2014.

[Martin et al. 13] Sam Martin, Marius Bjorge, Sandeep Kakalapudi, and Jan-Harald Fredriksen. "Challenges with High Quality Mobile Graphics ." In *ACM SIGGRAPH 2013 Mobile*, p. Article no. 7. New York: ACM, 2013.

Efficient Morph Target Animation Using OpenGL ES 3.0

James L. Jones

4.1 Introduction

Demand for impressive graphics in mobile apps has given rise to ever-more powerful GPUs and new graphics APIs such as OpenGL ES 3.0. These advances enable programmers to write cleaner and more efficient implementations of computer graphics algorithms than ever before. One particular area that stands to benefit is the facial animation of characters in mobile games, a technique that is commonly implemented using morph targets.

Morph target animation requires artists to pre-create multiple poses of a model offline. Later on, during application execution, these poses are mixed together in varying quantities to create animation sequences such as blinking eyes or a frowning face. When used in conjunction with skinning, the technique can serve as the foundation of a feature-rich character animation system. Historically, morph target animation has seen heavy use in PC and console games but a lack of flexibility in earlier graphics APIs has led to complicated or expensive implementations on mobile platforms. This chapter describes an efficient implementation of morph target animation that makes use of the transform-feedback API introduced in OpenGL ES 3.0. The application in this chapter is a continuation of the Gremlin demo, which was first introduced in a previous article [Senior 09]. The demo has been entirely rewritten and has been updated to take advantage of OpenGL ES 3.0 on PowerVR Series6 mobile GPUs.

4.2 Previous Work

An interesting geometry texturing approach was suggested for mobile GPUs that made use of the OpenGL ES 2.0 API [Senior 09]. This approach used a vertex encoding scheme to store vertex displacements between target poses in textures.

The morphing procedure would be performed entirely on textures bound to frame-buffer objects, with the final texture then being used to displace mesh vertices using vertex texture fetch operations. There are problems with this approach, most notably the fact that the maximum number of texture units provided by a platform is allowed to be zero [Munshi and Leech , pp. 40–41]. This means that on some platforms an alternative approach would need to be used. Transform-feedback functionality, which is standardized in OpenGL ES 3.0, allows for a simpler implementation and removes the need for wasteful vertex texture encoding and decoding operations.

4.3   Morph Targets

Morph target animation is used in cases where many small, per-vertex changes need to be applied to a model. This is in contrast to large, sweeping motions normally handled by skeletal animation systems. A good use-case for morph targets is the animation of facial muscles required to create believable facial expressions for video game characters. (See Figure 4.1.)

An implementation typically operates on multiple versions of a stored mesh, known as target poses or key poses. These poses are stored in conjunction with a base pose, which serves as a representation of the animation in a neutral state. To create different animation sequences, the position of each mesh vertex is blended with one or more target poses using a weight vector. The components of this vector are associated with a corresponding target pose and denote how much this target pose influences the result.

To be able to blend between target poses, a difference mesh is used. This is a mesh that is created for each target pose that gives the per-vertex difference between the target pose and the base pose [Senior 09, Lorach 08]. These difference

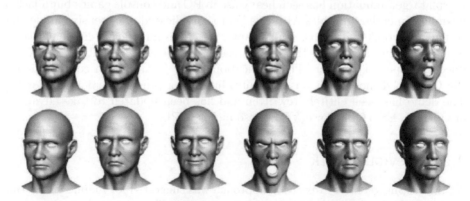

Figure 4.1. Multiple target poses showing a range of facial expressions.

vectors are used as bases in a vector space (i.e., each vertex in an output mesh can be constructed by taking a linear combination of these bases using a weight vector). More precisely, for each output vertex v_i at time t in N morph targets with base target vertex b_i, weight vector w, and target pose vertex p_i, we have

$$v_i(t) = b_i + \sum_{k=0}^{N} w_k(t) \cdot (p_{k,i} - b_i).$$

The formula above summarizes all that is necessary for a morph target implementation. However, for many scenes, it is often the case that only some of the total possible weights change every frame. Because of this, we want to avoid wastefully re-calculating the entire contribution from all target poses every frame. A better idea is to instead keep track of the changes in the weight vector along with the current pose in memory. For a change in frame time h, the new position is equal to the current pose position plus the change in this position:

$$v_i(t + h) = v_i(t) + \Delta_h[v_i](t).$$

We also see that the per-frame change in the position depends only on the per-frame changes in the weights:

$$\Delta_h[v_i](t) = \sum_{k=0}^{N} \Delta_h[w_k](t) \cdot (p_{k,i} - b_i).$$

Using this information, we develop an approach where we only need to compute and update the pose with the per-frame contribution for weights that have changed, i.e., when $\Delta_h[w_k](t) \neq 0$.

4.4 Implementation

This implementation uses vertex buffers that are bound to a transform feedback object to store and update the current pose across frames. Unfortunately, OpenGL ES 3.0 prevents reading and writing to the same buffer simultaneously so a secondary vertex buffer is used to ping-pong the current pose (i.e., the output buffer is swapped with the input buffer every frame). The difference meshes are computed in a pre-processing pass by iterating through the vertices and subtracting the base pose. Sensible starting values are loaded into the feedback vertex buffers (in this case the base pose is used). Every frame, we update the current pose in the vertex buffers using the changes in the weights. This update can be performed with or without batching. Finally, we render the contents of the updated vertex buffer as usual. We perform the computation on vertex normals in the same fashion as vertex positions; this gives us correctly animated normals for rendering. (See Figure 4.2.)

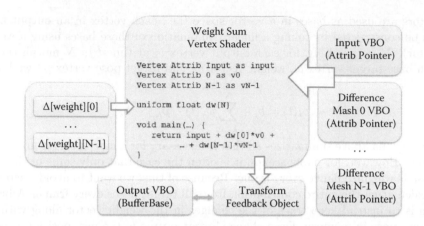

Figure 4.2. Technique overview.

4.4.1   Pose Update

Before we update the pose, we must first compute the changes in the weights. The following pseudo code illustrates how this can be done.

```
// Inputs:
// w[]  : current frame weight vector
// p[]  : previous frame weight vector
// dw[] : delta weight vector

// Per-Frame Weight Update:
animate(w)
for i = 0 to length(w):
    dw[i] = w[i] - p[i]
    p[i] = w[i]
```

Using the delta weights we can now check to see what components of the weight vector have changed. For those weights that have changed, do a transform feedback pass using the key-pose.

```
// Inputs:
// q[]  : array of difference mesh VBOs
// dw[] : delta weight vector
// vbo[]: array of vertex buffer objects for storing current
//        pose
// tfo  : transform feedback object
// shader : shader program for accumulation

// Per-Frame Pose Update:
glBindTransformFeedback(tfo)
glEnable(RASTERIZER_DISCARD)
```

```
glUseProgram(shader)
for(i = 0, i < length(q), i++):
    // Only for weights that have changed...
    if (abs(dw[i]) != 0):
        // Set the weight uniform
        glUniform1f(..., dw[i])
        // Bind the output VBO to TBO
        glBindBufferBase(GL_TRANSFORM_FEEDBACK_BUFFER,0,vbo[1])
        // Bind the inputs to vertex shader
        glBindBuffer(GL_ARRAY_BUFFER,vbo[0])
        glVertexAttribPointer(ATTRIBUTE_STREAM_0,...)
        glBindBuffer(GL_ARRAY_BUFFER,q[i])
        glVertexAttribPointer(ATTRIBUTE_STREAM_1,...)
        // Draw call performs per-vertex accumulation in vertex
        // shader.
        glEnableTransformFeedback()
        glDrawArrays(...)
        glDisableTransformFeedback()
        // Vertices for rendering are referenced with vbo[0]
        swap(vbo[0],vbo[1])
```

4.4.2 Batching

For efficiency, further improvements can be made. In this version, updates are batched together into fewer passes. Instead of passing in the attributes and weight uniform for one pose at a time, we can instead use a vertex shader that processes multiple key-poses per update pass. We then perform the update with as few passes as possible.

```
// Inputs:
// q[] : difference mesh VBOs, where corresponding dw != 0
// vbo[] : array of vertex buffer objects for storing current
//         pose
// dw[] : delta weight vector
// shader[] : shader programs for each batch size up to b
// b : max batch size

// Per-Frame Batched Pose Update:
// ... Similar setup as before ...
for(i = 0, i < length(q), ):
    k = min(length(q),i+b) - i
    glUseProgram(shader[k])
    glBindBufferBase(GL_TRANSFORM_FEEDBACK_BUFFER,0,vbo[1])
    // Bind attributes for pass
    for(j = 0, j < b, j++):
        if (j < k):
            glEnableVertexAttribArray(ATTRIBUTE_STREAM_1+j)
            glBindBuffer(GL_ARRAY_BUFFER,q[i+j])
            glVertexAttribPointer(ATTRIBUTE_STREAM_1+j,...)
        else:
            glDisableVertexAttribArray(ATTRIBUTE_STREAM_1+j)
    // Set the delta weights
    glUniform1fv(...)
    // Bind current pose as input and draw
    glEnableVertexAttribArray(ATTRIBUTE_STREAM_0)
    glBindBuffer(GL_ARRAY_BUFFER,vbo[0])
```

```
glVertexAttribPointer ( ATTRIBUTE_STREAM_0 ,...)
glEnableTransformFeedback ()
glDrawArrays (...)
glDisableTransformFeedback()
swap ( vbo [0] , vbo [1])
i = i + k
```

This technique requires multiple versions of the shader where each version executes the summation on incrementally more input attributes up until the maximum batch size. It is important to note that the maximum number of input attributes available is limited by the API. This value (which must be at least 16) can be retrieved by querying `glGetIntegerv` with the argument `GL_MAX_VERTEX_ATTRIBS`.

4.4.3   Results

While gathering the data for the graph in Figure 4.3, a maximum batch size of seven targets was used (batch size indicates the number of additions being performed in the vertex shader). The demo was executed multiple times for varying batch sizes. For each run the average frame rate was taken.

These results show that batching the passes reduces the overhead cost of redrawing the geometry during the animation update. Depending on the number of targets used during a given frame, an adequately large batch size should be chosen to reduce this cost.

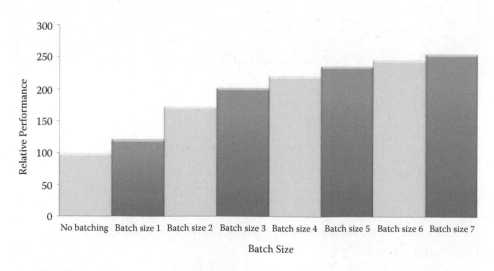

Figure 4.3. Relative performance against batch size when running the demo app.

4.5 Conclusion

This chapter has demonstrated an efficient morph target animation system using transform-feedback. The technique can be computed as a separate pass before rendering, and additional techniques such as skinning can be easily implemented on top of this system.

4.6 Acknowledgements

I would like to thank my colleagues Ken Catterall, Kristof Beets, and Peter Quayle of Imagination Technologies for their consistent support and encouragement.

Bibliography

[Lorach 08] Tristan Lorach. "DirectX 10 Blend Shapes: Breaking the Limits." In *GPU Gems 3*, edited by Hubert Nguyen, pp. 53–67. Upper Saddle River, NJ: Addison-Wesley, 2008.

[Munshi and Leech] Aaftab Munshi and Jon Leech, editors. *OpenGL ES Common Profile Specification*. Khronos Group Inc.

[Senior 09] Andrew Senior. "Facial Animation for Mobile GPUs." In *ShaderX7: Advanced Rendering Techniques*, edited by Wolfgang Engel, pp. 561–569. Boston: Charles River Media, 2009.

Tiled Deferred Blending

Ramses Ladlani

5.1 Introduction

Desktop and mobile GPUs are designed with very different goals in mind. While the former mainly focuses on performance, the latter must strive for controlled power consumption. This directly impacts the memory bandwidth, which often constitutes the main performance bottleneck on mobile devices, especially when using fillrate intensive effects such as alpha blending.

Some GPU manufacturers have come up with designs centered around a tile-based architecture (e.g., Imagination Technologies PowerVR, ARM Mali, Qualcomm Adreno) allowing for a fraction of the original bandwidth to be used. On those *tile-based renderers* (TBR), the blending operation in itself is very cheap because it is entirely performed using the on-chip memory [Merry 12].

Other manufacturers, such as NVIDIA and its Tegra family of SoCs, have opted for a more traditional *immediate mode rendering* (IMR). On those systems, the read-modify-write cycle to the framebuffer required by alpha blending places a significant additional burden on the memory system, and it is of critical importance to use it sparingly while trying to minimize overdraw [NVIDIA 13].

This discrepancy between platform capabilities provides an extra challenge for developers to offer a similar and interesting experience to the end users.

This chapter describes a technique that has been developed at Fishing Cactus while porting *After Burner Climax* from Xbox360/PS3 onto mobile (iOS and Android) to efficiently support effects with lots of alpha blending (e.g., the clouds seen during level transitions) on all the target platforms. Figure 5.1 shows some screenshots showcasing this effect.

The basic idea behind the technique is to leverage the programmability of OpenGL ES 2 and the multiple texture units available on those devices to render several layers of transparency at once with minimal overdraw. The grouping scheme is somewhat inspired by *tiled shading techniques* where lights affecting a scene are bucketed into screen-space tiles [Pranckevičius 12, Olsson and Assarsson 11] so that they can be rendered more efficiently later. This tech-

Figure 5.1. Cloud level transitions in *After Burner Climax* (iOS).

nique is essentially the application of the "use multi-texturing instead of multiple passes" [Apple 13b] recommendation to the blending problem.

While being a natural fit for rendering particle systems, this method is generic enough to be used for rendering any combination of transparent textured quads (e.g., sprites, interface elements). The main goal of the technique is to optimize memory bandwidth consumed by blending operations, but it also provides a good opportunity to reduce the number of batches sent to the GPU.

In the following sections, we will briefly outline the algorithm before peeking into more details about its implementation. This will be followed by a section focusing on some optimizations and we will end with a discussion around the results obtained with the proposed solution.

5.2   Algorithm

The algorithm is based on a division of the rendering area into smaller screen-space tiles. Tile layouts are discussed in Section 5.3.1.

Once a layout has been defined, the general algorithm can be summarized in the following steps (see Figure 5.2).

1. Project vertices on CPU to find the screen-space extent of each sprite quad.

2. For each quad, find intersecting tiles and store their ID in each affected cell.

3. (optional) Optimize grid by grouping compatible cells (see Section 5.4.1).

4. For each tile, compute required information to render aggregated sprites.

5. For each non empty tile, for each fragment use interpolated texture coordinates to sample bound textures and blend results manually.

First, the sprites vertices are transformed on the CPU to figure out where they will land on screen after projection. Once the screen-space positions are known, we can compute, for each tile, the list of sprites affecting it. The lack of compute shader on OpenGL ES forces us to make all those computations on CPU.

For complex scenes containing lots of sprites to blend together, SIMD instructions (e.g., ARM NEON[1] Instruction Set) provide a good opportunity to reduce the extra CPU overhead induced by the technique. Libraries[2] are available to get you started quickly.

After having computed the list of sprites affecting each tile, we can, for each cell and for each sprite, compute the texture coordinate transform that will transform the tile texture coordinates into those of each sprite it aggregates. Those 3×2 transform matrices (2D rotation + translation) will be passed later as uniforms to the vertex shader.

Finally, the render phase itself simply consists in rendering the tiles, one at a time, using the interpolated texture coordinates to sample each texture (the same texture can be bound to several samplers if desired) and to blend the intermediate results manually, respecting the transparency order.

An optional optimization phase (step 3) can take place after building the per-tile sprite lists and before computing the extrapolated texture coordinates; this optimization consists in merging together cells that share the exact same sprites, thus lowering the number of primitives sent to the GPU.

---

[1]ARM is a registered trademark of ARM Limited (or its subsidiaries) in the EU and/or elsewhere. NEON is a trademark of ARM Limited (or its subsidiaries) in the EU and/or elsewhere. All rights reserved.

[2]https://code.google.com/p/math-neon/

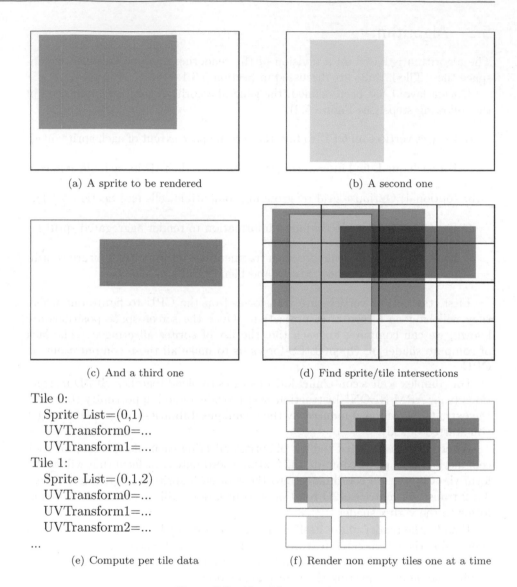

(a) A sprite to be rendered

(b) A second one

(c) And a third one

(d) Find sprite/tile intersections

Tile 0:
   Sprite List=(0,1)
   UVTransform0=...
   UVTransform1=...
Tile 1:
   Sprite List=(0,1,2)
   UVTransform0=...
   UVTransform1=...
   UVTransform2=...
...

(e) Compute per tile data

(f) Render non empty tiles one at a time

Figure 5.2. Algorithm overview.

5.3   Implementation

5.3.1   Tile Layout

Choosing the right tile layout is crucial for achieving good performance; a good choice depends heavily on the positioning and size of the sprites to be rendered.

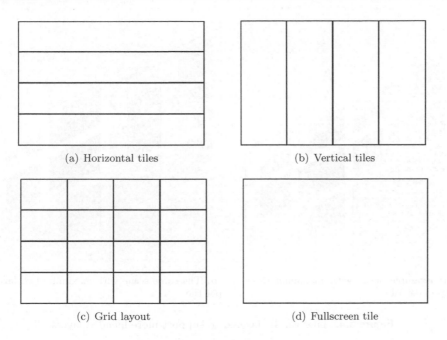

(a) Horizontal tiles   (b) Vertical tiles

(c) Grid layout   (d) Fullscreen tile

Figure 5.3. Different tile layouts.

Make the tiles too big compared to the underlying geometry and too many fragments will unnecessarily be shaded (using a stencil can come in handy here as
described in Section 5.4.3).

A good layout is a layout that minimizes partially covered tiles (fully transparent fragments) and that keeps the number of draw calls as low as possible.
Depending on the number of sprites to be rendered, a well-chosen layout can even
help reduce the total draw call count considerably (in the best case, up to eight
times fewer draw calls on current gen mobile GPUs).

Simple useful common layouts include vertical slices, horizontal slices, the
grid, or even the single fullscreen tile as demonstrated in Figure 5.3.

In Section 5.4.1, we describe a simple approach to dynamically reduce the
number of tiles to be rendered.

5.3.2 Supporting More Layers

When the number of sprites to blend in a single tile is above the maximum it can
hold (see Section 5.3.4), new screen-space tiles can be instantiated as required at
the exact same position to support the extra layers to blend. Figure 5.4 shows
how a second tile layer was added to support the example scene if each tile could
only blend two layers.

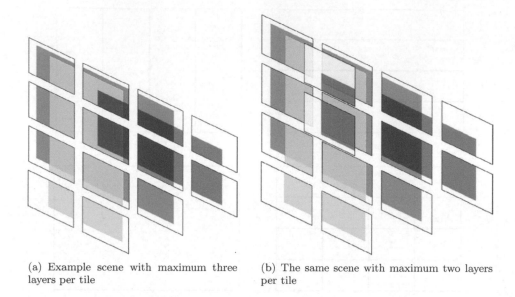

(a) Example scene with maximum three layers per tile

(b) The same scene with maximum two layers per tile

Figure 5.4. Tiles can be layered to support more blended layers.

5.3.3   Sprite-Tile intersection

The relatively low complexity of our tile layout in *After Burner Climax* (eight vertical tiles) and the small amount of clouds to render (a few dozens) allowed us to use a simple (SIMD) axis aligned rectangle-rectangle intersection test on CPU with no performance problem.

When using a higher density grid, it could prove to be useful to use a rasterization strategy as suggested by [Olsson and Assarsson 11] in the context of tiled shading. This would also allow for arbitrary shapes to be used instead of just regular quads.

5.3.4   Rendering

The number of layers aggregated by each tile is only limited by the number of texture units and the number of interpolators supported by the device.[3] For the sake of the example, we will consider a maximum of eight varyings and eight texture units for the rest of this chapter (these values match current generation devices such as the iPhone5 equipped with a PowerVR SGX 543 [Apple 13a]).

To reduce unnecessary work when not all possible layers are being used, we select among eight different programs (one for each number of blended layers

---

[3]Calling `glGet()` with `GL_MAX_VARYING_VECTORS` and `GL_MAX_TEXTURE_IMAGE_UNITS` retrieves those values.

supported by the tile). This not only lowers the amount of computations to perform, it also diminishes the number of texture fetches as well as the number of interpolators being used.

The rendering phase uses a single static vertex buffer object (VBO) and performs a draw call for each non empty tile to be rendered.

By first sorting the tiles by the number of aggregated layers (1 to 8), we also minimize the number of `glUseProgram()` calls.

1. Sort tiles by number of layers being used.

2. For $i = 1$ to 8,

   (a) enable program corresponding to i blended layers;
   (b) for each tile,
       i. set uniforms,
       ii. bind textures,
       iii. render tile quad.

The uniforms being used by the program are the following as follows:

- `uPositionTransform`: A `vec4` containing the scaling and offset to apply to the positions in the VBO to properly position the tile on screen.

- `uCoordinateTransformX/Y`: Two tables of eight `vec3`, each pair representing a 3×2 matrix (2D rotation followed by a translation) used to transform the tile "unit" texture coordinates into layer coordinates.

The vertex shader is shown in Listing 5.1 and uses the aforementioned uniforms to transform the (static) attributes of the VBO and pass them as varyings to the fragment shader. A preprocessor define directive is used to ease the management of the multiple programs; each program is compiled with `LAYER_COUNT` being defined to a value ranging from 1 to 8.[4]

The fragment shader shown in Listing 5.2 is not a lot more complex. It basically samples all textures, carefully avoiding dependent texture reads by not using `.zw` components to fetch texture data [Imagination Technologies 12], and performs the blending manually. This manual blending offers the possibility, if desired, to implement more exotic blending modes than the regular lerp.

Again, `LAYER_COUNT` is used for controlling the number of layers blended by the program.

You might have noticed that the blending formula assumes premultiplied alpha. Premultiplied textures provide lots of desirable properties (e.g., blending

---

[4]To keep reasonable performances on the iPhone 4S (iOS 6.0.1), we had to unroll the fragment shader loop manually.

```
multiple_draw_call_VS ]
attribute vec2
  Position ,
  TextureCoordinates ;

uniform mediump vec4
  uPositionTransform ;
uniform mediump vec3
  uCoordinateTransformX [ LAYER_COUNT ] ,
  uCoordinateTransformY [ LAYER_COUNT ];

varying mediump vec2
  vTextureCoordinates [ LAYER_COUNT ];

void main ()
{
  gl_Position.xy =
    Position.xy * uPositionTransform.xy + uPositionTransform.zw;
  gl_Position.zw = vec2( 0.0, 1.0 );
  mediump vec3 texcoord = vec3( TextureCoordinates , 1.0 );
  for( int i = 0; i < LAYER_COUNT; i++ )
  {
    vTextureCoordinates [i].x =
      dot( uCoordinateTransformX [i] , texcoord );
    vTextureCoordinates [i].y =
      dot( uCoordinateTransformY [i] , texcoord );
  }
}
```

Listing 5.1. The vertex shader.

associativity) [Forsyth 06], but care must still be taken to preserve transparency order. The previous shader assumes that we have sorted the transparent layers back to front.

```
varying mediump vec2
  vTextureCoordinates [ LAYER_COUNT ];

uniform sampler2D
  Textures [ LAYER_COUNT ];

void main ()
{
  mediump vec4 result = vec4( 0.0, 0.0, 0.0, 0.0 );

  for( int i = 0; i < LAYER_COUNT; i++ )
  {
    mediump vec4 contribution =
      texture2D( Textures [i] , vTextureCoordinates [i] );
    result = contribution + ( 1.0 - contribution.a ) * result;
  }

  gl_FragColor = result;
}
```

Listing 5.2. Multiple draw call fragment shader.

5.3.5 Sampler Configuration

The above shader works fine when setting the samplers' wrap modes to `GL_CLAMP` `_TO_EDGE` and when using textures that have a fully transparent border. If this is not the case (or if repeat mode is required), the shader must take care of discarding the layer contribution if it falls out of the accepted range. The following is an example on how to discard values outside the $[0.0, 1.0]$ range.

```
contribution =
  texture2D( Textures[i], vTextureCoordinates[i] );
result = contribution + ( 1.0 - contribution.a ) * result;
result *= step( 0.0, vTextureCoordinates[i].x );
result *= step( vTextureCoordinates[i].x, 1.0 );
result *= step( 0.0, vTextureCoordinates[i].y );
result *= step( vTextureCoordinates[i].y, 1.0 );
```

5.3.6 Simulating Depth

If depth testing is required, it needs to be handled manually because we are now rendering screen-space tiles. After binding the depth texture and sampling it in the fragment shader, it is now possible to compare the depth value to each tile's depth (passed in as an extra vertex attribute) in order to modulate the intermediate results using a call to `step()`. Compared to regular blending, the depth buffer needs to be sampled only once per pixel (per screen-space tile affecting it) instead of once per primitive.

```
mediump float depth;
depth = texture2D( DepthTexture, tileTextureCoordinates.xy );

// ...

contribution =
  texture2D( Textures[ i ], vTextureCoordinates[i] );
result = contribution + ( 1.0 - contribution.a ) * result;
result *= step( vTextureCoordinates[i].z, depth );
```

Using `gl_FragCoord` to compute the coordinates to sample the depth textures would result in a dependent texture fetch; a better solution consists of passing the screen-space coordinates as varyings.

From here, we can get soft particles almost for free by using an alpha ramp instead of the previous `step()` function.

For all this to work, the device must of course support depth textures (`OES_` `depth_texture` extension).

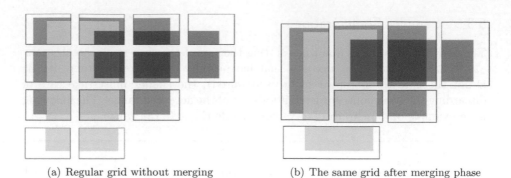

(a) Regular grid without merging   (b) The same grid after merging phase

Figure 5.5. Adaptive tile layout.

5.4   Optimizations

5.4.1   Minimize Number of Batches

Adaptive tile layout. The initial tile layout can be optimized dynamically by analyzing it to merge adjacent compatible cells together (see Figure 5.5). Two tiles are compatible if they share the same list of aggregated sprites.

This merging operation results in fewer primitives being sent down to the GPU. Fewer primitives means less memory traffic (lighter vertex buffer and smaller Parameter Buffer usage) and also less vertex shader work.

Single draw call. When using the same texture for all layers (e.g., when rendering a particle system) or when all tiles are using the same textures in the same order, we can drastically reduce the number of batches by constructing a single dynamic VBO to render the whole grid at once.

For each tile, and for each transparent layer it aggregates, the sprite texture coordinates are extrapolated to the corners of each cell. This computation is performed on CPU and the values are appended into the vertex buffer. Thus, each vertex now contains one `vec2` position and eight `vec2` texture coordinates; no uniforms are required anymore.

The vertex shader being used is a simple pass-through, which will allow all attributes to be interpolated and passed to the fragment shader (see Listing 5.3).

We can notice that, even when all eight layers that can be rendered by a tile are not used, this shader will still consume eight interpolators. That many varyings can affect performance negatively as the large amount of memory required to store the interpolated values might lower the number of fragments in flight and could also trash the post-transform cache [McCaffrey 12].

When the maximum number of layers is not being used in a given tile, a solution can be found through dynamic branching to early out and not take the

```
attribute vec2
  Position ,
  TextureCoordinates [LAYER_COUNT];

varying mediump vec2
  vTextureCoordinates [LAYER_COUNT];

void main ()
{
  gl_Position = vec4( Position.xy, 0.0, 1.0 );

  for ( int i = 0; i < LAYER_COUNT; i++ )
  {
    vTextureCoordinates [i] = TextureCoordinates [i];
  }
}
```

Listing 5.3. Single draw call vertex shader.

superfluous layers into account; this solution requires packing an extra attribute containing the number of layers aggregated by the current primitive.

We did not need to implement this, but it should be possible to address the texture limitation mentioned before (one texture or same textures in same order for all tiles) by using texture atlases at the cost of a more complex handling of texture coordinates and wrap modes. A better solution would have been to use *Array Textures* if they were available on all platforms [OpenGLWiki 13]. Starting with OpenGL ES 3.0, this will become a valid option [Khronos 13].

The fragment shader is the same as the one of the multiple draw calls approach.

Table 5.1 summarizes the main differences between the two approaches. The main argument for choosing one or the other is related to the number of tiles to render. When using a high number of tiles (e.g., 64 or more) or if your application is already sending too many batches, the single draw call approach should perform better (provided your scene fits its limitations). When using a relatively low number of tiles, we would recommend using the multiple draw calls approach, as it is much more flexible, easier to implement and provides more opportunities to lower memory traffic.

5.4.2 Render Target Resolution

For effects such as clouds and smoke, which use textures of relatively low frequencies, a commonly used optimization consists in rendering the effect to a lower resolution offscreen render target before upsampling it to the final framebuffer.

	Single Draw Call	Multiple Draw Calls
Draw calls	1	1 per tile
VS data	dynamic VBO	static VBO + uniforms
Texcoord transforms	on CPU	on GPU
Number of textures	1 (up to 8 for whole grid)	8 per tile
Unused layers	dynamic branching	different programs
Interpolators usage	high	low to high depending on aggregated layer count

Table 5.1. Single versus multiple draw calls summary.

5.4.3   Stencil

Stencil test is another common optimization for effects that affect only portions of the screen [Weber and Quayle 11].

5.5   Results

The savings achieved with this technique depend greatly on the scene complexity, the tile layout and, first and foremost, the underlying architecture. We can, however, estimate a best case scenario by comparing the cost of rendering several fullscreen quads using regular blending versus rendering the same amount of fullscreen quads using deferred tile blending. The results are presented in Figure 5.6 and in Table 5.2.

We can observe a linear relationship between the number of fullscreen layers to blend and the time it takes to render the frame. As expected, we did not notice any improvement on TBR architectures and the technique was even a bit slower than simple blending on some devices. However, on IMR GPUs such as the Tegra 3 equipping the Nexus 7, rendering time was approximately 35% shorter than without using tile-based blending.

Fullscreen layer count	SB (Nexus7)	TDB (Nexus7)	SB (iPhone4S)	TDB (iPhone4S)
8	23	16	7	8
16	45	30	13	14
24	66	44	19	21
32	87.5	58	24	28
40	109	72	32	34

Table 5.2. Tiled deferred blending (TDB) and simple blending (SB) rendering times (in ms).

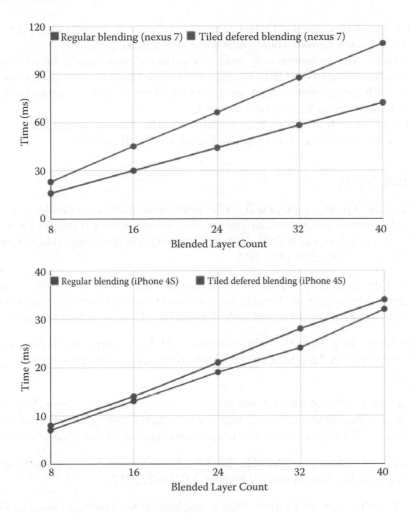

Figure 5.6. Comparing rendering time for tiled deferred blending and simple blending for Nexus 7 (top) and iPone 4S (bottom).

5.6 Conclusion

This chapter has presented a technique based on tile bucketing to reduce the memory bandwidth consumed by blending operations.

This technique is not a "one solution fits all" and should not be used blindly. For example, we would not recommend using it to render all your particle systems, as it would quickly become too expensive when the number of particles increases. However, a hybrid approach combining regular blending for small sprites and tiled deferred blending for those covering a screen area above a given threshold, à la *contribution culling*, could show some substantial gains.

Actually, the technique only works for screen-aligned quads, but, by passing depth information to the GPU, it could be extended to support arbitrary oriented sprites with perspective correct interpolation of the texture coordinates (at the price of using dependent texture fetches).

It is my hope that this technique will serve others in developing better looking effects while achieving their target performance on all devices.

Bibliography

[Apple 13a] Apple. "OpenGL ES Hardware Platform Guide for iOS." http://developer.apple.com/library/ios/documentation/OpenGLES/ Conceptual/OpenGLESHardwarePlatformGuide_iOS/OpenGLESHardware PlatformGuide_iOS.pdf, 2013.

[Apple 13b] Apple. "OpenGL ES Programming Guide for iOS." http:// developer.apple.com/library/ios/documentation/3DDrawing/Conceptual/ OpenGLES_ProgrammingGuide/OpenGLES_ProgrammingGuide.pdf, 2013.

[Forsyth 06] Tom Forsyth. "Premultiplied Alpha." http://home.comcast.net/ ~tom_forsyth/blog.wiki.html#%5B%5BPremultiplied%20alpha%5D%5D, 2006.

[Imagination Technologies 12] Imagination Technologies. "PowerVR Performance Recommendations." http://www.imgtec.com/powervr/insider/docs/ PowerVR.Performance%20Recommendations.1.0.28.External.pdf, 2012.

[Khronos 13] Khronos. "OpenGL ES 3.0.2 Specification." http://www.khronos. org/registry/gles/specs/3.0/es_spec_3.0.2.pdf, 2013.

[McCaffrey 12] Jon McCaffrey. "Exploring Mobile vs. Desktop OpenGL Performance." In *OpenGL Insights*, edited by Patrick Cozzi and Christophe Riccio, Chapter 24, pp. 337–352. Boca Raton, FL: A K Peters/CRC Press, 2012.

[Merry 12] Bruce Merry. "Performance Tuning for Tile-Based Architectures." In *OpenGL Insights*, edited by Patrick Cozzi and Christophe Riccio, pp. 323–336. Boca Raton, Fl: A K Peters/CRC Press, 2012.

[NVIDIA 13] NVIDIA. "Optimize OpenGL ES 2.0 Performance for Tegra." http://docs.nvidia.com/tegra/data/Optimize_OpenGL_ES_2_0_ Performance_for_Tegra.html, 2013.

[Olsson and Assarsson 11] Ola Olsson and Ulf Assarsson. "Tiled Shading." *Journal of Graphics, GPU, and Game Tools* 15:4 (2011), 235–251.

[OpenGLWiki 13] OpenGLWiki. "Array Texture." http://www.opengl.org/wiki/Array_Texture, 2013.

[Pranckevičius 12] Aras Pranckevičius. "Tiled Forward Shading Links." http://aras-p.info/blog/2012/03/27/tiled-forward-shading-links/, 2012.

[Weber and Quayle 11] Marco Weber and Peter Quayle. "Post-Processing Effects on Mobile Devices." In *GPU Pro 2*, edited by Wolfgang Engel, pp. 291–305. Natick, MA: A K Peters, Ltd., 2011.

Adaptive Scalable Texture Compression

Stacy Smith

6.1 Introduction

Adaptative Scalable Texture Compression (ASTC) is a new texture compression format that is set to take the world by storm. Having been accepted as a new Khronos standard, this compression format is already available in some hardware platforms. This chapter shows how it works, how to use it, and how to get the most out of it. For more in-depth information, there is a full specification provided with the encoder [Mali 14a].

6.2 Background

ASTC was developed by ARM Limited as the flexible solution to the sparsely populated list of texture compression formats previously available. In the past, texture compression methods were tuned for one or more specific "sweet spot" combinations of data channels and related bit rates. Worsening the situation was the proprietary nature of many of these formats, limiting availability to specific vendors, and leading to the current situation where applications have to fetch an additional asset archive over the internet after installation, based on the detected available formats. The central foundation of ASTC is that it can compress an input image in every commonly used format (Table 6.1) and output that image in any user selected bit rate, from 8 bpp to 0.89 bpp, or 0.59 bpp for 3D textures (Table 6.2).

Bitrates below 1 bpp are achieved by a clever system of variable block sizes. Whereas most block-based texture compression methods have a single fixed block size, ASTC can store an image with a regular grid of blocks of any size from 4×4 to 12×12 (including nonsquare block sizes). ASTC can also store 3D textures, with block sizes ranging from $3 \times 3 \times 3$ to $6 \times 6 \times 6$.

Raw Input Format	Bits per Pixel
HDR RGB+A	64
HDR RGBA	64
HDR RGB	48
HDR XY+Z	48
HDR X+Y	32
RGB+A	32
RGBA	32
XY+Z	24
RGB	24
HDR L	16
X+Y	16
LA	16
L	8

Table 6.1. Bitrates of raw image formats.

Output Block Size[a]	Bits per Pixel
4×4	8.000
5×5	5.120
6×6	3.556
8×8	2.000
10×10	1.280
12×12	0.889
$3 \times 3 \times 3$	4.741
$4 \times 4 \times 4$	2.000
$5 \times 5 \times 5$	1.024
$6 \times 6 \times 6$	0.593
4×6	5.333
8×10	1.600
12×10	1.067

[a] This is by no means an exhaustive list of available block sizes, merely the square/cube block sizes to show data rates, with a few nonsquare examples.

Table 6.2. Bitrates of ASTC output.

Regardless of the blocks' dimensions, they are always stored in 128 bits, hence the sliding scale of bit rates.

6.3   Algorithm

Each pixel in these blocks is defined as a quantized point on a linear gradient between a pair of boundary colors. This allows for fairly smooth areas of shading. For blocks containing boundaries between areas of completely different colors, the block can use one of 2048 color partitioning patterns, which split the block into different designs of 1–4 color gradients. (See Figure 6.1.)

These blocks are algorithmically generated, and selecting the right one is where the majority of the compression time goes. This technique allows a block to contain areas of completely different hues with arbitrary shading or multiple intersecting hard-edged patches of different tones. Each block defines up to four pairs of colors and a distribution pattern ID, so that each pixel knows which of those pairs it uses to define its own color. The individual pixels then have a quantized value from 0 to 1 to state where they are on the gradient between the given pair of colors.[1] Due to the variable number of bounding colors and individual pixels in each 128 bit block, the precision of each pixel within the block is quantized to fit in the available remaining data size.

---

[1] Indices are encoded at variable resolution using a scheme developed by researchers at Advanced Micro Devices, Inc.

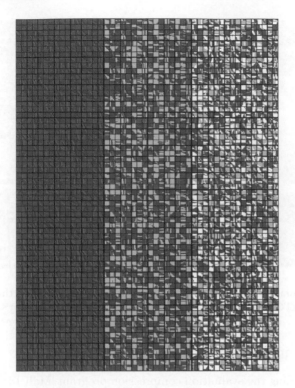

Figure 6.1. Different partition patterns.

During compression, the algorithm must select the correct distribution pattern and boundary color pairs, then generate the quantized value for each pixel. There is a certain degree of trial and error involved in the selection of patterns and boundary colors, and when compressing, there is a trade-off between compression time and final image quality. The higher the quality, the more alternatives the algorithm will try before deciding which is best. However long the compression takes, the decompression time is fixed, as the image data can always be re-extrapolated from the pattern and boundary colors in a single pass.

The compression algorithm can also use different metrics to judge the quality of different attempts, from pure value ratios of signal to noise, to a perceptual judgement weighted toward human visual acuity. The algorithm can also judge the channels individually rather than as a whole, to preserve detail for textures where the individual channels may be used as a data source for a shader program, or to reduce angular noise, which is important for tangent-space normal maps.

Overall, correct usage of these options can give a marked improvement over existing compression algorithms, as shown in Figure 6.2.

Figure 6.2. From top to bottom on the right we see a close up of the original image, the 2 bpp PVRTC [Fenney 03] compressed image, then the 2 bpp ASTC image at the bottom.

6.4 Getting Started

After downloading the evaluation compression program [Mali 14a], the command line interface can be used to compress textures. This program supports input images in PNG, Targa, JPEG, GIF(non-animated only), BMP, Radiance HDR, Khronos Texture KTX, DirectDraw Surface DDS, and Half-Float-TGA. There is also limited support for OpenEXR.

The `astcenc` application provides a full list of available command line arguments. The most basic commands are

```
astcenc −c <input.file> <output.file> <rate> [options]
```

The `-c` tells the program to compress the first file and save the compressed form into the second file. The rate is used to decide a block size. A block size can either be directly chosen as block size, such as 5×4 or $3 \times 3 \times 3$, or the algorithm can be given the bpp to aim for and it will choose automatically. The bit rate must always have one decimal place, in the range 8.0 to 0.8 (or as low as 0.6 for 3D textures).

When wishing to decompress a texture to view, use the following command:

```
astcenc −d <input.file> <output.file> [options]
```

In this case, the -d denotes a decompression, the input file is a texture that has already been compressed, and the output file is one of the uncompressed formats.

To see what a texture would look like compressed with a given set of options, use the command

```
astcenc -t <input.file> <output.file> <rate> [options]
```

The -t option compresses the file with the given options then immediately decompresses it into the output file. The interim compressed image is not saved, and the input and output files are both in a decompressed file format.

The options can be left blank, but to get a good result, there are a few useful ones to remember.

The most useful arguments are the quality presets:

```
-veryfast
-fast
-medium
-thorough
-exhaustive
```

Many options are available to set various compression quality factors, including

- the number and scope of block partition patterns to attempt,

- the various signal-to-noise cutoff levels to early out of the individual decision-making stages,

- the maximum iterations of different bounding color tests.

Most users won't explore all of these to find the best mix for their own needs. Therefore, the quality presets can be used to give a high-level hint to the compressor, from which individual quality factors are derived.

It should be noted that veryfast, although almost instantaneous, gives good results only for a small subset of input images. Conversely, the exhaustive quality level (which does exactly what it says and attempts every possible bounding pattern combination for every block) takes a very much longer time, but it will often have very little visible difference to a file compressed in thorough mode.

6.5 Using ASTC Textures

ASTC capability is a new hardware feature available starting in late 2013. To get started with ASTC right away, the ARM Mali OpenGL ES 3.0 Emulator [Mali 14b] is available from ARM's website, and this is compatible with ASTC

```
struct astc_header
{
  uint8_t magic[4];
  uint8_t blockdim_x;
  uint8_t blockdim_y;
  uint8_t blockdim_z;
  uint8_t xsize[3];
  uint8_t ysize[3];
  uint8_t zsize[3];
};
```

Listing 6.1. ASTC header structure.

texture formats and as such can be used to test ASTC-based programs on a standard desktop GPU.

Loading a texture in ASTC format is no different from loading other compressed texture formats, but the correct internal format must be used. Files output by the compressor have a data header containing everything needed to load the compressed texture.

Using the data structure in Listing 6.1, the application can detect the important information needed to load an ASTC texture. Please see the Mali Developer Center website for source code examples.

6.6   Quality Settings

This chapter has already mentioned some of the high-level quality settings, but there are far more precisely targeted ways to tweak the quality of the compressor's output. The command line compressor has two main categories of argument, search parameters and quality metrics.

The algorithm for compressing a texture relies heavily on trial and error. Many combinations of block partition and boundary colors are compared and the best one is used for that block. Widening search parameters will compare more combinations to find the right one, enabling the algorithm to find a better match but also lengthening search time (and therefore compression time).

- `plimit` is the maximum number of partitions tested for each block before it takes the best one found so far.

- `dblimit` is the perceptual signal-to-noise ratio (PSNR) cutoff for a block in dB. If the PSNR of a block attempt exceeds this, the algorithm considers it good enough and uses that combination. This PSNR may not be reached, since the algorithm may hit the other limits first.

- `oplimit` implements a cutoff based on comparing errors between single and dual partitioning. That is, if the dual partition errors are much worse than the single partition errors, it's probably not worth trying three or four partitions. The `oplimit` defines how much worse this error must be to give up at this point.

- `mincorrel` defines the similarity of color coefficients that the algorithm will try to fit in a single color plane. The smaller this number, the more varied colors on the same plane can be; therefore, the block will not be tested with higher numbers of partitions.

- `bmc` is a cutoff for the count of block modes to attempt. The block mode defines how the individual color values are precision weighted using different binary modes for each partition.

- `maxiters` is the maximum cutoff for the number of refining iterations to colors and weights for any given partition attempt.

These values can be set individually to extend searching in specific directions: for example,

- A texture that has lots of subtle detail should probably have a high `oplimit` to ensure subtle color variations don't get bundled into the same partition plane.

- A texture that has very busy randomized patterns should probably search more partition types to find the right one.

Usually, however, these are set to default levels based on the general quality setting, as seen in Table 6.3.

Improving quality with these factors is a trade-off between compression time and quality. The greater the search limits and the less willing the algorithm is to accept a block as "good enough" the more time is spent looking for a better match. There is another way to get a better match, though, and that is to adjust the quality metrics, altering the factors by which the compressor judges the quality of a block.

preset	plimit	dblimit[a]	oplimit	Mincorrel	bmc	maxiters
veryfast	2	18.68	1.0	0.5	25	1
fast	4	28.68	1.0	0.5	50	1
medium	25	35.68	1.2	0.75	75	2
thorough	100	42.68	2.5	0.95	95	4
exhaustive	1024	999	1000.0	0.99	100	4

[a] dblimit defaults for levels other than exhaustive are defined by an equation based on the number of texels per block.

Table 6.3. Preset quality factors.

6.6.1 Channel Weighting

The simplest quality factors are channel weighting, using the command line argument:

```
-ch <red-weight> <green-weight> <blue-weight> <alpha-weight>
```

This defines weighting values for the noise calculations. For example, the argument -ch 1 4 1 1 makes error on the green channel four times more important than noise on any other given channel. The argument -ch 0.25 1 0.25 0.25 would appear to give the same effect, but that assumption is only partly correct. This would still make errors in the green channel four times more prevalent, but the total error would be lower, and therefore more likely to be accepted by a "good enough" early out.

Channel weighting works well when combined with swizzling, using the -esw argument. For textures without alpha, for example, the swizzle -esw rgb1 saturates the alpha channel and subsequently doesn't count it in noise calculations.

6.6.2 Block Weighting

Though human eyesight is more sensitive to variations in green and less sensitive to variations in red, channel weighting has limited usefulness. Other weights can also improve a compressed texture in a number of use cases. One of these is block error checking, particularly on textures with compound gradients over large areas. By default there is no error weight based on inter-block errors. The texels at the boundary of two adjacent blocks may be within error bounds for their own texels, but with noise in opposing directions, meaning that the step between the blocks is noticeably large. This can be countered with the command line argument:

```
-b <weight>
```

The equation to judge block suitability takes into account the edges of any adjacent blocks already processed. Figures 6.3 and 6.4 show this in action. However, this simply makes the search algorithm accept blocks with better matching edges more readily than others, so it may increase noise in other ways. Awareness of adjacent smooth blocks can be particularly helpful for normal maps.

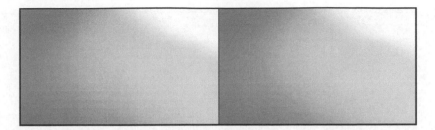

Figure 6.3. An example of block weighting. The left image shows block errors, the right image is recompressed with `-b 10`.

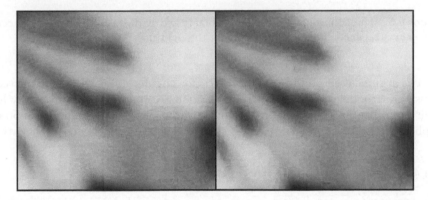

Figure 6.4. A second example of improvements from block weighting, using the same settings as Figure 6.3.

6.6.3 Normal Weighting

When compressing normal maps or maps used as a data source rather than color information, there are arguments that implement a number of additional settings all in one. These are `-normal_psnr`, `-normal_percep`, and `-mask`. Only one of these should be used at a time, as they override each other.

The first two of these are geared toward the compression of two-channel normal maps, swizzling the X and Y into luminance and alpha, overriding the default oplimit and mincorrel, and adding weight on angular error, which is far more important in normal maps. `-normal_percep` is similar but has subtly different weighting for better perceptual results. These can be seen in Figure 6.5.

.5 Both of these functions swizzle the X and Y into luminance and alpha, with an implied `-esw rrrg` argument, and also have an internal decode swizzle of `-dsw raz1` placing the luminance into X, placing the alpha into Y, and reconstructing Z using

$$z = \sqrt{1 - r^2 - a^2}.$$

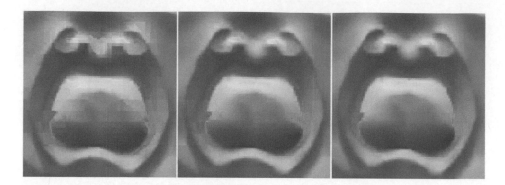

Figure 6.5. The leftmost normal map is compressed with default settings, the center uses `-normal_psnr`, and the normal map on the right uses `-normal_percep`

The argument `-rn`, adds an error metric for angular noise. Other texture compression methodologies have lacked this option. Normal maps traditionally have been a problem to compress, as the minor variations in the angular component implied by the X and Y value can get ignored in pure signal to noise calculations.

6.6.4   Masking Channel Errors

The argument `-mask` tells the compressor to assume that the input texture has entirely unrelated content in each channel, and as such it is undesirable for errors in one channel to affect other channels.

This is shown in Figure 6.6, an example of a bitmap font where the red channel represents the characters, the blue is a rear glow, and the green is a drop shadow.

The perceptual and mask filters are based on combinations of the `-v` and `-va` arguments. These two arguments give low-level access to the way an error value for a block is collected from its individual texel differences. The full syntax is

Figure 6.6. The left image is the uncompressed data, the center is compressed with default settings, and the right image uses the `-mask` argument.

```
−v <radius> <power> <baseweight> <avgscale> <stdevscale>
   <mixing−factor>
```

The radius is the area of neighboring texels for which the average and standard deviations in error are combined using the equation

$$weight = \frac{1}{baseweight + avgscale * average^2 + stdevscale * stdev^2}.$$

The individual error values are raised to power before average and standard deviation values are calculated. The mixing factor is used to decide if the individual channel errors are combined before or after averaging. If the mixing factor is 0, each color channel has its own average and standard deviation calculated, which are then combined in the equation above. If the mixing factor is 1, the errors of each channel are combined before a single average is calculated. A value between 1 and 0 provides a combination of these two values.

The result is an erratic error value that, if just averaged over a block, can lead to a fairly noisy output being accepted. Using the standard deviation over a given radius gives the error calculations visibility of any added noise between texels, in much the same way that step changes between blocks can be checked with the block weighting (see Section 6.6.2) argument.

This equation of average noise works on the color channels, the alpha channel is controlled separately, with a similar set of values in the command line arguments:

```
−va <baseweight> <power> <avgscale> <stdevscale>
−a <radius>
```

The alpha channel is controlled separately as, particularly with punch through textures, a little bit of quantization noise may be preferable to softening of edges.[2]

6.7   Other color formats

ASTC supports images with one to four channels, from luminance only all the way to RGBA. Additionally, the algorithm has support for different color-space encodings:

---

[2]It's worth reassuring the reader that yes, that is quite a lot of powers and coefficients to throw at a somewhat chaotic system, so manual adjustments can often feel like a stab in the dark—hence the presets.

- Linear RGBA,[3]

- sRGB + linear A,

- HDR RGB + A,[4]

- HDR RGBA.

6.7.1 sRGB

ASTC supports nonlinear sRGB color-space conversion both at compression and decompression time.

To keep images in sRGB color space until the point that they are used, simply compress them in the usual way. Then when they're loaded, instead of the regular texture formats, use the sRGB texture formats. These are the ones that contain `SRGB8_ALPHA8` in the name. There's an sRGB equivalent of every RGBA format.

Helpfully the constants for the sRGB formats are always `0x0020` greater than the RGBA constants, allowing an easy switch in code between the two.

As an alternative to using sRGB texture types at runtime, there is also a command line argument for the compressor to transform them to linear RGBA prior to compression. The `-srgb` argument will convert the color space and compress the texture in linear space, to be loaded with the usual RGBA texture formats.

6.7.2 HDR

ASTC also supports HDR image formats. Using these requires no additional effort in code and the same loading function detailed above can be used. When encoding an image in a HDR format, the encoder doesn't use HDR encoding by default. For this, one of two arguments must be used:

```
-forcehdr_rgb
-forcehdr_rgba
```

In this mode, the encoder will use a HDR or LDR as appropriate on a per-block basis. In `-forcehdr_rgb` mode, the alpha channel (if present) is always encoded LDR. There are also the simpler arguments:

```
-hdr
-hdra
```

---

[3]The most commonly understood and supported color space.
[4]HDR RGB channels with an LDR alpha.

which are equivalent to `-forcehdr_rgb` and `-forcehdr_rgba` but with additional alterations to the evaluation of block suitability (a preset `-v` and `-va`) better suited for HDR images. Also available are

```
—hdr_log
—hdra_log
```

These are similar but base their suitability on logarithmic error. Images encoded with this setting typically give better results from a mathematical perspective but don't hold up as well in terms of perceptual artifacts.

6.8   3D Textures

The compression algorithm can also handle 3D textures at a block level. Although other image compression algorithms can be used to store and access 3D textures, they are compressed in 2D space as a series of single texel layers, whereas ASTC compresses 3D blocks of texture data, improving the cache hit rate of serial texture reads along the Z axis. Currently there are no suitably prolific 3D image formats to accept as inputs, as such encoding a of 3D texture has a special syntax:

```
—array <size>
```

With this command line argument, the input file is assumed to be a prefix pattern for the actual inputs and decorates the file name with `_0`, `_1`, and so on all the way up to `_<size-1>`. So, for example, if the input file was "slice.png" with the argument `-array 4`, the compression algorithm would attempt to load files named "slice_0.png," "slice_1.png," "slice_2.png," and "slice_3.png." The presence of multiple texture layers would then be taken as a signal to use a 3D block encoding for the requested rate (see Table 6.2).

6.9   Summary

This chapter shows the advantages of ASTC over other currently available texture compression methodologies and provides code to easily use ASTC texture files in an arbitrary graphics project, as well as a detailed explanation of the command line arguments to get the most out of the evaluation codec.

Additionally, ARM provides a free Texture Compression Tool [ARM 14] that automates the ASTC command line arguments explained in this chapter via a Graphical User Interface (GUI) to simplify the compression process and provide visual feedback on compression quality.

Bibliography

[ARM 14] ARM. "Mali GPU Texture Compression Tool." http://malideveloper
.arm.com/develop-for-mali/mali-gpu-texture-compression-tool/, 2014.

[Fenney 03] Simon Fenney. "Texture Compression Using Low-Frequency Signal
Modulation." In *Proceedings of the ACM SIGGRAPH/EUROGRAPHICS
Conference on Graphics Hardware*, pp. 84–91. Aire-la-Ville, Switzerland: Eu-
rographics Association, 2003.

[Mali 14a] Mali. "ASTC Evaluation Codec." http://malideveloper.arm.com/
develop-for-mali/tools/astc-evaluation-codec/, 2014.

[Mali 14b] Mali. "OpenGL ES SDK Emulator." http://malideveloper.arm.com/
develop-for-mali/sdks/opengl-es-sdk-for-linux/, 2014.

[Nystad et al. 12] J. Nystad, A. Lassen, A. Pomianowski, S. Ellis, and T. Olson.
"Adaptive Scalable Texture Compression." In *Proceedings of the Fourth
ACM SIGGRAPH/Eurographics Conference on High-Performance Graph-
ics*, pp. 105–114. Aire-la-Ville, Switzerland: Eurographics Association, 2012.

Optimizing OpenCL Kernels for the ARM® Mali™-T600 GPUs

Johan Gronqvist and Anton Lokhmotov

7.1   Introduction

OpenCL is a relatively young industry-backed standard API that aims to provide *functional portability* across systems equipped with computational accelerators such as GPUs: a standard-conforming OpenCL program can be executed on any standard-conforming OpenCL implementation.

OpenCL, however, does not address the issue of *performance portability*: transforming an OpenCL program to achieve higher performance on one device may actually lead to lower performance on another device, since performance may depend significantly on low-level details, such as iteration space mapping and data layout [Howes et al. 10, Ryoo et al. 08].

Due to the popularity of certain GPU architectures, some optimizations have become hallmarks of GPU computing, e.g., coalescing global memory accesses or using local memory. Emerging mobile and embedded OpenCL-capable GPUs, however, have rather different organization. Therefore, even seasoned GPU developers may need to forgo their instincts and learn new techniques when optimizing for battery-powered GPU brethren.

In this chapter, we introduce the ARM Mali-T600 GPU series (Section 7.3) and discuss performance characteristics of several versions of the Sobel edge detection filter (Section 7.4) and the general matrix multiplication (Section 7.5).[1]

We make no claim that the presented versions are the fastest possible implementations of the selected algorithms. Rather, we aim to provide an insight into

---

[1]Source code for some versions is available in the Mali OpenCL SDK [ARM 13].

which transformations should be considered when optimizing kernel code for the Mali-T600 GPUs. Therefore, the described behavior may differ from the actual behavior for expository purposes.

We perform our experiments on an Arndale development board[2] powered by the Samsung Exynos 5250 chip. Exynos 5250 comprises a dual-core Cortex-A15 CPU at 1.7 GHz and a quad-core Mali-T604 GPU at 533 MHz. The OpenCL driver is of version 3.0 Beta.

7.2   Overview of the OpenCL Programming Model

In the OpenCL programming model, the host (e.g., a CPU) manages one or more devices (e.g., a GPU) through calls to the OpenCL API. A call to the `clEnqueueND Range()` API function submits a job that executes on a selected device the same program (*kernel*)[3] as a collection of *work-items*.

Each work-item has a unique index (*global ID*) in a multidimensional iteration space (*ND-range*), specified as the *global work size* argument to `clEnqueueND Range()`. The *local work size* argument to `clEnqueueNDRange()` determines how the ND-range is partitioned into uniformly sized *work-groups*. Work-items within the same work-group can synchronize using the `barrier()` built-in function, which must be executed by all work-items in the work-group before any work-item continues execution past the barrier.

In our examples, the ND-range is two-dimensional: work-items iterate over the pixels of the output image (Section 7.4) or the elements of the output matrix (Section 7.5), while work-groups iterate over partitions (or *tiles*) of the same. For example, the local work size of $(4, 16)$ would result in 64 work-items per work-group, with the first work-group having global IDs (x, y), where $0 \leq x < 4$ and $0 \leq y < 16$.

7.3   ARM Mali-T600 GPU Series

The ARM Mali-T600 GPU series based on the Midgard architecture is designed to meet the growing needs of graphics and compute applications for a wide range of consumer electronics, from phones and tablets to TVs and beyond. The Mali-T604 GPU, the first implementation of the Mali-T600 series, was the first mobile and embedded class GPU to pass the OpenCL v1.1 Full Profile conformance tests.

---

[2]http://www.arndaleboard.org

[3]The kernel is typically written in the OpenCL C language, which is a superset of a subset of the C99 language standard.

7.3.1 Architecture Overview

The Mali-T604 GPU is formed of four identical cores, each supporting up to 256 concurrently executing (*active*) threads.[4]

Each core contains a tri-pipe containing two arithmetic (A) pipelines, one load-store (LS) pipeline, and one texture (T) pipeline. Thus, the peak throughput of each core is two A instruction words, one LS instruction word, and one T instruction word per cycle. Midgard is a VLIW (Very Long Instruction Word) architecture, so that each pipe contains multiple units and most instruction words contain instructions for multiple units. In addition, Midgard is a SIMD (Single Instruction Multiple Data) architecture, so that most instructions operate on multiple data elements packed in 128-bit vector registers.

7.3.2 Execution Constraints

The architectural maximum number of work-items active on a single core is $\max(I) = 256$. The actual maximum number of active work-items I is determined by the number of registers R that the kernel code uses

$$I = \begin{cases} 256, & 0 < R \le 4, \\ 128, & 4 < R \le 8, \\ 64, & 8 < R \le 16. \end{cases}$$

For example, kernel A that uses $R_A = 5$ registers and kernel B that uses $R_B = 8$ registers can both be executed by *no more than* 128 work-items.[5]

7.3.3 Thread Scheduling

The GPU schedules work-groups onto cores in batches, whose size is chosen by the driver depending on the characteristics of the job. The hardware schedules batches onto cores in a round-robin fashion. A batch consists of a number of "adjacent" work-groups.[6]

Each core first creates threads for the first scheduled work-group and then continues to create threads for the other scheduled work-groups until either the maximum number of active threads has been reached or all threads for the scheduled work-groups have been created. When a thread terminates, a new thread can be scheduled in its place.

---

[4]In what follows, we assume that a single hardware thread executes a single work-item. A program transformation known as *thread coarsening* can result in a single hardware thread executing multiple work-items, e.g., in different vector lanes.

[5]Therefore, the compiler may prefer to spill a value to memory rather than use an extra register when the number of used registers approaches 4, 8, or 16.

[6]In our examples using 2D ND-ranges, two "adjacent" work-groups have work-items that are adjacent in the 2D space of global IDs (see Section 7.5.6 for a more detailed description).

Created threads enter the tri-pipe in a round-robin order. A core switches between threads on every cycle: when a thread has executed one instruction, it then waits while all other threads execute one instruction.[7] Sometimes a thread can stall waiting for a cache miss and another thread will overtake it, changing the ordering between threads. (We will discuss this aspect later in Section 7.5.)

7.3.4 Guidelines for Optimizing Performance

A compute program (kernel) typically consists of a mix of A and LS instruction words.[8] Achieving high performance on the Mali-T604 involves the following:

- Using a sufficient number of active threads to hide the execution latency of instructions (pipeline depth). The number of active threads depends on the number of registers used by kernel code and so may be limited for complex kernels.

- Using vector operations in kernel code to allow for straightforward mapping to vector instructions by the compiler.

- Having sufficient instruction level parallelism in kernel code to allow for dense packing of instructions into instruction words by the compiler.

- Having a balance between A and LS instruction words. Without cache misses, the ratio of 2:1 of A-words to LS-words would be optimal; with cache misses, a higher ratio is desirable. For example, a kernel consisting of 15 A-words and 7 LS-words is still likely to be bound by the LS-pipe.

In several respects, programming for the Mali-T604 GPU embedded on a System-on-Chip (SoC) is easier than programming for desktop class GPUs:

- The `global` and `local` OpenCL address spaces get mapped to the same physical memory (the system RAM), backed by caches transparent to the programmer. This often removes the need for explicit data copying and associated barrier synchronization.

- All threads have individual program counters. This means that branch divergence is less of an issue than for warp-based architectures.

---

[7]There is more parallelism in the hardware than this sentence mentions, but the description here suffices for the current discussion.

[8]The texture (T) pipeline is rarely used for compute kernels, with a notable exception of executing barrier operations (see Section 7.5). The main reason is that when performing memory accesses using vector instructions in the LS pipeline results in higher memory bandwidth (bytes per cycle) than using instructions in the T pipeline for kernels requiring no sampling.

7.3.5 A Note on Power

We discuss performance in terms of the time it takes to complete a computation. When analyzing the performance of an OpenCL kernel running on a mobile device, it is also important to consider the power and energy required for the execution. Often, the mobile device's thermal dissipation capacity will determine the maximum DVFS operating point (voltage and frequency) at which the GPU can be run. On Mali-T600 GPUs, it is often sufficient to characterize the performance of the *kernel* in terms of the number of cycles required for the execution. To determine the overall performance, one also has to factor in the GPU clock rate.

We focus on the cycle count of kernel execution and consider this sufficient for our optimization purposes. We posit that GPU power is (to a broad approximation) constant across sustained GPGPU workloads at a fixed operating point.[9] Energy consumed for a given workload is therefore determined by performance— both the number of cycles for that workload and the operating point required to meet the required performance target.

7.4 Optimizing the Sobel Image Filter

7.4.1 Algorithm

Our first example is the Sobel 3×3 image filter used within edge-detection algorithms. Technically speaking, the Sobel filter is a $(2K+1) \times (2K+1)$ convolution of an input image $\mathbf{I}$ with a constant mask $\mathbf{C}$:

$$\mathbf{O}_{y,x} = \sum_{u=-K}^{K} \sum_{v=-K}^{K} \mathbf{I}_{y+u,x+v} \cdot \mathbf{C}_{u,v},$$

taking an image containing the luminosity values and producing two images containing the discretized gradient values along the horizontal and vertical directions:

$$\mathbf{O}_{y,x}^{\mathbf{dx}} = \sum_{u=-1}^{1} \sum_{v=-1}^{1} \mathbf{I}_{y+u,x+v} \cdot \mathbf{C}_{u,v}^{\mathbf{dx}}, \quad \text{where} \quad \mathbf{C}^{\mathbf{dx}} = \begin{pmatrix} -1 & 0 & 1 \\ -2 & 0 & 2 \\ -1 & 0 & 1 \end{pmatrix},$$

$$\mathbf{O}_{y,x}^{\mathbf{dy}} = \sum_{u=-1}^{1} \sum_{v=-1}^{1} \mathbf{I}_{y+u,x+v} \cdot \mathbf{C}_{u,v}^{\mathbf{dy}}, \quad \text{where} \quad \mathbf{C}^{\mathbf{dy}} = \begin{pmatrix} 1 & 2 & 1 \\ 0 & 0 & 0 \\ -1 & -2 & -1 \end{pmatrix}.$$

---

[9]This assumption holds broadly on the Mali-T600 GPU series, as a result of the pipeline architecture, aggressive clock gating, and the GPU's ability to hide memory latency effectively.

7.4.2   Implementation Details

In our implementation, the input image $\mathbf{I}$ is an $H \times W$ array of unsigned 8-bit integers (uchar's) and the output images $\mathbf{O^{dx}}$ and $\mathbf{O^{dy}}$ are $H \times W$ arrays of signed 8-bit integers (char's). The results are computed as signed 16-bit integers (short's) and are normalized by dividing by 8 (i.e., shifting right by 3). The results are only computed for $(H - 2) \times (W - 2)$ inner pixels of the output images, leaving pixels on the one-pixel wide border intact.[10]

7.4.3   Performance Characteristics

Table 7.1 shows the results for all the kernel versions discussed in this section on a 512×512 input image. We present the following numbers for each kernel version:

- the number of input pixels per work-item,

- the maximal local work size, max(LWS), i.e., the maximal number of active work-items per core,

- the number of arithmetic and load-store instruction words per work-item,

- the number of arithmetic and load-store instruction words per cycle,

- the number of pixels processed per cycle.

Achieving a high proportion of the peak numbers of A-words and LS-words executed per cycle (8 and 4, respectively, for the Mali-T604) may be challenging due to memory and other effects.

7.4.4   Using Scalars

The char kernel in Listing 7.1 is a naïve, scalar version. Each work-item reads a 3×3 square of input pixels around its coordinate. The computation is performed using 16-bit integer arithmetic to avoid overflow. No vector operations are used.

Table 7.1 shows that each work-item has to pass 13 times through an A-pipe, and at least 7 times through a LS-pipe (possibly more due to cache misses). Having 256 active work-items ensures good utilization: indeed, this version reaches the highest number of LS-words per cycle. However, the overall performance is poor (0.3 pixels per cycle) due to not using vector operations.

---

[10]Our test image has a size of 512×512, which means that the interior has a size of only 510×510. We have vectorized versions that handle 8 or 16 pixels per work-item, and for those implementations, we have an (interior) image size that is not a multiple of the number of pixels per work-item. In a real application, we would have to take care to handle the border separately, but as this affects only a small percentage of the image, we will instead ignore that discussion, as it is not important for our qualitative performance considerations.

```
kernel void sobel_char (
  global const uchar * restrict in,   //< Input.
  global char * restrict dx,          //< X gradient.
  global char * restrict dy,          //< Y gradient.
  const int width)
{
  // X and Y gradient accumulators.
  short _dx, _dy;

  // Left, middle and right pixels: loaded as
  // unsigned 8-bit, converted to signed 16-bit.
  uchar lLoad, mLoad, rLoad;
  short lData, mData, rData;

  // Compute (column,row) position and offset.
  const int column = get_global_id(0);
  const int row    = get_global_id(1);
  const int offset = row * width + column;

  // Compute contribution from first row.
  lLoad = *(in + (offset + width * 0 + 0));
  mLoad = *(in + (offset + width * 0 + 1));
  rLoad = *(in + (offset + width * 0 + 2));

  lData = convert_short(lLoad);
  mData = convert_short(mLoad);
  rData = convert_short(rLoad);

  _dx = rData - lData;
  _dy = rData + lData + mData * (short)2;

  // Compute contribution from second row.
  lLoad = *(in + (offset + width * 1 + 0));
  rLoad = *(in + (offset + width * 1 + 2));

  lData = convert_short(lLoad);
  rData = convert_short(rLoad);

  _dx += (rData - lData) * (short)2;

  // Compute contribution from third row.
  lLoad = *(in + (offset + width * 2 + 0));
  mLoad = *(in + (offset + width * 2 + 1));
  rLoad = *(in + (offset + width * 2 + 2));

  lData = convert_short(lLoad);
  mData = convert_short(mLoad);
  rData = convert_short(rLoad);

  _dx += rData - lData;
  _dy -= rData + lData + mData * (short)2;

  // Store the results.
  *(dx + offset + width + 1) = convert_char(_dx >> 3);
  *(dy + offset + width + 1) = convert_char(_dy >> 3);
}
```

Listing 7.1. Initial scalar implementation: `char`.

Version Name	Pixels/WI	max(LWS)	A-words/WI	LS-words/WI	A-words/Cycle	LS-words/Cycle	Pixels/Cycle
char	1	256	13	7	3.9	2.1	0.3
char8	8	128	17	9	3.8	2	1.8
char16	16	64	21	7	2.3	0.8	1.8
char8_load16	8	128	18	5	5	1.4	2.2
char16_swizzle	16	128	32	8	5.1	1.3	2.6
2xchar8	16	128	29	14	3.8	1.9	2.1
2xchar8_load16	16	128	32	7	4.9	1.1	2.5
3xchar8	24	64	39	19	2.2	1.1	1.4

Table 7.1. Performance characteristics of all Sobel versions running on a 512×512 image (see Section 7.4.3 for a description of the columns). Note that our implementations compute two output pixels for each input pixel (i.e., double the output of a standard 3×3 convolution filter), but we only count the number of input pixels per work-item (WI).

7.4.5   Using Vectors

Eight components. Each work-item of the char8 kernel in Listing 7.2 performs eight char8 load operations to read a 3×10 region of input pixels and computes two char8 vectors of output pixels. The conversion and compute instructions operate on short8 data in 128-bit registers.

Table 7.1 shows that while the char8 kernel computes eight times more data, it performs only about 30% more arithmetic and memory instructions than the char kernel, resulting in a six times increase in performance (1.8 pixels per cycle). The ratio between the arithmetic and memory instructions is close to the 2:1, optimal for cases with few cache misses. Due to the increase in complexity, the kernel max(LWS) is 128, limiting the number of simultaneously active work-items per core to 128. Still, the number of instruction words executed per cycle is nearly the same as for the scalar version, which shows that we can accept a max(LWS) of 128 without significant performance problems for this kind of workload.

Sixteen components. The number of operations per pixel is reduced even further by using char16 memory operations (full vector register width) and short16 arithmetic operations (broken into short8 operations by the compiler) in the char16 kernel partially shown in Listing 7.3. Performance, however, does not increase, because this kernel can only be executed with up to 64 simultaneous work-items per core (max(LWS) = 64), which introduces bubbles into the pipelines due to reduced latency-hiding capability.

```
kernel void sobel_char8(
  global const uchar * restrict in,  //< Input.
  global char * restrict dx,         //< X gradient.
  global char * restrict dy,         //< Y gradient.
  const int width)
{
  // X and Y gradient accumulators.
  short8 _dx, _dy;

  // Left, middle and right pixels: loaded as
  // unsigned 8-bit, converted to signed 16-bit.
  uchar8 lLoad, mLoad, rLoad;
  short8 lData, mData, rData;

  // Compute (column,row) position and offset.
  const int column = get_global_id(0) * 8;
  const int row    = get_global_id(1) * 1;
  const int offset = row * width + column;

  // Compute contribution from first row.
  lLoad = vload8(0, in + (offset + width * 0 + 0));
  mLoad = vload8(0, in + (offset + width * 0 + 1));
  rLoad = vload8(0, in + (offset + width * 0 + 2));

  lData = convert_short8(lLoad);
  mData = convert_short8(mLoad);
  rData = convert_short8(rLoad);

  _dx = rData - lData;
  _dy = rData + lData + mData * (short8)2;

  // Compute contribution from second row.
  lLoad = vload8(0, in + (offset + width * 1 + 0));
  rLoad = vload8(0, in + (offset + width * 1 + 2));

  lData = convert_short8(lLoad);
  rData = convert_short8(rLoad);

  _dx += (rData - lData) * (short8)2;

  // Compute contribution from third row.
  lLoad = vload8(0, in + (offset + width * 2 + 0));
  mLoad = vload8(0, in + (offset + width * 2 + 1));
  rLoad = vload8(0, in + (offset + width * 2 + 2));

  lData = convert_short8(lLoad);
  mData = convert_short8(mLoad);
  rData = convert_short8(rLoad);

  _dx += rData - lData;
  _dy -= rData + lData + mData * (short8)2;

  // Store the results.
  vstore8(convert_char8(_dx >> 3), 0, dx + offset + width + 1);
  vstore8(convert_char8(_dy >> 3), 0, dy + offset + width + 1);
}
```

Listing 7.2. Initial vector implementation: char8.

```
41   // Compute contribution from third row.
42   lLoad = vload16(0, in + (offset + width * 2 + 0));
43   mLoad = vload16(0, in + (offset + width * 2 + 1));
44   rLoad = vload16(0, in + (offset + width * 2 + 2));
45
46   lData = convert_short16(lLoad);
47   mData = convert_short16(mLoad);
48   rData = convert_short16(rLoad);
49
50   _dx += rData - lData;
51   _dy -= rData + lData + mData * (short16)2;
52
53   // Store the results.
54   vstore16(convert_char16(_dx >> 3), 0, dx + offset + width + 1);
55   vstore16(convert_char16(_dy >> 3), 0, dy + offset + width + 1);
```

Listing 7.3. Computing contribution from the third row: `char16`.

7.4.6 Reusing Loaded Data

Larger load operations. The `char8` kernel performed eight `char8` load operations. The `char8_load16` kernel, partially shown in Listing 7.4, performs only three `char16` load operations: the required subcomponents are extracted by swizzle operations, which are often free on the Midgard architecture. Table 7.1 confirms that the number of memory operations per pixel is decreased, while still allowing the kernel to be launched with up to 128 simultaneous work-items per core.

Eliminating redundant loads. The `char16` kernel performed three `char16` load operations to read 18 bytes for the first and third rows. The `char16_swizzle` kernel, partially shown in Listing 7.5, performs two `char16` load operations for the leftmost and rightmost vectors and reconstructs the middle vector by swizzle operations.

```
41   // Compute contribution from third row.
42   load = vload16(0, in + (offset + width * 2 + 0));
43
44   lData = convert_short8(load.s01234567);
45   mData = convert_short8(load.s12345678);
46   rData = convert_short8(load.s23456789);
47
48   _dx += rData - lData;
49   _dy -= rData + lData + mData * (short8)2;
50
51   // Store the results.
52   vstore8(convert_char8(_dx >> 3), 0, dx + offset + width + 1);
53   vstore8(convert_char8(_dy >> 3), 0, dy + offset + width + 1);
```

Listing 7.4. Computing contribution from the third row: `char8_load16`.

```
41  // Compute contribution from third row.
42  lLoad = vload16(0, in + (offset + width * 2 + 0));
43  rLoad = vload16(0, in + (offset + width * 2 + 2));
44
45  lData = convert_short16(lLoad);
46  mData = convert_short16(
47    (uchar16)(lLoad.s12345678, rLoad.s789abcde));
48  rData = convert_short16(rLoad);
49
50  _dx += rData - lData;
51  _dy -= rData + lData + mData * (short16)2;
52
53  // Store the results.
54  vstore16(convert_char16(_dx >> 3), 0, dx + offset + width + 1);
55  vstore16(convert_char16(_dy >> 3), 0, dy + offset + width + 1);
```

Listing 7.5. Computing contribution from the third row: `char16_swizzle`.

While the number of instruction words increases in comparison to the `char16` kernel (by nearly 50% for A-words and even slightly for LS-words due to instruction scheduling effects), this kernel can be launched with 128 simultaneous work-items per core. This leads to the highest utilization of the A-pipes of all the versions in this study, as well as the best overall performance.

7.4.7 Processing Multiple Rows

The kernels presented so far have loaded pixels from three input rows to compute pixels in a single output row. In general, to compute pixels in n output rows, $n + 2$ input rows are needed.

```
43  // Compute contribution from third row.
44  lLoad = vload8(0, in + (offset + width*2 + 0));
45  mLoad = vload8(0, in + (offset + width*2 + 1));
46  rLoad = vload8(0, in + (offset + width*2 + 2));
47
48  lData = convert_short8(lLoad);
49  mData = convert_short8(mLoad);
50  rData = convert_short8(rLoad);
51
52  _dx1 += rData - lData;
53  _dy1 -= rData + lData + mData * (short8)2;
54  _dx2 += (rData - lData) * (short8)2;
```

```
68  // Store the results.
69  vstore8(convert_char8(_dx1 >> 3), 0, dx1 + offset + width + 1);
70  vstore8(convert_char8(_dy1 >> 3), 0, dy1 + offset + width + 1);
71  vstore8(convert_char8(_dx2 >> 3), 0, dx2 + offset + width*2 + 1);
72  vstore8(convert_char8(_dy2 >> 3), 0, dy2 + offset + width*2 + 1);
```

Listing 7.6. Computing contribution from the third row: `2xchar8`.

```
41    // Compute contribution from third row.
42    load = vload16(0, in + (offset + width*2 + 0));
43
44    lData = convert_short8(load.s01234567);
45    mData = convert_short8(load.s12345678);
46    rData = convert_short8(load.s23456789);
47
48    _dx1 += rData - lData;
49    _dy1 -= rData + lData + mData * (short8)2;
50    _dx2 += (rData - lData) * (short8)2;
```

```
62    // Store the results.
63    vstore8(convert_char8(_dx1 >> 3), 0, dx1 + offset + width + 1);
64    vstore8(convert_char8(_dy1 >> 3), 0, dy1 + offset + width + 1);
65    vstore8(convert_char8(_dx2 >> 3), 0, dx2 + offset + width*2 + 1);
66    vstore8(convert_char8(_dy2 >> 3), 0, dy2 + offset + width*2 + 1);
```

Listing 7.7. Computing contribution from the third row: `2xchar8_load16`.

Computing two rows of output. The `2xchar8` and `2xchar8_load16` kernels load from four input rows to compute results for two output rows ($n = 2$). They are partially shown in Listing 7.6 and Listing 7.7 and are modifications of the `char8` and `char8_load16` kernels, respectively. Both kernels can be launched with up to 128 simultaneous work-items per core and both kernels perform better than the single-row variants. As before, the `load16` version is faster, and indeed achieves the second best performance in this study.

Computing three rows of output. The `3xchar8` kernel, partially shown in Listing 7.8, has grown too complex and can only be launched with up to 64 simultaneous work-items per core. Therefore, exploiting data reuse by keeping more than two rows in registers is suboptimal on the Mali-T604.

7.4.8   Summary

We have presented several versions of the Sobel filter, and discussed their performance characteristics on the Mali-T604 GPU. Vectorizing kernel code and exploiting data reuse are the two principal optimization techniques explored in this study. The fastest kernel, `char16_swizzle`, is nearly nine times faster than the slowest kernel, `char`, which reiterates the importance of target-specific optimizations for OpenCL code.

To summarize, we note that although the theoretical peak performance is at the ratio of two arithmetic instruction words for every load-store instruction word, the best performance was obtained in the versions with the highest number of arithmetic words executed per cycle. Restructuring the program to trade load-store operations for arithmetic operations has thus been successful, as long as the kernel could still be launched with 128 simultaneous work-items per core.

```
43   // Compute contribution from third row.
44   lLoad = vload8(0, in + (offset + width*2 + 0));
45   mLoad = vload8(0, in + (offset + width*2 + 1));
46   rLoad = vload8(0, in + (offset + width*2 + 2));
47
48   lData = convert_short8(lLoad);
49   mData = convert_short8(mLoad);
50   rData = convert_short8(rLoad);
51
52   _dx1 += rData - lData;
53   _dy1 -= rData + lData + mData * (short8)2;
54   _dx2 += (rData - lData) * (short8)2;
55   _dx3 = rData - lData;
56   _dy3 = rData + lData + mData * (short8)2;
```

```
83   // Store the results.
84   vstore8(convert_char8(_dx1 >> 3), 0, dx1 + offset + width + 1);
85   vstore8(convert_char8(_dy1 >> 3), 0, dy1 + offset + width + 1);
86   vstore8(convert_char8(_dx2 >> 3), 0, dx2 + offset + width*2 + 1);
87   vstore8(convert_char8(_dy2 >> 3), 0, dy2 + offset + width*2 + 1);
88   vstore8(convert_char8(_dx3 >> 3), 0, dx3 + offset + width*3 + 1);
89   vstore8(convert_char8(_dy3 >> 3), 0, dy3 + offset + width*3 + 1);
```

Listing 7.8. Computing contribution from the third row: 3xchar8.

7.5 Optimizing the General Matrix Multiplication

The Sobel filter implementations have hightlighted the importance of using vector instructions and a high number of active work-items. We next study implementations of the general matrix multiplication (GEMM) to elucidate the importance of using caches effectively. We first discuss aspects of the caches and how we optimize for them. At the end, we look at the runtimes on an Arndale development board and compare to our discussions.

7.5.1 Algorithm

The general matrix multiplication is a function of the Basic Linear Algebra Subprograms (BLAS) API[11] that computes

$$C = \alpha AB + \beta C,$$

where A, B, C are matrices of floating-point numbers and α, β are scalars.

7.5.2 Implementation Details

In our implementation, the matrices are $N \times N$ arrays of single-precision floating-point numbers (SGEMM). We consider two common SGEMM variants:

---

[11] http://www.netlib.org/blas

- NN: A is non-transposed, B is non-transposed:

$$C[i,j] = \alpha \sum_{k=0}^{N-1} A[i,k] \times B[k,j] + \beta C[i,j].$$

- NT: A is non-transposed, B is transposed:

$$C[i,j] = \alpha \sum_{k=0}^{N-1} A[i,k] \times B[j,k] + \beta C[i,j],$$

where $i = 0, \ldots, N-1$ and $j = 0, \ldots, N-1$.

CPU implementations of the NN variant often first transpose B and then perform the NT variant, which has a more cache-friendly memory access pattern, as we show in Section 7.5.4.

7.5.3 Scalar Implementations

We first consider scalar implementations with an $N \times N$ ND-range covering all elements of C. From our experience with optimizing the Sobel filter, these versions are clearly suboptimal as they do not use any vector operations. We will (due to their simplicity) use them to introduce our notation for describing memory access patterns of kernels, and we will also use them as examples in some qualitative discussions later.

Non-transposed. Each work-item of the `scalarNN` version in Listing 7.9 produces one element of C by computing the dot product of a row of A and a column of B.

```
kernel void
sgemm(global float const *A, global float const *B,
      global float *C, float alpha, float beta, uint n)
{
  uint j = get_global_id(0);
  uint i = get_global_id(1);

  float ABij = 0.0f;
  for (uint k = 0; k < n; ++k)
  {
    ABij += A[i*n + k] * B[k*n + j];
  }
  C[i*n + j] = alpha * ABij + beta * C[i*n + j];
}
```

Listing 7.9. Initial scalar implementation: `scalarNN`.

```
kernel void
sgemm(global float const *A, global float const *B,
      global float *C, float alpha, float beta, uint n)
{
  uint j = get_global_id(0);
  uint i = get_global_id(1);

  float ABij = 0.0f;
  for (uint k = 0; k < n; ++k)
  {
    ABij += A[i*n + k] * B[j*n + k];
  }
  C[i*n + j] = alpha * ABij + beta * C[i*n + j];
}
```

Listing 7.10. Initial scalar implementation: `scalarNT`.

Transposed. Each work-item of the `scalarNT` version in Listing 7.10 produces one element of C by computing the dot product of a row of A and a column of B^T (or equivalently a row of B).

7.5.4   Memory Access Patterns of Scalar Implementations

A single work-item of the `scalarNN` version sequentially reads (within the k loop) from pairs of locations $(A[i,0], B[0,j])$, $(A[i,1], B[1,j])$, ..., $(A[i, N-1], B[N-1,j])$. We will abbreviate this access pattern to

$$\overset{N-1}{\underset{k=0}{\text{;}}}(A[i,k], B[k,j]),$$

which denotes that the accesses happen sequentially for $0 \leq k < N$.

Similarly, the access pattern of a single work-item of the `scalarNT` version is

$$\overset{N-1}{\underset{k=0}{\text{;}}}(A[i,k], B[j,k]).$$

With the row-major array layout used in the C language, the `scalarNT` variant reads both A and B with stride 1, while the `scalarNN` variant reads B with stride N.

Let us assume a core executes a single work-group of dimensions (λ_0, λ_1). Since work-items execute in an interleaved order (Section 7.3.3), the actual memory access pattern of the `scalarNN` variant on the core will be

$$\overset{N-1}{\underset{k=0}{\text{;}}}\left[\left(\overset{\lambda_1-1}{\underset{i=0}{\text{;}}}\overset{\lambda_0-1}{\underset{j=0}{\text{;}}} A[i,k]\right), \left(\overset{\lambda_1-1}{\underset{i=0}{\text{;}}}\overset{\lambda_0-1}{\underset{j=0}{\text{;}}} B[k,j]\right)\right],$$

which means that on each iteration $0 \leq k < N$ all work-items first read from A and then from B. The $,$ operator for $0 \leq j < \lambda_0$ is the innermost one, due to the order in which threads are created by the device.[12]

7.5.5   Blocking

As a first step towards better implementations, we will introduce *blocking*, a program transformation that will allow us to use vector operations for memory accesses and arithmetic operations. We will later exploit blocking to improve cache usage.

Let us assume that matrix order N is divisible by blocking factors ΔI, ΔJ and $\Delta K_{\text{reg.}}$. Imagine that

- matrix A consists of $\frac{N}{\Delta I} \times \frac{N}{\Delta K_{\text{reg.}}}$ submatrices of $\Delta I \times \Delta K_{\text{reg.}}$ elements each,

- matrix B consists of $\frac{N}{\Delta K_{\text{reg.}}} \times \frac{N}{\Delta J}$ submatrices of $\Delta K_{\text{reg.}} \times \Delta J$ elements each,

- matrix C consists of $\frac{N}{\Delta I} \times \frac{N}{\Delta J}$ submatrices of $\Delta I \times \Delta J$ elements each.

Now, instead of writing the SGEMM NN algorithm as

$$C[i,j] = \alpha \sum_{i,j} A[i,k] \times B[k,j] + \beta C[i,j],$$

where $A[i,k]$, $B[k,j]$ and $C[i,j]$ were individual elements, we can write it as

$$C[I,J] = \alpha \sum_{I,J} A[I,K] \times B[K,J] + \beta C[I,J],$$

where $A[I,K]$, $B[K,J]$ and $C[I,J]$ are submatrices as above and $\times$ is the matrix multiplication operation.

Our kernels will still have the same structure, but each work-item will now compute one $\Delta I \times \Delta J$ submatrix of $C[I,J]$. Each iteration of the k loop will multiply a $\Delta I \times \Delta K_{\text{reg.}}$ matrix by a $\Delta K_{\text{reg.}} \times \Delta J$ matrix.

For the NN variant, where both A and B use normal matrix layout, we implement the matrix multiplication between a 1×4 block from A and the 4×4 block from B as[13]

---

[12]The GPU increments the ID associated with λ_0 as the innermost index, and by assigning `get_global_id(0)` to j, we have chosen j as the innermost index in our implementation. This choice will be discussed in Section 7.5.6

[13]In code snippets such as these, we gloss over some details, such as the fact that we need $4k$ instead of k as the offset in the reads from B.

```
float4 a  =  A[i,    k];
float4 b0 =  B[k+0, j];
float4 b1 =  B[k+1, j];
float4 b2 =  B[k+2, j];
float4 b3 =  B[k+3, j];
ab += a.s0*b0 + a.s1*b1 + a.s2*b2 + a.s3*b3;
```

where `ab` (of type `float4`) is the accumulator for the 1×4 block of C and all operations are vector operations. The kernel is shown in Listing 7.11.

For the NT variant, we instead select ($\Delta I = 2$, $\Delta J = 2$, $\Delta K_{\mathrm{reg.}} = 4$) and implement the multiplication between the 2×4 block of A and the 2×4 block of the transposed B as

```
float4 a0 = A[i   , k];
float4 a1 = A[i+1, k];
float4 b0 = B[j   , k];
float4 b1 = B[j+1, k];
ab.s01 += (float2) (dot(a0, b0), dot(a0, b1));
ab.s23 += (float2) (dot(a1, b0), dot(a1, b1));
```

where `ab` is an accumulator variable of type `float4` for the 2×2 block of the matrix C.[14] The full kernel is shown in Listing 7.12

```
kernel void
sgemm(global float4 const *A, global float4 const *B,
      global float4 *C, float alpha, float beta, uint n)
{
  uint j = get_global_id(0);
  uint i = get_global_id(1);
  uint nv4 = n >> 2;

  float4 accum = (float4) 0.0f;
  for (uint k = 0; k < nv4; ++k)
  {
    float4 a = A[i*nv4 + k];

    float4 b0 = B[(4*k+0)*nv4 + j];
    float4 b1 = B[(4*k+1)*nv4 + j];
    float4 b2 = B[(4*k+2)*nv4 + j];
    float4 b3 = B[(4*k+3)*nv4 + j];

    accum += a.s0*b0+a.s1*b1+a.s2*b2+a.s3*b3;
  }
  C[i*nv4 + j] = alpha * accum + beta * C[i*nv4 + j];
}
```

Listing 7.11. Vectorized implementation: `blockedNN`.

---

[14]The components `ab.s01` accumulate the top row and the components `ab.s23` accumulate the bottom row of the 2×2 block.

```
kernel void
sgemm(global float4 * const A, global float4 * const B,
      global float2 *C, float alpha, float beta, uint n)
{
  uint i = get_global_id(0);
  uint j = get_global_id(1);
  uint nv4 = n >> 2;

  float4 ab = (float4)(0.0f);
  for (uint k = 0; k < nv4; ++k)
  {
    float4 a0 = A[ 2*i     *nv4 + k];
    float4 a1 = A[(2*i+1)*nv4 + k];

    float4 b0 = B[ 2*j     *nv4 + k];
    float4 b1 = B[(2*j+1)*nv4 + k];

    ab += (float4)(dot(a0, b0), dot(a0, b1),
                   dot(a1, b0), dot(a1, b1));

  }
  uint ix = 2*i*(n>>1) + j;
  C[ix]          = alpha * ab.s01 + beta * C[ix];
  C[ix + (n>>1)] = alpha * ab.s23 + beta * C[ix + (n>>1)];
}
```

Listing 7.12. Vectorized implementation: `blockedNT`.

We saw the need to introduce blocking to enable the use of vector operations, but register blocking also decreases the number of loads necessary. Our scalar implementations (both the NN and NT variants) loaded N elements of A and N elements of B to compute one element of C, so we needed to load $(N+N)N^2 = 2N^3$ elements from A and B. in general, we need to load one $\Delta I \times \Delta K_{\text{reg.}}$ block from A and one $\Delta K_{\text{reg.}} \times \Delta J$ block from B per iteration, and we need $N/\Delta K_{\text{reg.}}$ iterations. We need one work-item for each of the $(N/\Delta I)(N/\Delta J)$ blocks in C, which gives us a total of

$$(\Delta I \Delta K_{\text{reg.}} + \Delta K_{\text{reg.}} \Delta J)\frac{N}{\Delta K_{\text{reg.}}} \frac{N}{\Delta I} \frac{N}{\Delta J} = N^3 \left(\frac{1}{\Delta J} + \frac{1}{\Delta I} \right)$$

elements to be loaded into registers.

The above result tells us that we should want to choose ΔI and ΔJ large and similar, while the choice of $\Delta K_{\text{reg.}}$ is less important. We always set $\Delta K_{\text{reg.}}$ to 4, as this is the smallest value that allows us to use vector operations.[15]

In NN implementations, we have to also choose ΔJ as a multiple of 4, to allow for the use of vector operations, whereas $\Delta I = \Delta J = 2$ is one option we may choose in the NT case. We can compute the difference in load requirements between the $1 \times 4 \times 4$ and $2 \times 4 \times 2$ implementations[16] by computing $1/\Delta I + 1/\Delta J$

---

[15]We note that the scalar version corresponds to $\Delta I = \Delta J = \Delta K_{\text{reg.}} = 1$.

[16]We will sometimes refer to a blocking by writing it $\Delta I \times \Delta K_{\text{reg.}} \times \Delta J$.

for them, and we find 1.25 and 1, respectively, showing that the second blocking needs fewer load operations. We see that the added flexibility we are given to choose blocking widths in the NT version can help us decrease the number of memory operations, and this is one reason to expect that the NT variants will perform better on the GPU.

In both cases, however, we perform $O(N^3)$ load operations from data of size $O(N^2)$, which means that each datum is reloaded into registers $O(N)$ times. Effective cache usage will clearly be important, as it allows us to access data from caches rather than from main memory.

7.5.6   L1 Cache Analysis of the $1 \times 4 \times 4$ Blocked NN SGEMM

Overview.   To estimate the cache usage of our kernels, we have to take into account the order of reads within a work-item, as well as the fact that many work-items are active at the same time. We will first look at one specific choice of program and local work size and then try to extend the analysis to be able to compare the cache usage of different implementations and local work sizes.

In the program we choose to analyze first, the $1 \times 4 \times 4$ blocked NN implementation, every work-item performs five memory operations per iteration in its loop, and we will assume that the memory operations take place in the same order as they appear in the program (i.e., the compiler does not change their order), and that, for a given work-item, memory operations never execute in parallel. Another restriction that we will also make in our analysis, and which is important, is that we are able to perfectly predict the order in which work-items execute on the GPU. Finally, this section will only focus on the L1 cache, which allows us to restrict the analysis to a single core, as each core has its own L1 cache.

Thread order.   A single work-item loops over the variable k, and for every value of k, it performs one memory load from A and four memory loads from B. With our assumptions, we know that the work-item[17] will enter the load-store pipeline once for each of those instructions, in the order they appear in the program source. We also know that we schedule one work-group of work-items at a time, that those work-items execute their memory operations in an interleaved fashion one after the other, and that they always do this in the order they were spawned by the GPU. We will now see what how we can use that knowledge to analyze the L1 data cache that we need to use.

---

[17]From a hardware point of view, we of course discuss the behavior and order of threads, but we continue to use the term work-item, remembering that one work-item in OpenCL corresponds to one thread in the GPU.

Fixed local work size. Using our notation introduced previously, work-item (j, i) performs the following reads in loop iteration k:

$$A[i, k], B[4k + 0, j], B[4k + 1, j], B[4k + 2, j], B[4k + 3, j],$$

where each memory access now loads a `float4` vector. With many active threads, we will first see all threads performing their first reads from A, and thereafter we will see all threads performing their first read from B, etc. This implies that reads that are executed after each other correspond to different threads executing the same instruction in the program code. With a local work size of $(4,32)$, the GPU initiates the work-items for work-group (m, n) by incrementing the first index first, i.e., in the order

$$(4m, 32n), (4m + 1, 32n), (4m + 2, 32n), (4m + 3, 32n),$$
$$(4m, 32n + 1), (4m + 1, 32n + 1), (4m + 2, 32n + 1), (4m + 3, 32n + 1),$$
$$(4m, 32n + 2), (4m + 1, 32n + 2), (4m + 2, 32n + 2), (4m + 3, 32n + 2),$$
$$\ldots,$$
$$(4m, 32n + 31), (4m + 1, 32n + 31), (4m + 2, 32n + 31), (4m + 3, 32n + 31),$$

where we have again used the comma as a sequencing operation to describe the ordering of `global_id` values of the work-items.

This means that the memory reads for loop iteration k will execute in the following order:

$$\left(\overset{32n+31}{\underset{i=32n}{,}} \overset{4m+3}{\underset{j=4m}{,}} A[i, k] \right),$$

$$\left(\overset{32n+31}{\underset{i=32n}{,}} \overset{4m+3}{\underset{j=4m}{,}} B[4k + 0, j] \right), \left(\overset{32n+31}{\underset{i=32n}{,}} \overset{4m+3}{\underset{j=4m}{,}} B[4k + 1, j] \right),$$

$$\left(\overset{32n+31}{\underset{i=32n}{,}} \overset{4m+3}{\underset{j=4m}{,}} B[4k + 2, j] \right), \left(\overset{32n+31}{\underset{i=32n}{,}} \overset{4m+3}{\underset{j=4m}{,}} B[4k + 3, j] \right),$$

where the ID variable j is incremented before i as it corresponds to `get_global_id(0)`, and it is therefore written as the innermost $,$ operator.

We see that the reads from A do not depend on j and are therefore repeated for each group of four consecutive work-items, and we introduce the $\times$ operation to reflect repetition of the same memory access as in

$$\overset{4m+3}{\underset{j=4m}{,}} A[i, k] = A[i, k] \times 4$$

This notation allows us to write a single iteration over k as

$$\left(\begin{matrix} 32n+31 \\ \text{,} \\ i=32n \end{matrix} A[i,k] \times 4 \right), \left(\begin{matrix} 4m+3 \\ \text{,} \\ j=4m \end{matrix} B[4k+0,j] \right) \times 32, \left(\begin{matrix} 4m+3 \\ \text{,} \\ j=4m \end{matrix} B[4k+1,j] \right) \times 32,$$

$$\left(\begin{matrix} 4m+3 \\ \text{,} \\ j=4m \end{matrix} B[4k+2,j] \right) \times 32, \left(\begin{matrix} 4m+3 \\ \text{,} \\ j=4m \end{matrix} B[4k+3,j] \right) \times 32.$$

As a cache line has space for four `float4` elements, we see that the reads from A read the first quarter of 32 consecutive cache lines and the reads from B read four full cache lines. To get full cache lines instead, we consider four consecutive iterations in k together, and we see that those four iterations read 32 full cache lines from A and 16 full cache lines from B. For the moment, we restrict ourselves to considering a single work-group, and we note that these cache lines will never be reused by later operations in the same work-group. We have now arrived at our conclusion for the L1 cache requirements of the loop. If our L1 cache has enough space for 48 cache lines, then we will never read the same value into the L1 cache twice while executing the loop for all work-items in a work-group, as all subsequent uses will be able to reuse the value that is stored in the cache.

After the loop has completed, the work-group additionally has to load and store to C, which needs access to a 32×4 block of 1×4 blocks of C, spanning 32 complete cache lines, meaning that (as long as our L1 cache is at least 32 cache lines large) we will not see any lack of reuse for the elements of C within a work-group.

If we continue to assume that we only have a single work-group at a time, and consider the possibilities for cache reuse between consecutively scheduled work-groups on the same core, we need to consider the state of the L1 cache when work-group (n, m) finishes execution. The L1 cache contains 256 cache lines in total, and the operations on C will have filled 32 of those, so 224 remain for A and B. Each sequence of four iterations needs 48 cache lines, so the number of iterations that have their cache lines still in cache at work-group completion is $4(256 - 32)/48$, or 16, and this lets us see that the work-group size where we may have reuse between work-groups is when we only need 16 sequences of four iterations each in the loop, or 64 iterations, which corresponds to a matrix size of 256×256 (as we chose $\Delta K_{\text{reg.}} = 4$). For larger matrices, no reuse between consecutively scheduled work-groups on the same core is possible.

Arbitrary local work size. For an arbitrary local work size, we have two reasons to redo the above analysis. First, we have the obvious reason that we get a different interleaved read pattern between the work-items within a work-group. Second, we can have more than one work-group simultaneously active on the same core, if we choose a smaller local work size.

With a local work size of (λ_0, λ_1), we need to look at all work-groups that are running simultaneously on the same core. If the total number of work-items on the core is 128 (which seemed optimal in the Sobel study), and if $\lambda_0\lambda_1 = 128$, then we have only a single work-group on the core, but we could have chosen $\lambda_0 = \lambda_1 = 4$, which would give us $128/16 = 8$ work-groups executing simultaneously on a core. As before, it will be beneficial to look at the cache usage over four iterations over k, and we can easily generalize the results we had before to see that a single work-group reads λ_1 full cache lines from A and $4\lambda_0$ full cache lines from B for every four iterations (provided that λ_0 is a multiple of 4).

If $\lambda_0\lambda_1 \leq 64$, we have more than one work-group executing simultaneously on the core. In this case, the work-groups that are simultaneously active on a code will have consecutive values of m and identical values of n. We see that the reads from A read from the same cache lines, so they are reused between the work-groups. We said above that a few work-groups are sent to each core, and we assume that the work-groups we are having active at the same time belong to this set, as we would otherwise not have consecutive group IDs (m, n).[18]

This means that the 128 work-items executing simultaneously on one core use

$$\lambda_1 + 4\lambda_0 \, [\text{number of work-groups}] = \lambda_1 + 4\lambda_0 \frac{128}{\lambda_0\lambda_1} = \lambda_1 + 512/\lambda_1$$

cache lines from the L1 cache for four consecutive iterations in k. As this expression is independent of λ_0, we can select our λ_0 freely (as long as it is a multiple of 4), and the only effect we see (from our analysis so far) is that a larger λ_0 restricts our possible choices for λ_1. With $\lambda_1 = 1, 2, 4, 8, 16, 32, 64, 128$, we see that we require $513, 258, 132, 72, 48, 48, 72, 132$ cache lines, and with room for 256 lines in the L1 cache of each core, the fraction of L1 we need to use is[19] $2.0, 1.0, 0.52, 0.28, 0.19, 0.19, 0.28, 0.52$. Under our assumptions of fully associative cache and perfect execution order between work-items, we would expect all options with a value below 1 to have the same performance (disregarding the effects of L2 and RAM).

As we know that our assumptions are incorrect, though, we need to discuss what happens when executing on a real GPU. First, due to the design of the cache, we will see cache misses before the cache is 100% filled, i.e., earlier than our analysis above would have predicted. The more complicated aspect of execution is that the work-items that are spawned in the order we describe here do not keep the order. When one work-item is stalled on a cache miss, other work-items may overtake it, so we will have active work-items that are executing different iterations (different values of k) at the same time. We refer to this as thread divergence (or work-item divergence), and the fraction of L1 we need is a measure of our robustness to keep having good performance in cases of thread divergence. Thread divergence always happens and is difficult to measure and quantify, but

---

[18]With work-group divergence, i.e., with a few work-items each from many work-groups partially finished on the same core, we might have work-groups with very different `group_ids` simultaneously active on the same core.

[19]The numbers are also shown in Table 7.2.

we can qualitatively say that the longer the program runs, the stronger divergence we see. This implies that the benefits of a low L1 cache utilization fraction have a stronger impact on performance for large matrix sizes.

The innermost index. Now that we have discussed cache usage, we will return to one aspect of the NN variant that we did not discuss before, namely the choice to use j as the innermost index in the sequencing of operations. We have chosen the order by using `global_id(0)` for the index j and `global_id(1)` for the index i in our CL C kernels. The argument we will provide here holds only for the NN versions, and is not applicable for the NT versions.

If we again consider the memory read sequence for the scalar NN variant, and only look at a single iteration and a single work-group, we see

$$\left(\overset{\lambda_1-1}{\underset{i=0}{?}} \overset{\lambda_0-1}{\underset{j=0}{?}} A[i,k] \right), \left(\overset{\lambda_1-1}{\underset{i=0}{?}} \overset{\lambda_0-1}{\underset{j=0}{?}} B[k,j] \right)$$

$$= \left(\overset{\lambda_1-1}{\underset{i=0}{?}} A[i,k] \times \lambda_0 \right), \left(\overset{\lambda_0-1}{\underset{j=0}{?}} B[k,j] \right) \times \lambda_1,$$

but we could instead have swapped the roles of the `global_id`s and gotten

$$\left(\overset{\lambda_1-1}{\underset{j=0}{?}} \overset{\lambda_0-1}{\underset{i=0}{?}} A[i,k] \right), \left(\overset{\lambda_1-1}{\underset{j=0}{?}} \overset{\lambda_0-1}{\underset{i=0}{?}} B[k,j] \right)$$

$$\left(\overset{\lambda_0-1}{\underset{i=0}{?}} A[i,k] \right) \times \lambda_1, \left(\overset{\lambda_1-1}{\underset{j=0}{?}} B[k,j] \times \lambda_0 \right).$$

We will now look for the number of cache-line switches in the execution of those reads. For the former case, the reads from A are described by $\overset{\lambda_1-1}{\underset{i=0}{?}} A[i,k] \times \lambda_0$, which switches cache line λ_1 times (and between those switches, we read from the same matrix element λ_0 times). For different values of i we read from different rows of the matrix, and separate rows are always on separate cache lines.[20] Staying with the first version, but looking at B, we see that we switch matrix element $\lambda_0\lambda_1$ times, as every read is from a different element than the previous read, and we perform $\lambda_0\lambda_1$ reads. We note, however, that we switch between consecutive elements in memory, which means that we only have $\lambda_0\lambda_1/16$ cache line switches, as we can fit 16 matrix elements into a cache line. For the second version, with the indices in the other order, analogous considerations show that we switch matrix element $\lambda_0\lambda_1$ times for A and λ_1 times for B, but

---

[20]Except for very small matrices, of course, but those cases do not require cache analysis anyway.

we again step between consecutive memory locations in B, which means that the number of cache-line switches is only $\lambda_1/16$ for B. If we add the cache line switches together for A and B, we have $\lambda_0\lambda_1/16 + \lambda_1$ and $\lambda_0\lambda_1 + \lambda_1/16$ for the two versions, respectively. With λ_0 and λ_1 between 4 and 64, the first version will always need fewer cache-line switches than the latter.[21] In cases where we do have cache misses (e.g., due to thread divergence), this should improve the performance by reducing the concurrent cache needs within an iteration.

7.5.7   L1 Cache Analysis of Blocked NT Kernel

For the blocked NT kernel, we can analyze the L1 cache utilization in the same way as for the NN kernel. We start by noting that work-item (j, i), in iteration k, performs the memory accesses

$$A[2i, k], A[2i + 1, k], B[2j, k], B[2j + 1, k],$$

and we see that we should again consider four iterations over k, to get full cache lines:

$$A[2i, k + 0], A[2i + 1, k + 0], B[j, k + 0], B[2j + 1, k + 0];$$
$$A[2i, k + 1], A[2i + 1, k + 1], B[j, k + 1], B[2j + 1, k + 1];$$
$$A[2i, k + 2], A[2i + 1, k + 2], B[j, k + 2], B[2j + 1, k + 2];$$
$$A[2i, k + 3], A[2i + 1, k + 3], B[j, k + 3], B[2j + 1, k + 3].$$

During execution of the first four iterations, the first work-group, with its $\lambda_0\lambda_1$ work-items, accesses

$$\overset{4}{\underset{k=0}{?}} \left[\left(\overset{\lambda_1-1}{\underset{i=0}{?}} \overset{\lambda_0-1}{\underset{j=0}{?}} A[2i, k] \right), \left(\overset{\lambda_1-1}{\underset{i=0}{?}} \overset{\lambda_0-1}{\underset{j=0}{?}} A[2i + 1, k] \right), \right.$$
$$\left. \left(\overset{\lambda_1-1}{\underset{i=0}{?}} \overset{\lambda_0-1}{\underset{j=0}{?}} B[2j, k] \right), \left(\overset{\lambda_1-1}{\underset{i=0}{?}} \overset{\lambda_0-1}{\underset{j=0}{?}} B[2j + 1, k] \right) \right]$$

and the first set of M simultaneous work-groups accesses

$$\overset{4}{\underset{k=0}{?}} \left[\left(\overset{M-1}{\underset{m=0}{?}} \overset{\lambda_1-1}{\underset{i=0}{?}} \overset{m\lambda_0+\lambda_0-1}{\underset{j=m\lambda_0}{?}} A[2i, k] \right), \left(\overset{M-1}{\underset{m=0}{?}} \overset{\lambda_1-1}{\underset{i=0}{?}} \overset{m\lambda_0+\lambda_0-1}{\underset{j=m\lambda_0}{?}} A[2i + 1, k] \right), \right.$$
$$\left. \left(\overset{M-1}{\underset{m=0}{?}} \overset{\lambda_1-1}{\underset{i=0}{?}} \overset{m\lambda_0+\lambda_0-1}{\underset{j=m\lambda_0}{?}} B[2j, k] \right), \left(\overset{M-1}{\underset{m=0}{?}} \overset{\lambda_1-1}{\underset{i=0}{?}} \overset{m\lambda_0+\lambda_0-1}{\underset{j=m\lambda_0}{?}} B[2j + 1, k] \right) \right],$$

---

[21]The roles of λ_0 and λ_1 are interchanged between the two versions, but the first one is still always better.

λ_1	1	2	4	8	16	32	64	128
Cache lines (NN)	513	258	132	72	48	48	72	132
L1 fraction (NN)	2.0	1.0	0.52	0.28	0.19	0.19	0.28	0.52
Cache lines (NT)	258	132	72	48	48	72	132	258
L1 fraction (NT)	1.0	0.52	0.28	0.19	0.19	0.28	0.52	1.0

Table 7.2. L1 cache utilization for the $1 \times 4 \times 4$ blocked NN and the $2 \times 4 \times 2$ blocked NT kernels. We note that if we want to choose $\lambda_0 = 4$, we are restricted to $\lambda_1 \leq 32$.

where m was incremented as an outer index to both i and j, as we create all work-items in the first work-group before creating the first work-item in the second work-group. We again share the accesses to A, and these four iterations over k will need $2\lambda_1$ cache lines from A and $2M\lambda_0$ cache lines from B, and as before, we have $M = 128/(\lambda_0\lambda_1)$, giving a total L1 usage of

$$2\lambda_1 + 2\lambda_0 \frac{128}{\lambda_0\lambda_1} = 2\lambda_1 + \frac{256}{\lambda_1}.$$

If we compare with the result of the NN implementation, we get the L1 utilization fractions shown in Table 7.2. By comparing with the results with the previous ones, we see that while we had a preference for $\lambda_1 = 16$ or $\lambda_1 = 32$ for the $1 \times 4 \times 4$ blocked (NN) version, the $2 \times 4 \times 2$ blocked (NT) implementation works better with smaller work-groups.

7.5.8 L1 Cache Blocking

We saw above that the L1 cache utilization determined our robustness against thread divergence, but every program will, if we do not interfere with thread scheduling in any way, experience thread divergence. For large enough matrices, this will always lead to performance degradations in the kernels we have discussed so far. Our strategy to get around this issue is to introduce yet another level of blocking and to rewrite the algorithm with this additional level of block-matrix multiplication.

As a means of relating this level of blocking to the discussion about register blocking, we now introduce a much larger ΔK, so that we have two: the $\Delta K_{\text{reg.}}$ introduced previously, and the new ΔK_{cache}. After each set of ΔK_{cache} iterations in the loop, we reassemble all work-items in the work-group to ensure that no thread divergence appears within the work-group.

Relating the change to the actual code, we insert a barrier operation between every ΔK_{cache} iterations in the loop. As this only limits thread divergence within a work-group, we will still have to take into account the divergence between work-groups that will limit L1 cache sharing between different work-groups. It therefore seems as if we should expect that this method will work best when there is only one simultaneously active work-group on each core. The full kernel is shown in Listing 7.13.

```
#define  di  ((uint)2)
#define  dj  ((uint)2)
#define  dk  ((uint)32)

kernel  void
sgemm(global  float4  const  *A,  global  float4  const  *B,
   global  float2  *C,  float  alpha,  float  beta,  uint  n)
{
  uint  j  =  get_global_id(0);
  uint  i  =  get_global_id(1);
  uint  nv4  =  n  >>  2;

  float4  ab  =  (float4)  0.0f;
  for  (uint  k  =  0;  k  <  nv4;  k  +=  dk)
  {
    for  (uint  kk  =  0;  kk  <  dk;  ++kk)
    {
      float4  a0  =  A[  2*i    *nv4  +  kk+k];
      float4  a1  =  A[(2*i+1)*nv4  +  kk+k];

      float4  b0  =  B[  2*j    *nv4  +  kk+k];
      float4  b1  =  B[(2*j+1)*nv4  +  kk+k];

      ab  +=  (float4)(dot(a0,  b0),  dot(a0,  b1),
                 dot(a1,  b0),  dot(a1,  b1));
    }
    barrier(CLK_GLOBAL_MEM_FENCE);
  }

  uint  ix  =  2*i*(n>>1)  +  j;
  C[ix]          =  alpha  *  ab.s01  +  beta  *  C[ix];
  C[ix  +  (n>>1)]  =  alpha  *  ab.s23  +  beta  *  C[ix  +  (n>>1)];
}
```

Listing 7.13. Cache-blocked implementation: `cacheblockedNT`. The constants `di`, `dj`, and `dk` correspond to our ΔI, ΔJ, and ΔK_{cache}, respectively.

The benefit of the barrier is that we can get the same L1 cache sharing for large matrices as we had for small matrices. The cost of executing the barrier is due to the fact that we have to reassemble all work-items of the work-group at regular intervals. If no thread divergence occurs, this means that all work-items need to enter into the barrier, which takes time proportional to the number of work-items, and then all work-items need to exit from the barrier, which again takes a number of cycles proportional to the number of work-items involved. This means that the effective cost of a barrier is the number of cycles it takes, times the number of work-items that are taking part in the barrier, or at least[22] $2\lambda_0^2\lambda_1^2$. It is therefore beneficial for the actual execution time of the barrier to

[22]Executing the **barrier** instruction takes $2\lambda_0\lambda_1$ cycles, and in this time the $\lambda_0\lambda_1$ work-items involved are prevented from performing other work, which means that the work lost due to the **barrier** instruction is $2\lambda_0^2\lambda_1^2$. Again, the description is simplified but sufficient for our needs (e.g., while the last work-item exits from the barrier, the first work-item is already performing work again).

have small work-groups. As the work-group divergence that is a consequence of small work-groups will hurt cache sharing between work-groups, we have two competing behaviors, and we need to find a good compromise. We may therefore want to select a small work-group size to ensure that barriers are cheap (and an NT algorithm, as we say that it goes better with small work-groups). On the other hand, we will want to choose a large work-group size, as we want to keep work-group divergence small, and therefore want to have only a small number of active work-groups.

We also have to find a good compromise for the value of the parameter ΔK_{cache}. It must be small enough to keep thread divergence low, but we also need to ensure that we do not execute the barrier too often (to keep the cost of executing the barriers low).

The barrier is executed $N/(\Delta K_{\text{reg}}.\Delta K_{\text{cache}})$ times, with a cost of $2\lambda_0^2\lambda_1^2$ cycles each time, and we want to ensure that this cost is small compared to the number of memory operations. The number of memory operations performed by the work-group between two consecutive barriers is $\Delta K_{\text{cache}}(\Delta I\Delta K_{\text{reg}}. + \Delta K_{\text{reg}}.\Delta J)\lambda_0\lambda_1$, and our condition for ΔK_{cache} becomes

$$\Delta K_{\text{cache}}(\Delta I\Delta K_{\text{reg}}. + \Delta K_{\text{reg}}.\Delta J)\lambda_0\lambda_1 > 2\lambda_0^2\lambda_1^2,$$

which we rewrite as

$$\Delta K_{\text{cache}} > \frac{2\lambda_0\lambda_1}{(\Delta I\Delta K_{\text{reg}}. + \Delta K_{\text{reg}}.\Delta J)}.$$

For the $2 \times 4 \times 2$ blocking with a large work-group size, we find that we need

$$\Delta K_{\text{cache}} > \frac{2[\#\text{active threads}]}{8 + 8} = \frac{256}{16} = 16.$$

For our kernel, we have chosen $\Delta K_{\text{cache}} = 32$.

7.5.9 Page Table Lookups

One aspect that we have not yet discussed but that is important for the performance of the NN and NT versions, is the way they affect the memory management unit. The physical memory is partitioned into areas called *pages*, and the abstract pointer space is also partitioned into pages in a similar way. Every page that we use in the pointer space must correspond to a page in physical memory, and information about this mapping is stored in page tables. When we try to access memory using a pointer, we need to find out which page it points to in pointer space, and which page that corresponds to in the physical memory space. The process of looking up a page in the page tables is costly, and we want to perform as few page table lookups as possible when executing our kernel.[23] Going back

---

[23]This description is simplified but sufficient for our current purposes.

to the scalar kernels, to keep the discussion simple, the memory accesses of a work-group of the scalar NN kernel looks like

$$
\overset{N}{\underset{k=0}{,}} \left[\left(\overset{\lambda_1-1}{\underset{i=0}{,}} \overset{\lambda_0-1}{\underset{j=0}{,}} A[i,k] \right), \left(\overset{\lambda_1-1}{\underset{i=0}{,}} \overset{\lambda_0-1}{\underset{j=0}{,}} B[k,j] \right) \right],
$$

and we see that it needs to access data from all rows of B but only from a single row of A. The scalar NT kernel instead reads from

$$
\overset{N}{\underset{k=0}{,}} \left[\left(\overset{\lambda_1-1}{\underset{i=0}{,}} \overset{\lambda_0-1}{\underset{j=0}{,}} A[i,k] \right), \left(\overset{\lambda_1-1}{\underset{i=0}{,}} \overset{\lambda_0-1}{\underset{j=0}{,}} B[j,k] \right) \right],
$$

which accesses only one row each of A and B. This means that, if the matrices are much larger than the size of a page, the work-group in the NN variant needs to access memory from many more pages than the NT variant, although they access the same number of bytes. We must expect that the need to access more pages implies a need to perform a larger number of page table lookups, which decreases performance.

We should look at the memory accesses for the work-groups that are active at the same time, and not just a single work-group, but the conclusion will be the same: the NN version needs to perform a larger number of page table lookups than the NT version. The conclusion also remains the same when we look at blocked versions, as we are still in the situation that all work-items access the entire column from B in the NN versions.

If we turn to a cache-blocked NN version, we have a barrier that we introduced to prevent thread divergence, and although we still need a larger number of lookups in the NN version than in the NT version, we do not need as many at the same time as in the scalar and blocked NN versions, as the barrier ensures that the work-items that are simultaneously active only want to access a limited number of pages at once.

To summarize the discussion of page tables, cache-blocking should improve the situation slightly over the scalar and blocked NN versions, but for large matrices, we must expect the NT versions to have a performance advantage over the NN versions.

7.5.10   Performance

Performance metrics. The primary performance metric is the number of floating-points operations (nflops) per second (FLOPS). For each output element $C[i,j]$, $(2N-1)+1 = 2N$ FLOPS are required to compute the dot product of $A[i,*] \cdot B[*,j]$ and scale it by α, one multiplication to scale $C[i,j]$ by β, and one addition to obtain the final result. Thus, nflops $= 2N^2(N+1)$. Dividing nflops by execution time in nanoseconds (10^{-9} seconds) gives GFLOPS (10^9 FLOPS).

Size	sNN	sNT	bNN	bNT	cbNN	cbNT
96	2.0	2.0	8.0	11.2	5.1	7.4
192	2.0	2.1	8.4	13.0	5.1	8.1
384	2.0	2.1	7.6	13.2	6.4	10.1
768	2.0	2.1	7.5	13.1	6.6	10.0
1440	2.0	2.1	7.4	13.1	6.5	9.3
2880	1.6	2.0	6.8	10.8	6.1	9.2

Table 7.3. Performance in GFLOPS for some variants and matrix sizes. For each matrix size and kind of implementation, we have only selected one number, and it may, e.g., use different blocking parameters at different sizes. The columns show the best performance we see in GFLOPS for scalar (s), blocked (b), and cache-blocked (cb) variants of non-transposed (NN) and transposed (NT) SGEMM implementations.

Overall trends. In Table 7.3, we show performance numbers for different kinds of implementations and different matrix sizes. Variation within one kind is not shown, and different rows in the same column can contain results for different variants of the same kind (e.g., different blocking parameters or work-group sizes).

We see that the NT versions perform better than NN versions and that blocked versions are better than scalar versions, as expected. While already the smallest shown matrix size appears sufficient for the scalar versions, the blocked and (more strongly) the cache-blocked variants need larger amounts of work to reach their best performance.

Our experiments with larger matrices, where performance is heavily influenced by system effects like thread-divergence, are not shown in the table, due to variations in results.

Cache-blocking. One surprising result in the table is the large difference between the blocked and cache-blocked variants, where the introduction of cache-blocking seems to come at a large cost. This impression is misleading and due to our selection of data. We only display the best performance achieved for each kind of implementation, and we saw in the Sobel results that the number of registers plays a crucial role in determining performance. For the best blocked NT implementation we have, the corresponding cache-blocked versions use more registers, which prevents us from keeping 128 simultaneous threads per core. Due to the limited number of threads, this version is not our best cache-blocked implementation, as we have other variants that use fewer registers. The columns bNT and cbNT therefore display results for different implementations. If we instead consider (nearly) identical implementations of $1 \times 4 \times 4$ blocked and cache-blocked NT variants (shown in Table 7.4), we see much larger similarities in the top results, and we also see the large difference in the median result for large matrices.

Work-group divergence. For large workloads, work-group divergence will start to appear, and this will affect performance. The occasional very good performance

Size	Blocked		Cache-Blocked	
	Median	High	Median	High
96	9.3	9.4	7.0	7.4
192	10.5	10.6	8.0	8.1
384	9.9	10.0	9.9	10.0
768	9.7	9.9	9.7	10.0
1440	9.6	9.9	9.1	9.3
2880	1.1	9.4	9.2	9.2

Table 7.4. Performance in GFLOPS for $1 \times 4 \times 4$ blocked and cache-blocked NT implementations. Each implementation was run three times for each matrix size and each local work-group size. The median and best results from the nine runs are listed in the table.

results with blocking versions probably appear in runs where we see no or very little work-group divergence, whereas the much lower median result shows that the typical case has lower performance.

Cache-blocking, introduced to stifle thread divergence, also has an effect in preventing work-group divergence, thereby decreasing the variability.

The cost of a barrier. In our previous estimate of the cost of executing a barrier instruction, we assumed that we would have one work-item per cycle entering into the barrier, and then one work-item per cycle exiting. In reality, with thread divergence, we do not have the ideal case of one work-item entering the barrier every cycle, as the first work-item will be a few instructions ahead of the last one. Instead, all work-items will have to wait for the last one to arrive at the barrier. The actual cost of the barrier can therefore be significantly higher than our estimate, if a few work-items of the work-group are far behind in executing the program.

7.5.11 Summary

We started from scalar versions of a generic matrix multiplication and then transformed the initial kernels, successively arriving at more elaborate implementations. We discussed the reason behind the transformations, and we discussed how the transformations took advantage of aspects of the hardware. We started by introducing vector operations, and then we focused on the memory system and in particular on the L1 cache. We also discussed execution times, as measured on an Arndale development board, and we found that the qualitative results were as we expected, although a quantitative comparison shows that our simplifying assumptions are not always satisfied.

Acknowledgments

The authors gratefully acknowledge the work of their colleagues at ARM's Media Processing Group.

Bibliography

[ARM 13] ARM. "Mali OpenCL SDK v1.1." http://malideveloper.arm.com/develop-for-mali/sdks/mali-opencl-sdk, 2013.

[Howes et al. 10] Lee Howes, Anton Lokhmotov, Alastair F. Donaldson, and Paul H. J. Kelly. "Towards Metaprogramming for Parallel Systems on a Chip." In *Workshop on Highly Parallel Processing on a Chip (HPPC)*, LNCS 6043, pp. 36–45. Berlin: Springer-Verlag, 2010.

[Ryoo et al. 08] Shane Ryoo, Christopher I. Rodrigues, Sam S. Stone, John A. Stratton, Sain-Zee Ueng, Sara S. Baghsorkhi, and Wen-mei W. Hwu. "Program optimization carving for GPU computing." *Journal of Parallel and Distributed Computing* 68:10 (2008), 1389–1401.

3D Engine Design

Welcome to the 3D Engine Design section of this edition of *GPU Pro*. The selection of chapters you will find here covers a range of engine design problems.

First, Peter Sikachev, Vladimir Egorov, and Sergey Makeev share their experience using quaternions in an MMORPG game engine. Their chapter, "Quaternions Revisited," illustrates the use of quaternions for multiple purposes in order to replace bulky 3×3 rotation and tangent space matrices throughout the entire engine, most notably affecting aspects such as normal mapping, generic transforms, instancing, skinning, and morph targets. The chapter shows the performance and memory savings attributable to the authors' findings.

Second, Fabrice Robinet, Rémi Arnaud, Tony Parisi, and Patrick Cozzi present the chapter "glTF: Designing an Open-Standard Runtime Asset Format." This chapter introduces work by the COLLADA Working Group in the Khronos Group to provide a bridge between interchange asset formats and the OpenGL-based runtime graphics APIs (e.g., WebGL and OpenGL ES). The design of the glTF open-standard transmission-format is described, along with open-source content pipeline tools involved in converting COLLADA to glTF and REST-based cloud services.

Finally, Bartosz Chodorowski and Wojciech Sterna present the chapter "Managing Transformations in Hierarchy," which provides a study on this basic 3D engine component. In addition to presenting the theory, it describes and addresses some of the issues found in common implementations of the transformation hierarchy system. It also describes how to achieve some useful operations within this system such as re-parenting nodes and global positioning.

I hope you enjoy this edition's selections, and I hope you find these chapters inspiring and enlightening to your rendering and engine development work.

—Wessam Bahnassi

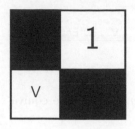

Quaternions Revisited

Peter Sikachev, Vladimir Egorov, and Sergey Makeev

1.1 Introduction

Quaternions have been extensively used in computer graphics in the last few years. One defines a quaternion as a hypercomplex number, $w + xi + yj + kz$, but in practice it is convenient to consider it to be a 4D vector (x, y, z, w) with a special operation of multiplication defined for it. In 3D computer graphics, quaternions can be used to encode rotations and coordinate systems.

In this chapter we describe the experience of using quaternions in the MMO-RPG engine. In comparison with [Malyshau 12], we propose a quaternion interpolation solution that does not increase vertex count. Besides, we go deeper in detail regarding precision and performance issues. Finally, we strive to cover a broader range of problems, including normal mapping, skinning, instancing, morph targets, and nonuniform scale.

1.2 Quaternion Properties Overview

While strict wording may be found in the excellent book [Lengyel 11], we will summarize some key quaternion properties below. The quaternion $\mathbf{q}$ is called *normalized* if $\|\mathbf{q}\| = \sqrt{x^2 + y^2 + z^2 + w^2} = 1$. The geometric meaning of a normalized quaternion (x, y, z, w) can be easily perceived if we re-write it as

$$(x, y, z, w) = \left(x' \sin\left(\frac{\alpha}{2}\right), y' \sin\left(\frac{\alpha}{2}\right), z' \sin\left(\frac{\alpha}{2}\right), \cos\left(\frac{\alpha}{2}\right) \right).$$

This quaternion encodes an α radians rotation around the axis (normalized vector) (x', y', z'). This notation immediately provides us with the following properties for quaternions:

- The quaternion $\mathbf{q}$ is equivalent to the quaternion $k\mathbf{q}$ where $k \in \mathbb{R}$.

- The normalized quaternions (x, y, z, w) and $(-x, -y, -z, -w)$ are equivalent.

- The inverse rotation for the quaternion (x, y, z, w) is denoted by the quaternion $(x, y, z, -w)$.

The angle between two normalized quaternions $\mathbf{q_1}$, $\mathbf{q_2}$ can be found as $\theta = 2\arccos(q_1, q_2)$, where (q_1, q_2) is a per-component dot product of q_1 and q_2. In this chapter all quaternions are implied to be normalized if not noted otherwise.

1.3   Quaternion Use Cases

In our engine we used quaternions for multiple purposes. Our goal was to replace bulky 3×3 rotation and tangent-space matrices throughout the entire engine. This affected the following engine components:

- normal mapping,

- generic transforms,

- instancing,

- skinning,

- morph targets.

For each of these cases we discuss the implications in the following individual sections.

1.4   Normal Mapping

Normal mapping was an initial reason to use quaternions engine-wide. Normal mapping requires one to define a so-called tangent space at each surface location: a coordinate system, which is defined by tangent, bi-tangent (often erroneously called bi-normal), and normal (TBN).

Usually, these basis vectors are defined per model vertex and then interpolated inside triangles, and this is where the problems arise. First, TBN occupies at least six interpolator channels (provided we reconstruct the third vector using a `cross` instruction and pack a handedness bit without wasting an extra interpolator channel). This may be alleviated by packing TBN, but it comes at a pixel shader additional cost.

Second, TBN might need orthonormalization multiple times throughout the pipeline. In the case of a model-view matrix containing a nonuniform scale, we need to use inverse-transpose of the model-view matrix to transform TBN (tangents and bi-tangents use the same transform as normals). It is very expensive to invert a matrix in a shader, and in the case of a model-view inverse-transpose matrix pre-computation, we would need to pass this matrix through vertex attributes per instance in case of instancing. One possible hack is to re-use the original model-view matrix to transform TBN, but in this case we need to orthonormalize TBN afterwards to avoid lighting artifacts.

Moreover, TBN becomes unnormalized and loses orthogonality during interpolation. Hence, orthogonalization and normalization also need to be performed in a pixel shader. In our experience, this takes a significant amount of ALUs in vertex and pixel shaders.

We tried several methods enabling normal mapping without TBN in our engine. [Mikkelsen 10] needs so-called derivative maps as an input, which can be obtained from normal maps. However, on our assets this method was capable of conveying much less detail than regular normal mapping, which was unacceptable for artistic reasons.

We also tried the method in [Schüler 06]. It implies additional ALU cost for differential chain rule application. However, the greatest limitation appeared to be pipeline issues: the TBN basis generated by Autodesk Maya did not coincide with one derived from the texture-coordinate gradient. This resulted in different parameterizations, making it impossible to reuse already existing normal maps.

Encoding TBN with quaternions allows us to overcome these problems. However, there are several problems with this approach. One is TBN matrix *handedness*, which we will not discuss here as it is covered in detail in [Malyshau 12].

The other problem is quaternion interpolation. Quaternion *spherical linear interpolation* (SLERP) produces correct results without a prior alignment. However, since vertex attribute interpolation is not programmable, we interpolate quaternions linearly, which causes issues. [Malyshau 12] proposes a solution that increases the original vertex count by 7.5% and polygon count by 0.14%. Below, we propose a solution, which works for any correctly UV-mapped model, that does not change vertex and polygon count at all. Let us first explain the ground for this problem.

Let us consider quaternions $\mathbf{q}_1 = (x_1, y_1, z_1, w_1)$ and $\mathbf{q}_2 = (x_2, y_2, z_2, w_2)$. If their dot product $(\mathbf{q}_1, \mathbf{q}_2)$ is positive, the quaternions will interpolate along the shortest arc; otherwise they interpolate along the longest. That being said, if we take a $-\mathbf{q}_1$ quaternion (instead of an equivalent $\mathbf{q}_1$), the interpolation arc will be reversed. For vertex normals inside the triangles, we will expect to interpolate along the shortest arc. Yet, for a closed model, that might not always be the case. A natural solution to this will be to *align* all quaternions at the model's neighboring vertices by multiplying one of them by -1 so that their dot product becomes positive. However, this will not solve the problem in most cases.

Let us consider a cylinder model as in Figure 1.1. We will take a quaternion $\mathbf{q} = (0, 0, 0, 1)$ at the point A as a reference and start aligning all the quaternions

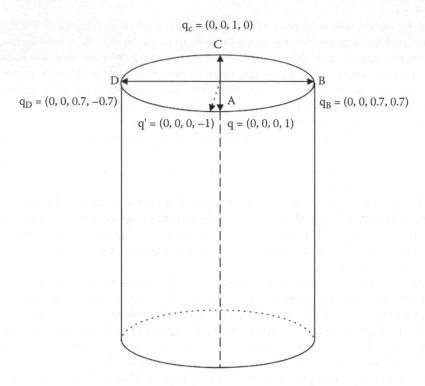

Figure 1.1. Aligning quaternions for the cylinder object.

on the cylinder surface one after another in the counterclockwise direction. As one can observe, when we return to point A after a turn around, the respective quaternion at this point will be $\mathbf{q}' = (0, 0, 0, -1)$. This means that neighboring vertices at point A will be *misaligned*, resulting in the long-arc quaternion interpolation as shown in Figure 1.2.

The geometrical justification for this effect lies in the quaternion nature. If we recall that a quaternion $\mathbf{q} = (x \sin(\frac{\alpha}{2}), y \sin(\frac{\alpha}{2}), z \sin(\frac{\alpha}{2}), \cos(\frac{\alpha}{2}))$, it becomes clear that while our turn around the angle α (and respective normal) made a complete 360°, which corresponds to the full period of the function, it only made a half-period (since we have $\frac{\alpha}{2}$ as an argument) for the quaternion.

In the general case, this problem is unsolvable without a topology alteration. However, for a real in-game UV-mapped asset, we will never have a situation when we can find a closed chain of adjacent vertices on the surface of a model so that a normal makes a 360° rotation when we traverse this chain. This is true because a closed mesh cannot be correctly UV-mapped so that a texture, unique at each point, can be applied to this mesh. If we get back to the cylinder sample and try to map a 2D texture to the cylindrical surface (Figure 1.3), this would mean that,

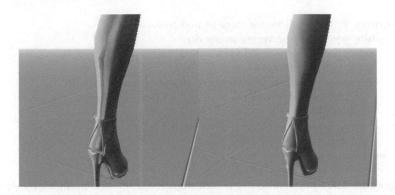

Figure 1.2. Normal rendering. Incorrectly interpolated quaternions (left) and correctly interpolated quaternions after alignment (right). [Image courtesy of Mail.Ru Group.]

at some point, a u-coordinate will change from 0 to 1 at the neighboring vertices, resulting in the whole texture u-range being mapped to the single triangle. To avoid this, artists duplicate the vertices of the model, having as a result vertices $\mathbf{v}$ and $\mathbf{v}'$ with the same position but different texture coordinates. This fact allows us to align quaternions at neighboring vertices without any further vertex duplication, which is described in Algorithm 1.1.

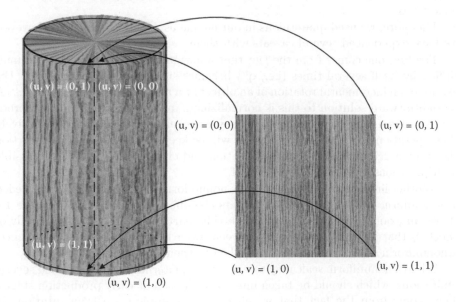

Figure 1.3. Textured cylinder object.

Require: Initialize all vertex flags as *non-traversed*
1: **while** *non-traversed* vertex exists **do**
2:     select any *non-traversed* vertex as $\mathbf{q}$
3:     set $\mathbf{q}$ flag as *traversed*
4:     **for** every *non-traversed* vertex $\mathbf{q}'$ sharing edge with $\mathbf{q}$ **do**
5:         set $\mathbf{q}'$ flag as *traversed*
6:         align $\mathbf{q}'$ to $\mathbf{q}$
7:         repeat recursively from step 4 for $\mathbf{q}:=\mathbf{q}'$
8:     **end for**
9: **end while**

Algorithm 1.1. Quaternion alignment algorithm for UV-mapped meshes.

1.5   Generic Transforms and Instancing

If we compare encoding transformations with quaternions and with matrices, quaternions will have several advantages. First, a transformation matrix needs 4×3 values to encode position, rotation and scale, while with *SQTs* (scale-quaternion-translation) we need only eight values provided we assume the scale to be uniform. Second, reverse rotation comes virtually for free in the case of quaternions, while for matrices this is a quite costly operation. Finally, multiplying two 3×3 rotation matrices will result in 45 scalar operations (additions and multiplications), while quaternions can be multiplied using a total of 28 scalar operations.

Therefore, we used quaternions in our engine as widely as possible. However, we have experienced several caveats with them.

The first one comes from the fact that a normalized quaternion $\mathbf{q}$ being multiplied by itself several times (i.e., $\mathbf{q}^n$) becomes significantly unnormalized. For example, an incremental rotation of an object at a same angle may lead to this. A straightforward solution to this is normalizing a quaternion multiplication product, but this significantly reduces efficiency, as normalization is usually a relatively slow operation. An alternative solution will be keeping a normalization assertion check for a debug version of an application and eliminating cases of all possible multiplications of a quaternion on itself.

Another limitation for quaternions is nonuniform scale. In *Skyforge* we needed a nonuniform scale for a family of effects classified as "channeling." Figure 1.4 shows an example of a channeling effect. The particular feature of this family of effects is that an effect is stretched between two arbitrary points in space. Hence, a nonuniform scale is needed to be applied to them.

While a nonuniform scale may co-exist with quaternions, we have faced several limitations, which should be taken into consideration at early production stages. They come from the fact that we effectively decouple scale from rotation (in contrast to conventional 3×3 scale-rotation matrices).

Figure 1.4. Channeling spell being cast. [Image courtesy of Mail.Ru Group.]

First, only *axis-aligned nonuniform* scale may be encoded. Figure 1.5 shows the difference between encoding the same transform with an SQT and a scale-rotation matrix. While a single scale-rotation transform performed by a scale-rotation matrix can also encode only an axis-aligned nonuniform scale, a superposition of these transforms can encode a non-axis-aligned scale, while a superposition of SQTs will always keep all scales axis-aligned. This means, for instance, that a box will always remain a box after any SQT transformations (keeping straight angles around its corners), but this is not a case for an arbitrary scale-rotation matrices superposition. In our experience, we did not have a strong need for such transformations. However, this can slightly increase the mesh count, as, for instance, different rhombi can no longer be encoded with a single mesh with different transformations applied.

Second, with SQTs all scale transformations are done in the *object space*. For instance, if you rotate an object at a 90° angle in the xy-plane and then scale along the x-axis, it will be scaled along the y-axis instead, as shown in Figure 1.6. In terms of channeling effects, this imposed a restriction on the content. All objects that a channeling effect consists of should be aligned along the major axis of the effect; otherwise, they will be stretched orthogonally to the effect direction.

For instanced objects, encoding rotation with quaternions worked straightforwardly. We provide more details on this in Section 1.8.

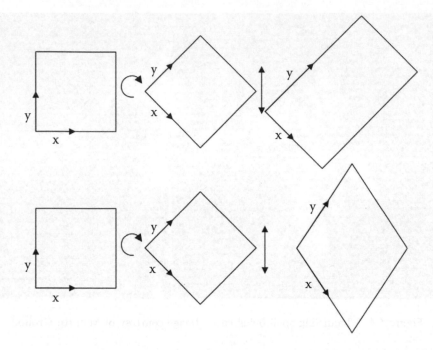

Figure 1.5. A box being rotated and scaled using SQT (top) and scale-rotation matrix (bottom). Object xy-axis is shown.

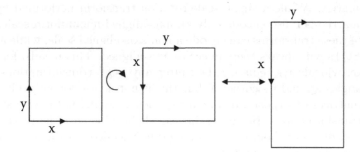

Figure 1.6. 90° rotation and scaling with SQT.

1.6 Skinning

In our engine we pack bone data for skinning into a texture. There are several reasons for this. First, as the game is supposed to run on a DirectX 9 compatible hardware, only 256 constants are available in the general case. Second, we wanted to enable character instancing: in the case of storing skinning data in a single texture, we need to store only a texture offset per instance. Thus, we

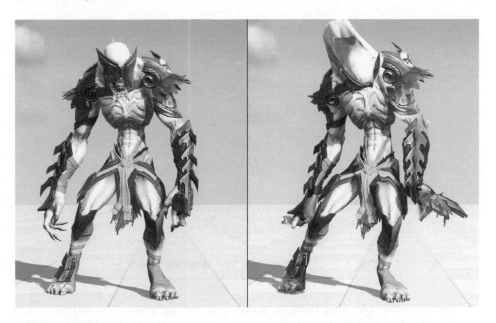

Figure 1.7. Matrix palette skinning (left) and direct quaternion blending (right). [Image courtesy of Mail.Ru Group.]

pack all bones of all characters in a single 2D texture, the format of which is discussed below. In fact, we use this texture as a "large constant buffer" which we dynamically address using an instance ID, in order to make skinning work for many characters on DirectX 9 compatible hardware.

A straightforward solution for using quaternions in skinning would be to interpolate quaternions, corresponding to different bones, *before* applying rotation; in the same way as matrices are interpolated in the *matrix palette skinning* approach, as proposed in [Hejl 04]. However, our experience shows that this method produces incorrect results when a vertex is skinned to several bones, which have significant rotation from a bind pose, as shown in Figure 1.7.

The mathematical reason for this lies in the fact that quaternions *cannot be correctly blended*. Provided quaternions can be very effectively *interpolated*, this sounds a bit controversial; therefore we provide a proof below.

Let us consider Figure 1.8. A quaternion $\mathbf{q}_2$ defines a $180 - \epsilon^\circ$ rotation in an xy-plane and $\mathbf{q}_3$ corresponds to a $180 + \epsilon^\circ$ rotation. If we blend quaternions $\mathbf{q}_1$, $\mathbf{q}_2$ and $\mathbf{q}_1$, $\mathbf{q}_3$ with weights $\lambda_1 = \lambda_2 = \lambda_3 = 0.5$, resulting quaternions $\mathbf{q}_4$ and $\mathbf{q}_5$ will point in significantly different directions if we use shortest-arc interpolation for blending. Taking ϵ infinitely small proves that the blending result of $\mathbf{q}_1$ and $\mathbf{q}_2$ ($\mathbf{q}_3$) is not *continuous*.

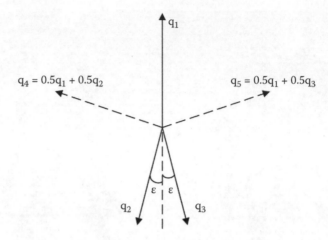

Figure 1.8. Discontinuity of blending two quaternions.

Furthermore, blending three or more quaternions is not *commutative*. Let us consider Figure 1.9. Quaternions $\mathbf{q}_1$, $\mathbf{q}_2$, and $\mathbf{q}_3$ specify $0°$, $140°$, and $220°$ rotations in the xy-plane, respectively. Let us set quaternion weights to $\lambda_1 = \lambda_2 = \lambda_3 = \frac{1}{3}$. The case where we blend quaternions in order $\mathbf{q}_4 = (\lambda_1 \mathbf{q}_1 + \lambda_2 \mathbf{q}_2) + \lambda_3 \mathbf{q}_3$ will differ from the result when we blend them in order $\mathbf{q}_5 = (\lambda_1 \mathbf{q}_1 + \lambda_3 \mathbf{q}_3) + \lambda_2 \mathbf{q}_2$.

Having said that, we do not blend quaternions directly. Instead, we blend final transformed vertex positions. This, obviously, slightly increases ALU count in the shader code, but we benefit from a reduced skinning texture size and fewer vertex texture fetches, as shown in Section 1.8.

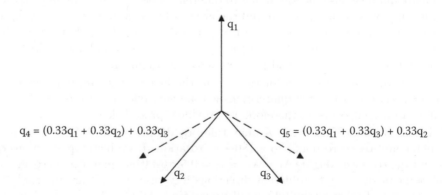

Figure 1.9. Ambiguity of blending three quaternions.

Figure 1.10. Original character (left) and two extreme morph targets (center, right). [Image courtesy of Mail.Ru Group.]

1.7 Morph Targets

As *Skyforge* is an MMORPG game, we want to give players as many opportunites to customize characters as possible. One of the most interesting customizations enables a player to change body proportions of his or her character in a continuous fashion. This is implemented via interpolation of each vertex between two so called *morph targets*, i.e., separate vertex streams. An example of such an interpolation is shown in Figure 1.10.

Regarding quaternions, only a few considerations should be kept in mind for morph targets. First, meshes, corresponding to different targets between which we are interpolating, should have the same topology and *uv*-mapping. This obviously includes handedness of initial TBN in vertices. Second, after we convert TBNs to quaternions, we should align quaternions, corresponding to the same vertex in different targets. This can be obtained naturally, if we start Algorithm 1.1 for both targets at the same vertex, as meshes share the same topology.

1.8 Quaternion Format

In this section we discuss how we store quaternions in memory and how we pack them when sending to GPU. Table 1.1 shows layouts we use for quaternions in our engine.

The most interesting case is a vertex quaternion. Our experiments have shown that 8-bit precision is enough for per-vertex quaternions. However, since TBNs can have different handedness, we also need to store a handedness bit. We did not want to spend another channel on it, so we came up with two solutions.

Case	Channels				
Vertex Quaternion	x (int8)	y (int8)	z (int8)	h (1b)	w (7b)
Model Transform	x (float32)	y (float32)	z (float32)	w (float32)	
Instance Data	x (int16)	y (int16)	z (int16)	w (0, calculated)	
Bone Transform	x (float16)	y (float16)	z (float16)	w (float16)	

Table 1.1. Quaternion packing for different scenarios. h stands for quaternion handedness.

First, we could store in the same byte a handedness bit and a sign bit for w and then reconstruct w in the shader as we operate onto normalized quaternions. We abandoned this approach, as unpacking w would lead to the sqrt instruction, which is costly and should be avoided in the shader.

Instead, we packed a handedness into the first bit and packed w into the remaining seven last bits (as an unsigned integer). It turned out that even seven bits is enough in the case of vertex quaternion. Furthermore, this approach resulted in a very fast unpacking, as shown in Listing 1.1. A nice property of this packing is that it interpolates correctly in all cases of vertex quaternions and morph targets. We implicitly use the fact that it is never a case in practice to interpolate quaternions with different handedness. In this case, the first bit of quaternions to be interpolated would always be the same, resulting in correct interpolation of low seven bits.

For model transforms, as we operate them on the CPU side, we store the quaternion values in float32 format. To pack a quaternion of instance rotation, we opted for int16 for several reasons. First, we wanted to keep instance vertex layout as small as possible, and 32-bit formats are definitely an overkill for a quaternion in terms of precision. Quaternion's values are limited to the $[-1, 1]$ domain, so we need only fixed-point precision. Unfortunately, 8-bit formats were not enough as they provide around 1–2° angle steps. While this was enough for a vertex quaternion, in the case of encoding an instance's position, such a

```
float UnpackFirstBitFromByte ( float argument )
{
   return saturate((argument * 255.0f - 127.5f) * 100.0f);
}

float UnpackLow7BitsFromByte ( float firstBit , float argument )
{
   return (argument * 255.0f - 128.0f * firstBit) / 127.0f;
}
```

Listing 1.1. Vertex quaternion unpacking.

```
inline uint16 Float2fp16( float x )
{
  uint32 dwFloat = *((uint32 *)&x);
  uint32 dwMantissa = dwFloat & 0x7fffff;
  int32 iExp = (int)((dwFloat>>23) & 0xff) - (int)0x70;
  uint32 dwSign = dwFloat>>31;


  int result = ( (dwSign<<15)
  | (((uint32)(max(iExp, 0)))<<10)
  | (dwMantissa>>13) );
  result = result & 0xFFFF;
  return (uint16)result;
}
```

Listing 1.2. `float32` to `float16` fast conversion.

large angle step resulted in non-smooth rotation and difficulties in aligning static instanced geometry for map designers.

Finally, we experimented with quaternion packing for skinning. Initially, we stored a skinning bone 3×3 scale-rotation matrix and position (12 values in total) in a `float32` RGBA texture. Therefore, we needed three vertex texture fetches per bone and we wasted 25% of the skinning texture for better alignment, resulting in four `float32` RGBA texels per bone. After switching to quaternions, we used SQT encoding with a uniform scale: this resulted in eight values in total. That allowed us to store a single bone information only in two texels, thus making two vertex texture fetches per bone. As we packed skinning values in a texture, the format of different SQT components had to stay the same. Scale and transform needed a floating-point format; this is why we picked `float16` (a.k.a. `half`). The only issue we tackled in packing was a low speed of a standard DirectX fp16 packing function, which resulted in significant CPU stalls. To address this, we used a fast packing method similar to [Mittring 08]. However, we enhanced this method, making it work for all domain values, unlike the original one. The resulting code is shown in Listing 1.2.

1.9 Comparison

After the transition to quaternions had been done, we made a comparison, shown in Table 1.2. As could be observed, using quaternions significantly reduces memory footprint. In the case of normal mapping, the number of `nrm`, `rsq`, and `rcp` instructions is also decreased, which provides better performance increase than one could be expected from the raw ALUs figures. In the case of skinning and instancing, instruction count increases, but in our experience, ALUs have not been a bottleneck in vertex shaders.

Case	Matrix/TBN				Quaternion			
Measured Value	ALUs		Memory		ALUs		Memory	
Pipeline Stage	VS	PS	VS	VS→PS	VS	PS	VS	VS→PS
Normal Mapping	15	12	7	7	13	12	4	5
Instancing (Scale+Rot)	15	-	20	-	21	-	12	-
Skinning	33	-	64	-	71	-	16	-

Table 1.2. Comparison of 3×3 rotation matrices/TBN and quaternions performance (in ALUs) and memory footprint (vertex attributes (TBN, instance data)/vertex texture fetch (skinning) size in bytes (VS)/interpolator channels count (VS→PS)).

1.10   Conclusion

In this chapter we tried to fully cover our experience with quaternions. We have used quaternions throughout the whole engine, significantly reducing memory and bandwidth costs. There are, however, certain pitfalls, which we described, that we hope will not prevent quaternions from replacing matrices in modern engines.

1.11   Acknowledgements

The authors would like to thank Victor Surkov for helping with the illustrations for this chapter.

Bibliography

[Hejl 04] Jim Hejl. "Hardware Skinning with Quaternions." In *Game Programming Gems 4*, edited by Andrew Kirmse, pp. 487–495. Boston: Cengage Learning, 2004.

[Lengyel 11] Eric Lengyel. *Mathematics for 3D Game Programming and Computer Graphics*, Third edition. Boston: Cengage Learning PTR, 2011.

[Malyshau 12] Dzmitry Malyshau. "A Quaternion-Based Rendering Pipeline." In *GPU Pro 3*, edited by Wolfgang Engel, pp. 265–273. Boca Raton, FL: A K Peters/CRC Press, 2012.

[Mikkelsen 10] Morten S. Mikkelsen. "Bump Mapping Unparametrized Surfaces on the GPU." *Journal of Graphics, GPU, and Game Tools* 1 (2010), 49–61.

[Mittring 08] Martin Mittring. "Advanced Virtual Texture Topics." In *ACM SIGGRAPH 2008 Games*, pp. 23–51. New York: ACM, 2008.

[Schüler 06] Christian Schüler. "Normal Mapping without Precomputed Tangents." In *ShaderX5: Advanced Rendering Techniques*, edited by Wolfgang Engel, pp. 131–140. Boston: Cengage Learning, 2006.

gITF: Designing an Open-Standard Runtime Asset Format
Fabrice Robinet, Rémi Arnaud, Tony Parisi, and Patrick Cozzi

2.1 Introduction

This chapter presents work by the COLLADA Working Group in the Khronos Group to provide a bridge between interchange asset formats and the runtime graphics APIs. We present the design of gITF, an open-standard transmission-format that bridges the gap between COLLADA and engines based on WebGL, OpenGL, and OpenGL ES. gITF strives to provide a common foundation for developers to efficiently load assets into their engine. We discuss the format itself, the open-source content pipeline tool that converts COLLADA to gITF, and REST-based cloud services.

2.2 Motivation

Art assets account for a significant amount of the development costs of modern games and graphics applications. In 2003, the effort to provide a common asset description format for content pipeline tools started at Sony Computer Entertainment, and led to the COLLADA spec a few years later. Although the compatibility of assets among modeling packages is now largely solved, engine developers still need to build their own content pipelines and transmission format to produce optimized assets for their engines.

While work on COLLADA continued, the Khronos Group released new specifications for runtime APIs to provide hardware accelerated graphics. This includes WebGL, OpenGL, and OpenGL ES. Even though the asset format and GL APIs emanate from the same group, there is no easy way for a developer to take assets and use them in their engine. Two major issues create a gap. The content has to be processed to fit within the data format that is required by the GL APIs, and the content has to be formatted for transmission and parsing performance.

The idea of creating a new spec focusing on the runtime use rather than content-creation needs was raised a few years ago in the working group, and it finally resulted in the work done by the authors of this chapter to introduce glTF—the GL Transmission Format. By analogy, this format is in the same category as the audio and video formats, such as MP3 and MPEG, that have been key in supporting the consumption of media content and dramatically impacted the ecosystem and consumers. We hope that glTF will help 3D content be easily deployed and consumed.

Although significant work has been done, at the time this book goes to press, glTF is still a work in progress; it is not an official Khronos-ratified specification yet.

2.3   Goals

2.3.1   Easy and Efficient to Render

A glTF asset is composed of a .json file for the structure, .bin files for numerical data, .glsl (text) files for shaders, and image files. The .json file references the other files. The .bin files store data as little endian since this covers the vast majority of the market.

glTF uses JSON to define the node hierarchy, materials, lights, and cameras and the binary blobs to store geometry and textures. (See Figure 2.1.) JSON is cross-platform, compact, and readable, allows validation, and minifies and compresses well. Binary blobs, unlike JSON data, allow efficient creation of GL buffers and textures since they require no additional parsing, except perhaps decompression. glTF specifically targets the GL APIs, so the runtime engine can efficiently load and render the asset because most of the data processing is done by the content pipeline.

2.3.2   Balanced Feature Set and Extensible

Only allowing features directly supported by the GL APIs would make glTF too limited. Likewise, including all features in interchange formats would make glTF too complex for runtime use. We carefully selected features, such as the node hierarchy, materials, animation, and skinning, to balance the trade-offs between simplicity and completeness.

Unlike interchange formats, which need to preserve data used for authoring, glTF only preserves data used for rendering. For example, COLLADA allows

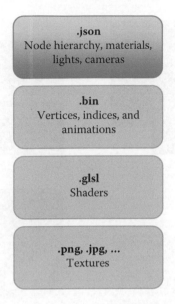

Figure 2.1. Set of files defining a glTF asset.

several transforms and transform representations per node; glTF only has one transform per node and fewer representations.

We recognize that many engines will need features beyond what glTF defines. For this, glTF is extensible to support engine-specific features by allowing metadata on all JSON object properties.

2.3.3 Code, Not Just Spec

A spec alone is not sufficient to make glTF successful. We believe that an open-source content pipeline that converts COLLADA to glTF is important for adoption. We developed such a tool, COLLADA2GLTF, as open-source on GitHub [Khronos 14a]. COLLADA2GLTF provides developers an accessible on-ramp for getting content into their engine and serves as a reference implementation for converters for other model formats. We selected COLLADA because of our familiarity with it, its open-standard, and its widely available exporters.

To ensure that a glTF renderer is easy to implement, we developed several glTF renderers while working on the spec, including JavaScript open-source implementations in Three.js [Mrdoob 14], Cesium [Analytical Graphics 14], rest3d viewer [AMD 14], and Montage with straight WebGL [Fabrobinet 14]. (See Figure 2.2.) In many cases, we implemented a renderer multiple times as spec work progressed.

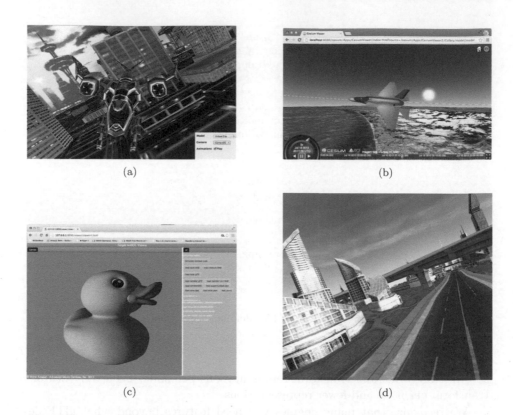

Figure 2.2. (a) glTF asset in Three.js. [Model from 3drt.com.] (b) glTF asset in Cesium being driven by Cesium's animation engine. (c) glTF and COLLADA assets can be loaded and displayed in the rest3d viewer. (d) glTF asset in the MontageJS viewer. [Model from 3drt.com.]

2.3.4   Community

To enable early community involvement, we also used the public GitHub repo for spec work [Khronos 14a]. We used GitHub issues to discuss spec details and wrote the draft spec in a markdown file in the repo. As expected, the working group still did the majority of the work, but community feedback is valuable and also gives developers more buy-in since their voices are heard. In addition, the public archives are a useful resource for why design decisions were made.

2.3.5   WebGL, OpenGL, and OpenGL ES

glTF is a runtime format for WebGL, OpenGL, and OpenGL ES. However, we are pragmatic about where we expect initial adoption—by the WebGL community.

WebGL engines are still young, and most either use an ad-hoc custom asset format or support a subset of COLLADA. WebGL engines will benefit from a carefully crafted runtime format and a supporting open-source content pipeline.

We spoke with game developers with established OpenGL and OpenGL ES engines, and their feedback on glTF is pretty consistent: it is a good idea but they usually have their own format and content pipeline already in place. However, for new engines and independent developers, whose growth has been phenomenal recently, glTF lowers the barriers to integrate 3D content without requiring heavier solutions.

2.4   Birds-Eye View

A glTF asset is made up of components familiar to most graphics developers such as nodes, meshes, and materials. Figure 2.3 shows the organization of the top-level glTF properties, i.e., properties whose parent is the glTF asset's root. A design goal is to provide the required structure without unnecessary indirection and overhead.

At the highest level, a scene is composed of one or more root nodes. Nodes have a transform, e.g., a 4×4 matrix, and an array of child nodes, forming a node hierarchy that positions each node in the scene. A node can contain either a camera, a light, or an array of meshes, which is the most common case.

A mesh contains an array of primitives (not shown in Figure 2.3 because they are not a top-level glTF property), each of which references attributes and indices defining the mesh's geometry, and a material defining its shading.

An attribute defines the section of a `bufferView` that contains data for one attribute in the mesh, including a stride, so multiple attributes can be interleaved in the same `bufferView`, and a bounding box, so the runtime engine doesn't need to recompute a bounding volume. Similarly, indices define a section of a `bufferView` containing index data for a mesh. Of course, different meshes may point to the same attributes or indices just like different nodes may point to the same mesh.

`bufferViews` point to a subset of a buffer, which can reference an external .bin file or have the binary data encoded in the JSON. There can be one or more buffers, and a single buffer can contain heterogeneous data, e.g., vertex attributes and indices.

In addition to referencing attributes and indices, a primitive in a mesh also references a material, which is an instance of a technique, i.e., a technique plus its parameter inputs, which correspond to GL uniforms, including textures and their sampler state. A technique defines the parameter inputs and a pass that defines the attribute inputs, the shader program containing vertex and fragment shaders, and the render states. Like buffers, shader source and image files may be stored in external files or embedded in the JSON.

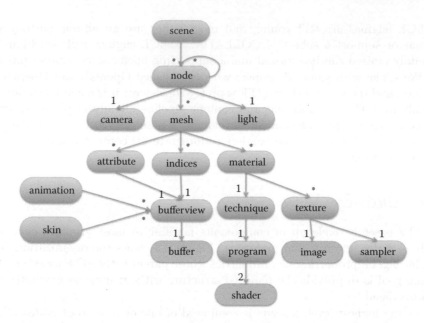

Figure 2.3. Structure of top-level glTF JSON properties. Properties in gray may reference external files or have embedded data.

Animations and skins reference `bufferViews` in a similar fashion to attributes and indices. They also reference nodes and other properties to change their values over time.

A glTF asset may use most or all of these top-level properties to define a scene, or it could contain just meshes or techniques, for example. Next, we'll look at buffers, materials, and animations in more detail.

2.5   Integration of Buffer and Buffer View

Buffers and their associated buffer views are fundamental building blocks of glTF assets. A glTF JSON file relies on binary data for heavy payloads such as vertices and indices. Consequently, glTF needs to describe these data. The typed array specification [Vukicevic 11] is a natural choice because

- it was created by capturing the requirements of a GL-based API, namely WebGL,

- it provides a relevant API to describe arrays whether glTF is implemented using JavaScript or C++,

- when possible, glTF relies on proven APIs from widely adopted specs.

To implement buffers, glTF borrowed two fundamental types from typed arrays:

- `ArrayBuffer` for entries in buffers property, and

- `ArrayBufferView` for entries in the `bufferViews` property.

Both `buffers` and `bufferViews` implement the same interface of their respective typed-array counterpart. However, types are not named exactly the same because glTF `buffers` and `bufferViews` contain additional properties. In the JSON snippets in Figure 2.4, properties in blue come directly from typed arrays. Properties in red are not part of typed arrays and were added to provide

- external storage via a path property,

- a hint about the kind of data stored via a target property, which is optional but a useful optimization for binding the corresponding VBO once and just updating the offset for subsequent draw calls.

```
"buffers":
{
  "office": {
    "byteLength": 829958,
    "path": "office.bin"
  }
},
"bufferViews": {
  "bufferView_7958": {
    "buffer": "office",
    "byteLength": 686264,
    "byteOffset": 0,
    "target": "ARRAY_BUFFER"
  },
  "bufferView_7959": {
    "buffer": "office",
    "byteLength": 143694,
    "byteOffset": 686264,
    "target": "ELEMENT_ARRAY_BUFFER"
  }
}
```

While buffers and `bufferViews` provide access to data, other concepts are needed:

- *Types:* In order to map directly to GL APIs, glTF reuses existing GL types.

- *Interleaving:* Typed arrays deal with contiguous buffers, but to interleave vertex attributes, other properties like stride are needed. Also, semantically, count fits better than length.

For these reasons, and in order to get the best of typed arrays and GL worlds, vertex attributes and indices wrap buffer views as follows:

```
{
    "bufferView": "bufferView_29",
    "byteOffset": 0,
    "byteStride": 12,
    "count": 2399,
    "type": "FLOAT_VEC3"
}
```

Finally, it's up to the runtime engine to define how buffers are loaded, e.g., using multiple accesses to files at different offset for progressive loading or by loading all data at once. The number of external files storing buffers is up to the content pipeline.

The same flexibility applies to the way GL resources are created. It's up to the engine to create a vertex buffer that contains all the attributes of the scene or to create multiple buffers. `bufferViews` and their wrappers allow adapting any resource management scheme.

2.6   Code Flow for Rendering Meshes

In glTF, a mesh is simply an array of primitives to be rendered. A primitive specifies its type, matching the GLenum type used by `drawElements`; indices; a material; and vertex attributes, which are shared for a given mesh. This design for meshes is due to modeling tools grouping primitives that share vertex attributes into a single mesh.

Special care is made to make sure that the "flow" of glTF maps well with the "code flow" when implementing using a GL API. For meshes, Figure 2.4 shows how glTF properties map to actual GL APIs concepts.

For clarity, Figure 2.4 omits reordering primitives to render opaque primitives before primitives requiring blending. Next we look at materials, techniques, and passes. By implementing them, rendering order comes naturally.

2.7   From Materials to Shaders

Modern GL APIs require binding a program and setting up shaders. Here, we walk through the layers between materials at the highest level and programs at the lowest levels.

Most shaders take uniform inputs. At the highest level, these values come from parameters within materials. To specify which implementation of shaders these parameters should use, a material refers to a technique. This design allows multiple materials to share the same technique. Thus, multiple materials are

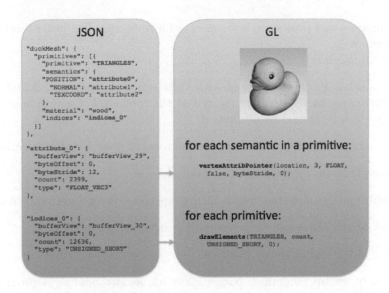

Figure 2.4. Mapping glTF to GL APIs.

naturally ordered by techniques, shaders, and even GL states since they are also specified within techniques under passes.

Figure 2.5 is a possible workflow. Advanced engines may differ, but this schema shows that even the most naive renderer following glTF flow of properties would de-facto apply fundamental GL principles for efficient rendering, such as minimizing the number of states changes.

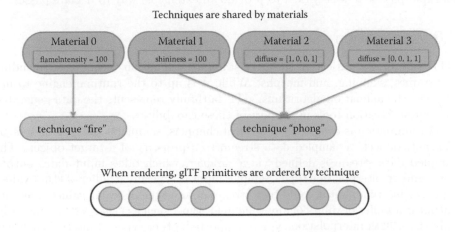

Figure 2.5. Materials share techniques.

Techniques and passes are key concepts for understanding lower-level rendering concepts.

A technique's role is

- to declare parameters along with their types and optional default values (technique parameters are located at the root level of a technique so that they can be shared by all passes),

- to refer to the first pass that acts as an entry point for the rendering.

A pass contains all the implementation details:

- which program to bind, which in turns specifies vertex and fragment shaders,

- list of attributes and uniforms both pointing to parameters,

- list of GL render states to be set.

To fully set up rendering, passes allow atomically binding a program and enabling GL states along with their associated functions. Properties such as double-sided or transparency from higher-level properties emphasize that generating shaders from high-level material definitions cannot be dissociated from generating states on their side.

Not all engines will want to import shaders and states, especially for lighting shaders relying on deferred rendering. For such engines, within passes, a `details` property can be generated by COLLADA2GLTF to specify every relevant aspect to be able to regenerate the shaders and states on the fly.

Both the specification and COLLADA2GLTF currently only support a single pass using forward rendering. However, considering further evolutions and multiple passes, it was critical to provide an extensible way to declare passes.

2.8   Animation

glTF supports a variety of industry-standard animation techniques, including key frames, skinning, and morphs. While it is up to the runtime engine to implement the animation algorithms, glTF faithfully represents the data generated by content-creation tools in support of these capabilities.

An animation is composed of a set of channels, samplers, and parameters. A *channel* connects a sampled data stream to a property of a target object. The sampled data stream is defined via a *sampler,* which takes input data, output data, and an interpolation type. Sampler input is typically a buffer of `FLOAT` values representing time, but it could be a stream of any type of scalar values. Sampler output is a buffer of values of any valid glTF type, such as `FLOAT_VEC3`. Currently, only the `LINEAR` interpolation type is supported; other types of interpolation will be possible via future extensions.

The channel's *target* object contains the ID of a node in the glTF node hierarchy. The property to be animated is represented via a *path*, a string that contains a value such as `translation`, `rotation`, or `scale`. It is up to the runtime engine to map these standardized names to its own properties. For example, the Three.js viewer maps `translation` to `position`, the internal name for translation of a 3D object in the Three.js scene graph.

The sampler's input and output data are supplied by referencing *parameters*. Parameters are named objects defined in the animation's `parameters` property. The scope for parameter names is local to the containing animation. Each parameter references a named `bufferView` from the `bufferViews` section of the glTF file, specifying an offset, data type, and size.

Listing 2.1 shows the JSON for animating the translation of node `node-cam01 -box` using key frames. The animation defines one channel that connects the sampler `animation_0_translation_sampler` to the `translation` property of the node. The sampler uses the parameter `TIME` as its input to linearly interpolate one of the properties. Note that the `TIME` parameter can be shared among other samplers, such as for animation rotation and scale; this is a typical usage scenario that keeps all properties synchronized and represents the data compactly.

Channels are also used to drive skinned animations. With skinning, channels define animations of nodes representing joints in a skeleton. Skins, joints, and vertex weights are defined to be friendly for hardware-accelerated skinning. For example, glTF defines a `WEIGHT` semantic type for use with hardware techniques:

```
"weight" : {
  "semantic" : "WEIGHT" ,
  "type" : "FLOAT_VEC4"
}
```

2.9   Content Pipeline

The content pipeline, as shown in Figure 2.6, is the process by which the content is optimized and formatted for a specific runtime. Typically, processing involves creating objects that are directly consumable by the runtime engine, such as creating triangles out of surfaces and other primitives, and then splitting and formatting in bundles that are efficient for loading and parsing.

Figure 2.6. A typical content pipeline.

```
"animation_0": {
"channels": [{
  "sampler": "animation_0_translation_sampler",
  "target": {
  "id": "node-cam01-box",
  "path": "translation"
}],
"count": 901,
"parameters": {
  "TIME": {
    "bufferView": "bufferView_4509",
    "byteOffset": 0,
    "count": 901,
    "type": "FLOAT"
  },
  "translation": {
    "bufferView": "bufferView_4509",
    "byteOffset": 3604,
    "count": 901,
    "type": "FLOAT_VEC3"
  }
},
"samplers": {
  "animation_0_translation_sampler": {
    "input": "TIME",
    "interpolation": "LINEAR",
    "output": "translation"
  }
}
}
```

Listing 2.1. Animation listing.

glTF targets GL APIs by creating structures that can be sent directly to a runtime engine built with WebGL, OpenGL ES, or OpenGL. glTF consists of a set of files that are directly compatible with web technology—a JSON file, binary files, GLSL shaders, and images. COLLADA2GLTF is the open-source converter from COLLADA to glTF. As shown in Figure 2.7, it can be used as-is, be incorporated into a content pipeline, or serve as a reference implementation for other converters.

2.9.1 COLLADA2GLTF

COLLADA2GLTF content processing incorporates several stages that progressively transform the content into the data structure accepted by GL APIs:

- *Triangulate:* Geometry is transformed into primitives accepted by GL. The most common one is TRIANGLES.

- *Single index:* Only one index per vertex attribute can reference all the attributes associated. Modelers often use one index per attribute, which

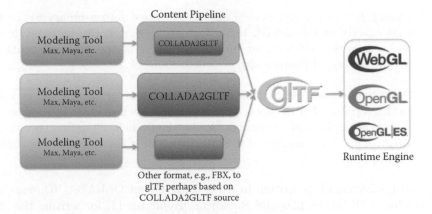

Figure 2.7. glTF content pipeline examples.

avoids vertex data duplication. This step reorganizes the data and duplicates vertices when necessary so that only one index per vertex is used.

- *Split:* Without extensions, WebGL and OpenGL ES 2.0 have indices range limitations, so meshes need to be split when they exceed the UNSIGNED_SHORT type.

- *Skinning optimizations:* In a modeler, skinned meshes may have any number of influences per bone. In GL, the limitation is given by the vertex shader, where the number of influences has to be fixed to fit inside a vertex attribute. Typically, this step creates four influences per bone, providing good performance and matching what is usually found in interactive applications. In order to host all the referred "bone matrices," the mesh may also be split to comply with the maximum number of vector uniforms that a destination GL API supports.

- *Shaders:* Taking into account all parameters impacting rendering (e.g., lights, lighting model, skinning, etc.), this step generates shaders that match the material description, which is typically the "common profile" for COLLADA. Along with shaders, this step also generates GL states. Shaders are provided with no further formatting, they are saved as the ASCII .glsl file that can be passed directly to the GLSL compiler.

- *JSON formatting:* The data structure created by the converter is finally serialized into a JSON file. The JSON file is relatively small as the bulk of the content will be stored in the binary file.

- *Image conversion:* As of now, the converter only performs alpha channel checks to know whether blending should be enabled.

- *Binary formatting:* Numerical data is serialized into a binary file or files that exactly match the GL buffer format, so that it can be easily loaded and sent to the API without any parsing or further processing by runtime, except perhaps decompression.

- *Additional steps:* Additional content processing of formatting can be added to this pipeline. For instance, when the content is provided via a web server, servers generally (zlib) compress files on the fly before sending them to the client. This is an example of the integration of glTF in an existing runtime environment.

COLLADA2GLTF is written in C++ using OpenCOLLADA [Khronos 14b] for reading COLLADA files and Rapidjson [Kennytm 11] for writing the glTF .json files. The conversion and optimization stages are written from scratch.

2.9.2   rest3d

glTF closes the gap between content creation and content deployment and provides core technology to enable moving the content pipeline in the cloud. More and more workflows are moving to the cloud. There are many benefits including the following:

- *Safety:* Data is not stored locally, so it is safe no matter what happens to your computer.

- *Security:* Data access can easily be restricted to those with access rights.

- *No install:* Software is always up to date and there is no need to install it.

- *Sharing:* All data are available to all users. This makes global collaboration easier.

- *Content management:* Data is cheap in the cloud, so there is no problem keeping a copy of everything and enabling users to go back in time.

- *Cloud processing:* Once the content is in the cloud, processing can happen in the cloud, so complex operations are possible using any device.

- *Deployment:* Deploying content and web applications is as easy as sending a URL out.

- *SaaS:* The Software as a Service (SaaS) business model makes it possible for customers to pay for only what they need and enables service providers to tailor to individual needs.

Figure 2.8. Managing content in the cloud.

There are also disadvantages such as trusting the cloud provider to keep our data secure and initially moving our data to the cloud. But those are manageable; for instance, data can be encrypted.

Moving workflows into the cloud requires new technologies and trade-offs. Not having direct access to data on the local disk, asynchronous processing, and latency are issues that need to be addressed. Before being practical and effective, a majority of the ecosystem has to be available and interoperable in the cloud.

Cloud service providers have been very successful at providing an interface to their data and services through an API designed to follow the REST protocol [Fielding 00]. rest3d's goal is to research how such a cloud API can be designed to enable a 3D content ecosystem to be moved to the cloud [AMD 14].

The first step is to enable tools to dialog with the cloud as shown in Figure 2.8. COLLADA works well for transmitting data between various modeling tools and the cloud. Existing content-management systems can handle XML documents, as well as provide queries and search, i.e., XQUERY, inside the document. Additional metadata can be attached to the content and provide specific services, for example geo-specific information added to COLLADA for 3D content placed on Google Earth. Modeling tools as a cloud service are already available, such as http://clara.io/, https://tinkercad.com/, and http://home.lagoa.com/.

Once the content is available in the cloud, we can move the content pipeline, and more specifically, glTF conversion, into the cloud. Content can be processed on-demand for a particular device's needs. This solves the fragmentation of devices issue that is inherent in cloud computing and the explosion of devices that consumers expect to be able to use to access the same content. This is mostly solved for video and audio, where the size and quality of content streamed is based on the capacity of the target device and the available bandwidth. rest3d and glTF work together to enable this for 3D content. (See Figure 2.9.)

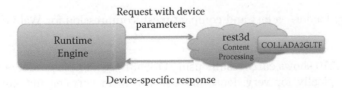

Figure 2.9. Moving the content pipeline into the cloud.

The rest3d open-source project is an experiment to provide client and server code to study the issues openly and converge toward a practical specification. Currently, it includes an XML database system, a nodejs http server, and client code for a basic UI, WebGL viewer, and model loaders. The system is able to fetch, parse, and display 3D content for both COLLADA and glTF. Parsing data and preparing it for WebGL visualization is an order of magnitude ($10\times$–$20\times$) faster with glTF than COLLADA. glTF becomes significantly better for models that need a lot of content processing.

A sample application was created to demonstrate using a web browser and server as a glTF conversion service. This shows that using these technologies, it is straightforward to create an easy-to-use tool that would always be up to date with the latest runtime format, and that can keep the content uploaded to be automatically converted when needed. The URL of the converted content can be used to be incorporated in the assets. Since it is a cloud service, a model converted a long time ago can keep the same URL, and it will automatically be reprocessed if needed so that it is always up to date.

Balancing the number of http requests, the size of each unit of content, and caching behavior is dependent on the type of application and content. rest3d aims to provide control over those parameters when running the converter and additional packaging on the server. One area of work, already available in the rest3d repo, is a geometry compression technique that can be applied to the geometry at the end of the COLLADA2GLTF processing pipeline. The client has the option to ask the server to compress the geometry, which will optimize the bandwidth and transfer time, at the cost of decompression on the client side.

2.10 Future Work

As we prepare the glTF spec for ratification, we are still finalizing the format itself and continuing to build open-source tools.

Compression is a promising area to expand on. At the time of writing this chapter, two early integrations of compression libraries have been tested with COLLADA2GLTF:

- Open3DGC—an efficient TFAN compression [Mammou et al. 09],

- webgl-loader—a fast and compact mesh compression for WebGL [Wonchun 14].

Figure 2.10 shows early results using Open3DGC. These numbers are promising, and typically for very dense meshes, the ratio between uncompressed and compressed data is even better. Our next integration step is to investigate memory footprint and processing impact while decoding compressed meshes.

Model	COLLADA		glTF		glTF+Open3DGC ascii		glTF+Open3DGC binary	
	XML	gzip	raw	gzip	raw	gzip	raw	raw bin gzip JSON
			bin:102k JSON:11k	bin:81k JSON:2kb	ascii:29k JSON:11k	ascii:19k JSON:2k	bin:18k JSON:11k	bin:18k JSON:2k
	336k	106k	113k	83k	40k	21k	29k	20k

Figure 2.10. Compression test with Open3DGC.

Similar to the GL APIs, glTF will support profiles and extensions to allow use of functionality not available everywhere. For example, a profile for modern OpenGL or OpenGL ES would allow using binary shaders to improve load times.

The current content pipeline in COLLADA2GLTF is a good start, but more stages are planned to fully support COLLADA and better optimize the output glTF. These stages include tessellating splines, flattening meshes and nodes, optimizing and minifying GLSL, and minifying JSON. There is also a lot of parallelism within and across stages that can be exploited to improve the latency of asset conversion. Finally, improving the architecture so the optimization stages can be done independent of converting to glTF will make the content pipeline useful beyond glTF. A high-quality open-source content pipeline for glTF is key for its adoption and success.

2.11 Acknowledgements

Khronos, WebGL, COLLADA, and glTF are trademarks of the Khronos Group Inc. OpenGL is a registered trademark and the OpenGL ES logo is a trademark of Silicon Graphics International used under license by Khronos.

Bibliography

[AMD 14] AMD. *rest3d GitHub Repo.* http://github.com/amd/rest3d, 2014.

[Analytical Graphics 14] Analytical Graphics, Inc. *Cesium GitHub Repo.* https://github.com/AnalyticalGraphicsInc/cesium, 2014.

[Fabrobinet 14] Fabrobinet. *MontageJS Viewer GitHub Repo.* https://github.com/fabrobinet/glTF-webgl-viewer, 2014.

[Fielding 00] Roy Thomas Fielding. "Architectural Styles and the Design of Network-based Software Architectures." PhD thesis, University of California, Irvine, CA, 2000.

[Kennytm 11] Kennytm. *Rapidjson GitHub Repo.* https://github.com/kennytm/rapidjson, 2011.

[Khronos 14a] Khronos Group. *glTF GitHub Repo.* https://github.com/
KhronosGroup/glTF, 2014.

[Khronos 14b] Khronos Group. *OpenCOLLADA GitHub Repo.* https://github.
com/KhronosGroup/OpenCOLLADA, 2014.

[Mammou et al. 09] K. Mammou, T. Zaharia, and F. Prêteux, "TFAN: A Low
Complexity 3D Mesh Compression Algorithm." *Computer Animation and
Virtual Worlds* 20:2–3 (2009), 343–354.

[Mrdoob 14] Mrdoob. *Three.js GitHub Repo.* https://github.com/mrdoob/three.
js, 2014.

[Vukicevic 11] Vladimir Vukicevic and Kenneth Russell, editors. *Typed Array Specification.* https://www.khronos.org/registry/typedarray/specs/1.0/,
2011.

[Wonchun 14] Wonchun. *webgl-loader*, Google Code project. https://code.google.
com/p/webgl-loader/, 2014.

3

Managing Transformations
in Hierarchy
Bartosz Chodorowski and Wojciech Sterna

3.1 Introduction

One of the most fundamental aspects of 3D engine design is management of
spatial relationship between objects. The most intuitive way of handling this
issue is to organize objects in a tree structure (hierarchy), where each node stores
its local transformation, relative to its parent.

The most common way to define the local transformation is to use a so-
called TRS system (present in most modeling packages or game engines like in
[Technologies 05]), where the transformation is composed of translation, rotation,
and scale.[1] This system is very easy to use for both programmers using the engine
as well as non-technical users like level designers. In this chapter we describe the
theory behind such a system.

To render an object described with TRS, we need to determine the final world
matrix to pass it to the render system. We thus merge translation, rotation, and
scale into one local transformation matrix and combine it with local transformations of the node's ancestors to obtain the node's final world matrix.

One problem with the system (and any other that merges rotation and scale
components into a single matrix) is decomposition of a matrix back to TRS. It
turns out that this problem is often ill-defined and no robust solution exists. We
present an approximate solution that works reasonably well in the majority of
cases.

Finally, tightly related to decomposition is switching a node's parent. Usually,
after that operation has been performed, we would most likely want to retain the
global transformation of the node. This problem can be alleviated using the
presented decomposition algorithm.

---

[1] As you will see later in this chapter's formulas, the term SRT would be more appropriate (because we are using row-major notation). However, we decided to stick to TRS to be
consistent with [Technologies 05].

3.2   Theory

In this section of the chapter all mathematical machinery will be presented. First, the hierarchy concept will be described. This will be followed by some basic theoretical formulations.

3.2.1   Hierarchy Concept

Keeping objects in hierarchy is a well-known concept. Every object (a hierarchy node) can have a number of *children* and only one *parent*. Technically, we want every object to store a pointer to its parent (or NULL value when we have no parent, i.e., the object is at the top of the hierarchy). It can also be convenient to store and manage a list of pointers to the children so that we have fast access to them. The aforementioned structure is in fact a *tree*.

We assume that a node stores its translation, rotation, and scale (*TRS*) that are relative to its parent. Therefore, we say these properties are *local*. When we move an object, we drag all its children with it. If we increase scale of the object, then all of its children will become larger too.

Let us consider an example of three unit cubes (of width, height, and length equal to 1). Figure 3.1 shows the objects and enlists their TRS values.

One interesting thing to note here is the location of object C. It is two units away on the X axis from object A despite the fact that its local translation is $x = -1$. That is because object A has the scale component $x = 2$.

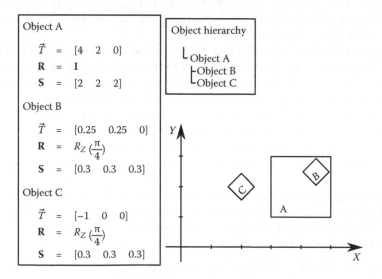

Figure 3.1. First example.

3.2.2   Transformations Composition

Local TRS uniquely defines a local transformation matrix $\mathbf{M}$. We transform vector $\vec{v}$ in the following way:

$$\vec{v'} = \vec{v}\mathbf{S}\mathbf{R} + \vec{T} = \vec{v}\mathbf{S}\mathbf{R}\mathbf{T} = \vec{v}\mathbf{M}, \tag{3.1}$$

where $\mathbf{S}$ is an arbitrary scale matrix, $\mathbf{R}$ is an arbitrary rotation matrix, $\mathbf{T}$ is a translation matrix, and $\vec{T}$ is the vector matrix $\mathbf{T}$ is made of.[2]

To render an object, we need to obtain its *global* (world) transformation by composing local transformations of all the object's ancestors up in the hierarchy.

The composition is achieved by simply multiplying local matrices. Given a vector v_0, its local matrix $\mathbf{M_0}$, and the local matrix $\mathbf{M_1}$ of v_0's parent, we can find the global position v_2:

$$\vec{v}_2 = \vec{v}_1\mathbf{M}_1 = \vec{v}_0\mathbf{M}_0\mathbf{M}_1.$$

Using vector notation for translation, we get

$$\vec{v}_2 = \vec{v}_1\mathbf{S}_1\mathbf{R}_1 + \vec{T}_1 = (\vec{v}_0\mathbf{S}_0\mathbf{R}_0 + \vec{T}_0)\mathbf{S}_1\mathbf{R}_1 + \vec{T}_1 \tag{3.2}$$
$$= \vec{v}_0(\mathbf{S}_0\mathbf{R}_0\mathbf{S}_1\mathbf{R}_1) + (\vec{T}_0\mathbf{S}_1\mathbf{R}_1 + \vec{T}_1)$$

Given that we store local transformations in TRS, it would be useful if we could decompose the global $\mathbf{M}_0\mathbf{M}_1$ matrix into TRS. We can easily extract the translation vector $\vec{T}_0\mathbf{S}_1\mathbf{R}_1 + \vec{T}_1$ but scale and rotation $\mathbf{S}_0\mathbf{R}_0\mathbf{S}_1\mathbf{R}_1$ is somehow combined. It turns out that in the general case we cannot extract the $\mathbf{S}$ and $\mathbf{R}$ matrices out of the $\mathbf{S}_0\mathbf{R}_0\mathbf{S}_1\mathbf{R}_1$ matrix. It stems from the following theorem.

Theorem 3.1. *There exist a rotation matrix $\mathbf{R}$ and a scale matrix $\mathbf{S}$ such that $\mathbf{R}\mathbf{S}$ cannot be expressed in the form of $\mathbf{S}'\mathbf{R}'$, where $\mathbf{S}'$ is a scale matrix and $\mathbf{R}'$ is a rotation matrix.*

Proof: Consider

$$\mathbf{S} = \begin{bmatrix} 1 & 0 & 0 \\ 0 & 2 & 0 \\ 0 & 0 & 1 \end{bmatrix}, \qquad \mathbf{R} = \begin{bmatrix} 1 & 0 & 0 \\ 0 & \frac{\sqrt{2}}{2} & -\frac{\sqrt{2}}{2} \\ 0 & \frac{\sqrt{2}}{2} & \frac{\sqrt{2}}{2} \end{bmatrix}.$$

Let us suppose by contradiction that there exist a scale matrix $\mathbf{S}'$ and a rotation matrix $\mathbf{R}'$ such that $\mathbf{R}\mathbf{S}=\mathbf{S}'\mathbf{R}'$. Moreover,

$$\mathbf{S}' = \begin{bmatrix} s'_1 & 0 & 0 \\ 0 & s'_2 & 0 \\ 0 & 0 & s'_3 \end{bmatrix}, \qquad \mathbf{R}' = \begin{bmatrix} r'_{11} & r'_{12} & r'_{13} \\ r'_{21} & r'_{22} & r'_{23} \\ r'_{31} & r'_{32} & r'_{33} \end{bmatrix}.$$

---

[2]In expression $\vec{v}\mathbf{S}\mathbf{R} + \vec{T}$ terms $\mathbf{S}$ and $\mathbf{R}$ are 3×3 matrices and $\vec{T}$ is a 3-component vector. In $\vec{v}\mathbf{S}\mathbf{R}\mathbf{T}$ all $\mathbf{S}$, $\mathbf{R}$ and $\mathbf{T}$ terms are 4×4 matrices.

We evaluate the left side of the equation

$$\mathbf{RS} = \begin{bmatrix} 1 & 0 & 0 \\ 0 & \sqrt{2} & -\frac{\sqrt{2}}{2} \\ 0 & \sqrt{2} & \frac{\sqrt{2}}{2} \end{bmatrix}$$

and the right side

$$\mathbf{S'R'} = \begin{bmatrix} s_1' r_{11}' & s_1' r_{12}' & s_1' r_{13}' \\ s_2' r_{21}' & s_2' r_{22}' & s_2' r_{23}' \\ s_3' r_{31}' & s_3' r_{32}' & s_3' r_{33}' \end{bmatrix}.$$

We compare entries from the first row and use the fact that $\mathbf{R'}$ is orthonormal. We get a system of equations

$$\begin{cases} 1 = s_1' r_{11}', \\ 0 = s_1' r_{12}', \\ 0 = s_1' r_{13}', \\ {r_{11}'}^2 + {r_{12}'}^2 + {r_{13}'}^2 = 1, \end{cases}$$

which we solve for s_1', thus yielding $s_1' = \pm 1$.

Considering the second and the third rows in a similar way, we get $s_2' = \pm \frac{\sqrt{2}\sqrt{5}}{2}$ and $s_3' = \pm \frac{\sqrt{2}\sqrt{5}}{2}$.

Since $\det(\mathbf{AB}) = \det(\mathbf{A})\det(\mathbf{B})$ and $\mathbf{RS} = \mathbf{S'R'}$ and $\det(\mathbf{S'}) = s_1' s_2' s_3'$,

$$\det(\mathbf{R'}) = \frac{\det(\mathbf{R})\det(\mathbf{S})}{\det(\mathbf{S'})} = \frac{1 \cdot (1 \cdot 2 \cdot 1)}{\pm 1 \cdot \frac{\sqrt{2}\sqrt{5}}{2} \cdot \frac{\sqrt{2}\sqrt{5}}{2}} = \pm \frac{4}{5} \neq 1,$$

which contradicts the assumption of $\mathbf{R'}$ being an orthonormal rotation matrix and finishes the proof. $\square$

3.2.3   Skew Problem

Let us go back for a minute to the example shown in Figure 3.1. If we change the x component of scale of object A, we will get a situation that is depicted by Figure 3.2.

Applying a *nonuniform scale* (coming from object A) that follows a local rotation (objects B and C) will cause objects (B and C) to be *skewed*. Skew can appear during matrices composition but it becomes a problem during the decomposition, as it cannot be expressed within a single TRS node. We give an approximate solution to this issue in Section 3.2.4.

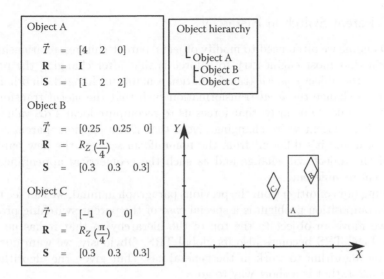

Figure 3.2. Modified example.

3.2.4 Decomposition of Global Transform to TRS

While we already know that in the standard TRS system, due to skew, we cannot always decompose a global transformation into global TRS values, we aim to find an algorithm that gives us at least an approximate solution.

Let an object have n ancestors in the hierarchy tree. Let $\mathbf{M}_1, \mathbf{M}_2, \cdots, \mathbf{M}_n$ be their local transformation matrices, $\mathbf{M}_0$ be a local transformation matrix of the considered object, and $\mathbf{M}_i = \mathbf{S}_i\mathbf{R}_i\mathbf{T}_i$.

Let us denote $\mathbf{M}_{TRS\Sigma} = \mathbf{M}_0\mathbf{M}_1\cdots\mathbf{M}_n$ ($TRS\Sigma$ means here that the matrix holds pretty much everything including translation, rotation, scale, and skew). We also define $\mathbf{M}_{TR} = \mathbf{R}_0\mathbf{T}_0\mathbf{R}_1\mathbf{T}_1\cdots\mathbf{R}_n\mathbf{T}_n$ (TR indicates that the matrix holds information about translation and rotation).

Global translation is easily extractible from $\mathbf{M}_{TRS\Sigma}$; we just look at the fourth row of the matrix.

Global rotation is determined simply by taking $\mathbf{M}_{TR}$ stripped of the translation vector, giving us $\mathbf{M}_R$ matrix. This matrix will usually have to be converted to a quaternion or to Euler angles. [Dunn and Parberry 02] provides extensive coverage on how to do this.

Global scale is the trickiest part. To get reasonable values for it, we determine $\mathbf{M}_{RS\Sigma}$ matrix (which is $\mathbf{M}_{TRS\Sigma}$ matrix with zeroed translation part). Then, we compute $\mathbf{M}_{S\Sigma} = \mathbf{M}_{RS\Sigma}\mathbf{M}_R^{-1}$. Voilà—here we have the skew and the scale combined. We use diagonal elements of $\mathbf{M}_{S\Sigma}$ to get the scale, and we choose to ignore the rest that is responsible for the skew.

3.2.5   Parent Switch in Hierarchy

In a 3D engine we often need to modify objects' parent-children relationship. One condition that most engines try to enforce is that after changing the parent of an object, the object's *global* transformation remains unchanged. In other words, we want to change the *local* transformation such that the *global* transformation is still the same. Obviously, that forces us to recompute local TRS values of the object whose parent we're changing. Note that if the previous parent's scale is nonuniform and it's different from the nonuniform scale of the new parent, the skew of the object will change and as such the geometrical appearance of the object will be different.

Having our condition from the previous paragraph in mind, we can see that the TRS decomposition problem is a special case of the parent switching problem— when we move an object to the top of the hierarchy so that it has no parent, its new local TRS becomes also its global TRS. Obviously, we want our parent switching algorithm to work in the general case, but given the algorithm from Section 3.2.4, that is a short way to go.

To get from the current local space to a new local space (parent changes, global transform stays the same), we first need to find the global transform of the object by going up in the hierarchy to the root node. Having done this we need to go down the hierarchy to which our new parent belongs.

Let $\mathbf{M}'_0$ be the new parent's local transformation matrix. Let that new parent have n' ancestors in the hierarchy tree with local transformations $\mathbf{M}'_1, \mathbf{M}'_2, \cdots,$ $\mathbf{M}'_{n'}$, where $\mathbf{M}'_i = \mathbf{S}'_i \mathbf{R}'_i \mathbf{T}'_i$. The new local transformation matrix can thus be found using the following formula:

$$\mathbf{M}_{TRS\Sigma} = \mathbf{M}_0 \mathbf{M}_1 \cdots \mathbf{M}_n (\mathbf{M}'_0 \mathbf{M}'_1 \cdots \mathbf{M}'_{n'})^{-1}$$
$$= \mathbf{M}_0 \mathbf{M}_1 \cdots \mathbf{M}_n \mathbf{M}'_{n'}{}^{-1} \mathbf{M}'_{n'-1}{}^{-1} \cdots \mathbf{M}'_0{}^{-1}.$$

Similarly,

$$\mathbf{M}_{TR} = \mathbf{R}_0 \mathbf{T}_0 \mathbf{R}_1 \mathbf{T}_1 \cdots \mathbf{R}_n \mathbf{T}_n (\mathbf{R}'_0 \mathbf{T}'_0 \mathbf{R}'_1 \mathbf{T}'_1 \cdots \mathbf{R}'_{n'} \mathbf{T}'_{n'})^{-1}$$
$$= \mathbf{R}_0 \mathbf{T}_0 \mathbf{R}_1 \mathbf{T}_1 \cdots \mathbf{R}_n \mathbf{T}_n (\mathbf{R}'_{n'} \mathbf{T}'_{n'})^{-1} (\mathbf{R}'_{n'-1} \mathbf{T}'_{n'-1})^{-1} \cdots (\mathbf{R}'_0 \mathbf{T}'_0)^{-1}.$$

Now we simply use the algorithm from Section 3.2.4 to get the new local TRS values.

3.2.6   Alternative Systems

Here we present some alternatives to the standard TRS system.

Uniform scale. This is probably the simplest solution proposed in [Eberly 07]. Instead of allowing the system to handle nonuniform scale, we might decide that we can get away with just using uniform scale. This can be a limiting constraint though. The good thing about it is that the skew problem is completely gone.

Let us reformulate equation (3.1) with uniform scale factor s:

$$\vec{v}' = \vec{v}s\mathbf{R} + \vec{T} = \vec{v}s\mathbf{RT} = \vec{v}\mathbf{M}.$$

Equation (3.2) now becomes

$$\vec{v}_2 = \vec{v}_1 s_1 \mathbf{R}_1 + \vec{T}_1 = (\vec{v}_0 s_0 \mathbf{R}_0 + \vec{T}_0) s_1 \mathbf{R}_1 + \vec{T}_1$$
$$= \vec{v}_0 (s_0 \mathbf{R}_0 s_1 \mathbf{R}_1) + (\vec{T}_0 s_1 \mathbf{R}_1 + \vec{T}_1).$$

Since matrix-scalar multiplication is commutative, we can thus write

$$\vec{v}_2 = \vec{v}_0 (s_0 s_1 \mathbf{R}_0 \mathbf{R}_1) + (\vec{T}_0 s_1 \mathbf{R}_1 + \vec{T}_1).$$

Term $\mathbf{R}_0 \mathbf{R}_1$ is an orthonormal rotation matrix. Scaling such a matrix by a scalar geometrically does nothing more but simply scales the basis vectors encoded in this matrix. This means that we can extract the scale factor from the $s_0 s_1 \mathbf{R}_0 \mathbf{R}_1$ matrix by just calculating length of one of its basis vectors.

Nonuniform scale in last node. This solution is an extension of the previous one and was also proposed in [Eberly 07]. The idea is to give the TRS system the ability to store nonuniform scale but only in the last nodes of the hierarchy. This solution still avoids the skew problem (because there is no parent that could store a nonuniform scale) but at the same time offers a little bit more flexibility.

The aforementioned alternatives just scratch the surface and in specific applications more complex systems might be needed.

3.3   Implementation

Here we shall discuss selected parts of the source code of a demo that accompanies this book. The demo contains a full implementation of the `Node` class, which is equipped with a rich set of functions for transform (node) manipulation. We will discuss the most interesting excerpts from that implementation, leaving the rest for self-study.

3.3.1   Class Fields

Listing 3.1 depicts the `Node` class's fields.

Fields `localTranslation`, `localRotation`, and `localScale` define the TRS system that we have discussed throughout this chapter. We choose to store all components in the local space but that does not have to be the case. We could equally well store just global components, or even both. All these fields are

```
public:
    string name;

private:
    Node* parent;
    vector<Node*> children;

    Vector3 localTranslation;
    Quaternion localRotation;
    Vector3 localScale;

    Matrix localMatrix;
```

Listing 3.1. Node class fields.

private so the class's users don't need to know what is actually stored inside the class; the implementation is up to us. Note, however, that the interface (discussed in the next section) exhibits functionality to set/get both local and global transforms. Choosing rotation representation in the form of a quaternion is also our implementation choice. Nothing prevents us from using here a 3×3 rotation matrix, but that would obviously be a waste of memory (four floats against nine). We could actually save one more float by storing Euler angles instead of a quaternion. However, quaternions are much neater to work with (in terms of composition and interpolation). More on this can be found in a thorough case study in [Dunn and Parberry 02].

The last field, `localMatrix`, is here to act as a sort of cache. It is expensive in terms of memory to store such a big matrix, but given how often we need to find the local matrix in code, we decided to have it here and recompute only when needed. Obviously, if memory is more precious to us than computations, we can remove this field and always compute the local matrix on the fly.

3.3.2   Class Interface

Listing 3.2 presents a list of public methods Node class exposes. Some have been skipped (marked with [...] comment) so that we can focus on functions that are of greatest interest to us as well as for compactness reasons.

There are two functions for altering the local translation vector. The difference is that `SetLocalTranslation` resets the old translation vector to completely new values while `LocalTranslate` just adds a new vector to the current `localTranslation`. The same scheme goes for local rotation functions.

There is also a `SetLocalScale` function, which does exactly what we can expect from it. However, there is no `SetGlobalScale` function. That is because when using the TRS system with nonuniform scale, there is just no single global scale value. Global scale is a combination of both local scales and local rotations of all nodes in the hierarchy. We can, however, get the global scale (function `GetGlobalLossyScale`) just as we did in Section 3.2.4.

```
void SetParent(Node* newParent);
void SetChild(Node* newChild) { newChild->SetParent(this); }

// local translation sets
void SetLocalTranslation(float x, float y, float z,
    bool useLocalRotation = false);
void LocalTranslate(float x, float y, float z,
    bool useLocalRotation = false);

// global translation sets [...]

// local rotation sets
void SetLocalRotation(const Quaternion& rotation);
void LocalRotate(const Quaternion& rotation);
void SetLocalEulerAngles(float x, float y, float z);

// global rotation sets [...]

// local scale sets
void SetLocalScale(float x, float y, float z);

// local gets [...]

// global gets

Vector3 GetGlobalTranslation() const;
Quaternion GetGlobalRotation() const;
Vector3 GetGlobalEulerAngles() const;
Vector3 GetGlobalLossyScale() const;

Vector3 GetGlobalRight();
Vector3 GetGlobalUp();
Vector3 GetGlobalBackward();
Vector3 GetGlobalForward();

Matrix GetGlobalMatrix() const;
Matrix GetGlobalMatrix_TranslationAndRotation() const;
Matrix GetGlobalMatrixWithoutLocalMatrix() const;
```

Listing 3.2. Node class interface.

All of the set functions that alter a node's local TRS call the `UpdateLocalMatrix` function, which updates the `localMatrix` cache matrix. That means that after calling functions that set local translation, rotation, and scale, `UpdateLocalMatrix` gets called more than once without actually being used anywhere. There are two optimizations available here. One is to use a dirty flag that would defer the call to `UpdateLocalMatrix` until any function that needs it is called. Another idea is to expose a function that sets all parameters (translation, rotation, and scale) one by one and then calls the update function. However, none of these are present in the demo application for the sake of simplicity.

Function `GetGlobalMatrix` returns the global transformation matrix. `GetGlobalMatrix_TranslationAndRotation` does this as well but does not involve scale. This is, in fact, matrix $\mathbf{M}_{TR}$ from Section 3.2.4. The last function, `GetGlobalMatrix`

```
inline void Node::SetGlobalTranslation(float x, float y, float z)
{
    localTranslation =
        Vector3(Vector4(x, y, z, 1.0f) *
        GetGlobalMatrixWithoutLocalMatrix().GetInversed());

    UpdateLocalMatrix();
}
```

Listing 3.3. Node::SetGlobalTranslation.

WithoutLocalMatrix, deserves a little bit more attention and will be discussed in the context of the SetGlobalTranslation function, whose implementation is in Listing 3.3. This method finds the node's local-to-global transform matrix but does not take the node's local transform into account (only its ancestors). Taking the inverse of this matrix creates a transform that goes from the global space to the node's parent space. Now, if we had some global coordinates and multiplied them by this matrix, we would find out what these coordinates are in the node parent's local space. This is exactly what we understand as setting global translation and this function implements that.

3.3.3   Demo Application

The demo application accompanying this chapter makes extensive use of the Node class that has just been described. The application can render up to four unit cubes whose local components we can change (through standard input; select each cube with keys 1, 2, 3, or 4). We can also change parent-child relationships.

The aforementioned four cubes can be reset to one of four initial coordinate configurations. The first configuration (F1 key) depicts the skew problem. When the green object's parent is set to 0 (no parent), the skew is gone. The remaining three configurations (keys F2, F3, and F4) all set local components to the same values but differ in the moment when the parent-child relationships are determined. Have a look at the code to examine those cases and see how they affect the global transforms of the objects.

One more interesting thing in the demo is the way the free camera movement is implemented. It uses Node class and needs very few easy-to-understand code lines to achieve the desired effect.

3.4   Conclusions

Managing transformations in hierarchy is one of the most fundamental aspects of every 3D engine. In this chapter we have thoroughly described a TRS system that is quite easy to both understand and implement and offers a lot of flexibility, while at the same time minimizing drawbacks related to using nonuniform scale.

Bibliography

[Dunn and Parberry 02] Fletcher Dunn and Ian Parberry. *3D Math Primer for Graphics and Game Development*, First edition. Plano, TX: Wordware Publishing, 2002.

[Eberly 07] David H. Eberly. *3D Game Engine Design*, Second edition. San Francisco, CA: Morgan Kaufmann Publishers, 2007.

[Technologies 05] Unity Technologies. "Unity 3D." http://unity3d.com/, 2005.

VI

Compute

Graphics processing units are becoming more capable every year of processing general purpose calculations. The new console generation is able to execute compute tasks asynchronously. The game industry re-thinks traditional algorithms to utilize the thread group shared memory or the on-chip cache in better ways and sees substantial gains in performance.

The Compute section starts with the chapter by Dongsoo Han, "Hair Simulation in TressFX." It describes the simulation algorithms used in the game *Tomb Raider* to animate Lara Croft's hair and in the AMD demo *Ruby*. TressFX can simulate 19,000 strands of hair, consisting of 0.22 million vertices in less than a millisecond on a high-end GPU.

The next chapter, "Object-Order Ray Tracing for Fully Dynamic Scenes" by Tobias Zirr, Hauke Rehfeld, and Carsten Dachsbacher, describes the implementation of a ray tracer that is capable of utilizing the same art assets as a rasterizer-based engine, which is one of the major obstacles in using ray tracers in games.

The chapter "Quadtrees on the GPU" by Jonathan Dupuy, Jean-Claude Iehl, and Pierre Poulin describes a quadtree implementation that is implemented with linear trees on the GPU. The chapter explains how to update linear trees, which are a pointer-free alternative to recursive trees on the GPU, and how to render multiresolution, crack-free surfaces with frustum culling using hardware tessellation and a distance-based LOD selection criterion.

A key feature for simulating rigid bodies on the GPU is the performance of the constraint solver. Takahiro Harada shows in his chapter "Two-Level Constraint Solver and Pipelined Local Batching for Rigid Body Simulation on GPUs" an implementation that uses pipelined batching to run the entire solver on the GPU. This constraint solver is also implemented in the Bullet Physics Engine.

The last chapter in the series, "Non-separable 2D, 3D, and 4D Filtering with CUDA" by Anders Eklund and Paul Dufort, covers the efficient implementation of filtering algorithms tailored to deal with 3D and 4D datasets, which commonly occur in medical imaging, and 2D datasets.

—Wolfgang Engel

Hair Simulation in TressFX

Dongsoo Han

1.1 Introduction

A human has around 120,000 strands of hair, and due to its high cost of rendering and lack of real-time simulation technique, it has been a challenge to present human hair inside real-time video games. Therefore, many artists and game developers have to choose alternative approaches such as simple polygons and textures.

In this chapter, I will explain the hair simulation method in TressFX, which has been used in the recent *Tomb Raider* and AMD *Ruby* demos. (See Figure 1.1.) It can simulate around 19,000 strands consisting of 0.22 million vertices in less than a millisecond in high-end GPUs. TressFX was developed specifically for video games. Therefore, performance was the highest concern, over physical accuracy.

Figure 1.1. Example of hair simulation in *Tomb Raider*.

1.2   Simulation Overview

When TressFX simulation was developed, the main focus was to simulate styled hair, which is much harder than straight hair because it requires strong bending and twisting effects. Regardless of hair style, it should be safe to consider human hair as inextensible. To simulate those three effects, there are generally two ways to represent them, as either stiff spring or constraint.

In VFX, stiff spring is commonly used for various simulations such as hair or cloth. However, for real-time physics simulation, stiff spring is not practical because the integration of strong spring force can easily make the mass-spring-damper system unstable unless a complicated integration scheme such as implicit backward integrator is used [Baraff and Witkin 98, Selle et al. 08]. Also, it becomes hard to deal with stretching, bending, and twisting springs in the same solver, especially in GPUs. In TressFX, all springs are replaced with hard and soft constraints. For inextensibility, we use a simple iterative position-based distance constraint. Bending and twisting are considered as a single effect for simplicity, and local and global shape constraints were developed. We also sometimes resort to ad-hoc constraints to deal with fast-moving characters.

Besides bending and twisting effects, the rest of hair simulation is similar to cloth simulation. However, in terms of GPU computing, hair has more benefits because there are a lot of hair strands and they are independent as long as inter-hair collisions are ignored. Also the topology of vertex connection is straightforward. By exploiting them, TressFX can achieve strand- and vertex-level parallelism without complex data structure.

> **Input**: hair data
> precompute rest-state values;
> **while** *simulation running* **do**
> > integrate;
> > apply Global Shape Constraints;
> > **while** *iteration* **do**
> > > apply Local Shape Constraints;
> >
> > **end**
> > **while** *iteration* **do**
> > > apply Edge Length Constraints;
> >
> > **end**
> > apply wind;
> > collision handling;
> > update position;
> > pass updated vertex buffer to rendering pipleine;
>
> **end**

Algorithm 1.1. Hair simulation outline.

1.3   Definitions

Basically, each hair strand is a poly line. We will use the terms *local* and *global* often when we explain local shape constraints. Global is in world frame and local is in local frame, which is attached to the starting point of a line segment.

The index of vertices starts from the root of a hair strand that is attached to a scalp. P_i is the position of vertex i in the current time step. The zeroth time step is the rest state, and we use a right superscript to express it explicitly (i.e., P_i^0). Here, we focus only on vertices in one strand when we explain algorithms. Therefore, vertex index i is always unique.

In case we need to explicitly clarify which coordinate system we are using, we specify it using a left superscript (i.e., $^{i-1}P_i$ means the position of vertex i in the current time step defined in the local frame $i-1$). When the position is defined in the world coordinate system, we can drop the frame index (i.e., $^wP_i = P_i$).

In terms of transforms, we define $^{i-1}T_i$ as a full transformation containing rotation $^{i-1}R_i$ and translation $^{i-1}L_i$. It transforms $^iP_{i+1}$ to $^{i-1}P_{i+1}$ such that $^{i-1}P_{i+1} = {}^{i-1}T_i \cdot {}^iP_{i+1}$. Because of careful indexing of vertices in the strand, the following equation holds:

$$^wT_i = {}^wT_0 \cdot {}^0T_1 \cdot {}^1T_2 .... {}^{i-2}T_{i-1} \cdot {}^{i-1}T_i.$$

In this chapter, we call $^{i-1}T_i$ a local transform and ^wT_i a global transform. In the case of vertex 0, local transform and global transform are the same such that $^{-1}T_0 = {}^wT_0$.

In Figure 1.2, local frames are defined at each vertex. Vectors x_i, y_i, and z_i are basis vectors of the local frame of vertex i in the current time step. x_i is simply defined as a normalized vector of $P_i - P_{i-1}$. As an exception, $x_0 = (P_1 - P_0) / \|P_1 - P_0\|$. In Figure 1.3, basis vectors are shown in red, yellow, and blue.

To describe the head transform, we use ^wT_H, which transforms the head from the rest state to the current state and is an input from user or predefined animations.

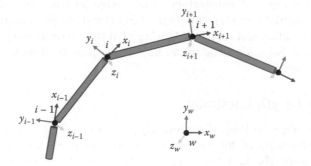

Figure 1.2. Local frames in a hair strand.

Figure 1.3. Black is a hair stand. Red, yellow, and blue are x, y, and z axes, respectively.

1.4 Integration

To integrate the motion of hair dynamics, we use the Verlet integration scheme because it is simple and shows good numerical stability compared to the explicit Euler method. External forces such as gravity are applied during this step. The damping coefficient is multiplied by velocity to simulate a damping effect.

We integrate only particles whose inverse mass is nonzero. If the inverse mass is zero, we consider it non-movable, update its positions following its attached objects (such as a head), and skip the rest of the steps for those particles. We assign zero inverse mass for vertex 0 and 1 so they can be animated following the head movement.

1.5 Constraints

There are three types of constraints. ELC (edge length constraint) is a hard constraint to simulate inextensible hair. LSC (local shape constraint) is a soft constraint for bending and twisting. GSC (global shape constraint) is complementary to LSC and helps keep the initial hair shape preserved with very minimum computation cost.

1.5.1 Edge Length Constraint

ELC enforces edges to keep their rest lengths. Figure 1.4 shows how position corrections are computed for each edge. To be simple, we set an equal mass to all vertices except the first two vertices. To apply this constraint in parallel, we create two batches. Each batch is independent of the other so that it is

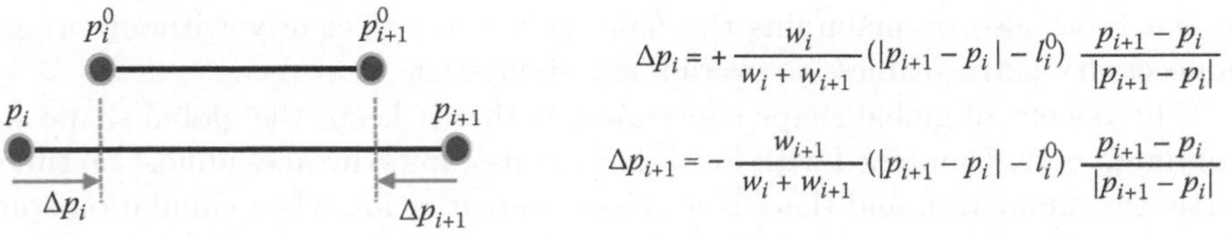

$$\Delta p_i = + \frac{w_i}{w_i + w_{i+1}} (|p_{i+1} - p_i| - l_i^0) \frac{p_{i+1} - p_i}{|p_{i+1} - p_i|}$$

$$\Delta p_{i+1} = - \frac{w_{i+1}}{w_i + w_{i+1}} (|p_{i+1} - p_i| - l_i^0) \frac{p_{i+1} - p_i}{|p_{i+1} - p_i|}$$

Figure 1.4. Edge length constraint: w_i and w_{i+1} are inverse masses of p_i and p_{i+1}, respectively.

safe to update vertex positions without conflict. In hair, it is easy to create the two batches as an even edge index group and an odd edge index group. We run the first batch followed by the second one. This approach gives us a good parallelism. Unfortunately, the trade-off is that it has poor convergence, so we iterate it multiple times to make all edges reach their rest lengths.

In *Tomb Raider*, the main character can move and turn very fast. Basically, users can create a strong acceleration, which causes very long elongation to hair. In this case, ELC does not converge well even with more than 20 iterations. It is easy to check the convergence by measuring the first movable edge length and comparing it with its rest length. To fix this problem, we switch to the ad-hoc constraints, which update only one vertex position, p_{i+} in Figure 1.4. By updating one vertex position per edge starting from the root of the hair strand, we can simply satisfy ELC by one iteration. However, this approach can add extra energy to the system and cause unnatural simulation results. To remove this extra energy, we add high damping. Due to this, we only use this approach when it is really necessary. The interested reader is referred to [Müller et al. 12] for deeper understanding of this problem and different solutions.

1.5.2 Global Shape Constraint

The main idea of GSC is quite simple. We take the initial hair shape as a target and try to move vertices to it. It is similar to shape matching. Probably the easy way to understand it is to think of the initial hair shape as a cage and GSC enforcing hair to trap inside it. Before simulation begins, we save the rest positions of vertices P_i^0. We use these rest positions as goal positions to apply global shape constraints. In equation (1.1), S_G is a stiffness coefficient for the global shape constraint. It ranges between 0 and 1. If S_G is 0, there is no effect; if it is 1, the hair becomes completely rigid, frozen to the initial shape:

$$P_i += S_G({}^w T_H \cdot P_i^0 - P_i). \tag{1.1}$$

In many cases, we apply global shape constraints on a part of the hair strand such as close to the root. We can also gradually reduce S_G from the root of the hair to the end. This is because hair seems to behave more stiffly close to the root; also, it maintains the hair style more efficiently without bringing unnecessary extra stiffness to overall hair simulation.

The benefit of global shape constraints is that it keeps the global shape with minimum cost. Combined with local shape constraints, it takes almost no time to settle the simulation and there is no visual perturbation when simulation starts. Designers can expect that their authored hair shape will be the initial shape. Global shape constraints also ensure that hair does not get tangled in weird shapes during fast-moving gameplay.

1.5.3   Local Shape Constraint

Even though GSC can effectively manage the hair shape, we need a way to simulate bending and twisting forces for individual hair strands. In real-time cloth simulation, the bending effect is often represented as a soft distance constraint connecting two vertices across the bent edge. It is also possible to use the same approach for a bending effect in hair, but twisting is not really easy.

For simplicity and high performance, we combine bending and twisting effects as one soft distance constraint. To define this constraint, the target goal positions are computed using the local frames as in Figures 1.2 and 1.3.

Equation (1.2) may look complex due to its subscripts and superscripts but the concept is the same as ELC. The first equation computes $^{i-1}d_i$, which is a distance between the current position and its target goal position. The left superscript $i-1$ indicates that those positions are defined within the local frames. In the end, when we calculate the position correction, we actually use world frame but equation (1.2) is written in local frame to simplify it:

$$^{i-1}d_i = \, ^{i-1}P_i^0 - ^{i-1}P_i$$

$$^{i-1}P_{i-1} \mathrel{-}= \frac{1}{2}S_L \, ^{i-1}d_i \qquad\qquad (1.2)$$

$$^{i-1}P_i \mathrel{+}= \frac{1}{2}S_L \, ^{i-1}d_i.$$

As explained in ELC, we divide the position correction by the mass ratio and apply it to two connected vertices ($^{i-1}P_{i-1}$ and $^{i-1}P_i$). Here, we already assume that all mass is equal so the ratio is $1/2$.

1.6   Wind and Collision

Wind is an important part of simulation since it makes the hair interact with the environment and gives the game character dynamics even during idle states. To generate more randomized effects and prevent hair from getting clumped, a single wind input gets converted to four cone-shape directions as in Figure 1.5. Also,

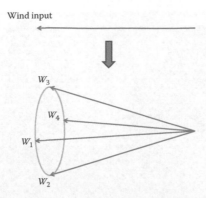

Figure 1.5. A single wind input is converted to four wind directions to generate randomized effects and prevent hair clumping.

wind magnitude gets modulated by using the sine function and frame number as below:

$$\text{wind magnitue} \times = (\sin^2(\text{frame} \times 0.05) + 0.5).$$

Equation (1.6) shows how wind force is calculated and applied to position update. W_1, W_2, W_3, and W_4 are the four wind vectors, and the strand index is used to add more randomization:

$$\begin{aligned}
a &= ((\text{strand index})\%20)/20, \\
W &= a \times W_1 + (1-a) \times W_2 + a \times W_3 + (1-a) \times W_4, \\
V &= P_i - P_{i+1}, \\
f &= -(V \times W) \times V, \\
P_i &+= f \times \Delta t^2.
\end{aligned} \qquad (1.3)$$

The number 20 in the first equation is an arbitrary choice, W is an interpolated wind vector by a from four wind vectors, and Δt is timestep.

The wind is applied after the shape constraints and is not a part of integration because shape constraints are too strong and could cancel its effect if it is applied as an external force during integration. The key point of calculating wind is to create randomized direction and periodic magnitude. So it is more empirical than physically correct.

1.7 Authoring Hair Asset

The TressFX demo and Lara Croft's hair assets were created using Autodesk Maya. (See Figure 1.6.) However, it can be authored using any DCC (digital

Figure 1.6. Authoring Lara Croft's hair in Autodesk Maya.

content creation) tools. Once the hair strands are authored as splines, a custom python script exports them as poly lines. In the TressFX demo, hair is divided into four groups as front, top, side, and ponytail and each group is saved as a separate file.

1.8   GPU Implementation

TressFX uses compute shader in DirectX 11 to run hair simulation in the GPU. There are a total of five compute shader kernels. Listing 1.1 shows the `Simulate Hair_A` kernel, which handles integration and GSC. This kernel computes one vertex per thread. Since `GROUP_SIZE` is defined as 64, one thread group can compute four hair strands if one strand has 16 vertices. With `maxPossibleVertsInStrand`, it is possible to control how many strands can be computed in one thread group. Since `GROUP_SIZE` is 64, the maximum number of vertices in a strand is 64. By changing `GROUP_SIZE` to 128 or 256, we can have more vertices. However, more vertices could take a longer time to enforce ELC and LSC. Therefore, it is recommended to use 16 or 32 vertices per strand for real-time purposes.

Listing 1.2 shows the `SimulateHair_A` kernel, which does LSC. This kernel computes one strand per thread and thus there is a `for` loop. `strandType` is a variable showing to which group the strand belongs. With this, we can assign different simulation parameters such as stiffness or damping to hair groups.

The `SimulateHair_C` kernel computes one vertex per thread, enforces ELC, and applies wind. Finally, `SimulateHair_D` takes care of collision and computes tangents of line segments for the rendering pipeline.

```
// Integrate and global shape constraints
// One thread computes one vertex
[numthreads(GROUP_SIZE, 1, 1)]
void SimulateHair_A(uint GIndex : SV_GroupIndex,
                    uint3 GId : SV_GroupID,
                    uint3 DTid : SV_DispatchThreadID)
{
    int offset = 0;
    int strandType = 0;

    uint globalStrandIndex = 0;
    uint localVertexIndex = 0;
    uint indexForSharedMem = GIndex;
    uint numOfStrandsPerThreadGroup = 2;
    uint maxPossibleVertsInStrand = (GROUP_SIZE /
      numOfStrandsPerThreadGroup);

    // If maxPossibleVertsInStrand is 64, one thread group
    // computes one hair strand.
    // If it is 32, one thread group computes two hair
    // strands. Below code takes care of strand and vertex
    // indices based on how many strands are computed
    // in one thread group.
    if ( GIndex < maxPossibleVertsInStrand )
    {
        globalStrandIndex = 2 * GId.x;
        localVertexIndex = GIndex;
    }
    else
    {
        globalStrandIndex = 2 * GId.x + 1;
        localVertexIndex = GIndex - maxPossibleVertsInStrand;
    }

    if( globalStrandIndex > 0 )
    {
        offset = g_GuideHairVerticesOffsetsSRV
                            .Load(globalStrandIndex - 1);
        strandType = g_GuideHairStrandType
                            .Load(globalStrandIndex - 1);
    }

    uint globalVertexIndex = offset + localVertexIndex;
    uint numVerticesInTheStrand = g_GuideHairVerticesOffsetsSRV
                            .Load(globalStrandIndex) - offset;

    // Copy data into shared memory
    // Integrate
    // Global shaping matching style enforcement
    // update global position buffers
}
```

Listing 1.1. SimulateHair_A compute shader kernel.

In case hair simulation should be skipped, SkipSimulateHair kernel does this job. It may be possible to assign 1.0 GSC stiffness but it would waste lots of computation. The SkipSimulateHair kernel applies only the head transform to vertices and makes the hair do rigid motion.

```
// Local shape constraints
// One thread computes one strand
[numthreads(GROUP_SIZE, 1, 1)]
void SimulateHair_B(uint GIndex : SV_GroupIndex,
                    uint3 GId : SV_GroupID,
                    uint3 DTid : SV_DispatchThreadID)
{
    uint globalStrandIndex = GROUP_SIZE*GId.x;
    globalStrandIndex += GIndex;

    int offset = 0;
    int strandType = 0;

    if ( globalStrandIndex > 0 )
    {
        offset =   g_GuideHairVerticesOffsetsSRV
                                .Load(globalStrandIndex - 1);
        strandType = g_GuideHairStrandType
                                .Load(globalStrandIndex - 1);
    }

    uint numVerticesInTheStrand = g_GuideHairVerticesOffsetsSRV
                            .Load(globalStrandIndex) - offset;

    // Local shape constraint for bending/twisting
    {
        float4 pos_minus_one = g_GuideHairVertexPositions
                                                    [offset];
        float4 pos = g_GuideHairVertexPositions[offset+1];
        float4 pos_plus_one;
        uint globalVertexIndex = 0;
        float4 rotGlobal = g_GlobalRotations[offset];

        for ( uint localVertexIndex = 1; localVertexIndex <
                numVerticesInTheStrand-1; localVertexIndex++ )
        {
            globalVertexIndex = offset + localVertexIndex;
            pos_plus_one = g_GuideHairVertexPositions
                                [globalVertexIndex+1];

            // Update position i and i_plus_1

            // Update local/global frames
        }
    }

    return;
}
```

Listing 1.2. `SimulateHair_B` compute shader kernel.

1.9   Conclusion

The hair simulation of TressFX is optimized for real-time games in many aspects, such as using shape constraints and limits on the number of vertices per strand. Therefore, it is required to understand its basic approaches to maximize its performance and quality.

Lastly, for readers who want to know more details, we refer them to [Han and Harada 12].

Bibliography

[Baraff and Witkin 98] David Baraff and Andrew Witkin. "Large Steps in Cloth Simulation." In *Proceedings of the 25th Annual Conference on Computer Graphics and Interactive Techniques*, pp. 43–54. New York: ACM, 1998.

[Han and Harada 12] Dongsoo Han and Takahiro Harada. "Real-Time Hair Simulation with Efficient Hair Style Preservation." In *VRIPHYS*, edited by Jan Bender, Arjan Kuijper, Dieter W. Fellner, and Eric Guérin, pp. 45–51. Aire-la-Ville, Switzerland: Eurographics Association, 2012.

[Müller et al. 12] Matthias Müller, Tae-Yong Kim, and Nuttapong Chentanez. "Fast Simulation of Inextensible Hair and Fur." In *VRIPHYS*, edited by Jan Bender, Arjan Kuijper, Dieter W. Fellner, and Eric Guérin, pp. 39–44. Aire-la-Ville, Switzerland: Eurographics Association, 2012.

[Selle et al. 08] Andrew Selle, Michael Lentine, and Ronald Fedkiw. "A Mass Spring Model for Hair Simulation." In *ACM SIGGRAPH 2008 Papers*, pp. 64:1–64:11. New York: ACM, 2008.

Object-Order Ray Tracing
for Fully Dynamic Scenes

Tobias Zirr, Hauke Rehfeld,
and Carsten Dachsbacher

2.1 Introduction

This chapter presents a method for tracing incoherent secondary rays that integrates well with existing rasterization-based real-time rendering engines. (See Figure 2.1.) In particular, it requires only linear scene access and supports fully dynamic scene geometry. All parts of the method that work with scene geometry are implemented in the standard graphics pipeline. Thus, the ability to generate, transform, and animate geometry via shaders is fully retained. Our method does not distinguish between static and dynamic geometry.

Figure 2.1. Arbitrary reflection rays traced using our method.

Moreover, shading can share the same material system that is used in a deferred shading rasterizer. Consequently, our method allows for a unified rendering architecture that supports both rasterization and ray tracing. The more expensive ray tracing can easily be restricted to complex phenomena that require it, such as reflections and refractions on arbitrarily shaped scene geometry. Steps in rendering that do not require the tracing of incoherent rays with arbitrary origins can be dealt with using rasterization as usual.

2.1.1   The Classic Divide between Rasterization and Ray Tracing

Ray tracing is a robust and flexible approach to image synthesis that elegantly solves many problems that are hard to solve using rasterization. Since light typically travels in straight lines, most light transport problems can be decomposed into finding the next point along a straight line, starting at a point that emits or receives light. The ability to determine intersections with the scene geometry for arbitrary rays therefore allows for a trivial implementation of many light transport phenomena.

Recent advances in the performance and flexibility of graphics processing hardware have made ray tracing a viable option even for real-time rendering applications. Yet, integrating ray tracing into existing rasterization-based real-time rendering solutions poses significant challenges. Modern rasterization-based rendering engines (Figure 2.2) typically use the capabilities of modern GPUs to generate, transform, and amplify geometry on the fly. In contrast, efficient ray tracing techniques typically depend on pre-built spatial acceleration data structures that allow for fast random access to the scene geometry (Figure 2.3).

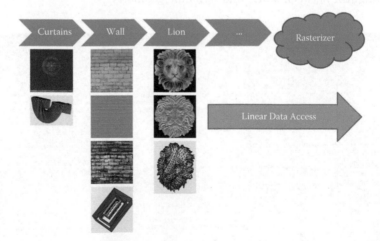

Figure 2.2. Linear batch-based rendering. A rasterizer sequentially iterates over all primitives and their resources to project them onto the image plane.

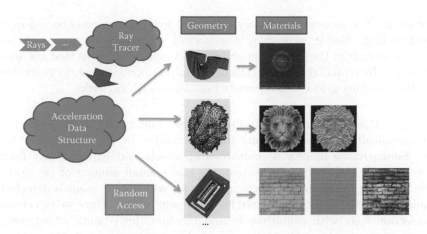

Figure 2.3. Ray-order ray tracing using a global acceleration data structure accesses the primitives and their resources in quasi-random order.

Our method bridges this divide: It allows for the precise tracing of arbitrary rays while only using linear render passes of triangle soups, just like rasterizing renderers do. Thus, it remains trivial to render dynamic geometry. Both geometry and shading can even be manipulated on the fly by shaders as usual. Hence, enhancing existing graphics engines with ray tracing becomes much easier.

2.2 Object-Order Ray Tracing Using the Ray Grid

To determine which pixels are overlapped by geometric primitives (typically triangles), rasterization projects them onto an image raster. Similarly, our algorithm determines which rays potentially intersect geometric primitives using a *ray grid*. Grid- and tree-based ray scheduling has been explored before in work on out-of-core ray tracing [Pharr et al. 97, Hanika et al. 10] and coherent image-order ray tracing [Guntury and Narayanan 12, Bikker 12].

The ray grid is a coarse voxel grid that encloses the scene. Each cell in the grid stores links to all rays that intersect it. Before any actual intersection testing is performed, the grid is filled by ray marching through the grid and storing a link to the traversing ray in each of the traversed grid cells.

In a subsequent intersection testing stage, all primitives in the scene are rendered into this ray grid. For every grid cell intersected by a primitive, we simply look up all the rays that traversed this particular grid cell during the prior ray grid construction stage and then test the primitive for intersection with only those rays. If an intersection is detected, the corresponding ray is updated with the nearest hit information.

Sparseness. The amount of memory consumed by a naively constructed ray grid would be high. Hence, we employ a conservative binary voxel approximation of the scene to restrict the generation of ray links to only those cells that are actually overlapped by geometry. Empty cells are simply skipped during ray marching, so that the resulting grid is only sparsely populated with ray links.

Occlusion. Rasterization typically uses a depth buffer with early depth testing to economically discard fragments that are hidden by geometry closer to the eye. Similarly, we employ a multi-pass approach that expands rays front to back: In each pass, rays are inserted only into a small number of ray grid cells each, and then tested for intersection. Rays for which a hit point is detected are terminated and no longer considered in subsequent passes. Thus, we can eliminate intersection tests with primitives behind the first (few) points of intersection. Moreover, this further reduces the size of the ray grid. In each pass, only very few links per ray (typically four) need to be stored, which makes our technique viable even in memory-constrained environments (about 14 MiB of ray links at 720p with full-resolution reflections).

2.3 Algorithm

Our algorithm consists of the following steps, illustrated in Figure 2.4:

1. *Scene voxelization:* We first build a coarse binary *voxel representation* of the scene by conservatively voxelizing all primitives. Affected voxels are flagged occupied.

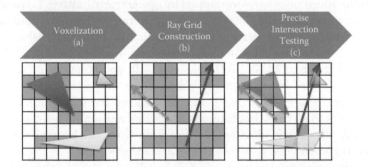

Figure 2.4. Algorithm steps: (a) Conservative binary voxel approximation of the scene (occupied voxels are marked in grey). (b) Links to traversing rays are inserted into the cells of a ray grid using ray marching (marked in the color of the rays). Unoccupied grid cells are skipped. (c) The scene is rendered into the ray grid. Each primitive is tested against the rays stored in all cells it overlaps.

2. *Ray grid construction:* Given a list of rays, we march along every ray to construct the *ray grid*. For every traversed grid cell, we first check if this cell is occupied by geometry by looking up the corresponding voxel in our voxel representation. A ray link is enqueued if the grid cell is occupied; empty cells are ignored.

3. *Intersection testing:* Using the ray grid, we perform precise intersection testing with the actual scene geometry. Again, we voxelize all scene geometry conservatively. For every voxel affected by a primitive, we look up all the rays that were enqueued in the corresponding ray grid cell during ray grid construction. We test the primitive for intersection only with these rays.

Note that in none of the steps are there any global dependencies on the primitives in the scene. Each batch of triangles can be rendered independently just as with rasterization.

2.3.1 Intersect Early: Multi-pass Scheme

Ray marching and intersection testing are repeated alternately to allow for front-to-back expansion of rays. Figure 2.5 illustrates this multi-pass scheme. Clearly, the right-hand ray (marked red) is obstructed by the second triangle it encounters. As we are only interested in the closest hit, intersection tests and ray links behind that triangle would be wasted.

Therefore, in the first pass, we start by expanding all rays into only the first few occupied cells of the ray grid each. Then, we immediately perform intersection testing using the resulting (incomplete) ray grid. A lot of rays will already intersect primitives in these first few occupied cells and are terminated. These rays can be ignored in subsequent passes, as we are progressing front to back. The remaining rays are expanded further in the next pass. Since the red ray in Figure 2.5 is terminated in the first pass, we only consider the yellow ray in the subsequent passes.

Bounded memory. We repeat intersection testing and ray grid construction alternately until all rays have either hit some geometry or have traversed the entire grid. The number of layers expanded in each pass can be increased as the number of active rays decreases. The fewer active rays that remain, the more ray links can be stored per ray without increasing the overall memory consumption of the ray grid. In the last pass, all remaining rays are fully expanded. Thus, we achieve both bounded time (typically three passes) and bounded memory (typically four links per ray).

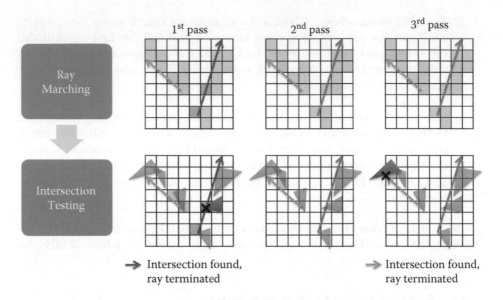

Figure 2.5. Three-pass intersection testing. Each pass builds a different partial ray grid (ray links are marked in the color of the rays). The red ray intersects a triangle in the first pass and is no longer considered afterward (grayed-out). The voxel representation of the scene is underlaid in grey to improve readability.

2.4   Implementation

In the following, we provide details on the implementation of our method. While some remarks may be specific to DirectX 11, everything that is required has its counterparts in other GPU programming APIs and thus can easily be implemented in different environments just as well.

2.4.1   Voxelization

We make use of voxelization both to build the coarse voxel representation of the scene and to identify overlapped ray grid cells during intersection testing. In both cases, voxelization has to be conservative, i.e., every voxel fully or partially overlapped by a triangle needs to be identified. Thus, we ensure that a *voxel fragment* (pixel shader thread) is generated for every voxel touched by a primitive. Otherwise, we could miss intersections with the rays of cells that are only partially overlapped.

Projection to 2D rasterization.   We have implemented conservative voxelization in the standard graphics pipeline, similar to [Crassin et al. 11]. We use the hardware rasterizer to rasterize primitives into a two-dimensional othographic projection of the voxel grid. Every pixel corresponds to one column of voxels that expands into the third dimension. As we only get one linearly interpolated depth value per pixel, the third dimension needs to be discretized manually.

To make effective use of parallel rasterization, we want to maximize the number of fragments per triangle. Since the rasterizer parallelizes over two dimensions only, this number depends on the orientation of the triangle and the chosen direction of projection. Fortunately, we can easily change the projection direction per triangle in the geometry shader. The triangle's normal tells us which of the three cardinal axes best fits the triangle's plane and thus will allocate the most fragments.

Conservative triangle modification. Rasterization has to be altered in a way that ensures that a pixel shader thread is executed for each intersected voxel column, even those where the fragment center itself is not covered by the projected triangle. Such modification of standard rasterization is appropriately called *conservative rasterization* and has been described in some detail in [Hasselgren et al. 05].

We use the vertex shader to transform positions into grid space. The geometry shader ensures conservative rasterization, essentially shifting all triangle edges outward by half a pixel diagonal. The resulting triangle will cover the *centers* of all pixels that were only partially covered by the original triangle (see Figure 2.6).

We do not construct a precise and minimal conservative hull for each voxelized triangle, as this would result in multiple triangles per input triangle. Instead, we only construct one over-conservative triangle and manually clip fragments outside the minimal conservative hull in the pixel shader. For this, an axis-aligned bounding box (AABB) of the minimal conservative triangle hull is computed alongside

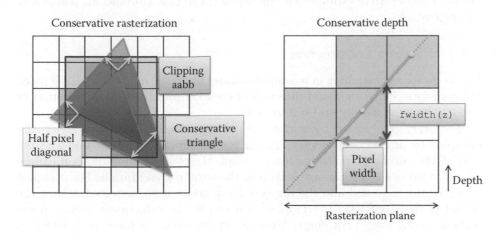

Figure 2.6. Over-conservative triangle modification with screen-space bounding box to clip unneeded fragments in the pixel shader (left). Depth bounds estimation using the derivatives of the linear triangle depth values (right).

the overestimating conservative bounding triangle in the geometry shader and is passed to the pixel shader as well. Note that modifying the triangle may change its depth derivatives, unless the resulting triangle is realigned with the plane of the original triangle.

To be able to reconstruct the proper grid space coordinates of a rasterized triangle, we also need to pass the chosen direction of projection to the pixel shader. This only requires two bits, so we reuse the storage of the four `float`s required to pass the clipping AABB to the pixel shader. As all fragment coordinates in screen space are nonnegative, we encode the three possible directions in the unused sign bits of two of the AABB components.

Conservative depth bounds estimation. During rasterization, a pixel shader is executed for each voxel column covered by the projected triangle. To conservatively find which voxels are intersected, we need to compute a depth range spanning from the closest to the farthest point on the projected triangle inside each voxel column. We can then iterate over all (fully or partially) overlapping voxels in the pixel shader.

To compute this depth range we use the pixel shader gradient instructions provided by HLSL. The intrinsic function `fwidth` returns the sum of the absolute partial derivatives for a given variable. The derivatives are evaluated at the location for which the pixel shader was executed, scaled to pixel steps. Since our projection is orthographic and thus our depth values are linear, this sum coincides with the maximum depth delta of the triangle inside a fully covered voxel column. As rasterization yields depth values interpolated at pixel centers (green in Figure 2.6), we add and subtract one half of the depth derivative to obtain a conservative estimate for the depth range that contains all potentially touched voxels.

2.4.2   Ray Grid Construction

We do classic ray marching in a compute shader to fill the ray grid with ray links. We transform both origin and direction of each ray into the grid and then work our way through the ray grid cell by cell.

For every cell crossed by a given ray, we first check if that cell is actually occupied by any scene geometry. In our implementation, the ray grid and the grid of the voxel representation always align, therefore this information can be retrieved using a single texture lookup in the voxel representation. For occupied cells, the ray is queued into the respective ray grid cell, to be tested against the actual triangle geometry overlapping that cell in the subsequent precise intersection testing stage. For empty cells, no further action is taken and marching simply continues to the next cell.

Note that filling the ray grid requires a conservative ray marching that does not skip cells in passing. Hence, it would not be sufficient to use a fixed step size,

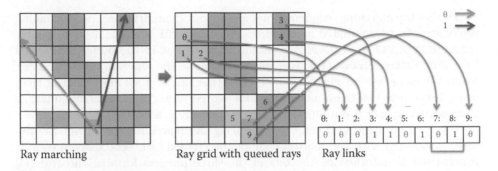

Ray marching   Ray grid with queued rays   Ray links

Figure 2.7. Ray grid construction by ray marching, adding ray links to traversed cells.

but rather the distance to the next cell has to be recalculated in every marching step. This is easily achieved by maintaining a vector of the three offsets to the next cell on every axis, always choosing the smallest of these as the next step offset. Thus, we ensure that no ray-cell intersection is missed.

Storage options. We can queue the rays into ray grid cells in several ways; the most straightforward solution is to construct linked lists. Every time a new ray is enqueued, a volumetric list head texture is atomically updated with the link to a new head element. HLSL's `InterlockedExchange()` also yields the previous head link, which can be stored in the new element to establish a singly linked list.

However, we have found that in our case a more compact and coherent layout is desirable: Once we enter the intersection testing stage, primitives will be intersected with all rays in each overlapped ray grid cell. For optimal memory access patterns, the links to rays enqueued in the same cell should lie next to each other in memory. As primitives typically come in connected batches of triangles, we can furthermore expect that a lot of them occupy similar sets of neighboring cells. To make good use of caches, the rays of neighboring cells should also lie next to each other in memory.

Storing the rays enqueued in the ray grid consecutively along a space-filling Z curve fulfills these requirements (see Figure 2.7). Such a Z layout can be directly obtained by applying a 3D parallel prefix sum scan to a grid of cell ray counts. However, for decently sized grids, this approach would have to work through too many empty cells to be efficient.

Construction using sorting. Recent research has shown that it is feasible to use sorting for grid construction [Kalojanov and Slusallek 09].[1] Using the optimized GPU sorting implementation provided by the B40C library [Merrill and Grimshaw 11], this turns out to be both simple and efficient.

---

[1]Also see [Kalojanov et al. 11] for multi-level grids.

During ray marching, enqueued rays are output in an arbitrary order, making use of structured unordered access views enhanced with a global atomic counter (`D3D11_BUFFER_UAV_FLAG_COUNTER` creation flag). A slot in the buffer is reserved by calling `RWStructuredBuffer.IncrementCounter()`. The function yields an index where the enqueued ray may be stored. Note that this is much more efficient than using `InterlockedAdd()` on a counter value stored in a global memory buffer, as `IncrementCounter()` is optimized for highly concurrent access.

For each occupied grid cell crossed during ray marching, we output the ray index annotated with the morton code of the crossed cell. The morton code is constructed by interleaving the bits of the three integers forming the grid cell index. Sorting data by morton code yields the desired coherent Z-order memory layout described in Section 2.4.2.

After sorting, each grid cell's range of ray links (ray indices with cell codes) is extracted in another compute shader pass. This pass simply compares the morton codes of successive ray links. Whenever these differ, the end of the previous cell's range and the beginning of the next cell's range have been found. Decoding the morton codes yields the grid indices of each cell, which allows for the begin and the end ray link indices to be stored in the respective cells of a volume texture.

Compacted ray inlining. During intersection testing all rays stored in a ray grid cell need to be fetched and tested against each overlapping primitive. Following the ray indices stored as ray links, this would repeatedly cause random indirect memory accesses. To further increase memory access coherency, we therefore *compact and inline* enqueued rays after sorting. Instead of following ray links again and again for each primitive, we follow the ray links in every cell once up front and store compacted clones of the referenced rays in an array parallel to the ray link array.

For compacted storage, we pack the ray origins into cell-relative 21-bit triples. The ray directions are packed into 16-bit tuples using the octahedron normal vector encoding described in [Meyer et al. 10]. Together, these require a total of three 32-bit integers per ray.

Persistent threads. During ray marching, we make use of the observations by Aila et al. regarding GPU work distribution [Aila and Laine 09]: just like in their BVH ray traversal algorithm, ray lengths in our ray marching stage may vary. On current GPUs, the work distribution unit always waits for an entire unit of work to be finished before distributing new units. For that reason, a single thread working on a particularly long ray may block all other processing units in the same processing group.

We therefore launch a fixed number of persistent GPU worker threads that continually fetch new rays whenever ray-marching along a previous ray has been finished. This alleviates work distribution delays. Due to the SIMD nature of GPUs, the problem cannot be completely avoided, but we can at least take advantage of more fine-grained scheduling mechanisms.

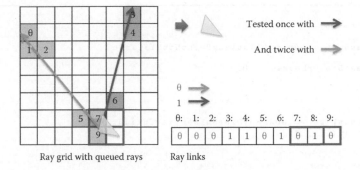

Figure 2.8. Intersection testing with one triangle using the ray grid. Ray grid cells are marked in the colors of the rays enqueued. Voxelization of the light-blue triangle generates the blue-framed voxel fragments. A lookup in the array of ray links returns both rays in one cell and only the yellow ray in another cell.

2.4.3 Precise Intersection Testing

After the ray grid has been constructed, we have direct access to all rays intersecting a particular cell just by indexing into a volume texture using the cell coordinates. In order to compute precise ray-triangle intersections with all triangles in the scene, we simply re-voxelize the scene into the ray grid as described in Section 2.4.1: For every fragment generated by conservative rasterization, we iterate over all cells in the corresponding voxel column that are touched by the respective triangle. For each cell, we check for intersection with all rays that have been enqueued there. Figure 2.8 shows an example.

Whenever a ray-triangle intersection is detected, the intersection information of the corresponding ray has to be updated. If the new intersection is closer than a previous intersection, the ray intersection information is locked, triangle attributes are interpolated, hit data is stored, and finally the closest distance is updated. If a thread finds the intersection information locked by another thread, it temporarily skips ray update and re-checks the ray state in a subsequent iteration (see Listing 2.1).

Ray hit information. Our ray hit information records consist of the distance, normal, and color(s) of each ray's current closest hit point. The records are stored in an array parallel to that storing the ray descriptions and may thus be indexed by ray links.

Apart from the distance attribute, these attributes may be replaced or extended freely to suit any rendering engine's need. We store typical G-buffer information to allow for simple deferred shading as described in Section 2.4.6.

To allow for atomic updating and synchronization with minimal memory overhead, we reuse the distance attribute to mark records locked. A negative sign indicates that the record is locked, while the absolute value of the attribute

```
1  // Distance of the new hit point,
2  // asuint() retains the order of positive floats
3  int newDist = asuint(floatingPointHitDistance);
4
5  int lastDistOrLocked = 0;
6  do
7  {
8    // The absolute value always corresponds to the current
9    // closest hit. Immediately discard farther hits
10   if (newDist >= abs(RayDistBuffer[rayIdx]))
11     break;
12
13   // Atomically compare new hit to the current closest hit
14   // and check if the ray is locked at the same time
15   InterlockedMin(
16       RayDistBuffer[rayIdx], newDist, lastDistOrLocked);
17
18   // Only entered if ray is unlocked (lastDistOrLocked >= 0)
19   // and new distance is less than old distance
20   if (newDist < lastDistOrLocked)
21   {
22     // Atomically lock ray via the distance buffer
23     // (= set distance to a negative value)
24     int lastDist = 0;
25     InterlockedCompareExchange(
26         RayDistBuffer[rayIdx], newDist, -newDist, lastDist);
27
28     // Check if exchg successful and new distance still closest
29     if (lastDist == newDist)
30     {
31       <Update hit data>
32       // Unlock the ray by updating the distance buffer
33       InterlockedExchange(RayDistBuffer[rayIdx], newDist);
34     }
35   }
36 // Re-iterate until the ray has been unlocked
37 } while(lastDistOrLocked < 0);
```

Listing 2.1. HLSL code for the ray update synchronization.

always corresponds to the current distance to the closest hit point. This enables us to both atomically compare the distance of a new hit point against the current closest distance and check the respective record's lock state at the same time.

Ray update synchronization. We make use of the atomic operations on unordered access views that have become available in shader model 5.0 to implement a spin lock mechanism that allows for the atomic updating of more than just one unsigned integer quantity. Listing 2.1 shows the HLSL code skeleton.

We first check whether the distance of the new hit point is actually smaller than the current absolute value of the record's distance attribute (line 8). Hits with greater distances are skipped right away. We then use InterlockedMin() in its *signed* integer version to atomically update the distance attribute with the *positive* distance of the new hit point (line 13). If the record is currently locked, the update fails, as negative values are always smaller than the given positive distance. In this case, updating is temporarily skipped (line 18) and will be retried in a subsequent loop iteration (`while` checks the lock state in line 37).

Note that just waiting for the record to become unlocked by looping until all other concurrent updates have been finished would not work. The SIMT execution model of current GPUs implies that threads skipping certain instructions have to wait on other threads that execute these instructions until all threads are back in sync and can continue to operate in *lockstep*. Therefore, it is important to implement the spin lock by skipping instructions in the waiting threads. Otherwise, waiting threads would actively hold back the unlocked threads from performing the work they are waiting on.

In case of a successful atomic distance update, the entire record is locked using `InterlockedCompareExchange()` (line 22). The distance of the hit point is passed for comparison. If no closer point of intersection has been found in the meantime, the negated distance will be written to the record, acquiring the lock on the hit data. If the exchange fails, the hit point is discarded. In this case, a closer point has already been found by some other thread. If the exchange succeeds, all the other hit information is updated. Afterwards, the record is unlocked using `InterlockedExchange()` to reset the distance attribute to the positive distance value (line 32).

Input register pressure and incoherence. Our first implementation simply passed entire triangles from geometry to pixel shader using many `nointerpolation` registers. This proved to be problematic in two ways. Firstly, as we exceeded a certain number of pixel shader input registers, performance greatly deteriorated. High register pressure limits the number of concurrent pixel shader threads that can be started. Secondly, the number of rays enqueued per voxel varies. It turned out to be too incoherent for SIMD parallelism to work on a per-voxel level: some threads were looping through large numbers of rays while others were mostly idling.

Load balancing using geometry shaders. To keep threads from idling, we implemented a two-pass load balancing scheme that makes use of geometry shaders to achieve full parallelism on a per-ray and per-triangle level. The scheme is illustrated in Figure 2.9.

In the first pass, the current batch of triangles is voxelized. During this pass, both the transformed triangles and pairs of ray grid cell and triangle indices for all touched voxels are streamed out into auxiliary buffers. In the second pass, all cell-triangle pairs are read in parallel using null-input vertex and geometry shaders. The primitive ID (retrieved using the `SV_PrimitiveID` shader system value input semantic) indicates which pair to process.

DirectX 11 provides `DrawInstancedIndirect()` to issue draw calls where the number of vertices and instances resides in a GPU buffer. This allows us to trigger

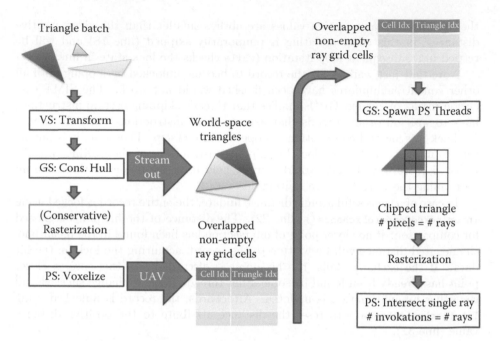

Figure 2.9. Intersection testing load balancing using the geometry shader.

the right number of vertex shader executions and thus process the right number of cell-triangle pairs without having to do a CPU read back. In the geometry shader of the second pass, a rectangle is generated for each pair. This *dispatch rectangle* is scaled to make the number of covered viewport pixels equal to the number of rays queued in the pair's ray grid cell. Consequently, for each *ray*, a fragment is generated and a pixel shader thread is spawned. We have to make sure that the viewport we rasterize the *dispatch rectancles* into is large enough to contain pixels for every ray in the fullest ray grid cell.

In each of the pixel shader threads, we now only have to perform intersection testing with one single ray against one single triangle. This way, we achieve fully concurrent intersection testing, independent of the number of rays queued per ray grid cell.

Unfortunately, we have to provide auxiliary buffers, one (created with `D3D11_BIND_STREAM_OUTPUT`) to store the streamed out pre-transformed geometry and another one (bound via counter-enhanced UAV) to store the intermediate cell-triangle pairs for one batch of triangles. However, these buffers only need to provide storage for the largest batch of triangles in the scene. The amount of storage can be strictly limited by enforcing a maximum triangle batch size, e.g., by partitioning larger batches using multiple draw calls.

2.4.4 Multi-pass Tracing

To properly implement the multi-pass intersection testing scheme described in Section 2.3, we need to store some additional information and take some additional precautions. First of all, we need to remember the ray grid cell in which the expansion of each ray stopped in the previous pass of ray grid construction. As we only ever continue ray expansion for rays that have not yet hit any geometry in the previous passes, we can simply reuse some of the ray hit information storage for that purpose. In each ray-marching pass we store the ray offset of the last grid cell each ray was expanded to and continue expansion with that offset in the next pass.

Active ray filtering. To keep track of which rays are still active and which rays may be terminated, we check the distance attribute of their hit information record. We use two special values to distinguish between rays that have already left the scene bounds without any intersections and rays for which no intersection has been found yet, but which are still in bounds. Recall that for atomic ray update to work, our distance attribute is a signed integer. Therefore, we may use `MissedRayDepth = 0x7ffffffe` and `MaxRayDepth = 0x7fffffff`, respectively. Before we continue expanding rays in subsequent ray grid construction passes, we filter out all terminated rays and compact the indices of remaining active rays into one consecutive array. This array is then processed by the ray marching shader.

Hit point ordering. Finally, it is important to enforce strict front-to-back intersection testing. Just like in classic ray tracing where an acceleration data structure is traversed in an ordered fashion, we may find intersection points that lie beyond the cells that the ray has been expanded to in the current pass. In other words, the intersection is found on a section of the ray that would only be tested in a later pass.

This is especially likely for large triangles that span many ray grid cells, when rays slowly converge toward the triangle plane and are inserted into several cells that hold the triangle but not the actual point of intersection. If we accepted these premature hit points, we would be prone to missing other in-between geometry that lies only in cells beyond those the ray has thus far been expanded to. We can remedy this problem by strictly accepting only those hit points that lie inside the cell that caused their detection. Rejected points will then be re-detected in the proper cells, possibly during a later pass. Thus, rays will not be terminated prematurely.

2.4.5 Ray Generation

In our implementation, we demonstrate the tracing of incoherent secondary rays with reflection rays. We simply generate these rays from the G-buffer created by

our traditional deferred shading pipeline. We reconstruct reflecting surface points
using the depth and the normal stored in the G-buffer and reflect the camera rays
to spawn reflection rays.

2.4.6 Shading

We use standard deferred shading to process the closest hit point information
collected for each ray. The result is composited with the shading of the point
that spawned the ray, blended using Schlick's fresnel approximation.

We implemented sunlight for demonstration purposes. For other, spatially
bounded light sources, it would make sense to limit the influence of these lights
to a certain subset of grid cells. Shading can then be restricted to few lights per
cell just like in screen-space deferred shading approaches.

2.5 Results

We have implemented the described algorithm with DirectX 11 Graphics and
Compute, and we use the radix sorting implementation provided by the B40C
library implemented in CUDA 5 [Merrill and Grimshaw 11]. The algorithm is
implemented in a typical rasterization-based deferred shading engine, using rasterization for primary and shadow rays and using the described method for tracing
reflection rays. All tests were run on a NVIDIA GeForce GTX 560 GPU and an
Intel Core i7-2600K CPU. Images were rendered at a resolution of 1280 × 720.
The ray and voxel grids had a resolution of 128 × 128 × 128 each.

We tested our method in the Crytek Sponza scene (270k tris), the Sibenik
Cathedral scene (75k tris), and a simple test scene composed of a bumpy reflective
cube and some low-poly objects (2k tris). The Sponza scene generates highly
incoherent reflection rays due to the heavy use of normal maps on the scene's
brickwork. Reflection rays were spawned everywhere except on the curtains and
the sky.

To increase the data locality of spacially adjacent geometry, we have used
the mesh optimization post-processing step provided by the Open Asset Import
Library [Gessler et al. 09]. All quantities were measured for a selection of view
points that vary in complexity by both ray coherence and surrounding geometry.

Table 2.1 shows the average time spent per frame in each of the major stages.
With less than 2 ms, conservative voxelization is rather cheap. Naive ray marching and ray sorting are pretty much independent of the scene complexity, constantly taking about 10 ms each. Intersection testing, on the other hand, is highly
sensitive to the number of triangles, as all triangles are processed linearly.

Table 2.2 details the time spent in the intersection testing stage. Together,
stream out (GS) and emission of cell-triangle pairs (PS) in pass 1 make for a
cross-shader communication overhead of about 10 ms. This can likely be reduced
in future graphics pipelines (see Section 2.6). Intersection testing itself (pass 2)
is compute-bound. Due to our carefully chosen memory layout, this is to be

	Frame	Voxelize	Ray March	Ray Sort	Testing
Sponza	92.6 ms	2.0 ms	9.9 ms	12.7 ms	54.2 ms
Sibenik	65.9 ms	0.6 ms	12.7 ms	15.4 ms	24.5 ms
Simple	31.3 ms	0.1 ms	9.2 ms	7.7 ms	5.4 ms

Table 2.1. Time spent in each of the stages per frame. Total frame time includes G-buffer generation, rendering of shadow maps, and deferred shading.

	VS	GS	PS	Total
Pass 1 (trafo + cell-tri pairs)	0.9 ms	2.3 ms	7.8 ms	11.0 ms
Pass 2 (ray-tri intersections)	1.3 ms	3.0 ms	38.2 ms	42.4 ms

Table 2.2. Time spent in each of the shaders in the two-pass load-balancing scheme illustrated in Figure 2.9 (measured in the Sponza scene and summed for all batches of triangles).

expected. Both geometry and rays are processed linearly and are therefore always accessed in a perfectly coherent fashion.

Table 2.3 shows some additional figures for the number of ray links and intersection tests. As can be seen, storage requirements for the ray grid typically stay below four links per ray. Across all passes, rays are enqueued to four to eight occupied cells on average, depending on the scene complexity. As expected, the number of hit tests per ray greatly depends on the number of triangles in the scene.

Table 2.4 shows how rays and triangles are distributed across all ray grid cells that are occupied by geometry and traversed by at least one ray. These numbers vary greatly for different scenes. They depend on the way the geometry is laid out, what parts are occluded, and how evenly the scene is tessellated.

	Tests	Hits	Hit Ratio	Max Links	Total Links
Sponza	121.1	1.5	1.72%	3.8	7.5
Sibenik	27.9	1.1	4.1%	3.7	6.4
Simple	8.0	0.4	4.65%	2.5	3.9

Table 2.3. Per ray, the hit tests, hits, maximum number of ray links per pass, and total number of ray links (not stored) across all passes.

		# rays/cell				
	# cells	μ	σ	$> 10\mu$	max	# tris/cell
Sponza	150K	32.9	261.6	1.66%	11670	15.4
Sibenik	138K	45.5	282.1	1.37%	9180	4.4
Simple	43K	58.8	461.3	1.95%	4131	2.1

Table 2.4. Number of ray grid cells active during intersection testing, with distribution of rays and triangles per cell; μ is the expected value and σ the standard deviation.

The high average number of hit tests per ray as well as the high average number of triangles per grid cell in the Sponza scene suggests that a more adaptive ray grid could be beneficial for more complex scenes with uneven tessellation. The great number of small triangles on the Sponza curtains fill the rather coarse fixed-size grid cells with loads of unstructured geometry, resulting in many hit tests for the rays passing nearby.

2.6   Conclusion

In this chapter, we have proposed a GPU-based object-order ray-tracing algorithm that allows for the tracing of incoherent secondary rays at interactive speeds. We have shown that this is possible in the context of a typical rasterization-based deferred shading rendering engine, without changing the architecture from linear batch processing to global pooling of randomly accessible scene data.

The presented algorithm is another step toward mingling rasterization and ray-tracing approaches. In future work, this mingling could be taken even further by re-introducing fixed-size shallow geometric hierarchies inside triangle batches. This way, the coherency that is present in most chunks of triangles could be exploited further and the linear cost of crowded ray grid cells with many triangles could be improved upon.

Future work could also apply multi-level grids as described by [Kalojanov et al. 11] to adapt grid resolution to uneven tessellation. This would additionally help in skipping potentially larger empty spaces in vast scenes. Furthermore, transferring occlusion culling as it is commonly used in rasterization-based rendering to secondary ray tracing could be an interesting topic.

The presented algorithm makes extensive use of the flexibility that is offered by the DirectX 11 graphics pipeline. With the tessellation and geometry shader stages, the graphics pipeline currently offers two junction points for load balancing, redistributing work across parallel GPU threads on the fly. However, passing data between these stages is still difficult. Currently, there does not appear to be an efficient way of passing entire triangles down to the pixel shader stage without resorting to a separate geometry stream out pass. DirectX 11.1 introduced unordered resource writes in all shader stages, which slightly improves the situation. While the feature is not widely available on PCs yet, it is likely to spread with the introduction of the next console generation. Still, having to resort to global memory writes seems like a suboptimal solution considering the availability of fast on-chip shared memory on today's graphics hardware.

Bibliography

[Aila and Laine 09] Timo Aila and Samuli Laine. "Understanding the Efficiency of Ray Traversal on GPUs." In *Proceedings of the Conference on High Performance Graphics 2009*, pp. 145–149. New York: ACM, 2009.

[Bikker 12] J. Bikker. "Improving Data Locality for Efficient In-Core Path Tracing." *Computer Graphics Forum* 31:6 (2012), 1936–1947.

[Crassin et al. 11] Cyril Crassin, Fabrice Neyret, Miguel Sainz, Simon Green, and Elmar Eisemann. "Interactive Indirect Illumination Using Voxel-Based Cone Tracing: An Insight." In *ACM SIGGRAPH 2011 Talks*, p. Article no. 20, 2011.

[Gessler et al. 09] Alexander Gessler, Thomas Schulze, Kim Kulling, and David Nadlinger. "Open Asset Import Library." http://assimp.sourceforge.net, 2009.

[Guntury and Narayanan 12] Sashidhar Guntury and P.J. Narayanan. "Raytracing Dynamic Scenes on the GPU Using Grids." *IEEE Transactions on Visualization and Computer Graphics* 18 (2012), 5–16.

[Hanika et al. 10] Johannes Hanika, Alexander Keller, and Hendrik P. A. Lensch. "Two-Level Ray Tracing with Reordering for Highly Complex Scenes." In *Proceedings of Graphics Interface 2010*, pp. 145–152. Toronto: Canadian Information Processing Society, 2010.

[Hasselgren et al. 05] Jon Hasselgren, Tomas Akenine-Möller, and Lennart Ohlsson. "Conservative Rasterization." In *GPU Gems 2: Programming Techniques for High-Performance Graphics and General-Purpose Computation*, edited by Matt Pharr and Randima Fernando, Chapter 42. Upper Saddle River, NJ: Addison-Wesley Professional, 2005.

[Kalojanov and Slusallek 09] Javor Kalojanov and Philipp Slusallek. "A Parallel Algorithm for Construction of Uniform Grids." In *Proceedings of the Conference on High Performance Graphics 2009*, pp. 23–28. New York: ACM, 2009.

[Kalojanov et al. 11] Javor Kalojanov, Markus Billeter, and Philipp Slusallek. "Two-Level Grids for Ray Tracing on GPUs." In *EG 2011 Full Papers*, pp. 307–314. Aire-le-Ville, Switzerland: Eurographics Association, 2011.

[Merrill and Grimshaw 11] Duane Merrill and Andrew Grimshaw. "High Performance and Scalable Radix Sorting: A Case Study of Implementing Dynamic Parallelism for GPU Computing." *Parallel Processing Letters* 21:2 (2011), 245–272.

[Meyer et al. 10] Quirin Meyer, Jochen Sußmuth, Gerd Sußner, Marc Stamminger, and Günther Greiner. "On Floating-Point Normal Vectors." *Computer Graphics Forum* 29:4 (2010), 1405–1409.

[Pharr et al. 97] Matt Pharr, Craig Kolb, Reid Gershbein, and Pat Hanrahan. "Rendering Complex Scenes with Memory-Coherent Ray Tracing."

In *Proceedings of the 24th Annual Conference on Computer Graphics and Interactive Techniques, SIGGRAPH '97*, pp. 101–108. New York: ACM Press/Addison-Wesley Publishing Co., 1997.

Quadtrees on the GPU
Jonathan Dupuy, Jean-Claude Iehl, and Pierre Poulin

3.1   Introduction

Finding an appropriate mathematical representation for objects is a fundamental problem in computer graphics. Because they benefit from hardware acceleration, polygon meshes provide an appealing solution and are widely adopted by both interactive and high-quality renderers. But in order to maintain optimal rendering performance, special care must be taken to guarantee that each polygon projects into more than a few pixels. Below this limit, the Z-buffer starts aliasing, and the rasterizer's efficiency decreases drastically [AMD 10]. In the movie industry, this limitation is alleviated by using very high sampling rates, at the expense of dissuasive computation times. For applications that target interactivity, however, such as video games or simulators, such overhead is unaffordable.

Another solution is to adapt the mesh to produce optimal on-screen polygons. If it can be simplified and/or enriched on the fly, it is said to be a scalable representation. Quadtrees provide such a scheme for grids and have been used extensively since the early days of rendering, especially for terrain synthesis. Despite their wide adoption, though, the first full GPU implementation was only introduced last year [Mistal 13]. This is due to two main reasons. First, quadtrees are usually implemented recursively, which makes them hard to handle in parallel by their very nature (see the implementation of Strugar [Strugar 09], for instance). Second, they require a T-junction removal system, which may result in an increase of draw calls [Andersson 07], adding non-negligible overhead to the CPU. As an alternative to quadtrees, instanced subdivision patches have been investigated [Cantlay 11, Fernandes and Oliveira 12]. Although such solutions can run entirely on the GPU, their scalability is currently too limited by the hardware.

In this chapter, we present a new implementation suitable for the GPU, which completely relieves the CPU without sacrificing scalability. In order to update the quadtree in parallel, we use the linear quadtree representation, which is presented

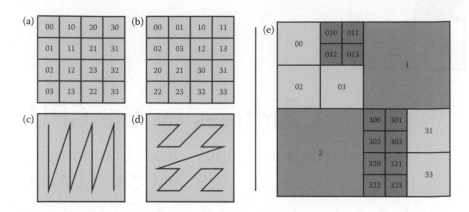

Figure 3.1. (a) Column major ordering versus (b) Morton ordering and (c,d) the curves they form. The curve formed by Morton ordering in (d) is often denoted as a Z-order curve. (e) Bit codes of a linear quadtree, built from the ordering of (b). The subdivision levels for the blue, green, and red nodes are respectively 1, 2, and 3.

in the next section. At render time, a square subdivision patch is instanced with a unique location and scale for each node. By employing a distance-based LOD criterion, we will show that T-junctions can be removed completely using a simple tessellation shader.

3.2   Linear Quadtrees

Linear quadtrees were introduced by Gargantini as a nonrecursive alternative to regular quadtrees [Gargantini 82]. In this data structure, each node is represented by its subdivision level and a unique bit code, and only the leaves are stored in memory. The code is a concatenation of 2-bit words, each identifying the quadrant in which the node is located relative to its parent. If these words are chosen so as to form a Z-order curve, then their concatenation forms a Morton code. In Figure 3.1, for instance, the codes 0, 1, 2, and 3 are mapped to the upper left (UL), upper right (UR), lower left (LL), and lower right (LR) quadrants, respectively. This last property allows direct translation to row/column major numbering (Figure 3.1(e)) by bit de-interleaving the code.

3.2.1   Representation

Similarly to Shaffer [Shaffer 90], we use a single integer to represent each node. The rightmost bits are reserved for the subdivision level, and the adjacent bits are left for the bit code. Below is the bit representation of the 32-bit word encoding the red node whose code is 321 in Figure 3.1. Bits irrelevant to the code are denoted by the "_" character.

```
// de-interleave a 32-bit word using the Shift-Or algorithm
uint lt_undilate_2(in uint x) {
    x = (x | (x >> 1u)) & 0x33333333;
    x = (x | (x >> 2u)) & 0x0F0F0F0F;
    x = (x | (x >> 4u)) & 0x00FF00FF;
    x = (x | (x >> 8u)) & 0x0000FFFF;
    return (x & 0x0000FFFF);
}

// retrieve column major position and level from a 32-bit word
void lt_decode_2_15(in uint key, out uint level, out uvec2 p) {
    level = key & 0xF;
    p.x = lt_undilate_2((key >> 4u) & 0x05555555);
    p.y = lt_undilate_2((key >> 5u) & 0x05555555);
}
```

Listing 3.1. GLSL node decoding routines. There are many ways to de-interleave a word. For a thorough overview of existing methods, we refer to [Raman and Wise 08].

```
msb                                          lsb
---- ---- ---- ---- ---- --11 1001 0011
```

The first four bits store the level ($0011_b = 3$ in this example), leaving the remaining 28 bits for the code. Using this configuration, a 32-bit word can store up to a $28/2 + 1 = 15$-level quadtree, including the root node. In Listing 3.1, we provide the procedures to retrieve the column major numbering from this representation. Naturally, more levels require longer words. Because longer integers are currently unavailable on many GPUs, we emulate them using integer vectors, where each component represents a 32-bit wide portion of the entire code. For more details, please see our implementation, where we provide a 30-level quadtree using the GLSL uvec2 datatype.

3.2.2 Updating the Structure

When relying on quadtrees to generate progressive meshes, efficient updates are critical. Fortunately, node splitting and merging can be accomplished in a very straightforward manner with linear trees. The following bit representations match the parent of the node given in the previous example with its four children:

```
          msb                                  lsb
parent:   ---- ---- ---- ---- ---- ---- 1110 0010
node:     ---- ---- ---- ---- ---- --11 1001 0011
UL:       ---- ---- ---- ---- ---- 1110 0100 0100
UR:       ---- ---- ---- ---- ---- 1110 0101 0100
LL:       ---- ---- ---- ---- ---- 1110 0110 0100
LR:       ---- ---- ---- ---- ---- 1110 0111 0100
```

```
// generate children nodes from a quadtree encoded
// in a 32-bit word
void lt_children_2_15(in uint key, out uint children[4]) {
  key = (++key & 0xF) | ((key & ~0xF) << 2u);
  children[0] = key;
  children[1] = key | 0x10;
  children[2] = key | 0x20;
  children[3] = key | 0x30;
}

// generate parent node from a quadtree encoded
// in a 32-bit word
uint lt_parent_2_15(in uint key) {
  return ((--key & 0xF) | ((key >> 2u) & 0x3FFFFFF0));
}
```

Listing 3.2. Splitting and merging procedures in GLSL.

Note that compared to the node representation, the levels differ by 1 and the bit codes are either 2-bit expansions or contractions. The GLSL code to generate these representations is shown in Listing 3.2. It simply consists of an arithmetic addition, a bitshift, and logical operations and is thus very cheap.

3.2.3   GPU Implementation

Managing a linear quadtree on the GPU requires two buffers and a geometry shader. During initialization, we store the base hierarchy (we start with the root node only) in one of the buffers. Whenever the nodes must be updated, the buffer is iterated over by the geometry shader, set to write into the second buffer. If a node needs to be split, it emits four new words, and the original code is deleted. Conversely, when four nodes must merge, they are replaced by their parent's code. In order to avoid generating four copies of the same node in memory, we only emit the code once from the UL child, identified using the test provided in Listing 3.3. For the nodes that do not require any intervention, their code is simply emitted, unchanged.

```
// check if node is the upper left child
// in a 32-bit word
bool lt_is_upper_left_2_15(in uint key) {
  return ((key & 0x30) == 0x00);
}
```

Listing 3.3. Determining if the node represents the UL child of its parent representation. Only the first 2-bit word of the Morton code has to be tested.

It is clear that this approach maps very well to the GPU. Note, however, that an iteration only permits a single split or merge operation per node. Thus when more are needed, multiple buffer iterations should be performed. At each new iteration, we swap the first and second buffer so that the newest hierarchy is processed by the geometry shader. This strategy is also known as double, or ping-pong, buffering. In our implementation, a single buffer iteration is performed at the beginning of each frame.

3.3 Scalable Grids on the GPU

So far, we have only discussed a parallel implementation of a quadtree. In this section, we present a complete OpenGL pipeline to extract a scalable grid from this representation, which in turn can be used to render terrains, as well as parametric surfaces.

3.3.1 LOD Function

Similarly to [Strugar 09], we essentially exploit the quadtree to build the final grid by drawing multiple copies of a static grid mesh. Each copy is associated with a node, so that it can be translated and scaled to the correct location. Listing 3.4 shows how the transformations are extracted from the codes and applied to each vertex of the instanced grid in a vertex shader.

```glsl
layout(location = 0) in vec2 i_mesh; // instanced vertices
layout(location = 1) in uint i_node; // per instance data

// retrieve normalized coordinates and size of the cell
void lt_cell_2_15(in uint key, out vec2 p, out float size) {
  uvec2 pos;
  uint level;

  lt_decode_2_15(key, level, pos);
  size = 1.0 / float(1u << level); // in [0,1]
  p = pos * size; // in [0,1)
}

void main() {
  vec2 translation;
  float scale;

  // pass on vertex position and scale
  lt_cell_2_15(i_node, translation, scale);
  vec2 p = i_mesh * scale + translation;
  gl_Position = vec4(p, scale, 1.0);
}
```

Listing 3.4. GLSL vertex shader for rendering a scalable grid.

In order to guarantee that the transformed vertices produce rasterizer-friendly polygons, a distance-based criterion can be used. Indeed, under perspective projection, the image plane size s at distance z from the camera can be determined analytically with the relation

$$s(z) = 2z \tan\left(\frac{\alpha}{2}\right),$$

where $\alpha \in (0, \pi]$ is the horizontal field of view. Thus if polygons scale proportionally to s, they are guaranteed to be of approximately constant size in screen space. Based on this observation, we derived the following routines to determine whether a node should be split or merged:

```
float  z1 = distance(eye, node_center);
float  z2 = distance(eye, parent_center);

if( k * node_size > s(z1) ) split();
else if( k * parent_size < s(z2) ) merge();
else keep();
```

Here, `k` is an arbitrary positive constant that controls the average number of on-screen cells. We found that using $k = 8$ produces good results, resulting in roughly 36 (6×6) cells in the image plane. Therefore, when the instanced grid has $n \times n$ polygons, the average on-screen polygon density is $36n^2$.

3.3.2   T-Junction Removal

The core of our meshing scheme closely resembles that of [Strugar 09]; both methods rely on mesh instancing and a distance-based LOD function to build a scalable grid. As such, Strugar's vertex morphing scheme can be used to avoid T-junctions. We suggest next an alternative solution, which relies on tessellation shaders.

Before transforming the vertices of the instanced grid, we invoke a tessellation control shader and evaluate the LOD function at each edge of its polygons. We then divide their length by the computed value and multiply the result by $\sqrt{2}$. This operation safely refines the grid polygons nearing neighbor cells of smaller resolution; its output is illustrated in Figure 3.2. Our GLSL tessellation control shader code is shown in Listing 3.5.

3.3.3   OpenGL Pipeline

Our OpenGL implementation consists of three passes. The first pass updates the quadtree, using the algorithm described in Section 3.2. After the tree has been updated, a culling kernel iterates over the nodes, testing their intersection with the view frustum. Note that we can reuse the buffer holding the nodes before

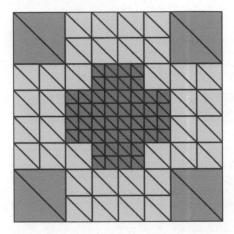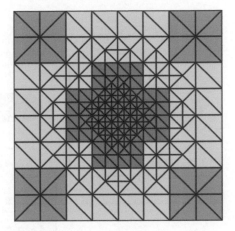

Figure 3.2. Multiresolution mesh before (left) and after (right) tessellation. T-junctions have been completely removed.

the first pass to store the results. Since we only have access to the leaf nodes, no hierarchical optimizations can be performed, so each node is tested independently. This scheme still performs very well nonetheless, as it is very adequate for the parallel architecture of the GPU. Finally, the third pass renders the scalable grid to the back buffer, using the algorithms described earlier in this section. The full pipeline is diagrammed in Figure 3.3.

```
layout(vertices = 4) out; // quad patches
uniform vec3 u_eye_pos; // eye position
void main() {
  // get data from vertex stage
  vec4 e1 = gl_in[gl_InvocationID].gl_Position;
  vec4 e2 = gl_in[(gl_InvocationID+1)%4].gl_Position;

  // compute edge center and LOD function
  vec3 ec = vec3(0.5 * e1.xy + 0.5 * e2.xy, 0);
  float s = 2.0 * distance(u_eye_pos, ec) * u_tan_fov;

  // compute tessellation factors (1 or 2)
  const float k = 8.0;
  float factor = e1.z * k * sqrt(2.0) / s;
  gl_TessLevelOuter[gl_InvocationID] = factor;
  gl_TessLevelInner[gl_InvocationID%2] = factor;

  // send data to subsequent stages
  gl_out[gl_InvocationID].gl_Position =
    gl_in[gl_InvocationID].gl_Position;
}
```

Listing 3.5. GLSL tessellation control shader for rendering a scalable grid.

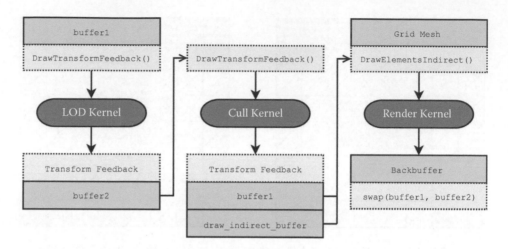

Figure 3.3. OpenGL pipeline of our method.

3.3.4   Results

To demonstrate the effectiveness of our method, we wrote a renderer for terrains and another one for parametric surfaces. Some results can be seen in Figures 3.4 and 3.5. In Table 3.1, we give the CPU and GPU timings of a zoom-in/zoom-out sequence using the terrain renderer at 720p. The camera's orientation was fixed, looking downward, so that the terrain would occupy the whole frame buffer, thus maintaining constant rasterization activity. The testing platform is an Intel Core i7-2600K, running at 3.40 GHz, and a Radeon 7950 GPU. Note that the CPU activity only consists of OpenGL uniform variables and driver management. On current implementations, such tasks run asynchronously to the GPU.

As demonstrated by the reported numbers, the performance of our implementation is both fast and stable. Naturally, the average GPU rendering time depends on how the terrain is shaded. In our experiment, we use solid wireframe shading [Gateau 07] which, despite requiring a geometry shader, is fairly cheap.

Kernel	CPU (ms)	GPU (ms)	CPU stdev	GPU stdev
LOD	0.096	0.067	0.039	0.026
Cull	0.068	0.077	0.035	0.032
Render	0.064	1.271	0.063	0.080

Table 3.1. CPU and GPU timings and their respective standard deviation over a zoom-in sequence of 1000 frames.

Figure 3.4. Crack-free, multiresolution terrain rendered from a quadtree implemented entirely on the GPU. The alternating colors show the different levels of the quadtree.

3.4 Discussion

This section provides a series of answered questions, which should give better insights on the properties and possible extensions of our implementation.

How much memory should be allocated for the buffers containing the nodes? This depends on the α and `k` values, which control how fast distant nodes should be merged. The buffers should be able to store at least $3 \times$ `max_level` $+1$ nodes and do not need to exceed a capacity of $4^{\texttt{max\_level}}$ nodes. The lower bound corresponds to a perfectly restricted quadtree, where each neighboring cell differs by one level of subdivision at most. The higher bound gives the number of cells at the finest subdivision level.

Is the quadtree prone to floating-point precision issues? There are no issues regarding the tree structure itself, as each node is represented with bit sequences only. However, problems may occur when extracting the location and scale factors applied to the instanced grid during the rendering pass, in Listing 3.4. The 15-level quadtree does not have this issue, but higher levels will, eventually. A simple solution to delay the problem on OpenGL4+ hardware is to use double precision, which should provide sufficient comfort for most applications.

Figure 3.5. Crack-free, multiresolution parametric surfaces produced on the GPU with our renderer.

Could fractional tessellation be used to produce continuous subdivisions? If the T-junctions are removed with the CDLOD morphing function [Strugar 09], any mode can be used. Our proposed alternative approach does not have restrictions regarding the inner tessellation levels, but the outer levels must be set to exact powers of two. Therefore, fractional odd tessellation will not work. The even mode can be used, though.

Are there any significant reasons to use tessellation rather than the CDLOD morphing function for T-junctions? The only advantage of tessellation is flexibility, since arbitrary factors can be used. For some parametric surfaces, tessellation turned out to be essential because the quadtree we computed was not necessarily restricted. The phenomenon is visible in Figure 3.5, on the blue portions of the trefoil knot. If we had used the CDLOD method, a crack would have occurred. For terrains, the distance-based criterion ensures that the nodes are restricted, so both solutions are valid.

There are two ways to increase polygon density: either use the GPU tessellator, or refine the instanced grid. Which approach is best? This will naturally depend on the platform. Our renderers provide tools to modify both the grid and the GPU tessellation values, so that their impact can be thoroughly measured. On the Radeon 7950, we observed that tessellation levels could be increased up to a factor of 8 without performance penalties, as long as the average on-screen polygon size remained reasonable.

3.5 Conclusion

We have presented a novel implementation for quadtrees running completely on the GPU. It takes advantage of linear trees to alleviate the recursive nature of common tree implementations, offering a simple and efficient data structure for parallel processors. While this work focuses on quadtrees, this representation can also be used for higher dimensional trees, such as octrees. Using the same distance-based criterion, the *Transvoxel* algorithm [Lengyel 10] could be employed to produce a crack-free volume extractor, running entirely on the GPU. We expect such an implementation to be extremely fast as well.

Acknowledgements

This work was partly funded in Canada by GRAND and in France by ANR. Jonathan Dupuy acknowledges additional financial support from an Explo'ra Doc grant from "région Rhône-Alpes," France.

Bibliography

[AMD 10] AMD. "Tessellation for All." http://community.amd.com/ community/amd-blogs/game/blog/2010/11/29/tessellation-for-all, 2010.

[Andersson 07] Johan Andersson. "Terrain Rendering in Frostbite Using Procedural Shader Splatting." In *ACM SIGGRAPH 2007 Courses*, pp. 38–58. New York: ACM, 2007.

[Cantlay 11] Iain Cantlay. "DirectX 11 Terrain Tessellation." White paper, http://developer.nvidia.com/sites/default/files/akamai/gamedev/files/ sdk/11/TerrainTessellation_WhitePaper.pdf, 2011.

[Fernandes and Oliveira 12] António Ramires Fernandes and Bruno Oliveira. "GPU Tessellation: We Still Have a LOD of Terrain to Cover." In *OpenGL Insights*, edited by Patrick Cozzi and Christophe Riccio, pp. 145–162. Boca Raton, FL: CRC Press, 2012.

[Gargantini 82] Irene Gargantini. "An Effective Way to Represent Quadtrees." *Communications of the ACM* 25:12 (1982), 905–910.

[Gateau 07] Samuel Gateau. "Solid Wireframe." http://developer. download.nvidia.com/SDK/10.5/direct3d/Source/SolidWireframe/Doc/ SolidWireframe.pdf, 2007.

[Lengyel 10] Eric Lengyel. "Voxel-Based Terrain for Real-Time Virtual Simulations." Ph.D. thesis, University of California, Davis, CA, 2010.

[Mistal 13] Benjamin Mistal. "GPU Terrain Subdivision and Tessellation." In *GPU Pro 4: Advanced Rendering Techniques*, edited by Wolfgang Engel, Chapter 1. Boca Raton, FL: A K Peters/CRC Press, 2013.

[Raman and Wise 08] Rajeev Raman and David Stephen Wise. "Converting to and from Dilated Integers." *IEEE Transactions on Computers* 57:4 (2008), 567–573.

[Shaffer 90] Clifford A. Shaffer. "Bit Interleaving for Quad or Octrees." In *Graphics Gems*, edited by Andrew S. Glassner, pp. 443–447. San Diego, CA: Academic Press, 1990.

[Strugar 09] Filip Strugar. "Continuous Distance-Dependent Level of Detail for Rendering Heightmaps." *Journal of Graphics, GPU, and Game Tools* 14:4 (2009), 57–74.

Two-Level Constraint Solver and Pipelined Local Batching for Rigid Body Simulation on GPUs
Takahiro Harada

4.1 Introduction

GPUs are attractive processors to execute large-scale dynamic physics simulations because of their high bandwidth and computational power. Studies on accelerating relatively simple simulations include particle-based [Harada et al. 07], cloth [Zeller 05], and grid-based fluid [Harris 04] simulations. However, there are few works on accelerating rigid body simulation using GPUs. Rigid body simulation in general consists of broad-phase collision detection, narrow-phase collision detection, and constraint solving [van den Bergen 03]. Each stage has challenges.

This chapter presents a two-level constraint solver designed for the GPU. We first give a general description of the solver and then present a GPU implementation. The two-level constraint solver performs two preparations: global split and local batching. Local batching is especially challenging for GPUs because the naïve implementation of batching is a serial algorithm. We present pipelined local batching, which parallelizes local batching by pipelining the operation and using a SIMD lane as a stage of the pipeline.[1] With pipelined local batching executed on the GPU, the entire constraint solver is completed on the GPU. Constraints in benchmark scenes are solved using the two-level constraint solver on the GPU to analyze the performance. This chapter is an extension of the work presented in [Harada 11]; this chapter also presents pipelined batching, which overcomes issues of local batching presented in [Harada 11], and a detailed performance analysis.

---

[1]We use terminology for AMD GPUs. A SIMD is a compute unit that can operate independently and is called a core on CPUs. An ALU unit in a SIMD is called a SIMD lane.

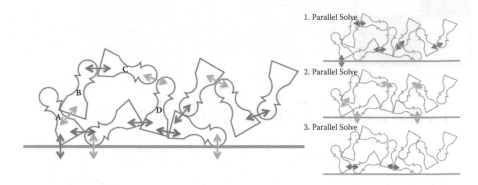

Figure 4.1. Batched constraints (left) and how they are solved in three steps (right).

4.2   Rigid Body Simulation

4.2.1   Simulation Pipeline

Rigid body simulation has been studied for decades. To realize interaction between bodies, colliding pairs must be detected dynamically, and a collision must be resolved for each of the detected pairs. Studies of implementing collision detection on GPUs include [Harada 07, Grand 07, Liu et al. 10].

After colliding pairs are detected, the normal directional component of relative velocity at each contact point must be greater than zero to prevent further penetration [Ericson 04]. This is a condition called velocity constraint and must be satisfied at all the contact points. Because the velocity constraint is not an equality, this is a linear complementarity problem (LCP) [Eberly 03]. LCPs can be solved using the projected Gauss-Seidel method, which is gaining popularity in a real-time application [Catto 05]. The Gauss-Seidel method can solve only a linear system, but the projected Gauss-Seidel method can solve LCP; it adds clamping a solution after solving a row of the system to the Gauss-Seidel method. However, the serial nature of the algorithm makes it difficult to implement in parallel.

4.2.2   Constraint Solver

Batched constraint solver. To solve constraints in parallel, dependency must be checked among the constraints. If we look at the constraints connecting A,B and C,D of the example shown in Figure 4.1, we see that they are independent constraints (i.e., they do not share any body), thus they can be solved in parallel.

We can collect those independent constraints and define a group of constraints, which is called a batch. These constraints in a batch can be solved in parallel because they are independent. After a batch is created, independent constraints are collected from the remaining constraints to create another batch. This operation is repeated until all the constraints are assigned to a batch. Once constraints are divided into batches, we can solve constraints within a batch in parallel, although synchronization is necessary among solving different batches because they have dependency. Figure 4.1 illustrates batched constraints in which constraints in the same batch are drawn using the same color.

Global batching. Batching classifies all the constraints into independent batches. An algorithm for batching is shown in Algorithm 4.1. It iterates through all the constraints in the simulation and checks the dependency of a constraint against the constraints stored in a batch. If a constraint does not have dependency to the constraints in the batch (line 7), the constraint is added to the batch (line 8); otherwise, the constraint is stored in another buffer as a remaining constraint (line 13).

Once all the constraints are checked, the batch is closed (line 16). Then the next batch is opened, the remaining constraints from the previous iteration are processed one by one, and dependency is checked against the current batch as for the first batch. This operation is repeated until all the constraints are assigned to a batch. We call this batching algorithm *global batching*, and a constraint solver that solves constraints using it a *global batch global constraint solver*.

```
 1: pairsSrc ← pairs
 2: pairsDst
 3: while pairsSrc.getSize() do
 4:     nConsumed = 0 // pair count scheduled in the batch
 5:     for pairsSrc.getSize() do
 6:         iPair = pairsSrc[i]
 7:         if !locked(iPair.x) and !locked(iPair.y) then
 8:             batch.add( iPair )
 9:             lock( iPair.x )
10:             lock( iPair.y )
11:             nConsumed++
12:         else
13:             pairsDst.add( iPair )
14:         end if
15:     end for
16:     if nConsumed = 0 then
17:         batch.close()
18:         clear( lockStatus )
19:     end if
20:     swap( pairSrc, pairsDst )
21: end while
22: batch.close()
```

Algorithm 4.1. Batch creation.

4.3   Two-Level Constraint Solver

This section presents the two-level constraint solver, which solves constraints in two stages. The reason for the split is to make the algorithm easy to parallelize and to localize expensive operations to improve the efficiency. This two-level approach is applicable for GPUs as well as for multi-core CPUs. Because the two-level constraint solver solves constraints in two steps, the batching, which is a serial computation, is also split into two steps (global split and local batching), each of which can be implemented in parallel.

4.3.1   Global Split

Constraints are split into several independent groups during the global split (a group is similar in concept to a simulation island). The objective of this split is to process groups in parallel. However, if all the constraints in the simulation are connected—as often happens—it just creates a single big group and we cannot split it into groups. Therefore, we first split constraints into groups, allowing some dependencies. Then independent groups are collected from all the groups to form a set of constraint groups. This operation is repeated until all the groups are assigned to one of the sets. After sets are created, constraint groups in a set can be processed in parallel; however, processing different sets must be serialized because they may depend on each other.

There are several spatial splits we can use, but we employ a two-dimensional regular split as shown in Figure 4.2 because the simplicity of the connectivity of cells of a regular split makes it easy to create sets of constraint groups. Constraints in a cell form a constraint group. Although adjacent cells can have a constraint sharing a body, one-ring neighbor cells do not have a connected constraint. Therefore, cells (or groups) are split into four independent sets (Figure 4.2).

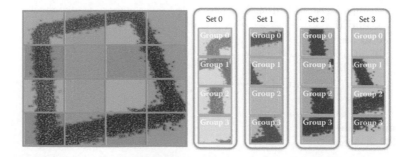

Figure 4.2. Global split creates sets of constraint groups.

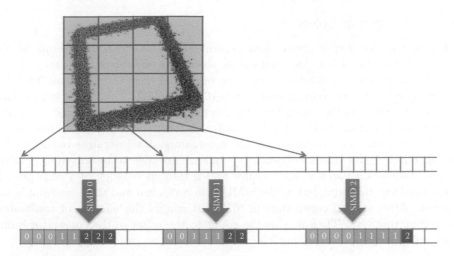

Figure 4.3. Constraints in a group are stored in a contiguous memory. Each group has the offset to the memory and number of constraints. Local batching sorts constraints for a group by batch index using a SIMD.

4.3.2 Local Batching

After the global split, constraint groups are independent in a set. In other words, groups in a set can be processed in parallel. A group is processed by a SIMD of the GPU. There are, however, still dependencies among constraints in a group. Therefore, batching is necessary to process them in parallel in each group. We call this *local batching*, in contrast to the global batching described in Section 4.2.2, because batching for this step must consider only the connectivity of constraints in a group that consists of localized constraints.

One big difference between global and local batching is the width of the batch we must create. For global batching, the optimal batch width is the hardware computation width. For a GPU, which executes thousands of work items concurrently, we have to extract thousands of independent constraints to fill the hardware. However, because we assign a SIMD to solve constraints in a group, local batching requires creating a batch only with the SIMD width (e.g., on a GPU with a 64-wide SIMD, only 64 independent constraints have to be extracted). Creating a narrower batch is easier and computationally cheaper because the wider the batch, the more expensive the dependency check of constraints becomes.

The input of local batching is a set of constraints. Batches are created at this stage and batch index is calculated for each constraint. For the convenience of the constraint solver, constraints are sorted by batch indices. Figure 4.3 illustrates how constraints are stored.

4.3.3   Constraint Solver

Because the global split creates four dependent sets of constraint groups, as discussed in Section 4.3.1, four sequential solves are executed. Within a set of constraint groups, constraint groups can be solved in parallel because they are independent. A constraint group is solved by a SIMD. The SIMD sequentially reads constraints of the group from the beginning of the section of the constraint buffer using a SIMD lane to read a constraint. Once constraints are read by all lanes, it compares batch indices of the constraints. If constraints belong to different batches, they have a dependency and are not able to be solved in parallel. Thus, it selects a batch index to solve and if the batch index of a constraint is different from the batch index, the SIMD lane is masked and the constraint is not solved. After solving constraints in SIMD, it counts the number of constraints solved at this step. Then it adds the count to the offset of the constraint buffer and repeats the operations until all constraints in the group are processed.

4.4   GPU Implementation

The two-level constraint solver has challenges when it comes to implementation on a GPU. In particular, batching described in Section 4.2.2 cannot be parallelized easily. Thus, we propose pipelined local batching that extracts parallelism on the batching by pipelining the algorithm to utilize wide SIMD architecture while keeping the quality of batches high.

4.4.1   Global Split

Because we use a two-dimensional grid for the split, the belonging cell of a constraint can be found from the world position of the constraint. As a unique cell index is assigned for each cell, cell indices are calculated for all constraints. Once that is done, constraints are sorted by cell index [Merrill and Grimshaw 11]. After the sort, bounds of constraints for cells are searched by comparing cell indices of adjacent constraints. We must ensure that the size of the cell is larger than the largest extent of rigid bodies; otherwise, non-adjacent cells can have a dependency because they share the same rigid body.

Host code can be written as follows. It uses parallel primitives such as radix sort and prefix scan. An OpenCL implementation can be found (for example, [Harada and Howes 12] and [Coumans 13]).

```
//    Compute sortData for each contact
execute(SetSortDataKernel, contacts, bodies, sortData);
//    Sort sortData. Keys are cell index
RadixSort(sortData);
//    Count number of entries per cell
BoundSearch(sortData, counts);
//    Convert counts to offsets
```

```
PrefixScan(counts, offsets);
//    Reorder contacts using sortData
execute(ReorderContactKernel, contacts, contactsSorted, sortData)↩
    ;
```

SetSortDataKernel computes the cell index and write a key value pair for each contact as follows.

```
__kernel
void SetSortDataKernel(__global Contact* gContact,
    __global Body* gBodies,
    __global int2* gSortDataOut)
{
    int gIdx = get_global_id(0);
    int aIdx = gContact[gIdx].m_bodyA;
    int bIdx = gContact[gIdx].m_bodyB;

    float4 p = gBodies[aIdx].m_pos;
    int xIdx = convertToCellIdx(p.x);
    int zIdx = convertToCellIdx(p.z);

    gSortDataOut[gIdx].x = computeUniqueId( xIdx, zIdx );
    gSortDataOut[gIdx].y = gIdx;
}
```

Once the key value pairs are sorted, contacts are reordered in `ReorderContactKernel`.

```
__kernel
void ReorderContactKernel(__global Contact* in,
    __global Contact4* out,
    __global int2* sortData)
{
    int gIdx = get_global_id(0);
    int srcIdx = sortData[gIdx].y;
    out[gIdx] = in[srcIdx];
}
```

4.4.2 Pipelined Local Batching

Each constraint group can be processed in parallel; thus, it is assigned to a SIMD of a GPU in a single kernel dispatch. However, the batching algorithm described in Section 4.2.2 is a completely serial process, which is inefficient if it is executed on a GPU. The proposed pipelined local batching transforms the serial batching algorithm into a pipelined parallel algorithm. Pipelined local batching decomposes the `while` loop of Algorithm 4.1 and processes them in parallel. However, each iteration of the `while` loop is dependent on the previous iteration and it is not straightforward to parallelize.

The proposed pipelined local batching uses a SIMD lane as a stage of the pipeline to create a batch. Pipelined local batching starts by reading a constraint of the group from the input buffer at the first stage by SIMD lane 0. The lane checks whether it can be inserted in batch 0. If the constraint is independent from constraints in batch 0, batch index 0 is assigned to the constraint and the constraint is deleted from the pipeline; otherwise, the constraint is forwarded to the next stage of the pipeline, which is processed by SIMD lane 1. This is one cycle of the pipeline. During the first cycle, only SIMD lane 0 is active. On the next cycle, SIMD lane 0 reads the next constraint from the input buffer and other lanes receive constraints from the previous stage of the pipeline. If the first constraint is forwarded from SIMD lane 0 after the first cycle, SIMD lane 1 receives the constraint. Then each lane checks the dependency of the constraint to the batch. If it is independent, it sets the batch index to the constraint and the data is deleted from the pipeline; otherwise, it is delivered to the next stage of the pipeline. As the number of cycles increases, more constraints flow on the pipeline and SIMD lanes at a deeper pipeline stage are filled with data.

While serial batching starts creation of the second batch once the first batch is created, pipelined local batching finishes batching soon after the first batch is created. When the last constraint of the group is processed by lane 0, most of the batches are completed and the pipeline finishes working once all the data in the pipeline is processed.

Figure 4.4 illustrates pipelined local batching, and Algorithm 4.2 shows pseudo code. Local data store (LDS) is used to forward data between stages processed by each lane of a SIMD. The SIMD width of the GPU used for this chapter is 64; therefore, it can create up to 64 batches. If a constraint could not be inserted in the last lane, it overflows the pipeline. Overflowed constraints can be stored in a buffer and processed after all the constraints are processed once. However, we did not implement this because we have not encountered an overflow for our test cases.

```
 1: nRemainings ← pairs.getSize() // number of pairs not batched yet
 2: while nRemainings > 0 do
 3:    iPair ← fetchFromBuffer()
 4:    if !locked(iPair.x) and !locked(iPair.y) then
 5:       batch.add( iPair )
 6:       lock( iPair.x )
 7:       lock( iPair.y )
 8:    else
 9:       forwardPairToNextLane( iPair )
10:    end if
11:    nRemainings = countRemainingPairs()
12: end while
```

Algorithm 4.2. Pipelined batching.

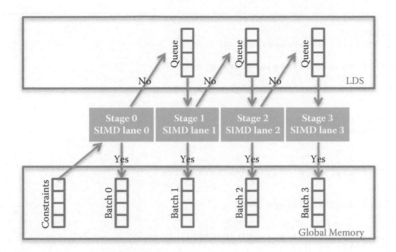

Figure 4.4. Pipelined local batching.

Pipelined local batching always creates the same batches as serial batching, whereas other parallel batching using atomics usually creates different batches and the number of batches is greater than the number created by the serial algorithm. Keeping the number of batches small is important to keep the computation time of the expensive constraint solver low, as discussed in Section 4.2.

OpenCL kernel code for pipelined batching can be found in Listing 4.1.

4.4.3 Constraint Solver

The constraints are solved by four subsequent kernel executions: one kernel execution for each set of constraint groups. Each dispatch assigns a SIMD for a constraint group within a set, and batched constraints are solved in parallel by checking batch indices. While the global constraint solver dispatches a kernel for each batch, the two-level constraint solver always executes four kernels in which a SIMD of the GPU repeats in-SIMD dispatches by itself until all the constraints belonging to the group are solved.

4.5   Comparison of Batching Methods

A batching method can be evaluated by two aspects: batching computation time and the performance of the constraint solver. Batching computation time is shorter when local batching is used because it can be executed in parallel and it needs to create batches only with the hardware SIMD width, while global batching must create batches with the processor width (the SIMD width times the number of SIMDs on the hardware).

```
__kernel
void PipelinedBatchingKernel ()
{
  int start = gOffsets [get_group_id (0)];
  int i = start;
  int lIdx = get_local_id (0);

  //  0.  initialize
  nPairsInQueue (lIdx) = 0;
  clearLocks ();

  if ( lIdx == 0 )
  {
    ldsNRemainings = countRemainingPairs ();
  }

  while ( ldsNRemainings != 0 )
  {
    //   1. fetch one pair from buffer
    int4 iPair = make_int4 (-1,0,0,0);
    if ( lIdx == 0 )
    {   //  SIMD lane 0 fetches from global memory
      iPair = make_int4 ( gPairs[i].x, gPairs[i].y, i, 0 );
    }
    else
    {   //  other lanes fetch from queues
      if ( nPairsInQueue (lIdx-1) != 0 )
      {
        iPair = ldsBuf [lIdx-1];
        nPairsInQueue (lIdx-1)--;
      }
    }

    //   2. check dependency of iPair to the batch
    bool notLocked = !locked( iPair.x ) && !locked( iPair.y );

    //   3. process iPair
    if ( iPair.x != -1 )
    {
      if ( notLocked )
      {   //  iPair was independent. add to the batch
        lock( iPair.x ); lock( iPair.y );
        gBatchOut [iPair.z] = lIdx;
      }
      else
      {   //  forward iPair to next lane
        ldsBuf [lIdx] = iPair;
        nPairsInQueue (lIdx)++;
      }
    }

    i++;
    if ( lIdx == 0 )
      ldsNRemainings = countRemainingPairs ();
  }
}
```

Listing 4.1. Simplified kernel code of pipelined local batching.

A measure of performance of a constraint solver is the total number of batches created by a batching method. As the number of batches increases, the number of serial computations and synchronization increases, which results in longer constraint solving time. When a rigid body in the simulation is connected by n constraints, at least n batches are necessary to batch these constraints because all of them must be executed in different batches. Thus, the number of batches created by global batching is more than $n_{\max}^{\text{global}} = \max(n_0, n_1, \cdots, n_m)$ for a simulation with m rigid bodies where n_i is the number of constraints connected to body i. When constraints are solved by the two-level constraint solver with local batching, it splits constraints into four constraint sets. The number of batches required for the set i is $n_{\max}^{\text{local}_i} = \max(n_0^i, n_1^i, \cdots, n_{m_i}^i)$. Constraint sets must be processed sequentially; thus, the number of batches for the two-level constraint solver is $\sum_0^4 n_{\max}^{\text{local}_i}$.

If all the constraints of the rigid body having $n_{\max}^{\text{global}}$ constraints belong to constraint set 0, $n_{\max}^{\text{local}_0} = n_{\max}^{\text{global}}$. Therefore, the total number of batches of the two-level constraint solver cannot be less than the number of batches created by global batching ($\sum_0^4 n_{\max}^{\text{local}_i} \geq n_{\max}^{\text{local}_0} = n_{\max}^{\text{global}}$).

If a simulation is executed on a highly parallel processor like a GPU, a large number of constraints can be solved at the same time. If the number of constraints in a batch is less than the hardware parallel width, the solving time for each batch should be roughly the same. Therefore, the number of batches can be an estimation of the computation time of a constraint solver. From the comparison of the number of batches, the two-level constraint solver cannot, in theory, outperform a parallel constraint solver using the optimal global batching.

4.6   Results and Discussion

The presented method is implemented on the GPU and constraints in six benchmark scenes (shown in Figure 4.5) are solved using an AMD Radeon HD7970 GPU. Table 4.1 shows the data from those simulations. We also implemented the global constraint solver, which uses the CPU for global batching and the GPU for solving constraints, to evaluate the performance of the two-level constraint solver. In our implementation, constraints are not stored one by one; instead, up to four constraints for a colliding pair are stored as a constraint pair.

4.6.1   Evaluation of Global Split

The space is split into 64×64 for a global split for all benchmarks. The number of splits is the only parameter we need to specify to implement our constraint solver, other than the physical parameters for a constraint solver. It is not likely that rigid bodies are distributed evenly in the simulation space (i.e., it is unlikely that all cells are populated in a simulation). Therefore, we want to set the number of

Figure 4.5. Test scenes.

nonempty cells to be about equal to the number of SIMDs on the GPU to assign
a computation for each SIMD.

We assumed that the ratio of non-empty cells to all cells is about 0.5. Thus,
when a 64×64 split is used, there are 2,048 non-empty cells in total, or 512
non-empty cells for each constraint set on average. The GPU we used for the
experiments has 128 SIMDs. Therefore, the number of non-empty cells for each
set is more than the number of SIMDs if the population ratio is 0.5. Figure 4.6

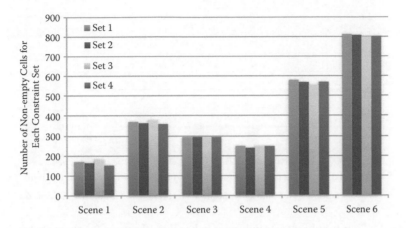

Figure 4.6. The number of non-empty cells for each scene.

shows the number of non-empty cells for each benchmark scene. Although scene 6 has about 800 non-empty cells for each set, scene 1 has less than 200 cells. Thus, all the SIMDs on the GPU are active. When the number of non-empty cells is small, we could increase the resolution of the spatial split. However, this results in a reduction of the number of constraints in a cell. At the same time, we do not want to reduce the number of constraints in a cell to fill SIMD lanes of each SIMD.

4.6.2 Computation Time

Computation times for pipelined local batching and constraint solvers are shown in Table 4.1. Pipelined local batching takes longer for a simulation with more constraints. Because constraints are processed by the pipeline one by one, the time taken for pipelined local batching is linear to the number of constraints in

	Scene 1	Scene 2	Scene 3	Scene 4	Scene 5	Scene 6
Number of bodies	1,200	6,240	12,640	19,040	9,600	38,400
Number of constraint pairs	1,763	13,203	21,904	33,209	16,684	67,263
Number of global batches	11	16	14	16	13	25
Pipelined local batching time	0.105	0.357	0.524	0.735	0.376	1.16
Global solver time (1 iter.)	0.264	0.415	0.45	0.552	0.367	0.999
Two-level solver time (1 iter.)	0.162	0.387	0.433	0.540	0.359	0.839
Max batch count in set1	6	12	11	16	13	17
Max batch count in set2	5	14	16	16	11	12
Max batch count in set3	5	12	14	14	11	13
Max batch count in set4	5	12	12	14	12	14

Table 4.1. Benchmark data (time in milliseconds).

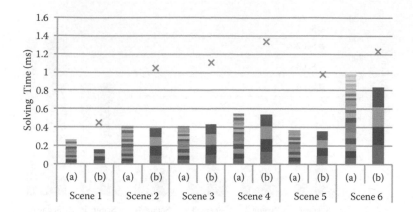

Figure 4.7. Time to solve constraints once in benchmarks using (a) the global and (b) the two-level constraint solvers. The plots show estimated time for the two-level constraint solver. Each color corresponds to a single-kernel execution. The global constraint solver requires several kernel executions, but the two-level constraint solver requires only four kernel executions. This graph plots the estimated computation time for the two-level constraint solver.

a group. Thus, batching for scene 6 takes longer than for other scenes.

A comparison of the computation time for the two-level and the global constraint solvers shown in Table 4.1 completely contradicts the expectation discussed in Section 4.5. For most scenes, the two-level constraint solver outperforms the global constraint solver, which needs the CPU for batching. The first potential explanation for the superior performance is that the number of batches for the two-level solver is smaller in the test scenes. We counted the number of batches for solvers for all scenes and confirmed that the total number of batches for the two-level constraint solver is more than that of the global constraint solver (Table 4.1).

To get a better understanding of this result, we performed more detailed analyses on the global constraint solver. The solving time for each batch is measured in Figure 4.8, and the number of constraints in each batch is counted in Figure 4.9. Figure 4.9 shows that no batch has more than 8,000 constraint pairs. The maximum number of concurrent works the GPU can execute is more than the number of SIMDs times the SIMD lane width: $128 \times 64 = 8,192$ for the GPU. Therefore, all constraints in a batch are processed concurrently. Batches with larger batch indices have constant computation times for all benchmarks; batches with smaller batch indices do not.

Figures 4.8 and 4.9 also show that batches that take longer to solve have more constraints. Batches with longer execution times, however, should have the same number of ALU operations per SIMD lane. The difference must come from memory access latency. As the number of constraint pairs increases, so does the

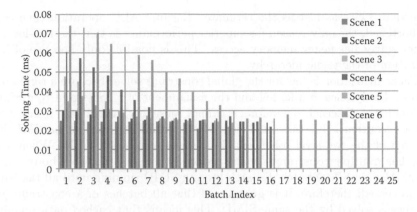

Figure 4.8. Solving time for a batch created by global batching.

demand for more memory operations. We can guess that the increase saturates the memory system at the point at which solver time exceeds the constant time.

We can also see solving time starts increasing when more than 2,000 constraint pairs are scheduled in a batch. As the number of constraints increases further, performance gradually decreases.

From Figure 4.8, we can get a lower bound of a batch's solving time as 0.021 ms. Multiplying the minimum time required to solve a batch by the number of batches for each benchmark scene, we can estimate the lower bound of the time required for the two-level constraint solver plotted in Figure 4.7. However, we can see that the measured solving time using the two-level constraint solver is

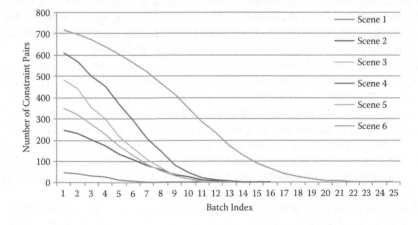

Figure 4.9. The number of constraint pairs in each batch when global batching is used.

more than twice as fast as the estimate. Because ALU operation time cannot be shortened, the only reason for superior performance is that the two-level constraint solver has faster memory access. This is possible only because of better utilization of the cache hierarchy.

Cache utilization is low for the global constraint solver because a rigid body is processed only once in a kernel and the assignment of a constraint to a SIMD is random for each kernel. Therefore, it cannot reuse any cached data from previous kernel executions. In contrast, localized constraint solving and in-SIMD batch dispatch of the two-level solver enable it to use cache efficiently. When a rigid body has multiple constraints in the region, it accesses the same body multiple times. Also, in-SIMD batch dispatch keeps a SIMD running until all the batches are processed; therefore, it is guaranteed that all batches of a constraint group are always solved by the same SIMD. This means that cached data remains in a SIMD, whereas the global constraint solver can assign any constraint from the entire simulation domain to a SIMD, which likely trashes the data in the cache for every batch solve.

Another advantage of in-SIMD dispatch is that it reduces GPU processing overhead by reducing the number of kernel dispatches. For scene 1, the global constraint solver executes 11 kernels (Table 4.1) while the two-level constraint solver executes four kernels to solve the system once. The two-level constraint solver has an advantage on the overhead as well.

From these analyses, we found that higher ALU occupancy is not the most important factor for achieving high performance of a constraint solver for a rigid body simulation on the GPU. To improve performance further, we need to reduce the memory traffic using optimizations such as memory compression and cache-aware ordering of constraint data.

The constraint solver using local batching is a persistent thread style implementation because a SIMD keeps processing until all constraints in a constraint group are solved [Aila and Laine 09]. They chose this implementation to improve the occupancy of the GPU, but we found that it has another positive impact: performance improvement because of better cache utilization.

Dispatching small kernels like the global constraint solver is simple to implement and worked well on old GPU architectures that do not have a memory hierarchy. However, today's GPUs have evolved and are equipped with a cache hierarchy. Our study has shown that the old GPU programming style, in which small kernels are dispatched frequently, cannot exploit current GPU architectures. Thus, a persistent thread style implementation is preferable for today's GPUs. An alternative solution would be to provide an API to choose a SIMD to run a computation so the GPU can benefit from the cache from different kernel executions.

This solver has been integrated to the Bullet 3 physics simulation library and it is used as a basis for the GPU rigid body simulation solver. Full source code is available at [Coumans 13].

Bibliography

[Aila and Laine 09] Timo Aila and Samuli Laine. "Understanding the Efficiency of Ray Traversal on GPUs." In *Proceedings of the Conference on High Performance Graphics 2009*, *HPG '09*, pp. 145–149. New York: ACM, 2009.

[Catto 05] E Catto. "Iterative Dynamics with Temporal Coherence." Presentation, Game Developers Conference, San Francisco, CA, March, 2005.

[Coumans 13] Erwin Coumans. "Bullet 3." http://bulletphysics.org/, 2013.

[Eberly 03] Dave H. Eberly. *Game Physics*. New York: Elsevier Science Inc., 2003.

[Ericson 04] Christer Ericson. *Real-Time Collision Detection*. San Francisco, CA: Morgan Kaufmann Publishers Inc., 2004.

[Grand 07] Scotte Le Grand. "Broad-Phase Collision Detection with CUDA." In *GPU Gems 3*, edited by Hubert Nguyen, pp. 697–722. Upper Saddle River, NJ: Addison-Wesley, 2007.

[Harada and Howes 12] Takahiro Harada and Lee Howes. "Heterogeneous Computing with OpenCL: Introduction to GPU Radix Sort." http://www.heterogeneouscompute.org/?page_id=7, 2012.

[Harada et al. 07] T. Harada, S. Koshizuka, and Y. Kawaguchi. "Smoothed Particle Hydrodynamics on GPUs." Presentation, Computer Graphics International Conference, Rio de Janeiro, Brazil, May, 2007.

[Harada 07] Takahiro Harada. "Real-Time Rigid Body Simulation on GPUs." In *GPU Gems 3*, edited by Hubert Nguyen, pp. 611–632. Upper Saddle River, NJ: Addison-Wesley, 2007.

[Harada 11] Takahiro Harada. "A Parallel Constraint Solver for a Rigid Body Simulation." In *SIGGRAPH Asia 2011 Sketches*, pp. 22:1–22:2. New York: ACM, 2011.

[Harris 04] Mark Harris. "Fast Fluid Dynamics Simulation on the GPU." In *GPU Gems*, edited by Randima Fernando, pp. 637–665. Upper Saddle River, NJ: Addison-Wesley, 2004.

[Liu et al. 10] Fuchang Liu, Takahiro Harada, Youngeun Lee, and Young J. Kim. "Real-Time Collision Culling of a Million Bodies on Graphics Processing Units." *ACM Transactions on Graphics* 29 (2010), 154:1–154:8.

[Merrill and Grimshaw 11] Duane Merrill and Andrew Grimshaw. "High Performance and Scalable Radix Sorting: A Case Study of Implementing Dynamic Parallelism for GPU Computing." *Parallel Processing Letters* 21:2 (2011), 245–272.

[van den Bergen 03] Gino van den Bergen. *Collision Detection in Interactive 3D Environments*. San Francisco, CA: Morgan Kaufmann, 2003.

[Zeller 05] Cyril Zeller. "Cloth Simulation on the GPU." In *ACM SIGGRAPH 2005 Sketches, SIGGRAPH '05*, p. Article no. 39. New York: ACM, 2005.

Non-separable 2D, 3D, and 4D
Filtering with CUDA
Anders Eklund and Paul Dufort

5.1 Introduction

Filtering is an important step in many image processing applications such as image denoising (where the goal is to suppress noise, see Figure 5.1), image registration (where the goal is to align two images or volumes, see Figure 5.2), and image segmentation (where the goal is to extract certain parts of an image or volume, see Figure 5.3). In medical imaging, the datasets generated are often 3D or 4D and contain a large number of samples, making filtering a computationally demanding operation. A high-resolution magnetic resonance (MR) scan of a human head normally contains on the order of $256 \times 256 \times 200$ voxels (a voxel is the 3D equivalent of a pixel). Functional magnetic resonance imaging (fMRI) is used for studying brain function, and the generated 4D datasets can easily contain 300 volumes over time with $64 \times 64 \times 30$ voxels each. Ultrasound machines are increasingly affordable and can output volume data at 20–30 Hz. Computed tomography (CT) scanners can yield even higher spatial resolution than MR scanners, at the cost of ionizing radiation. A 4D CT dataset of a beating heart can be of the size $512 \times 512 \times 445 \times 20$ samples [Eklund et al. 11]. Reducing the amount of radiation in CT leads to higher noise levels, but this can be remedied by applying image denoising algorithms. However, to apply 11 non-separable denoising filters with $11 \times 11 \times 11 \times 11$ coefficients to a dataset of size $512 \times 512 \times 445 \times 20$, for example, requires approximately 375,000 billion multiply-add operations using a convolution approach. Fortunately, graphics processing units (GPUs) can now easily be used to speed up a large variety of parallel operations [Owens et al. 07].

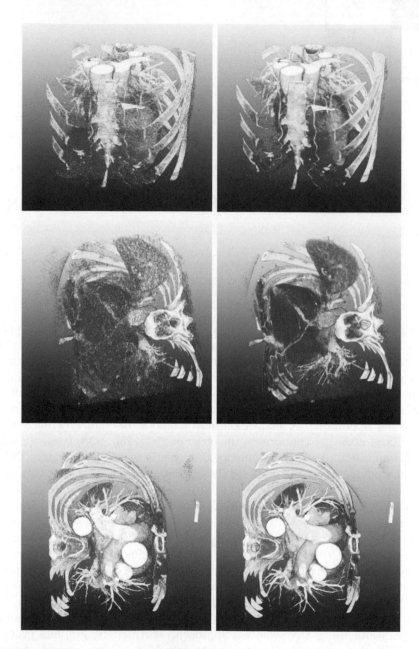

Figure 5.1. Results of denoising a 4D CT dataset, requiring convolution with 11 non-separable 4D filters of size $11 \times 11 \times 11 \times 11$. See [Eklund et al. 11] for further information about the denoising algorithm. The left images show the original data, and the right images show the denoised data.

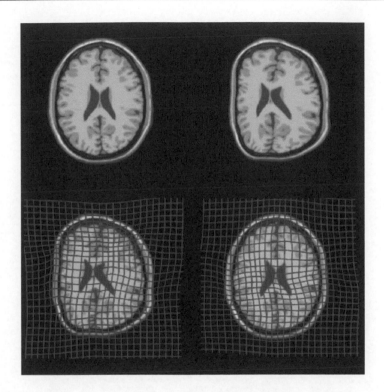

Figure 5.2. An example of image registration where the goal is to align two images or volumes. The registration algorithm used here is called the Morphon; it takes advantage of quadrature filters to detect edges and lines to estimate the displacement between two images or volumes. Quadrature filters are non-separable and can for example be of size $9 \times 9 \times 9$ voxels for volume registration. An axial brain MRI image is shown at the top left, with an artificially warped version of the same image at the top right. The task for the registration algorithm is to align the two images by finding an optimal field deforming one into the other. At the bottom left, the warped image is shown again, overlaid with the artificial deformation field used to create it. The output of the registration procedure appears at the bottom right, overlaid by its computed deformation field. The algorithm has recovered the original image and also generated a deformation field that inverts or cancels the artificial field. [This example was kindly provided by Daniel Forsberg.]

5.2 Non-separable Filters

Filtering can be divided into separable and non-separable variants. Popular separable filters are Gaussian filters (used for smoothing/blurring to reduce noise and details) and Sobel filters (used for detection of edges). Filter kernels for Gaussian (G) smoothing and edge detection along x and y using Sobel (S) filters can be

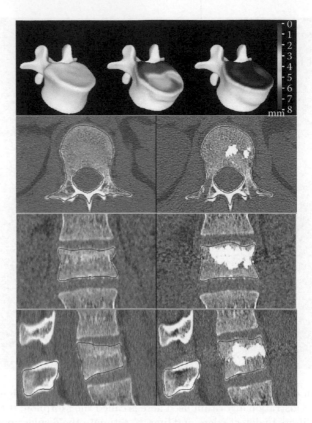

Figure 5.3. Three-dimensional segmentation of a fractured vertebra before and after a surgical procedure to restore its height, using the SpineJack device from Vexim SA of Toulouse, France. The bottom three rows show before (left) and after (right) images overlaid with the contours of the 3D segmentations. The top row shows 3D renderings of the segmentations, color-coded to indicate the change in height pre- and post-surgery. The reference (leftmost) 3D vertebra is a pre-trauma reconstruction—a prediction of the vertebra's shape before it was fractured. Filtering is used here to detect the edges of the vertebra. [Image used with permission courtesy of Dr. David Noriega, Valladolid, Spain, and Vexim SA.]

written as

$$
G = \begin{bmatrix} 1 & 2 & 1 \\ 2 & 4 & 2 \\ 1 & 2 & 1 \end{bmatrix} / 16 \,, \quad
S_x = \begin{bmatrix} 1 & 0 & -1 \\ 2 & 0 & -2 \\ 1 & 0 & -1 \end{bmatrix}, \quad
S_y = \begin{bmatrix} 1 & 2 & 1 \\ 0 & 0 & 0 \\ -1 & -2 & -1 \end{bmatrix}.
$$

Separability means that these filters can be decomposed as one 1D filter along x and one 1D filter along y. The Sobel filter used for edge detection along x can for example be decomposed as

$$S_x = \begin{bmatrix} 1 & 0 & -1 \\ 2 & 0 & -2 \\ 1 & 0 & -1 \end{bmatrix} = \begin{bmatrix} 1 \\ 2 \\ 1 \end{bmatrix} \begin{bmatrix} 1 & 0 & -1 \end{bmatrix}.$$

A separable filter of size 9×9 requires 18 multiplications per pixel and can be applied in two passes. One pass performs convolution along the rows, and the other pass performs convolution along the columns. A non-separable filter of size 9×9, on the other hand, requires 81 multiplications per pixel and is applied in a single pass.

While separable filters are less computationally demanding, there are a number of image processing operations that can only be performed using non-separable filters. The best-known non-separable filter is perhaps the Laplace (L) filter, which can be used for edge detection. In contrast to Gaussian and Sobel filters, it cannot be decomposed into two 1D filters. Laplace filters of size 3×3 and 5×5 can, for example, be written as

$$L_{3\times3} = \begin{bmatrix} 0 & 1 & 0 \\ 1 & -4 & 1 \\ 0 & 1 & 0 \end{bmatrix}, \quad L_{5\times5} = \begin{bmatrix} 1 & 1 & 1 & 1 & 1 \\ 1 & 1 & 1 & 1 & 1 \\ 1 & 1 & -24 & 1 & 1 \\ 1 & 1 & 1 & 1 & 1 \\ 1 & 1 & 1 & 1 & 1 \end{bmatrix}.$$

The quadrature filter is another popular non-separable filter, which is complex valued in the spatial domain. The real part of the filter is a line detector and the imaginary part is an edge detector. A 1D quadrature filter is given in Figure 5.4, but quadrature filters of any dimension can be created. The name *quadrature* comes from electronics and describes the relation between two signals having the same frequency and a phase difference of 90 degrees. An edge detector is an odd function similar to a sine wave, while a line detector is an even function similar to a cosine wave. A sine and a cosine of the same frequency always differ in phase by 90 degrees and a filter that can be described as one sine wave and one cosine wave is therefore called a *quadrature filter*. The interested reader is referred to [Granlund and Knutsson 95, Knutsson et al. 99] for further information about quadrature filters and filter design. Quadrature filters can be applied for a wide range of applications, such as image registration [Knutsson and Andersson 05, Eklund et al. 10, Forsberg et al. 11], image segmentation [Läthen et al. 10], and image denoising [Knutsson et al. 83, Knutsson 89, Granlund and Knutsson 95, Westin et al. 01]. Quadrature filters are very similar to Gabor filters [Granlund 78, Jain and Farrokhnia 91], which are also complex valued in the spatial domain.

For most algorithms using Gabor or quadrature filters, several filters are applied along different directions. For example, estimation of a structure tensor [Knutsson 89, Knutsson et al. 11] in 3D requires filtering with at least six complex valued quadrature filters, i.e., a total of 12 filters (six line detectors

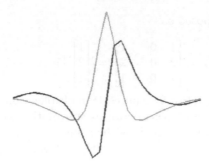

Figure 5.4. A 1D quadrature filter; the real part (green) is a line detector (a cosine modulated with a Gaussian window) and the imaginary part (blue) is an edge detector (a sine modulated with a Gaussian window).

and six edge detectors). The Morphon [Knutsson and Andersson 05] is an image registration algorithm that uses quadrature filters to estimate the displacement between two images or volumes. To improve the registration, estimation of a structure tensor is performed in each iteration, thus requiring an efficient implementation of filtering. Monomial filters [Knutsson et al. 11, Eklund et al. 11] are a good example of filters appropriate for non-separable filtering in 4D.

5.3   Convolution vs. FFT

Images and filters can be viewed directly in the image domain (also called the spatial domain) or in the frequency domain (also denoted Fourier space) after the application of a Fourier transform. Filtering can be performed as a convolution in the spatial domain or as a multiplication in the frequency domain, according to the convolution theorem

$$F[s * f] = F[s] \cdot F[f],$$

where $F[\ ]$ denotes the Fourier transform, s denotes the signal (image), f denotes the filter, $*$ denotes convolution, and $\cdot$ denotes pointwise multiplication. For large non-separable filters, filtering performed as a multiplication in the frequency domain can often be faster than convolution in the spatial domain. The transformation to the frequency domain is normally performed using the fast Fourier transform (FFT), for which very optimized implementations exist. However, FFT-based approaches for 4D data require huge amounts of memory and current GPUs have only 1–6 GB of global memory. Spatial approaches can therefore be advantageous for large datasets. Bilateral filtering [Tomasi and Manduchi 98], which is a method for image denoising, requires that a range function is evaluated for each filter coefficient during the convolution. Such an operation is hard to do with a FFT approach, since bilateral filtering in its original form is a nonlinear operation and the Fourier transform is linear. For optimal performance, FFTs often also require that the dimensions of the data are a power of 2. Additionally, there is no direct support for 4D FFTs in the Nvidia CUFFT library. Instead, one has to apply two batches of 2D FFTs and change the order of the data between these (since the 2D FFTs are applied along the two first dimensions).

5.4   Previous Work

A substantial body of work has addressed the acceleration of filtering using GPUs. Two of the first examples are the work by Rost, who used OpenGL for 2D convolution [Rost 96], and Hopf and Ertl, who used a GPU for separable 3D convolution [Hopf and Ertl 99]. For game programming, filtering can be used for texture animation [James 01]. A more recent example is a white paper from Nvidia discussing separable 2D convolution [Podlozhnyuk 07]. See our recent review about GPUs in medical imaging for a more extensive overview of GPU-based filtering [Eklund et al. 13]. GPU implementations of *non-separable* filtering in 3D, and especially 4D, are less common. For example, the NPP (Nvidia performance primitives) library contains functions for image processing, but for convolution it only supports 2D data and filters stored as integers. The CUDA SDK contains two examples of separable 2D convolution, one example of FFT-based filtering in 2D, and a single example of separable 3D convolution.

The main purpose of this chapter is therefore to present optimized solutions for non-separable 2D, 3D, and 4D convolution with the CUDA programming language, using floats and the fast shared memory. Our code has already been successfully applied to a number of applications [Eklund et al. 10, Forsberg et al. 11, Eklund et al. 11, Eklund et al. 12]. The implementations presented here have been made with CUDA 5.0 and are optimized for the Nvidia GTX 680 graphics card. Readers are assumed to be familiar with CUDA programming, and may avail themselves of the many books available on this topic if not (e.g. [Sanders and Kandrot 11]). All the code for this chapter is available under GNU GPL 3 at https://github.com/wanderine/NonSeparableFilteringCUDA.

5.5   Non-separable 2D Convolution

Two-dimensional convolution between a signal s and a filter f can be written for position $[x, y]$ as

$$(s * f)[x, y] = \sum_{f_x=-N/2}^{f_x=N/2} \sum_{f_y=-N/2}^{f_y=N/2} s[x - f_x, y - f_y] \cdot f[f_x, f_y], \qquad (5.1)$$

where $N + 1$ is the filter size. The most important aspect for a GPU implementation is that the convolution can be done independently for each pixel. To

```
__global__ void Convolution_2D_Texture(float* Filter_Response,
int DATA_W, int DATA_H)
{
    int x = blockIdx.x * blockDim.x + threadIdx.x;
    int y = blockIdx.y * blockDim.y + threadIdx.y;

    if (x >= DATA_W || y >= DATA_H)
        return;

    float sum = 0.0f;
    float y_off = -(FILTER_H - 1)/2 + 0.5f;
    for (int f_y = FILTER_H - 1; f_y >= 0; f_y--)
    {
        float x_off = -(FILTER_W - 1)/2 + 0.5f;
        for (int f_x = FILTER_W - 1; f_x >= 0; f_x--)
        {
            sum += tex2D(texture,x + x_off,y + y_off) *
            c_Filter[f_y][f_x];
            x_off += 1.0f;
        }
        y_off += 1.0f;
    }

    Filter_Response[Get2DIndex(x,y,DATA_W)] = sum;
}
```

Listing 5.1. Non-separable 2D convolution using texture memory: each thread calculates the filter response for one pixel. The filter kernel is stored in cached constant memory and the image is stored in cached texture memory. If the filter size is known at compile time, the inner loop can be unrolled by the compiler. The addition of 0.5 to each coordinate is because the original pixel values for textures are actually stored between the integer coordinates.

obtain high performance, it is also important to take advantage of the fact that filter responses for neighboring pixels are calculated from a largely overlapping set of pixels. We will begin with a CUDA implementation for non-separable 2D convolution that uses texture memory, as the texture memory cache can speed up local reads. Threads needing pixel values already accessed by other threads can thus read the values from the fast cache located at each multiprocessor (MP), rather than from the slow global memory. The filter kernel is put in the constant memory (64 KB) as it is used by all the threads. For Nvidia GPUs the constant memory cache is 8 KB per MP, and 2D filters can thus easily reside in the fast on-chip cache during the whole execution. The device code for texture-based 2D convolution is given in Listing 5.1.

The main problem with using texture memory is that such an implementation is limited by the memory bandwidth, rather than by the computational performance. A better idea is to instead take advantage of the shared memory available at each MP, which makes it possible for the threads in a thread block to cooperate very efficiently. Nvidia GPUs from the Fermi and Kepler architectures have 48 KB of shared memory per MP. If one only considers the number of valid filter responses generated per thread block, the optimal solution is to use all the shared memory for a single thread block, since this would waste a minimum of memory on the "halo" of invalid filter responses at the outer edges. According to the CUDA programming guide, GPUs with compute capability 3.0 (e.g., the Nvidia GTX 680) can maximally handle 1024 threads per thread block and 2048 concurrent threads per MP. Using all the shared memory for one thread block would therefore lead to 50% of the possible computational performance, as only 1024 threads can be used in one thread block. Full occupancy can be achieved by instead dividing the 48 KB of shared memory into two thread blocks. For floating point convolution, 96×64 pixel values can be fitted into 24 KB of shared memory. The 1024 threads per thread block are arranged as 32 threads along x and 32 threads along y, to achieve coalesced reads from global memory and to fit the number of banks in shared memory (32). Each thread starts by reading six values from global memory into shared memory ($96 \times 64/1024 = 6$). For a maximum filter size of 17×17 pixels, 80×48 valid filter responses can then be calculated from the 96×64 values in shared memory, since a halo of size 8 on all sides is required. All threads start by first calculating two filter responses, yielding 64×32 values. Half of the threads then calculate an additional three filter responses, giving a total of 48×32 filter responses. Finally, a quarter of the threads are used to calculate the filter responses for the last 16×16 pixels. The division of the 80×48 values into six blocks is illustrated in Figure 5.5. The first part of the code for non-separable 2D convolution using shared memory is given in Listing 5.2 and the second part is given in Listing 5.3. The device function that performs the 2D convolution is very similar to the kernel for texture-based convolution; interested readers are therefore referred to the repository.

If more than one filter is to be applied, e.g., four complex valued quadrature filters oriented along 0, 45, 90, and 135 degrees, all the filter responses can be calculated very efficiently by simply performing several multiplications and additions each time a pixel value has been loaded from shared memory to a register. This results in a better ratio between the number of memory accesses and floating point operations. By reducing the maximum filter size to 9×9, the number of valid filter responses increases to 88×56 since the halo size shrinks to 4. This will also result in a higher occupancy during the convolution. For the first case yielding 80×48 valid filter responses, the mean occupancy for the six blocks is $(32 \cdot 32 \cdot 2 + 32 \cdot 32 \cdot 2 + 32 \cdot 16 \cdot 2 + 32 \cdot 16 \cdot 2 + 16 \cdot 32 \cdot 2 + 16 \cdot 16 \cdot 2)/(6 \cdot 2048) = 62.5\%$, and for the second case yielding 88×56 valid filter responses, the mean occupancy increases to $(32 \cdot 32 \cdot 2 + 32 \cdot 32 \cdot 2 + 32 \cdot 24 \cdot 2 + 32 \cdot 24 \cdot 2 + 24 \cdot 32 \cdot 2 + 24 \cdot 24 \cdot 2)/(6 \cdot 2048)$ $= 80.2\%$.

The required number of thread blocks in the x- and y-directions are for the shared memory implementation *not* calculated by dividing the image width and height with the number of threads in each direction (32). The width and height should instead be divided by the number of valid filter responses generated in each

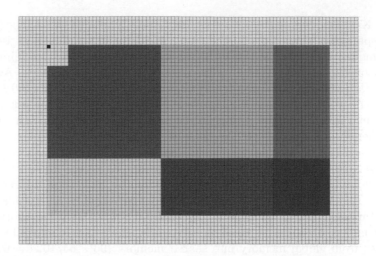

Figure 5.5. The grid represents 96×64 pixels in shared memory. As 32×32 threads are used per thread block, each thread needs to read six values from global memory into shared memory. The gray pixels represent the filter kernel and the black pixel represents where the current filter response is saved. A yellow halo needs to be loaded into shared memory to be able to calculate all the filter responses. In this case 80×48 valid filter responses are calculated, making it possible to apply at most a filter of size 17×17. The 80×48 filter responses are calculated as six runs, the first 2 consisting of 32×32 pixels (marked light red and light blue). Half of the threads calculate three additional filter responses in blocks of 32×16 or 16×32 pixels (marked green, dark blue, and dark red). A quarter of the threads calculates the filter response for a last block of 16×16 pixels (marked purple). If the halo is reduced from eight to four pixels, 88×56 valid filter responses can instead be calculated as two 32×32 blocks, one 24×32 block, two 32×24 blocks, and one 24×24 block. In addition to increasing the number of valid filter responses, such an implementation will also increase the mean occupancy during convolution from 62.5% to 80.2%. The only drawback is that the largest filter that can be applied drops from 17×17 to 9×9.

direction, since each thread block generates more than one valid filter response per thread. The calculation of the x- and y-indices inside the kernel also needs to be changed from the conventional

```
int x = blockIdx.x * blockDim.x + threadIdx.x;
int y = blockIdx.y * blockDim.y + threadIdx.y;
```

to

```
int x = blockIdx.x * VALID_RESPONSES_X + threadIdx.x;
int y = blockIdx.y * VALID_RESPONSES_Y + threadIdx.y;
```

```
#define HALO 8

__global__ void Convolution_2D_Shared(float* Filter_Response,
float* Image, int DATA_W, int DATA_H)
{
    int x = blockIdx.x * VALID_RESPONSES_X + threadIdx.x;
    int y = blockIdx.y * VALID_RESPONSES_Y + threadIdx.y;

    __shared__ float s_Image[64][96]; // y, x

    // Reset shared memory
    s_Image[threadIdx.y][threadIdx.x]           = 0.0f;
    s_Image[threadIdx.y][threadIdx.x + 32]      = 0.0f;
    s_Image[threadIdx.y][threadIdx.x + 64]      = 0.0f;
    s_Image[threadIdx.y + 32][threadIdx.x]      = 0.0f;
    s_Image[threadIdx.y + 32][threadIdx.x + 32] = 0.0f;
    s_Image[threadIdx.y + 32][threadIdx.x + 64] = 0.0f;

    // Read data into shared memory

    if ( ((x-HALO) >= 0) && ((x-HALO) < DATA_W)
      && ((y-HALO) >= 0) && ((y-HALO) < DATA_H) )
        s_Image[threadIdx.y][threadIdx.x] =
        Image[Get2DIndex(x-HALO,y-HALO,DATA_W)];

    if ( ((x+32-HALO) < DATA_W)
      && ((y-HALO) >= 0) && ((y-HALO) < DATA_H) )
        s_Image[threadIdx.y][threadIdx.x + 32] =
        Image[Get2DIndex(x+32-HALO,y-HALO,DATA_W)];

    if ( ((x+64-HALO) < DATA_W)
      && ((y-HALO) >= 0) && ((y-HALO) < DATA_H) )
        s_Image[threadIdx.y][threadIdx.x + 64] =
        Image[Get2DIndex(x+64-HALO,y-HALO,DATA_W)];

    if ( ((x-HALO) >= 0)
      && ((x-HALO) < DATA_W) && ((y+32-HALO) < DATA_H) )
        s_Image[threadIdx.y + 32][threadIdx.x] =
        Image[Get2DIndex(x-HALO,y+32-HALO,DATA_W)];

    if ( ((x+32-HALO) < DATA_W) && ((y+32-HALO) < DATA_H) )
        s_Image[threadIdx.y + 32][threadIdx.x + 32] =
        Image[Get2DIndex(x+32-HALO,y+32-HALO, DATA_W)];

    if ( ((x+64-HALO) < DATA_W) && ((y+32-HALO) < DATA_H) )
        s_Image[threadIdx.y + 32][threadIdx.x + 64] =
        Image[Get2DIndex(x+64-HALO,y+32-HALO,DATA_W)];

    __syncthreads();
```

Listing 5.2. Non-separable 2D convolution using shared memory. This listing represents the first part of the kernel, where data is loaded into shared memory. Each thread block consists of 32×32 threads, such that each thread has to read six values into shared memory (storing 96×64 values). The parameter HALO can be changed to control the size of the largest filter that can be applied (HALO*2 + 1). Before the actual convolution is started, synchronization of the threads is required to guarantee that all values have been loaded into shared memory.

```
if ( (x < DATA_W) && (y < DATA_H) )
  Filter_Response[Get2DIndex(x,y,DATA_W)] =
  Conv2D(s_Image,threadIdx.y+HALO,threadIdx.x+HALO);

if ( ((x + 32) < DATA_W) && (y < DATA_H) )
  Filter_Response[Get2DIndex(x+32,y,DATA_W)] =
  Conv2D(s_Image,threadIdx.y+HALO,threadIdx.x+32+HALO);

if (threadIdx.x < (32 - HALO*2))
{
  if ( ((x + 64) < DATA_W) && (y < DATA_H) )
    Filter_Response[Get2DIndex(x+64,y,DATA_W)] =
    Conv2D(s_Image,threadIdx.y+HALO,threadIdx.x+64+HALO);
}

if (threadIdx.y < (32 - HALO*2))
{
  if ( (x < DATA_W) && ((y + 32) < DATA_H) )
    Filter_Response[Get2DIndex(x,y+32,DATA_W)] =
    Conv2D(s_Image,threadIdx.y+32+HALO,threadIdx.x+HALO);
}

if (threadIdx.y < (32 - HALO*2))
{
  if ( ((x + 32) < DATA_W) && ((y + 32) < DATA_H) )
    Filter_Response[Get2DIndex(x+32,y+32,DATA_W)] =
    Conv2D(s_Image,threadIdx.y+32+HALO,threadIdx.x+32+HALO);
}

if ( (threadIdx.x < (32 - HALO*2)) &&
     (threadIdx.y < (32 - HALO*2)) )
{
  if ( ((x + 64) < DATA_W) && ((y + 32) < DATA_H) )
    Filter_Response[Get2DIndex(x+64,y+32,DATA_W)] =
    Conv2D(s_Image,threadIdx.y+32+HALO,threadIdx.x+64+HALO);
}
}
```

Listing 5.3. Non-separable 2D convolution using shared memory. This listing represents the second part of the kernel where the convolutions are performed, by calling a device function for each block of filter responses. For a filter size of 17×17, `HALO` is 8 and the first two blocks yield filter responses for 32×32 pixels, the third block yields 16×32 filter responses, the fourth and fifth blocks yield 32×16 filter responses and the sixth block yields the last 16×16 filter responses. The parameter `HALO` can easily be changed to optimize the code for different filter sizes. The code for the device function `Conv2D` is given in the repository.

5.6 Non-separable 3D Convolution

Three-dimensional convolution between a signal s and a filter f for position $[x, y, z]$ is defined as

$$(s * f)[x,y,z] = \sum_{f_x=-N/2}^{f_x=N/2} \sum_{f_y=-N/2}^{f_y=N/2} \sum_{f_z=-N/2}^{f_z=N/2} s[x - f_x, y - f_y, z - f_z] \cdot f[f_x, f_y, f_z].$$

This weighted summation can be easily implemented by using texture memory just as for 2D convolution. The differences between 3D and 2D are that an additional `for` loop is added and that a 3D texture is used instead of a 2D texture. The code will therefore not be given here (but is available in the github repository). Using shared memory for non-separable 3D convolution is more difficult, however. A natural extension of the 2D implementation would be, for example, to load $24 \times 16 \times 16$ voxels into shared memory. This would make it possible to calculate $16 \times 8 \times 8$ valid filter responses per thread block for a filter of size $9 \times 9 \times 9$. But the optimal division of the 1024 threads per thread block along x, y, and z is not obvious. One solution is to use $24 \times 16 \times 2$ threads per thread block, giving a total of 1536 threads per MP and 75% occupancy. However, only $16 \times 8 \times 2$ threads per thread block will be active during the actual convolution, giving a low occupancy of 25%. To use 24 threads along x will also result in shared memory bank conflicts, as there are 32 banks. To avoid these conflicts, one can instead load $32 \times 16 \times 12$ values into shared memory and, for example, use thread blocks of size $32 \times 16 \times 2$. The number of valid filter responses drops to $24 \times 8 \times 4 = 768$ per thread block (compared to 1024 for the first case) while the occupancy during convolution will increase to 37.5%. It is not obvious how the different compromises will affect the total runtime, making it necessary to actually make all the different implementations and test them. We will leave 3D convolution for now and instead move on to 4D convolution.

5.7   Non-separable 4D Convolution

There are no 4D textures in the CUDA programming language, so a simple texture implementation is impossible for non-separable 4D convolution. Possible solutions are to use one huge 1D texture or several 2D or 3D textures. One-dimensional textures can speed up reads that are local in the first dimension (e.g., x), but not reads that are local in the other dimensions (y, z, t). A solution involving many 2D or 3D textures would be rather hard to implement, as one cannot use pointers for texture objects. The use of shared memory is even more complicated than for 3D convolution, and here it becomes obvious that it is impossible to continue on the same path. The shared memory cannot even store $11 \times 11 \times 11 \times 11$ values required for a filter of size $11 \times 11 \times 11 \times 11$.

Let us take a step back and think about what a 4D convolution involves. To perform non-separable 4D convolution requires eight `for` loops, four to loop through all the filter coefficients and four to loop through all voxels and time points. To do all the `for` loops on the GPU is not necessarily optimal. A better way to divide the `for` loops is to do four on the CPU and four on the GPU, such that the four loops on the GPU correspond to a non-separable 2D convolution. Thus, four loops on the CPU are used to call the 2D convolution for two image dimensions and two filter dimensions (e.g., z and t). During each call to the 2D

```
// Loop over time points in data
for (int t = 0; t < DATA_T; t++)
{
  // Reset filter response for current volume
  cudaMemset(d_FR, 0, DATA_W * DATA_H * DATA_D * sizeof(float));

  // Loop over time points in filter
  for (int tt = FILTER_T - 1; tt >= 0; tt--)
  {
    // Loop over slices in filter
    for (int zz = FILTER_D - 1; zz >= 0; zz--)
    {
      // Copy current filter coefficients to constant memory
      CopyFilterCoefficients(zz,tt);

      // Perform 2D convolution and
      // accumulate the filter responses inside the kernel,
      // launch kernel for several slices simultaneously
      Convolution_2D_Shared<<<dG, dB>>>(d_FR);
    }
  }
}
```

Listing 5.4. Host code for non-separable 4D convolution, by performing non-separable 2D convolution on the GPU and accumulating the filter responses inside the kernel (`dG` stands for `dimGrid`, `dB` stands for `dimBlock`, and `FR` stands for filter responses). The CPU takes care of three `for` loops and the GPU five `for` loops.

convolution kernel, the filter responses are accumulated inside the kernel. Before each 2D convolution is started, the corresponding 2D values of the 4D filter are copied to constant memory.

A small problem remains; for a 4D dataset of size $128 \times 128 \times 128 \times 128$, the 2D convolution will be applied to images of size 128×128 pixels. If 80×48 valid filter responses are calculated per thread block, only five thread blocks will be launched. The Nvidia GTX 680 has eight MPs and each MP can concurrently handle two thread blocks with 1024 threads each. At least 16 thread blocks are thus required to achieve full occupancy. To solve this problem one can launch the 2D convolution for all slices simultaneously, by using 3D thread blocks, to increase the number of thread blocks and thereby the occupancy. This removes one loop on the CPU, such that three loops are taken care of by the CPU and five by the GPU. As some of the slices in the filter response will be invalid due to border effects, some additional time can be saved by only performing the convolution for the valid slices. The host code for non-separable 4D convolution is given in Listing 5.4 and the complete code is available in the github repository.

5.8 Non-separable 3D Convolution, Revisited

Now that an implementation for non-separable 4D convolution has been provided, 3D convolution is very easy. The host code is given in Listing 5.5 and

```
// Loop over slices in filter
for (int zz = FILTER_D - 1; zz >= 0; zz--)
{
  // Copy current filter coefficients to constant memory
  CopyFilterCoefficients(zz);

  // Perform 2D convolution and
  // accumulate the filter responses inside the kernel,
  // launch kernel for several slices simultaneously
  Convolution_2D_Shared<<<dG, dB>>>(d_FR);
}
```

Listing 5.5. Host code for non-separable 3D convolution, by performing non-separable 2D convolution on the GPU and accumulating the filter responses inside the kernel (`dG` stands for `dimGrid`, `dB` stands for `dimBlock`, and `FR` stands for filter responses). Just as for the non-separable 4D convolution, the 2D convolution is launched for all slices at the same time to increase the occupancy.

the complete code is available in the repository. The only difference compared to 4D convolution is that the CPU for 4D also loops over time points (for data and filters). Just as for 4D convolution, the 2D convolution is launched for all slices at the same time to increase the occupancy.

5.9 Performance

We will now list some performance measures for our implementations. All the testing has been done with an Nvidia GTX 680 graphics card with 4 GB of memory.

5.9.1 Performance, 2D Filtering

Performance estimates for non-separable 2D filtering are given in Figures 5.6–5.7. Time for transferring the data to and from the GPU is not included. The first plot is for a fixed image size of 2048×2048 pixels and filter sizes ranging from 3×3 to 17×17. The second and third plots are for fixed filter sizes of 9×9 and 17×17, respectively. The image sizes for these plots range from 128×128 to 4096×4096 in steps of 128 pixels. All plots contain the processing time for spatial convolution using texture memory (with and without loop unrolling), spatial convolution using shared memory (with and without loop unrolling), and FFT-based filtering using the CUFFT library (involving two forward FFT's, complex valued multiplication and one inverse FFT).

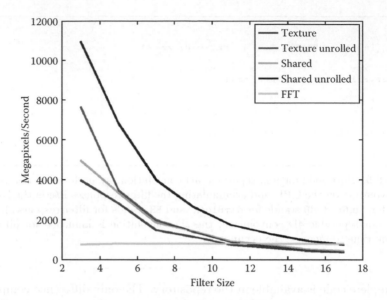

Figure 5.6. Performance, measured in megapixels per second, for the different implementations of 2D filtering, for an image of size 2048×2048 and filter sizes ranging from 3×3 to 17×17. The processing time for FFT-based filtering is independent of the filter size and is the fastest approach for non-separable filters larger than 17×17.

5.9.2   Performance, 3D Filtering

Performance estimates for non-separable 3D filtering are given in Figures 5.8–5.9. Again, time for transferring the data to and from the GPU is not included. The first plot is for a fixed volume size of $256 \times 256 \times 256$ voxels and filter sizes ranging from $3 \times 3 \times 3$ to $17 \times 17 \times 17$. The second and third plots are for fixed filter sizes of $7 \times 7 \times 7$ and $13 \times 13 \times 13$, respectively. The volume sizes for these plots range from $64 \times 64 \times 64$ to $512 \times 512 \times 512$ in steps of 32 voxels. All plots contain the processing time for spatial convolution using texture memory (with and without loop unrolling), spatial convolution using shared memory (with and without loop unrolling), and FFT-based filtering using the CUFFT library (involving two forward FFT's, complex-valued multiplication, and one inverse FFT).

5.9.3   Performance, 4D Filtering

Performance estimates for non-separable 4D filtering are given in Figures 5.10–5.11. Again, time for transferring the data to and from the GPU is not included. The first plot is for a fixed data size of $128 \times 128 \times 128 \times 32$ elements and filter sizes ranging from $3 \times 3 \times 3 \times 3$ to $17 \times 17 \times 17 \times 17$. The second and third plots

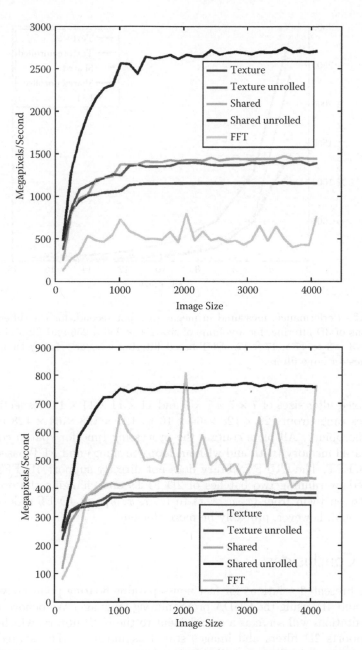

Figure 5.7. Performance, measured in megapixels per second, for the different implementations of 2D filtering and image sizes ranging from 128×128 to 4096×4096. Note the performance spikes for the FFT-based filtering for image sizes that are a power of 2. The results for a 9×9 filter are shown in the upper plot and the results for a 17×17 filter in the lower plot.

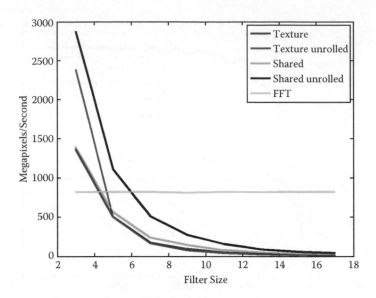

Figure 5.8. Performance, measured in megavoxels per second, for the different implementations of 3D filtering, for a volume of size $256 \times 256 \times 256$ and filter sizes ranging from $3 \times 3 \times 3$ to $17 \times 17 \times 17$. FFT-based filtering is clearly faster than the other approaches for large filters.

are for fixed filter sizes of $7 \times 7 \times 7 \times 7$ and $11 \times 11 \times 11 \times 11$, respectively. The data sizes range from $128 \times 128 \times 64 \times 16$ to $128 \times 128 \times 64 \times 128$ in steps of eight time points. All plots contain the processing time for spatial convolution using shared memory (with and without loop unrolling) and FFT-based filtering using CUFFT. The CUFFT library does not directly support 4D FFTs; it was performed by running two batches of 2D FFTs and changing the order of the data between them from (x, y, z, t) to (z, t, x, y). A 4D FFT developed by Nvidia would, however, probably be more efficient.

5.10   Conclusions

We have presented solutions for fast non-separable floating point convolution in 2D, 3D, and 4D, using the CUDA programming language. We believe that these implementations will serve as a complement to the NPP library, which currently only supports 2D filters and images stored as integers. The shared memory implementation with loop unrolling is approximately twice as fast as the simple texture memory implementation, which is similar to results obtained by Nvidia for separable 2D convolution [Podlozhnyuk 07]. For 3D and 4D data it might seem strange to use convolution instead of an FFT, but the convolution approach

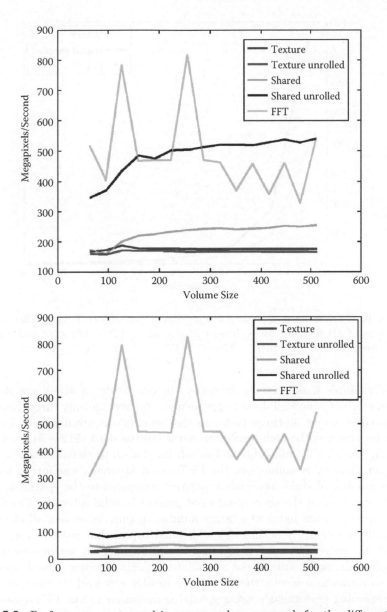

Figure 5.9. Performance, measured in megavoxels per second, for the different implementations of 3D filtering and volume sizes ranging from $64 \times 64 \times 64$ to $512 \times 512 \times 512$. FFT-based filtering is the fastest approach for large filters. The texture-based approach is actually slower for 3D with loop unrolling, which is explained by an increase in the number of registers used. The results for a $7 \times 7 \times 7$ filter are shown in the upper plot the results for a $13 \times 13 \times 13$ filter in the lower plot.

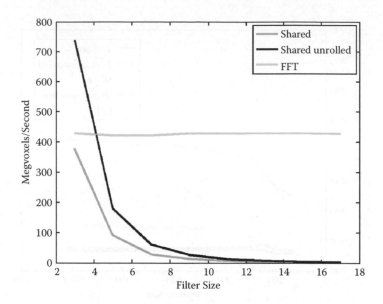

Figure 5.10. Performance, measured in megavoxels per second, for the different implementations of 4D filtering, for a dataset of size $128 \times 128 \times 128 \times 32$ and filter sizes ranging from $3 \times 3 \times 3 \times 3$ to $17 \times 17 \times 17 \times 17$.

can for example handle larger datasets. In our work on 4D image denoising [Eklund et al. 11], the FFT-based approach was on average only three times faster (compared to about 30 times faster in the benchmarks given here). The main reason for this was the high-resolution nature of the data ($512 \times 512 \times 445 \times 20$ elements), making it impossible to load all the data into global memory. Due to its higher memory consumption, the FFT-based approach was forced to load a smaller number of slices into global memory compared to the spatial approach. As only a subset of the slices (and time points) is valid after the filtering, the FFT-based approach required a larger number of runs to process all the slices.

Finally, we close by noting two additional topics that readers may wish to consider for more advanced study. First, applications in which several filters are applied simultaneously to the same data (e.g, six complex valued quadrature filters to estimate a local structure tensor in 3D) can lead to different conclusions regarding performance using spatial convolution versus FFT-based filtering. Second, filter networks can be used to speed up spatial convolution by combining the result of many small filter kernels, resulting in a proportionally higher gain for 3D and 4D than for 2D convolution [Andersson et al. 99, Svensson et al. 05]. All the code for this chapter is available under GNU GPL 3 at https://github.com/wanderine/NonSeparableFilteringCUDA.

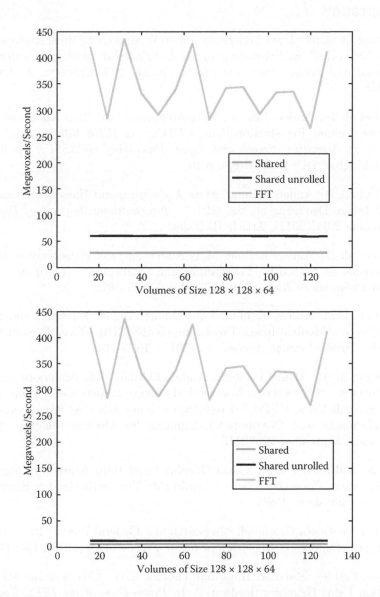

Figure 5.11. Performance, measured in megavoxels per second, for the different implementations of 4D filtering and data sizes ranging from $128 \times 128 \times 64 \times 16$ to $128 \times 128 \times 64 \times 128$. The FFT-based approach clearly outperforms the convolution approaches. The results for a $7 \times 7 \times 7 \times 7$ filter are shown in the upper plot and the results for a $11 \times 11 \times 11 \times 11$ filter in the lower plot.

Bibliography

[Andersson et al. 99] Mats Andersson, Johan Wiklund, and Hans Knutsson. "Filter Networks." In *Proceedings of the IASTED International Conference on Signal and Image Processing (SIP)*, pp. 213–217. Calgary: ACTA Press, 1999.

[Eklund et al. 10] Anders Eklund, Mats Andersson, and Hans Knutsson. "Phase Based Volume Registration Using CUDA." In *IEEE International Conference on Acoustics, Speech and Signal Processing (ICASSP)*, pp. 658–661. Washington, DC: IEEE Press, 2010.

[Eklund et al. 11] Anders Eklund, Mats Andersson, and Hans Knutsson. "True 4D Image Denoising on the GPU." *International Journal of Biomedical Imaging* 2011 (2011), Article ID 952819.

[Eklund et al. 12] Anders Eklund, Mats Andersson, and Hans Knutsson. "fMRI Analysis on the GPU—Possibilities and Challenges." *Computer Methods and Programs in Biomedicine* 105 (2012), 145–161.

[Eklund et al. 13] Anders Eklund, Paul Dufort, Daniel Forsberg, and Stephen LaConte. "Medical Image Processing on the GPU—Past, Present and Future." *Medical Image Analysis* 17 (2013), 1073–1094.

[Forsberg et al. 11] Daniel Forsberg, Anders Eklund, Mats Andersson, and Hans Knutsson. "Phase-Based Non-rigid 3D Image Registration—From Minutes to Seconds Using CUDA." Presentation, Joint MICCAI Workshop on High Performance and Distributed Computing for Medical Imaging, Toronto, Canada, September 22, 2011.

[Granlund and Knutsson 95] Gösta Granlund and Hans Knutsson. *Signal Processing for Computer Vision*. Dordrecht, The Netherlands: Kluwer Academic Publishers, 1995.

[Granlund 78] Gösta Granlund. "In Search of a General Picture Processing Operator." *Computer Graphics and Image Processing* 8 (1978), 155–173.

[Hopf and Ertl 99] Matthias Hopf and Thomas Ertl. "Accelerating 3D Convolution Using Graphics Hardware." In *Proceedings of the IEEE Conference on Visualization*, pp. 471–475. Los Alamitos, CA: IEEE Computer Society, 1999.

[Jain and Farrokhnia 91] Anil Jain and Farshid Farrokhnia. "Unsupervised Texture Segmentation Using Gabor Filters." *Pattern Recognition* 24 (1991), 1167–1186.

[James 01] Greg James. "Operations for Hardware-Accelerated Procedural Texture Animation." In *Game Programming Gems 2*, edited by Mark DeLoura, pp. 497–509. Cambridge, MA: Charles River Media, 2001.

[Knutsson and Andersson 05] Hans Knutsson and Mats Andersson. "Morphons: Segmentation Using Elastic Canvas and Paint on Priors." In *IEEE International Conference on Image Processing (ICIP)*, pp. 1226–1229. Los Alamitos, CA: IEEE Press, 2005.

[Knutsson et al. 83] Hans Knutsson, Roland Wilson, and Gösta Granlund. "Anisotropic Non-stationary Image Estimation and Its Applications—Part I: Restoration of Noisy Images." *IEEE Transactions on Communications* 31 (1983), 388–397.

[Knutsson et al. 99] Hans Knutsson, Mats Andersson, and Johan Wiklund. "Advanced Filter Design." In *SCIA '99: Proceedings of the 11th Scandinavian Conference on Image Analysis*, 1, 1, pp. 185–193. Kangerlussuaq, Greenland: IAPR, 1999.

[Knutsson et al. 11] Hans Knutsson, Carl-Fredrik Westin, and Mats Andersson. "Representing Local Structure Using Tensors II." In *Proceedings of the Scandinavian Conference on Image Analysis (SCIA)*, Lecture Notes in Computer Science, 6688, pp. 545–556. Berlin: Springer, 2011.

[Knutsson 89] Hans Knutsson. "Representing Local Structure Using Tensors." In *SCIA '89: Proceedings of the 6th Scandinavian Conference on Image Analysis*, pp. 244–251. Oulu, Finland: IAPR, 1989.

[Läthen et al. 10] Gunnar Läthen, Jimmy Jonasson, and Magnus Borga. "Blood Vessel Segmentation Using Multi-scale Quadrature Filtering." *Pattern Recognition Letters* 31 (2010), 762–767.

[Owens et al. 07] John Owens, David Luebke, Naga Govindaraju, Mark Harris, Jens Kruger, Aaron Lefohn, and Timothy Purcell. "A Survey of General-Purpose Computation on Graphics Hardware." *Computer Graphics Forum* 26 (2007), 80–113.

[Podlozhnyuk 07] Victor Podlozhnyuk. "Image Convolution with CUDA." White paper, Nvidia, 2007.

[Rost 96] Randi Rost. "Using OpenGL for Imaging." *SPIE Medical Imaging, Image Display Conference* 2707 (1996), 473–484.

[Sanders and Kandrot 11] Jason Sanders and Edward Kandrot. *CUDA by Example: An Introduction to General-Purpose GPU Programming*. Upper Saddle River, NJ: Addison-Wesley, 2011.

[Svensson et al. 05] Björn Svensson, Mats Andersson, and Hans Knutsson. "Filter Networks for Efficient Estimation of Local 3D Structure." In *IEEE International Conference on Image Processing (ICIP)*, pp. 573–576. Los Alamitos, CA: IEEE Computer Society, 2005.

[Tomasi and Manduchi 98] Carlo Tomasi and Roberto Manduchi. "Bilateral Filtering for Gray and Color Images." In *Proceedings International Conference on Computer Vision*, pp. 839–846. Los Alamitos, CA: IEEE Computer Society, 1998.

[Westin et al. 01] Carl-Fredrik Westin, Lars Wigström, Tomas Loock, Lars Sjöqvist, Ron Kikinis, and Hans Knutsson. "Three-Dimensional Adaptive Filtering in Magnetic Resonance Angiography." *Journal of Magnetic Resonance Imaging* 14 (2001), 63–71.

About the Editors

Marius Bjørge is a Staff Engineer at ARM's office in Trondheim, Norway. He currently looks at ways of enabling advanced real-time graphics on current and future mobile GPU technology. Previously he worked in the ARM Mali OpenGL ES driver team and before that he was a graphics programmer at Funcom Games, Canada.

Wessam Bahnassi is a software engineer and an architect (that is, for buildings not software). This combination drives Wessam's passion for 3D engine design. He has written and dealt with a variety of engines throughout a decade of game development. Currently, he is leading the programming effort at IN—Framez Technology, the indie game company he cofounded with his brother Homam. Their first game (*Hyper Void*) is a live shaders showcase (some of which have been featured previous *GPU Pro* volumes), and it is in the final development stages.

Carsten Dachsbacher is a full professor at the Karlsruhe Institute of Technology. Prior to joining KIT, he was an assistant professor at the Visualization Research Center (VISUS) of the University of Stuttgart, Germany, and post-doctoral fellow at REVES/INRIA Sophia-Antipolis, France. He received a MS in computer science from the University of Erlangen-Nuremberg, Germany, in 2002 and a PhD in computer science in 2006. His research focuses on real-time computer graphics, interactive global illumination, and perceptual rendering, on which he has published several articles at various conferences, including SIGGRAPH, I3D, EG, and EGSR. He has been a tutorial speaker at Eurographics, SIGGRAPH, and the Game Developers Conference and a reviewer for various conferences and journals.

Wolfgang Engel is the CEO of Confetti (www.conffx.com), a think tank for advanced real-time graphics for the game and movie industry. Previously he worked for more than four years in Rockstar's core technology group as the lead graphics programmer. His game credits can be found at http://www.mobygames.com/developer/sheet/view/developerId,158706/. He is the editor of the *ShaderX* and *GPU Pro* book series, the author of many articles, and a regular speaker at computer graphics conferences worldwide. He is also a DirectX MVP (since 2006), teaches at UCSD, and is active in several advisory boards throughout the industry. You can find him on twitter at @wolfgangengel.

Christopher Oat is the Associate Technical Director at Rockstar New England where he works on real-time rendering techniques used in Rockstar's latest games. Previously, he was the Demo Team Lead for AMD's Game Computing Applications Group. Christopher has published his work in various books and journals and has presented at graphics and game developer conferences worldwide. Many of the projects that he has worked on can be found on his website: www.chrisoat.com.

Michal Valient leads the technology team at Guerrilla in Amsterdam. He spends his time working on the core engine technology powering the highly acclaimed *Killzone* games on PS3 and PS4 as well as some yet unannounced projects. Previously he worked as a programmer and a lead at Caligari where he developed the shader-based real-time rendering engine for Caligari trueSpace7. His interests include many aspects of light transfer, shadows, and parallel processing in general. He believes in sharing the knowledge, and he gave talks at GDC and SIGGRAPH and wrote graphics papers published in *ShaderX* books and conference journals.

About the Contributors

Rémi Arnaud has worked on some of the most advanced real-time graphics systems. First at Thomson Training & Simulation, he designed a real-time visual system (Space Magic) for training purposes. Then at Silicon Graphics, he was part of the famous Iris Performer team working on the largest Infinite Reality systems. Then at Intrinsic Graphics, he worked on the Sony GsCube prototype system, which led to working at Sony Computer Entertainment R&D on the Playstation 3 SDK. He was at Intel working on gaming technology for the Larrabee and now is at AMD where CPUs and GPUs are finally working closely together thanks to him. He has been a witness of 3D technology making its way from multi-million-dollar systems to mainstream over the years. He is convinced 3D can be tamed and, once domesticated, make its way out of the niche into everyone's lives for the better.

Serge Bernier is a lead graphics engineer at Eidos Montreal, where his main focus is to work on rendering algorithms and graphics architecture. He has been involved with graphics-related optimizations for various projects on Playstation 3 since the platform was launched. Passionate about graphics innovations, what he loves the most is the fast evolving pace of specialization, where art and engineering meet to create great-looking worlds.

Bartosz Chodorowski started his programming journey in the mid-1990s when he played around with Schneider CPC6128, a German clone of Amstrad CPC. Then he switched to PCs and has been programming mostly in Pascal, Delphi, C, C++, and Perl. He graduated from Wrocław University of Technology with a master's degree in computer science in 2012. He is a Linux and open source enthusiast, a gamer, and, above everything, a game programmer. He was Lead Programmer at Madman Theory Games for over a year, working on a hack-and-slash mobile/PC game. Currently, He works as Engine Programmer at Flying Wild Hog. He also co-runs a game and middleware company, Blossom Games.

Ole Ciliox is an experienced freelance graphics programmer. Previously he worked on various technology at Unity and before that at IO Interactive.

Patrick Cozzi is coauthor of *3D Engine Design for Virtual Globes* (2011) and coeditor of *OpenGL Insights* (2012). At Analytical Graphics, Inc., he leads the graphics development of Cesium, a WebGL virtual globe. He teaches "GPU Programming and Architecture" at the University of Pennsylvania, where he received a master's degree in computer science. At Khronos, he is part of the COLLADA working group.

Michal Drobot is a game industry veteran specializing in rendering technology. Currently he shapes the future of 3D rendering at Ubisoft Montreal. Previously he worked at Guerrilla Games, designing and optimizing the renderer for the Playstation 4 launch title *Killzone: Shadow Fall*. Dancing pixels make him happy.

Paul Dufort earned BSc and MSc degrees from the Department of Physics at the University of Toronto and a PhD in computational biophysics from the U of T's Institute of Medical Science in 2000. He served as a computer graphics consultant to the U of T Institute for Aerospace Studies' Flight Simulation Laboratory from 1996 to 2009 and was a founding partner and Director of Research and Development at medical imaging start-up Tomographix IP from 2000 to 2009, before joining the University Health Network's Joint Department of Medical Imaging in Toronto as a Computational Imaging Scientist in 2009. He presently specializes in the development and application of high-performance image processing and computer vision algorithms to problems in medical imaging, with an emphasis on the application of machine learning algorithms and graphical models to problems in structural and functional neuroimaging.

Jonathan Dupuy is a French PhD student working on high-quality rendering under the supervision of Victor Ostromoukhov and Jean-Claude Iehl from the Université Claude Bernard de Lyon I and Pierre Poulin from the Université de Montréal. His PhD focuses on deriving and exploiting linearly filterable object representations that can be rendered at constant cost with very little memory overhead and benefit from GPU acceleration. In contrast to sampling-based methods whose computational costs increase proportionally to sub-pixel detail, this approach promises images of comparable quality at much higher frame rates.

Vladimir Egorov is a lead programmer at Mail.Ru Games LLC. He currently works on the *Skyforge* MMORPG. Before that, he had shipped *Allods Online*, *Heroes of Might and Magic 5*, *Blitzkrieg 2*, and other titles. He is now responsible for the entire client application architecture, from the auto-update system to the rendering engine.

Anders Eklund earned a MSc degree in applied physics and electrical engineering and a PhD degree in medical informatics from Linköping University, Sweden, and is currently a postdoctoral associate at Virginia Tech. His research interests include using functional magnetic resonance imaging (fMRI) to study brain activity, medical imaging, machine learning, and non-parametric statistics. He especially likes to combine these research areas with high-performance computing.

Johan Gronqvist has worked on OpenCL for ARM Mali GPUs over the last three years—writing benchmarks, analysing performance, teaching compute optimization, and optimizing applications for customers as well as for internal use. He is now working on the ARM Mali compiler, focusing on optimizations for GPU compute. From his pre-ARM history he has a PhD in physics, and his GPU interest revolves around understanding how to get more compute performance out of the devices.

Thorsten Grosch is a junior professor of computational visualistics at the University of Magdeburg, Germany. Prior to this appointment he worked as a postdoctoral fellow at MPI Informatik in Saarbruecken. Thorsten received his PhD at the University of Koblenz-Landau; his main research interest is in both the areas of physically accurate and real-time global illumination.

Martin Guay is a PhD student at INRIA Grenoble where he is conducting research on computer animation. His work includes techniques for physically based simulation as well as character control. Before graduate school, Martin worked as a graphics programmer at the game studio Cyanide in Montreal.

Tobias Günther received his master's degree in computer science at the University of Magdeburg in 2013. He is currently a scientific researcher at the Department of Simulation and Graphics in Magdeburg, working on his PhD. His research interests include scientific visualization, real-time rendering, and physically-based global illumination.

Dongsoo Han works as a software engineer and researcher in AMD's GPU Tech Initiatives Group. At AMD, he focuses on developing physics simulations such as rigid body, cloth, hair, and grass using GPU acceleration for real-time applications. His hair simulation technique is a part of TressFX and has been used for recent *Tomb Raider* game and *Ruby* demo. It became the first playable hair simulation in video games. His research focuses on parallelizing physics simulation algorithms in GPGPU such as a global constraint solver and collision response. He earned his master's degree in computer science at University of Pennsylvania where he focused on various fluid simulation methods.

Takahiro Harada is a researcher in AMD's office of the CTO, where he is exploring the possibility of GPU computing. Currently he is spending most of his time on research and development of physics simulation and rendering algorithms. Before joining AMD, he engaged in research and development on real-time physics simulation on PC and game consoles at Havok. Before coming to industry, he was in academics as an assistant professor at the University of Tokyo, where he also earned his PhD in engineering.

Samuel Hornus is a researcher at Inria in Nancy, France. He is interested in geometric problems that arise in computer graphics.

Jean-Claude Iehl is an associate professor at the LIRIS laboratory of the Université Claude Bernard de Lyon I. He holds a PhD and MSc from the Université de Saint-Etienne, both in computer science. His research interests are focused on efficiently rendering complex scenes using graphics hardware and off-line Monte Carlo methods.

James L. Jones graduated with a degree in computer science from Cardiff University and works on real-time graphics demos in the demo team at Imagination Technologies. He is currently focused on physically based rendering techniques for modern embedded graphics platforms and research for demos with Imagination's real-time ray-tracing technology.

Krzysztof Kluczek Krzysztof got his Masters degree in Computer Science at Gdansk University of Technology. Then, having worked for 5 years at Intel as a Graphics Software Engineer he set off to become a self-employed indie game developer. He is also currently pursuing his PhD degree at Gdansk University of Technology and doing graphics research. In his free time he is enjoying learning new technologies, making games, being a part of gamedev.pl community and Polish Demoscene.

Jason Lacroix has been involved in the games industry since 2000 and has worked for a wide range of companies including Artificial Mind and Movement (now bEhavior Interactive), Electronic Arts, Factor 5, and Crystal Dynamics. He has spent the last 9 years working on low level rendering code and shader programming for a variety of systems, including PC, Xbox/360, PS2/PS3, and Game-Cube/Wii. He is currently employed at Crystal Dynamics where he heads the rendering efforts for the Tomb Raider team.

Ramses Ladlani is lead engine programmer at Fishing Cactus, the video game company he co-founded in 2008 with three former colleagues from 10tacle Studios Belgium (a.k.a. Elsewhere Entertainment). When he is not working on the next feature of Mojito, Fishing Cactus's in-house cross-platform engine, he can be found playing rugby or learning his new role as a father. He received his master's degree in computer engineering from Université Libre de Bruxelles.

Anass Lasram received his PhD in computer science from INRIA in 2012 then joined Advanced Micro Devices, Inc. (AMD), where he develops software to interact with future GPUs. He is interested in hardware-accelerated rendering and animation.

Sylvain Lefebvre is a researcher at INRIA, France. He completed his PhD in 2004, on the topic of texturing and procedural texture generation using GPUs. He joined Microsoft Research (Redmond, WA) as a postdoctoral researcher in 2005. In 2006 he was recruited by INRIA as a permanent researcher. He is currently a member of the team ALICE in the Nancy Grand-Est INRIA center. His main research focuses are in procedural content generation—often starting from examples—end-user content manipulation, and compact GPU-friendly data structures for interactive applications, games, and 3D printing.

Anton Lokhmotov is the lead engineer responsible for designing, implementing, and tuning production (OpenCL, RenderScript) and research (EU-funded project CARP) compilers for the ARM Mali GPUs. Prior to joining ARM, he worked as a post-doctoral research associate at Imperial College London. His research interest span programming languages and tools, performance evaluation, and applications. He obtained an MSc in applied mathematics and physics from the Moscow Institute for Physics and Technology in 2004 and a PhD in computer science from the University of Cambridge in 2008.

Sergey Makeev is the technical director at Mail.Ru Games LLC, where he is currently working on the next-generation MMORPG *Skyforge*. One of his main work duties is to design and develop a proprietary game engine to reach maximum graphics quality on a wide variety of PC configurations. Before joining Mail.Ru Games LLC, he worked on several console games (Xbox 360, Xbox, PS3) at 1C Games and Akella. He also worked as a consultant for a variety of Russian game-development companies.

Timothy Martin works as a graphics programmer at Confetti Inc.

Gustavo Nunes is a Lead Tools/Pipeline Software Development Engineer in Test at Microsoft Turn 10 Studios. He received his BSc in computer engineering and MSc in computer graphics from Pontifícia Universidade Católica do Rio de Janeiro, Brazil. He has several articles published in the computer graphics field. He is passionate about games, computer graphics techniques, and developing tools to test game content in a smart and automated way. Gustavo was part of the teams that shipped Microsoft Office 2013, Xbox One, and *Forza Motorsport 5*.

David Pangerl is the CEO of Actalogic, where he is working as a lead researcher and engine architecture designer. He has been involved in computer graphics and engine research for over a decade.

Tony Parisi is an entrepreneur and career CTO/architect. He has developed international standards and protocols, created noteworthy software products, and started and sold technology companies. He may be best known for his work as a pioneer of 3D standards for the web. He co-created VRML and X3D, ISO standards for networked 3D graphics that were awesome but a bit ahead of their time. He is currently a partner in a stealth online gaming startup and has a consulting practice developing social games, virtual worlds, and location-based services for San Francisco Bay Area clients.

Emil Persson is the head of research at Avalanche Studios, where he is conducting forward-looking research, with the aim to be relevant and practical for game development, as well as setting the future direction for the Avalanche Engine. Previously, he was an ISV engineer in the Developer Relations team at ATI/AMD. He assisted tier-one game developers with the latest rendering techniques, identifying performance problems, and applying optimizations. He also made major contributions to SDK samples and technical papers. He also runs the website http://www.humus.name, where he blogs about graphics technology and posts demo applications and photographic skyboxes.

Pierre Poulin is a full professor in the Computer Science and Operations Research department of the Université de Montréal. He holds a PhD from the University of British Columbia and a MSc from the University of Toronto, both in computer science. He is associate editor for the journals *Computer Graphics Forum* and *Computer Animation and Virtual Worlds*; has been program co-chair of CASA 2014, Eurographics 2013, CGI 2011, EG Workshop on Natural Phenomena 2005, and GI 2000; and has served on program committees of more than 50 international conferences. His research interests cover a wide range of topics, including image synthesis, image-based modeling, procedural modeling, natural phenomena, scientific visualization, and computer animation.

David C. Schedl received his master's degree in the program of Interactive Media at the University of Applied Sciences Upper Austria Campus Hagenberg in 2011. He worked as a scientific researcher at the Institute of Computer Graphics and Algorithms at the Vienna University of Technology until 2012. He is currently a project assistant at the Institute of Computer Graphics at the Johannes Kepler University Linz. His research interests include real-time rendering, image processing, and light fields.

João Raza is a Program Manager at Microsoft's 343 Industries, where he works in the services cloud compute systems. Previously he was in the Windows Phone division, where he helped ship the SDK for game developers. An avid gamer, he has worked in the game industry for 5+ years. He holds a bachelor of computer science from Universidade Federal de São Carlos (UFSCar). He runs the blog www.versus-software.com, where he writes about his main interests in graphics, networking, and game design.

Hauke Rehfeld received his diploma in computational visualistics (computer science) at the University of Koblenz-Landau in 2011. He is currently a scientific researcher with the computer graphics group at Karlsruhe Institute of Technology, working on his PhD. His research interests include real-time rendering, light transport, visibility, ray tracing, GPU computing, and game design.

Fabrice Robinet works for MontageJS on seamlessly integrating 3D content on the web. He is also the COLLADA Working Group Chair at Khronos and lead for glTF (graphics library transmission format). Prior to joining the MontageJS team, he worked as an engineer at Apple where he co-created the Scene Kit framework.

Kai Rohmer works as a scientific researcher at the Department of Simulation and Graphics at the University of Magdeburg, Germany. His research interests include physically based real-time rendering as well as augmented reality on mobile devices. He received his MSc in computer science with distinction in 2012.

Peter Sikachev graduated from Lomonosov Moscow State University in 2009, majoring in applied mathematics and computer science. He started his career in academia, defending his thesis in gemstone rendering. After graduation, he moved to Vienna University of Technology, changing his research interests to scientific visualization. In 2011 he decided to switch to game development and joined Mail.Ru Games as a graphics programmer. He contributed to a range of rendering features of the *Skyforge* next-generation MMORPG. In 2013 he moved to Eidos Montreal as a research-and-development graphics programmer, finding a perfect balance between pure research and pure industry. As well as looking at emerging technologies and creating prototypes, he works closely with the game teams, contributing to the rendering engines of *Thief* and *Deus Ex: Universe*. He is a principal author of four publications in peer-reviewed international conference proceedings.

Ashley Vaughan Smith is an Applications Engineer at Imagination Technologies, developing and optimizing 3D graphical demos for PowerVR GPUs. Having previously achieved a BSc in computer games programming from the University of Derby and worked in the games industry on Xbox 360 and PS3 games, he now enjoys investigating new, up-coming technologies and graphical techniques.

Stacy Smith is technical lead of the Developer Education team and an engineer within the Demo Team at ARM. This dual role allows her to teach the effects and techniques implemented in the internal graphical demos seen on Mali platforms.

Wojciech Sterna has been an avid programmer since 2002. He started with simple programs made in Delphi but quickly moved towards C++, games, and graphics programming. From that time on, he has continuously (co-)worked (mostly) on private game projects. In 2011 he graduated with a Bachelor's degree in computer science from Wrocław University of Technology, writing a thesis on software rendering using CUDA. This led him to a three-month internship as a DevTech Engineer Intern at NVIDIA London's office. He had a short stint in Sweden, studying computer graphics for six months. Since that time he has worked professionally mostly on engine/rendering development at Madman Theory Games in Wrocław and most recently at Flying Wild Hog in Warsaw. He also co-runs a game and middleware company, Blossom Games.

Nicolas Thibieroz has spent all of his professional life working in developer relations for graphics hardware companies. He taught himself programming from an early age as a result of his fascination for the first wave of "real-time" 3D games such as *Ultima Underworld*. After living in Paris for 22 years, he decided to pursue his studies in England where he obtained a Bachelor of Electronic Engineering in 1996. Not put off by the English weather, Nicolas chose to stay and joined PowerVR Technologies to eventually lead the developer relations group, supporting game developers on a variety of platforms and contributing to SDK content. He then transitioned to ATI Technologies and AMD Corporation, where he is now managing the worldwide ISV Gaming Engineering group.

Yasin Uludag works as a rendering software engineer at EA DICE.

Nathan Vos is a principal graphics programmer at the core technology team at Guerrilla Games, where he works on the rendering engine used in the successful *Killzone* game series. Over the years he worked on various aspects of the rendering engine including particle simulation and rendering, post process effects, and other graphics-related features. He also developed the special effects rendering code used in the game *Little Big Planet* on PSP. In the last years his work was focused on extending the existing rendering engine with new features, including the volumetric light effects used in *Killzone: Shadow Fall*.

Jason C. Yang has been involved in the games industry since 2000, and he has worked for a wide range of companies including Artificial Mind and Movement (now bEhavior Interactive), Electronic Arts, Factor 5, and Crystal Dynamics. He has spent the last 11 years working on low-level rendering code and shader programming for a variety of systems, including PC, Xbox/360/One, PS2/PS3/PS4, and GameCube/Wii. He is currently employed at Crystal Dynamics where he heads the rendering efforts for the *Tomb Raider* team.

Egor Yusov is a graphics software engineer in Visual Computing Engineering group at Intel, where he has worked on a variety of 3D technologies including deformable terrain and physically based water rendering, shadows, and post-process effects. He received his PhD in computer science from Nizhny Novgorod

State Technical University, Russia, in 2011. His research interests include real-time visualization and rendering, data compression, GPU-based algorithms, and shader programming.

Renaldas Zioma is an experienced graphics programmer working at Unity. Prior to joining Unity, he worked on various technology at DICE.

Tobias Zirr is a student research assistant at Karlsruhe Institute of Technology (KIT), where he is currently pursuing a master's degree in computer science. A long-time computer graphics enthusiast, he started working in visualization at the age of 16. In 2013, he received a research scholarship for outstanding students at KIT. His current work includes visualization of particle-based simulations as well as novel real-time global illumination and rendering solutions. He is also an ex-demoscener. More of his work can be found at http://alphanew.net.

T - #0053 - 101024 - C522 - 235/191/28 [30] - CB - 9781482208634 - Gloss Lamination